ARCHIPELAGO TOURISM

New Directions in Tourism Analysis

Series Editor: Dimitri Ioannides, E-TOUR, Mid Sweden University, Sweden

Although tourism is becoming increasingly popular as both a taught subject and an area for empirical investigation, the theoretical underpinnings of many approaches have tended to be eclectic and somewhat underdeveloped. However, recent developments indicate that the field of tourism studies is beginning to develop in a more theoretically informed manner, but this has not yet been matched by current publications.

The aim of this series is to fill this gap with high quality monographs or edited collections that seek to develop tourism analysis at both theoretical and substantive levels using approaches which are broadly derived from allied social science disciplines such as Sociology, Social Anthropology, Human and Social Geography, and Cultural Studies. As tourism studies covers a wide range of activities and sub fields, certain areas such as Hospitality Management and Business, which are already well provided for, would be excluded. The series will therefore fill a gap in the current overall pattern of publication.

Suggested themes to be covered by the series, either singly or in combination, include – consumption; cultural change; development; gender; globalisation; political economy; social theory; sustainability.

Also in the series

Tourism and Violence
Edited by Hazel Andrews
ISBN 978-1-4094-3640-9

Tourism, Performance, and Place
A Geographic Perspective
*Jillian M. Rickly-Boyd, Daniel C. Knudsen, Lisa C. Braverman,
and Michelle M. Metro-Roland*
ISBN 978-1-4094-3613-3

Volunteer Tourism
Popular Humanitarianism in Neoliberal Times
Mary Mostafanezhad
ISBN 978-1-4094-6953-7

Tourism Destination Development
Turns and Tactics
Edited by Arvid Viken and Brynhild Granås
ISBN 978-1-4724-1658-2

Archipelago Tourism

Policies and Practices

Edited by

GODFREY BALDACCHINO

LONDON AND NEW YORK

First published 2015 by Ashgate Publishing

2 Park Square, Milton Park, Abingdon, Oxon OX14 4RN
711 Third Avenue, New York, NY 10017, USA

Routledge is an imprint of the Taylor & Francis Group, an informa business

First issued in paperback 2017

British Library Cataloguing in Publication Data
A catalogue record for this book is available from the British Library

The Library of Congress has cataloged the printed edition as follows:
Archipelago tourism : policies and practices / edited by Godfrey Baldacchino.
        pages cm
   Includes bibliographical references and index.
   ISBN 978-1-4724-2430-3 (hardback)
1. Tourism – Management – Case studies. 2. Archipelagos – Case studies.
I. Baldacchino, Godfrey, editor of compilation.

   G155.A1A637 2015
   910.68–dc23
                                                                    2014030612

ISBN 978-1-4724-2430-3 (hbk)
ISBN 978-1-138-08387-5 (pbk)

Contents

List of Figures

List of Tables

List of Plates

Notes on Contributors

Fathimath Amira is a doctoral researcher at New Zealand Tourism Research Institute/ Auckland University of Technology. She is currently completing her PhD thesis on the role of stakeholder collaboration in sustainable tourism competitiveness. Having achieved BPhil and MA in Hospitality Management at Birmingham College of Food and Creative Studies, UK, she gained an MPhil in Tourism Management from Auckland University of Technology. Her research interests include food tourism, tourism impacts, tourism and small island developing states, sustainable tourism, tourism promotion, culture and tourism and tourism competitiveness.

Rosemarie Ankre lectures in human geography and is a researcher at the European Tourism Research Institute (ETOUR), Mid Sweden University. She is also a PhD candidate in spatial planning at the Blekinge Institute of Technology, Sweden. Her research interests are in the areas of nature-based tourism and outdoor recreation in coastal, island and mountain areas, conflicts over land and water use, visitor attitudes, as well as zoning as a tool in planning and management. Her present research project involves natural quiet and noise related to motorised activities in the Swedish mountains.

Godfrey Baldacchino is Professor of Sociology at the University of Malta, Malta; Island Studies Teaching Fellow and outgoing Canada Research Chair (Island Studies) at the University of Prince Edward Island, Charlottetown, Canada; and Visiting Professor of Island Tourism at the Università di Corsica Pasquale Paoli, France. He is founding Executive Editor of *Island Studies Journal* (ISSN: 1715-2593). He is President of the International Small Islands Studies Association (ISISA); Council Member of the Islands Commission of the International Geographical Union (IGU); and a Director for Global Islands Network (GIN). Recently published books include: *Island Enclaves: Offshoring Strategies, Creative Governance and Subnational Island Jurisdictions* (2010); *Island Futures: Conservation and Development across the Asia-Pacific* (2011, with D. Niles); *Extreme Heritage Management: Practices and Policies from Densely Populated Islands* (2011); *Island Songs: A Global Repertoire* (2011); *A Taste of Islands* (2012, with A. Baldacchino); *The International Political Economy of Divided Islands* (2012) and *Independence Movements from Subnational Island Jurisdictions* (2013, with E. Hepburn).

Jennifer V. Barrow is a part-time lecturer in tourism, University of the West Indies (UWI), Cave Hill Campus, and is presently the Coordinator/Consultant with the Caribbean Tourism Organisation's Aviation Task Force. She is also doctoral candidate in Management Studies at UWI. As an experienced practitioner, she has worked in both the private and public sector within tourism and hospitality at senior management level in the Caribbean and its major tourism generating markets of USA, UK and Canada. She has a longstanding interest in small island development and integrated regions, strategic marketing and tourism. Jennifer's publications include 'Market positioning: the case of Barbados' (2010, with S. Roberts) in the edited volume *Marketing Island Destinations: Concepts and Cases*, and

'The development of sport and lifestyle tourism: going for gold in tourism niche markets' in *Business Barbados, 2005.*

Richard W. Butler is Emeritus Professor of International Tourism, Strathclyde University, Glasgow, UK. He holds degrees in geography and spent thirty years at the University of Western Ontario in Canada, before joining the University of Surrey, UK (1997 to 2005), and then moving to Strathclyde. He has published numerous journal articles and book chapters, and sixteen books on tourism. His principal research interests are the development of tourist destinations and the impacts of tourism. He is a former president of the International Academy for the Study of Tourism. He is probably best known for having developed the tourism area life cycle model in 1980.

Rita Cannas (PhD, Bologna) is a management researcher at the University of Cagliari, Italy, and a Marie Curie Fellow at the Institute for Tourism, Travel and Culture, University of Malta, Malta. Her research interests are in sustainable tourism development, authenticity and community empowerment in tourism, tourism policy and critical turn in tourism. She has been developing a three year research project on sustainable tourism models in Sardinia, funded by the Autonomous Region of Sardinia, within the Department of Economics Business of the University of Cagliari. She is the author of *Towards Sustainable Tourism Models: A Feasibility Study of an Eco-village Project in Scotland* (2012) and of several conference papers.

Samantha Chaperon is Senior Lecturer in Tourism and Events, University of Greenwich, London, United Kingdom. Research interests include destination management, tourism policy, tourism in islands and peripheral areas, tourism and dependency, core-periphery, and community responses to tourism. Her doctoral research examined community and actor responses to tourism development and tourism governance, in a core-periphery context, with the Maltese Islands as a case study. Recent publications include: a chapter in an edited collection entitled 'Views about the scale and types of tourism development in the rural periphery: the case of Gozo', in Macleod, D. and Gillespie, S. (eds) *Sustainable Tourism in Rural Europe: Approaches to Development* (2011, with B. Bramwell); 'Dependency and Agency in Peripheral Tourism Development' in *Annals of Tourism Research*, Vol. 40 (2013, with B. Bramwell); 'Analysis of the UK's Tourism Policy' in *Cultural Trends* (2013, with J. Kennell).

John Connell is Professor of Human Geography in the School of Geosciences, University of Sydney, Australia. He has been a consultant to the ILO, the WHO, the South Pacific Commission, the South Pacific Regional Environmental Program and the Asian Development Bank. His research interests cover development in the Pacific island region, migration of health workers, music tourism and the development of medical tourism. He has written more than 300 articles and over 20 books. The books include *Migration from Rural Areas* (with M. Lipton, R. Laishley and B. Dasgupta); *The Last Colonies* (with R. Aldrich); *Urbanisation in the Island Pacific: Towards Sustainable Development* (with J. Lea); *Music and Tourism: On the Road Again* (with C. Gibson); *Tourism at the Grass Roots* (with B. Rugendyke), and, most recently, *Islands at Risk* (2013).

Eduardo Costa Duarte Ferreira is PhD candidate and teaching assistant at the Centre for Social Studies, both at the University of the Azores, Portugal. He is interested in themes that deal with migration, development and the differential impact of tourism strategies in the Azorean archipelago. He is author of the book *Between Two Worlds: Emigration and Return to the Azores* (with G.P. Nunes Rocha and D. Mendes).

Ernestina Giudici is Full Professor of Management and Business Communication at the University of Cagliari, Sardinia, Italy. She is a member of the Board of Directors of the University of Cagliari and of the European Community Studies Association. She is also a member of the Editorial Advisory Board of the *International Journal of Quality and Services Sciences* (ISSN: 1756-669X) and of the Editorial Review Board of the *Transnational Marketing Journal* (ISSN: 2041-4684). Recent publications include: 'Can sustainable capitalism by achieved by 2020?' (2014, with A. Dettori); 'What should be the role of managers in organisations?' (2014, with F. Caboni and V. Niola); 'Can intangible cultural heritage promote sustainability in tourism?' (2013, with C. Melis, S. Dessì and B. Ramos); 'Towards a model of sustainable tourism for small hotels' (2012, with F. Caboni); 'Can a green brand determine customer choice?' (2012, with A. Dettori).

Dimitri Ioannides is Professor of Human Geography in the Department of Tourism Studies and Human Geography at Mid Sweden University, and Senior Fellow at Missouri State University, USA, where he taught for many years and held the rank of professor. He holds a PhD in Urban Planning and Policy Development from Rutgers University New Jersey, USA. His research interests include tourism and sustainable development, the equity dimension of sustainability, the rights of low-pay workers in the tourism sector. He has published various articles and book chapters on the economic geography of tourism. He is author of *Tourism in the USA: A Spatial and Social Synthesis* (2010, with D. Timothy). He is Series Editor for 'New Directions in Tourism Analysis' (Ashgate Publishing).

Henry Johnson is Professor of Music at the University of Otago, New Zealand. His research interests are in island studies, Asian studies and ethnomusicology, and he has carried out field research in a number of island cultures in Europe, Asia and Australasia. His books include *The Koto* (2004), *Asia in the Making of New Zealand* (2006; co-edited), *Performing Japan* (2008; co-edited), *The Shamisen* (2010), and *The Shakuhachi* (2014). His publications in the field of island studies have appeared in *Shima*, *Journal of Marine and Island Cultures*, and *Island Studies Journal*. He is from the Channel Islands.

Sofia Karampela is a PhD candidate and teaching assistant, Department of Environmental Studies, University of the Aegean, Greece. Her main research interest is the relationship of islands to regional and local development, sustainability and tourism planning. She is a member of the Laboratory of Local and Insular Development at the University of the Aegean. She has also worked in the private sector as a business consultant, producing financial and regional studies, as well as an investigator in the implementation of projects co-funded by the European Union.

Thanasis Kizos is Associate Professor of Rural Geography in the Department of Geography of the University of the Aegean, Greece. He holds an agricultural sciences bachelor's degree and a PhD in Environmental Policy and Planning. He has published on agricultural landscape change and farming systems, islands and insularity, analysis of cultural landscape change, ecosystem services assessment, temperate and Mediterranean agroforestry systems, and human-environment relations.

Pedro F. Marcelino is a researcher, writer, documentary filmmaker, and independent consultant, working primarily in human security. His research interests stretch from border narratives to migration nexuses. Having started his career as a journalist, he has since provided consultancy to the African Union, European Union and United Nations on migration issues and on peace-building. He is the CEO of Longyearbyen Consulting and Media. Recent publications include *The New Migratory Paradigm of African Migration* (2013). He has taken his social science experience to the field of film, having graduated from the Documentary Film Institute at Seneca College (Toronto, Canada) in 2012. He has since produced/directed two shorts and various institutional clips. *After the War: Memoirs of Exile*, his first feature film, premiered in May 2014. He is currently in pre-production for the documentary *Way Up North: An Arctic Symphony* (2015) filmed in northern Canada, and the TV-series *This Is Africa* (2016).

Luciano Minerbi is Professor of Urban and Regional Planning at the University of Hawai'i at Manoa, Hawai'i, USA. His research on sustainable island development uses human ecological and environmental approaches in place-based management, writing on responsible and alternative tourism, coastal zone management, heritage landscape, indigenous people, land use and watershed management, natural disaster mitigation, community based economic development, village planning and participatory research and serving local groups, neighbourhood and rural councils, city, county, state, territorial, and federal agencies, the East–West Center, United Nations agencies, and several Pacific island governments or organisations. Publications include: *A Framework for Integrated Socio-economic and Environmental Development Planning and Management* (1990); *Hawaiian Sanctuaries, Places of Refuge and Indigenous Knowledge in Hawai'i* (1992); *Hawaiian Subsistence and Community Sustainability* (1998, 2008); *Indigenous Management Models and the Protection of the Ahupua'a* (1999); *In the Face of Globalization: Two Decades of Insurgent Localism in Hawai'i* (2001); and *Hawai'i Tourism* (2012).

Per-Åke Nilsson is a member of the Department of Tourism, Hólar University College, Iceland. His research interests include the history of tourism, higher education, tourism studies, visual culture, and cultural tourism. He was affiliated to the Centre for Regional and Tourism Research, Nexø, Bornholm, Denmark.

Luzia Oca González is Lecturer and Researcher at the Centre for Transdisciplinary Development Studies (CETRAD), University of Trás-os-Montes e Alto Douro, Portugal. She holds a PhD in Social Anthropology from the University of Santiago de Compostela, Spain. She has worked in social intervention, especially with the Capeverdean community of Burela (Galicia), with women of Ribeira Grande de Santiago (Cape Verde), and with the Associação para a Cooperação com Cabo Verde. Her research interests focus on gender and migration, Capeverdean studies and applied anthropology. Her latest publications are 'Cabo Verde, um país insular de diáspora na confluência entre a Europa e África', in *Ordenamento e Planejamento territorial na África Ocidental: Cabo Verde, Senegal e Mali* (2011, with J. Piñeiro and C. Furtado); 'Capeverdians in Spain, in *Transnational Archipelago* (2008, with R. Moldes Farelo), and 'Badiu na Galiza: mar di homi; tera di mudjeres', in *Género e Migrações Cabo-verdianas* (2007).

Andreas Papatheodorou is Associate Professor in Industrial and Spatial Economics with Emphasis on Tourism and Director of the Laboratory for Tourism Research and Studies, both at the University of the Aegean, Greece. He is also a Dozent in the Aviation MBA Programme offered by Frankfurt University of Applied Sciences, Germany. An Oxford MPhil and DPhil graduate, Dr Papatheodorou started his academic career as a Lecturer in Tourism at the University of Surrey, UK. He is a member of the Executive Board of the International Association for Tourism Economics and of the Hellenic Aviation Society. He is Editor-in-Chief of the *Journal of Air Transport Studies*, a Resource Editor for *Annals of Tourism Research* and a member of the UNWTO Panel of Experts. He is a co-author (with M. Stabler and M.T. Sinclair) of *Economics of Tourism* (2010), while two of his papers were declared as the most downloaded in their year of publication by the respective journals (*Annals of Tourism Research*, 2001 and *Journal of Travel Research*, 2010).

Evangelia Petridou is Doctoral candidate in Political Science at Mid Sweden University, Sweden. Her research interests include theories of the policy process, political entrepreneurship, and urban governance. Her substantive policy area interests include economic development and territorial cohesion with a special interest in European peripheral areas. Her latest article has appeared in *Policy Studies Journal.* She is editor of *Entrepreneurship in Polis: Understanding Political Entrepreneurship* (2014, with I. Aflaki and L. Miles).

Sherma Roberts is Lecturer in Tourism at the University of the West Indies, Cave Hill Campus, Barbados. Having taught in the UK, she joined the Department of Management Studies at UWI in 2005, where she has raised the profile of tourism education. She also contributes to the public discourse on tourism as Chair of the Tourism Advisory Council and as a speaker at various local and regional tourism fora. She has published and presented papers on community participation, corporate social responsibility, sustainable tourism, diaspora tourism, e-marketing and tourism entrepreneurship. She is the editor of *Marketing Island Destinations* (with A. Lewis), *Tourism, Planning and Community Development* (with R. Phillips), and *Contemporary Caribbean Tourism: Concept and Cases* (forthcoming).

Sophia A. Rolle is Associate Professor of Tourism Management at The College of The Bahamas (CoB) and current Executive Director of the Culinary and Hospitality Management Institute at CoB. She conducts research over a number of genres in tourism and the social sciences, including the impact of tourism on small island states, the focus of which is sustainability of island destinations, acculturation and psycho-centric behaviour and capacity building. Other research areas include the macro-economic potential of small islands in The Bahamas, medical tourism, tourism marketing, socio-cultural and heritage tourism engagements, and sustainable tourism with an emphasis on ecotourism. Dr Rolle has developed a number of bachelor degree programmes in tourism, hospitality and ecotourism both locally and internationally. She is often consulted for advice on effective and efficient planning and process engagement in the areas of hospitality, sustainable tourism development and strategic implementation.

Stephen A. Royle is Professor of Island Geography at Queen's University Belfast in Northern Ireland, UK. He serves as Treasurer, International Small Islands Studies Association (ISISA); Deputy Editor, *Island Studies Journal*; Chair, Royal Geographical Society Northern Ireland Region; a member of the Council of British Geography; and member of the International Geographical Union's Commission on Islands. He is also a Member of the Royal Irish Academy. His books include *North America* (1999) (with Fred

Boal); *A Geography of Islands* (2001); *Enduring City: Belfast in the Twentieth Century* (2006, with Fred Boal); *The Company's Island: St. Helena, Company Colonies and the Colonial Endeavour* (2007*)*; *Doing Development Differently: Regional Development on the Atlantic Periphery* (2007, with Susan Hodgett and David Johnson); *Company, Crown and Colony: The Hudson's Bay Company and Territorial Endeavour in Western Canada* (2011), *Portrait of an Industrial City: 'Clanging Belfast', 1750–1914* (2011), and *Islands: Nature and Culture* (2014).

John N. Telesford is Lecturer and Associate Dean, School of Continuing Education, T.A. Marryshow College, Grenada. He recently (June 2014) completed doctoral research at the Robert Gordon University, Scotland, UK, on the thesis: 'Strategic sustainability and industrial ecology in an island context, with considerations for a green economy roadmap: a study in the tourism accommodation sector, Grenada.' His general research interest focuses on an inter-disciplinary approach to sustainable development in island contexts. His recent publications include 'Oil down' in *A Taste of Islands* (2012, edited by A. and G. Baldacchino); and a paper on best practice in facilities management in the *Journal of Education and Development in the Caribbean* (2010). He is a member of the International Sustainable Development Research Society (ISDRS), the International Small Islands Studies Association (ISISA) and the International Society for Industrial Ecology (ISIE).

Nadia Theuma is Senior Lecturer and Director, Institute for Tourism, Travel and Culture at the University of Malta, Malta. She holds degrees in Anthropology and Tourism Studies. She has taught courses and supervised post-graduate and undergraduate dissertations in the area of tourism studies and tourism management in Malta and the UK. She has conducted seminars and delivered lectures in Malta, Finland, Romania, UK and USA. She has held consultancy posts with the Ministries of Tourism, Malta Tourism Authority, Heritage Malta, Malta Crafts Council and the Ministry for Resources, Competitiveness and Communications. She was a board member of the Malta Tourism Authority where she helped develop a cultural tourism policy. She has also conducted research with and partnered in various EU funded projects. Her research interests include cultural heritage, community development, Maltese food and cultural products. She is author of *Le tourisme en Méditerranée: Une perspective socio-culturelle* (2005)*.*

Carsten Wergin is Senior Researcher at the Institute for Social and Cultural Anthropology, MLU Halle-Wittenberg, Germany. His general interests are in the areas of globalisation, media and transcultural studies with a particular focus on ethnographic research in the age of the anthropocene and beyond dichotomies such as nature/culture, material/immaterial, knowledge/science. Numerous publications in these domains stem from extensive fieldwork periods in the Indian Ocean region (The Mascarenes and Western Australia), in post-industrial spaces and at music festivals. Recent publications include the special section 'Songlines vs. Pipelines? Mining and Tourism Industries in Remote Australia' in *Australian Humanities Review* 53 (2012, with S. Muecke), the edited volume, *Musical Performance and the Changing City* (2013, with F. Holt), and a Special Issue of *Tourist Studies* on 'Materialities of Tourism' (2014, with S. Muecke).

Foreword
Archipelago Tourism: Some Thoughts and Reactions

Richard W. Butler

Introduction

A recent issue of the journal *Tourism Recreation Research* published a 'Research Probe' on the nature of island tourism (Sharpley, Butler, and Hall, 2012). Along with other aspects of that subject, it contained a discussion about whether there was such a phenomenon as *island tourism* as distinct from tourism to and on islands. The general conclusion was that this depends very much on the perceptions of each reader or discussant, the specific tourists involved, and also that 'a deeper understanding of how islands are consumed by tourists remains elusive and demands further scrutiny' (op. cit., p. 182). Clearly, there is both tourism *to* islands and tourism that takes place *on* islands, as all the chapters in this volume bear witness to.

Whether there is island tourism as a unique form or sub-category of tourism is much more of a perceptual problem. I strongly believe that island tourism – that is, visiting a destination specifically because it is an island, and perhaps a member of an archipelago – *is* a specific form of tourism, one that is quite distinct from simply participating in tourism at an island destination. It may appear pointless to consider whether one is examining island tourism or archipelago tourism (tourism to a group of islands); but again, there is an important perceptual issue involved in such a consideration. To tourism researchers, it is important to know what is motivating tourists to visit a specific destination, and what are their knowledge, understanding, and perceptions of that destination; that same information would presumably be useful also to tourism industry practitioners and relevant public sector agencies. In reality, knowledge of the mental processes of tourist destination choice is relatively poor, despite a number of models and concepts that have evolved over the past twenty years. In general, it is assumed that potential visitors have an initial idea of the kind of destination they wish to visit, presumably one which will provide the appropriate setting and opportunities for the type of vacation they wish to enjoy. They then work from a large set of possible destination choices (but as no tourist has complete knowledge of all potential destinations, their initial set is limited by their background, education, and information/knowledge) down to a smaller number of destinations that are given active consideration and then they finally choose one location from this smaller set. Depending on how they are arranging their holiday, they may go on-line to search for flights and accommodation, or visit a travel agent, in both cases perhaps unconsciously further limiting their options; in the first case by their own knowledge of what and how to search, and in the second by the experience and commercial integrity and values of the travel agent (reflecting their experience, their commissions from specific tour companies and their own company policies). Thus, the final selected destination may match the needs and preferences of the tourist perfectly or be a less than ideal compromise; it will fall somewhere on a continuum from perfection to failure and will have repercussions in terms of subsequent destination choices depending on the success of the holiday.

To the Archipelago

So far, I have not mentioned how archipelagos fit into this decision-making process, primarily because we have little or no such knowledge, a situation that hopefully this volume may help rectify. One can argue, in my own case from personal observation rather than from the academic literature (which really does not cover this topic), that some tourists are often unaware of whether they are even going to an island, let alone whether this is a solitary island or a member of an archipelago. This seems to be particularly so in the case of British tourists, with whom I am most familiar and of course on occasion, one myself. It is clear that many make little or no differentiation between whether a destination is on an island or not, let alone whether it is an island that is alone or is one member of an archipelago. In most cases, they are more concerned with what their destination can provide by way of services and opportunities. For those who are truly island tourists – that is, they are going to a destination specifically because it is an island – then its insular characteristics and qualities may well be of paramount importance. Even then, however, the question of single island or island group is, in many cases, still irrelevant. An example may clarify this situation.

As an enthusiastic bird watcher, I have spent several holidays and research visits to Fair Isle, the most remote (in terms of distance) of the inhabited British islands. It lies midway between the island archipelagos of Orkney and Shetland, belonging administratively and geologically to the latter group. I go to Fair Isle because it is probably the ultimate location in the United Kingdom from which to observe rare birds on migration, having recorded more 'first visits' to Britain by vagrant species than any other location. To visit the island, (unless I use a privately chartered plane as a few affluent bird-watchers do when a true vagrant or first record appears on the island), I have to travel first to what is known as the Shetland 'mainland', and from there travel to Fair Isle by boat or plane. Thus, being aware of the existence of and visiting the Shetland archipelago is inevitable. This awareness may even extend to the realisation that Shetland has its own 'mainland', which includes the capital city (Lerwick), and the main air and sea port terminals; with various other islands one or more ferry crossings away. These outliers have their own challenges in attracting tourists, their own multiple insular status creating both challenges (added distance, time and cost) and also opportunities (seclusion, rusticity and unique features) in developing themselves as boutique 'cold water' tourist destinations. However, as a more common 'sun, sea and sand' tourist, venturing to popular British foreign destinations, I could travel directly to Mallorca, or Ibiza (in the Balearics archipelago) or Lanzarote or Tenerife (in the Canaries archipelago), without any contact with any other island in their particular group and to all intents and purposes being ignorant of their very existence. Most of the islands in these groups are not visible from each other and travelling between them for a foreign tourist with minimal language or geographical abilities, let alone an interest in seeing other islands, is not easy or necessarily desirable.

If one's purpose on holiday is to spend most of one's time on a beach, any beach is as good as any other of equal quality (water temperature and purity, hours of sunshine, and clean sand in particular). Thus, there is little need or incentive to travel, at additional cost, to a neighbouring island. In the case of tourists whose primary or a major reason for travelling is related to culture and heritage, then visiting another island might be of considerable appeal and would justify any added cost and possible inconvenience. Thus the importance or added value of an island being a member of an archipelago may depend very much on the orientation and preferences of the tourist, as well as on their awareness of the characteristics and quality of the destination they are visiting. However, such tourists are generally in a minority, as most island tourists are on a sun, sea and sand type of holiday.

Does Awareness Matter?

Depending on the destination, however, tourists to some islands may be much more aware of the existence of an archipelago as well as the specific island they are visiting; but this is a point about which researchers would be justified in bemoaning the lack of detailed and reliable information on tourist mental images and awareness. It is likely that tourists to the Hawaiian archipelago are aware that there is more than the one island, whichever that may be, that they are visiting or contemplating visiting. They may not be aware that Waikiki is on the island of Oʻahu rather than on Hawaiʻi (the Big Island), but may well have heard of Maui and even Kauai, as well as Hawaiʻi if only because that is the name of the archipelago as a whole. (This alignment between the name of an archipelago and that of its main island is an issue taken up in this volume.) Such awareness is almost certainly higher among North American tourists than others as they are both the majority of visitors to Hawaiʻi and – in the case of residents of the United States – domestic tourists. In the case of the Caribbean, one has to consider if that archipelago includes all Caribbean islands or should be confined to specific groupings with the Caribbean Sea, such as the Bahamas, Turks and Caicos, Caymans, St. Kitts and Nevis, and Trinidad and Tobago, for example. Visitors to the Bahamas perhaps have greater awareness of the existence of other islands, although even there, despite the proximity to their major market, one might expect some vagueness and lack of knowledge of the names of many of the individual islands.

One might ask if this matters, and the answer is probably not in terms of tourist satisfaction. But it clearly does matter in terms of island visitation and awareness levels or visibility of individual islands within a group. It is a difficult issue with which to deal, as some of the following chapters indicate. Individual island sensitivities, archipelago politics, economic realities, transport and other aspects of accessibility, degree of development of tourist facilities and policies, and practices of intermediaries, including travel agents, tour operators, airlines and cruise lines are all involved. Some of the above agents will not be concerned about which specific islands tourists visit, while others may be greatly concerned and directly involved in influencing or controlling the pattern of visitation. Cruise line operators are perhaps the actor making most value out of the presences of archipelagos, as many tours/cruises visit island groups deliberately in order to offer the maximum number of ports of call in a cruise as possible and thus reduce sailing time, service demands and costs on each cruise. Their choice of destinations is governed by cost but also by the availability of adequate port facilities and policies in place with respect to number of cruise ships accepted at any one time, and other possible restrictions. As cruise vessels increase in size, some destinations may opt out or fall out of favour because of an inability to cater for the several thousands of visitors on an individual boat; they may be substituted by alternative islands within the same archipelago or elsewhere (e.g. Lawton and Butler, 1989).

The Archipelago and Island Hopping

Most of the previous discussion has related to tourists who are single-centre focused in their holiday choice; that is, they select a specific destination (an island, for example) and do not plan to relocate except possibly for part or all of a day. Indeed, many tourists do not leave even their hotel or resort complex during their stay except on arrival and departure. Thus to them the existence of an archipelago is irrelevant. For those tourists who are 'island hoppers', then an archipelago potentially is a considerable attraction and can be a major reason for visiting a specific island destination (Fennell, 1996). Much then depends on the accessibility of the islands within the archipelago being visited. For example, several of the Orkney Islands are linked by the Churchill Causeway constructed during the Second World War and it is easy to drive between several of the islands and the Orkney 'mainland' using this structure. In the case of the neighbouring Shetland archipelago, no islands are connected to each other by permanent structures (bridges, causeways, tunnels) and thus ferries or aircraft are necessary to move people, animals and cargo between individual islands. Much also depends on whether the tourists bring along their own transportation (most likely a car or bicycle, but also pleasure craft or yacht) with them. If they are not bringing their own transportation, then the availability of rental vehicles, taxis, ferries, air/seaplanes or similar services are essential if the desire is to encourage them to visit other islands. This then becomes an issue for both individual and archipelago agencies with responsibility for tourism, as well as tour agents and travel companies.

The relationships between individual islands and the other parts of their archipelago are often complex and sometimes controversial, as is amply shown in the following chapters of this timely book. Most such issues do not relate to tourism, although tourism may be a catalyst for the emergence or re-emergence of these issues because of the economic benefits (and costs) and its potential social, cultural and environmental impacts; as well as various related developments (such as transportation and other infrastructural facilities, medical, retail and other services) that tourism requires and stimulates. It is easier in general for specific islands to reject and refuse tourism and its associated developments than it is for any island to require an archipelago to deliver the infrastructure required to ensure tourist visitation. As the authors in this volume show, the island of primary access, often but not always the 'capital' island (in terms of political and administrative authority), is generally the one that is subject to most tourism development, thus making itself even more attractive to tourists, not only as the first point of call, but because to stay there avoids the need to trans-plane or trans-ship to another island. Success in tourism, if that is the correct term, tends to generate further tourism therefore, sometimes to the detriment of potential tourism to other islands in the archipelago. In this context, the interplay between endogenous and exogenous forces is of paramount importance, with extra-island players (airlines and cruise operators in particular) often in a more powerful position than the relevant island authorities to craft tourism policy. While the local authorities may limit or prohibit access or development (although few may wish to do this because of the potential loss of economic and employment benefits), it is much harder for them to insist on development in specific islands or parts of an archipelago if that is against the preferences of the external agencies (e.g. Hall, 1989).

Dealing with Neighbours

In many respects, therefore, the relationship between tourism to single islands and that to archipelagos mirrors the overall issues of tourism to islands in general: limitations and costs of access from markets, potential vulnerability to external forces, limited knowledge about the location by visitors, and inconsistency and often inequality in treatment by decision-makers, both within and external to the island destinations. This promising and timely volume reviews these salient and pertinent issues, and also delves into revealing discussions on logistic and infrastructural challenges, as well as specific versus generic island branding and marketing strategies, that bedevil island tourism. In tourism, as in many economic facets of life, one's neighbour may not be one's best friend, even if part of the 'family'.

References

Fennell, D.A. (1996). A tourist space-time budget in the Shetland Islands. *Annals of Tourism Research*, 23(4), 811–29.

Hall, C.M. (1989). Rethinking the prime minister's dilemma. *Annals of Tourism Research*, 16(3), 399–406.

Lawton, L.J. and Butler, R.W. (1989). Cruise ship industry: patterns in the Caribbean 1800–1986. *Tourism Management*, 8(4), 329–43.

Sharpley, R., Butler, R.W., and Hall, C.M. (2012). Research probe: island tourism or tourism on islands? *Tourism Recreation Review*, 37(2), 167–82.

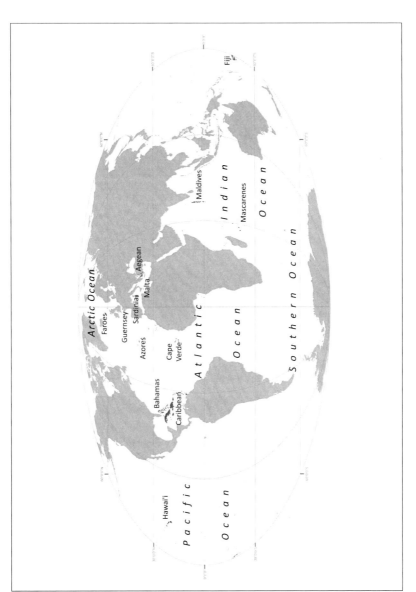

Figure E.1 World Map, showing location of the case study archipelagos, islands and regions

Editorial

More than Island Tourism: Branding, Marketing and Logistics in Archipelago Tourist Destinations

Godfrey Baldacchino

Introduction

> The sea, together with the boats which cross it … is crucial to issues of [island] survival; but it is a source of division in more ways than the purely geographical (Bethel, 2000, p. 244).

The association between islands and tourism goes much further than today's deliberate attempts by marketing agencies to position islands as earthy paradises. It can be traced to something much older: the millenary pursuit of especially beautiful places, like the Garden of Eden watered by running streams in both the Christian and Moslem traditions (Gillis, 2004; Scafi, 2006). This quest grounds the historically young business of vacationing and tourism within a culturally diffuse and well-established practice of longing for exclusive locales that bestow peace, security and deep communion with the divine and/or the natural (Royle, 2001; Löfgren, 2002). That we continue to desire such spaces for their putative transformative energies and powers explains much of the lingering, fundamental appeal of island tourism today.

And yet, this powerful allure must often come to terms with a reality on the ground that exudes a plurality of islands, each of which may be peddling its own identity, competing for its own specific tourist spend and lobbying for its own sea/air transport infrastructure. This is because, hidden behind the term 'island', we may have to contend with a full archipelago, and at different scales of analysis.

This introduction first dwells on the contemporary fascination of island tourism, but then argues that what one considers to be islands are usually archipelagos: and tourism on archipelagos has its own dynamics. We present the multiplicity of islands, the notion of an inner or domestic sea and a centrifugal tendency as three central features of archipelagos already established in the literature. To these, five additional interlocking attributes of archipelagos, specific to tourism, are proposed and discussed: in/visibility, tweaked representation, domination and subordination, liminality or layering, and the expression of inter-island differentiation. This conceptual review helps to frame the ensuing contributions which explore the implications of these nuances on the branding, marketing and unfolding of archipelago tourism; as well as on the logistics and transportation infrastructures that make it happen.

Island Tourism: Welcome to my Paradise

> The metaphoric deployment of 'island', with the associated attributes of small physical size and warm water, is possibly the central gripping metaphor within Western discourse (Hay, 2006, p. 26).

We speak of islands as exceptional places, easily identifiable because of their finite self-inscribed geography; and, while they are offshore and remote, they are never remote enough to make themselves inaccessible. Unless there is a fixed link, only a tantalising swim, a boat trip, a ferry crossing, or (more recently) a plane journey separates them from us; and assuming we are part of the 90% of humankind that does not live on islands. Islands are also spaces which invite visitors to enjoy experiences 'out of time', with a different tempo, even if briefly: perhaps one with a more relaxed, human way of life than that of the frenetic urban and hyper-technological modern metropolis, from which many are drawn to these island locales; or even one with a racier, wilder and glitzier schedule (Connell, 2013, pp. 97–110; Gillis and Lowenthal 2007; Gössling, 2003; Gössling and Wall, 2007; Lockhart and Drakakis-Smith, 1997; Pearce, 1989). Throughout history, ideas of Eden or Eden-like island paradises have been cyclically revitalised through such artefacts as works of art, religion, literature, pleasure gardens, television series, Hollywood movies, fun parks, children's toys, video games and tourism advertisements (Delumeau, 1992; Crouch et al., 2005; Picard, 2011, p. 11). Think of Homer's *Odyssey*, Shakespeare's *The Tempest*, Bernardin de Saint-Pierre's Paul et Virginie, R.M. Ballantyne's *Coral Island*, R.L. Stevenson's *Treasure Island*, J.M. Barrie's NeverNever Land (the dwelling place of Peter Pan and Tinker Bell) and *South Pacific* (the 1958 American romantic musical movie). Think also of the US television series *Fantasy Island* (with Mr Rourke welcoming guests who wish to have fantasies fulfilled); and, more recently, *Big Brother*, *Survivor* and *Lost* (Loxley, 1990). Even in the latest version of the popular video-game *Tomb Raider*, buxom heroine Lara Croft is stranded on a tropical island (Nyman, 2013a).

Thus, understanding what is it that attracts tourists to islands – to the extent that we can speak of 'small island tourist economies' (McElroy, 2003, 2006; McElroy and Hamma, 2010) – cannot be dismissed as merely speculative, banal or serendipitous (Baum et al., 2000: 214; World Tourism Organisation, 2005). The 'island lure' (Lockhart, 1997) and the fascination with islands as the stuff of dreams (Connell, 2003) have a rich and enduring pedigree:

> There is something special and different about getting into a boat or an aeroplane as a necessity in order to reach your [island] destination ... Once there, the feeling of separateness, of being cut off from the mainland, is also an important physical and psychological attribute of the successful vacation (Baum, 1997, p. 21).

Island tourism is not, however, just about tourism practices that happen to unfold in enisled spaces (e.g. Apostoulopoulos and Gayle, 2002; Briguglio et al., 1996a, 1996; Conlin and Baum, 1995). Butler (1993), one of the pioneers of the study of island tourism, proposes and discusses four key factors which seem to draw tourists specifically to island destinations. These are critically reviewed below.

The first, and most obvious, feature of island tourism is *physical separation*. The land-sea boundary is a crucial one that has been navigated physically and psychologically throughout history, in western and eastern traditions. This gives rise to notions of 'utopia' (More, 1516; *also* Cameron, 2012), and to the possibilities of exclusive and protected communities of those seeking a different life – from the monks formerly on Lindisfarne, Britain and Skellig Michael, Ireland; to the manufactured Palm Islands and 'The World', in Dubai, catering for the world's super-rich (Brown, 2003; Horn et al., 1990; Jackson and Della Dora, 2009, respectively). No wonder, therefore, that some organisations, including the European Union, will not recognise a piece of land surrounded by water at high tide as an island if it has been connected with a 'fixed link' – a causeway, tunnel or bridge – to a mainland (Baldacchino, 2007). The journey to, and from, or perhaps just around, an island – traditionally by boat or ship, now also by plane – is part of the basic package of 'doing' island tourism. Moreover, the journey to and from can be part of the fun or – as in the case of cruise ship tourism – intended to be most of the fun (Dowling, 2006).

A second characteristic of island tourism is *cultural difference.* Islanders often develop an identity that is different from that of contiguous mainlanders; indeed, the very existence of 'the mainland' as a constant reference point, nudges towards an ethno-cultural differentiation, to the extent that distinct dialects, dances, meals, rituals, musics, songs, customs and other behaviour patterns tend to evolve with time (e.g. Baldacchino, 2011). Emergent nationalist sentiments, often coalescing on distinct islands, intensify this process (e.g. Ballerino Cohen, 2010). Some 170 out of almost 1,000 of UNESCO's World Heritage sites are either on islands or are whole islands (UNESCO, 2014). The latter would include Chile's Easter island, Rapa Nui, Ecuador's Galápagos archipelago, Gambia's James Island, Greece's Patmos and Russia's Solovetsky, to name but a few. With the prospects of tourism, such cultural differences can be exaggerated and even invented, staged especially for tourist consumption, as part of the exoticisation of the island cultural landscape, rendering it more 'distant', 'different' and 'unique' than it actually is (Galani-Moutafi, 2000). In other island scenarios, the host-guest encounter has provided a new lease of life to archaic practices that may have easily disappeared, were it not for a sudden vigour and dynamism associated with their 'discovery' by enthusiastic tourists (Smith, 1989).

Important to island destinations are notions of an exclusive remoteness and a certain island magic (Picard, 2011). At the heart of this island thrill belongs the idea of a certain island *terroir* – a set of special, place-specific geographical and geological characteristics – offering a distinct island flavour – in cultural spectacle, in linguistic nuance, in specific mannerisms – but also literally, in locally produced food, beer, wine and spirits, all served in a growing number of restaurants dedicated to island specialties. Such products are fine examples of 'glocalisation' (Robertson, 1995), when the locally distinctive is produced and formatted to meet global standards, expectations and tastes (e.g. Baldacchino and Baldacchino, 2012).

Next, of course, is an *attractive climate and environment.* Nature is always experimenting, and it finds no better laboratory for such pursuits than islands, and especially oceanic islands. The biological diversity of the flora and fauna of islands is legendary. While the range of species on islands is typically more restricted, a larger proportion of native island species is likely to be endemic and unique; but that also means that any such species are more likely to be threatened or to have become extinct (Whittaker and Fernández-Palacios, 2007; Young, 1999). Of 724 known animal extinctions in the last 400 years, about half were of island species; and, of the bird species that have become extinct in that same period, at least 90% were island dwellers (Convention on Biological Diversity, 2010). The main causes of island species extinction have been identified as habitat destruction, invasive alien species, climate change, natural disasters, over-exploitation of natural resources, pollution and waste. Tourism development is implicated in many of these causal factors.

This status of an island as 'evolution's workshop' (Larson, 2001) is already a major attraction in itself. Now, combine this feature with so many islands being typically located in either tropical or temperate zones; they can offer pleasant climates, sandy beaches and what careless visitors might regard as happy natives itching to please, all the year round. No wonder that millions of 'the golden hordes' descend every year to inviting island paradises in the Pacific, Caribbean, Indian and Mediterranean seas/oceans to what has become the world's 'pleasure periphery' (Turner and Ash, 1975; also Lanfant et al., 1995). Tourism is now responsible for about one out of every 16 jobs available in the world (Schulz, 2011).

Butler's fourth, final, just as crucial yet less readily identifiable characteristic of island tourism is *political autonomy*. Nations make better, less ambiguous destinations. Forty five of the world's 193 sovereign states and members of the United Nations (UN) General Assembly are on islands, whole islands or archipelagos; almost one-fourth of all sovereign states (Baldacchino, 2006a, p. 3). These range from tiny Nauru to sub-continental Madagascar; from Barbados in the Caribbean to Fiji in the Pacific; and from tropical Samoa to much cooler Iceland. The number increases to 47 if Taiwan/Republic of China and the Turkish Republic of Northern Cyprus (not members of the UN) are included. Amongst these island states, Indonesia, Japan, the Philippines and the United Kingdom are the most heavily populated; while Australia is the world's only, single-state 'island continent'.

Moreover, over one hundred subnational island territories practise considerable degrees of autonomy: from constituent members of federal states (Hawai'i in the USA, Prince Edward Island in Canada, Tasmania in Australia); to those enjoying special status within their country (Jeju in South Korea; Madeira in Portugal; Hong Kong in China; Åland in Finland; the Canary Islands in Spain; Rodrigues in Mauritius; Svalbard in Norway), and finally others that linger as remnants of European or US (neo)colonialism, but with little appetite (so far) to become sovereign and independent states themselves (Aruba, Bermuda, Guam, Mayotte, Puerto Rico, Réunion, and the world's largest non-continental island, Greenland) (Baldacchino, 2006b, 2010; Bartmann, 2006). Each of these subnational island jurisdictions can bring to bear its resources to announce itself as a specific tourism destination. From a brand recognition perspective, these locations start with a net advantage: they have the political capacity to advertise themselves (as tourist destinations, among other things) in their own right. Nevertheless, there are various internationally renowned island tourism locales – Bali, Bora Bora, Key West and Venice, to name a few – that are not political jurisdictions unto themselves (Gregory, 2008).

More Than Meets the Eye? Enter the Archipelago

> The natural history of this archipelago is very remarkable: it seems to be a little world within itself (Darwin, 1839, p. 454).

Butler's diagnosis holds up very well to general scrutiny. But it needs to be deepened and refined in order to come to better terms with some of the real idiosyncrasies of island experiences. One of these is that of the archipelago.

Although we discuss and refer to islands, as in 'island tourism', the material reality is often one of multiple islands in some sort of relationship. Indeed, a careful examination of the world's islands reveals that most are actually members of archipelagos, assemblages that range from a minimum size of two (say, St. Kitts and Nevis), to over 50,000 in the archipelago sea of SW Finland, with the Åland mainland being the largest component therein (Depraetere and Dahl, 2007, p. 77). There are very few island jurisdictions that really are nothing but single land blocks: the Pacific island state of Nauru, perhaps, is one of these. Even places that might appear as unitary islands to a casual observer, such as Cyprus and Barbados, have rocks offshore that are significant components of their respective tourism appeal: at Petra tou Romiou, alleged birthplace of goddess Aphrodite, near Paphos, Cyprus;

and at Bethesda beach, on the wild east coast of Barbados. What appears to us today as the single land mass of Bermuda is actually a series of discrete islands inter-connected by bridges. And this observation flies in the face of a widespread practice that acts to camouflage the main islands of archipelagos as if they were single islands, by officially or colloquially ascribing the whole archipelago with the same name as that of its largest component, or the one that contains its main settlement. Åland, Chatham, Hawai'i, Madagascar, Madeira, Montreal, Pitcairn, Socotra, Svalbard, Tasmania and Zanzibar are some examples of this confusing, yet revealing, practice.

Indeed, contemporary scholarship tends to settle upon two rather overworked topological relations of islands. The first presents a clear focus on an island's singularity, its unique history and culture, crafted and inscribed by the border between *land* and *sea*. The second distinguishes an island from a *mainland/continent*, and dwells on its differences from, and dependencies on, the larger player. The concept of the archipelago evokes a third topological relation that is much less commonly deployed than the previous two. It foregrounds interactions between and among islands themselves. The relation of island to island is characterised by repetition and assorted multiplicity, which intensify, amplify and disrupt relations of land and water, as well as island and continent/mainland.

The archipelago is one component of the study of islands that is well established within the natural sciences, but much less beyond that. Thus, the juxtaposition of variation and similarity among the islands in the Galápagos archipelago played a key role in sharpening Charles Darwin's ideas on species evolution, speciation and natural selection. The Aru Islands of the Indonesian archipelago had a similar effect on Alfred Russell Wallace (Quammen, 1996). Other examples have included the study of birds in Indonesia (Mayr, 1942), Hawaiian honeycreepers (Wagner and Funk, 1995), and more on Galápagos finches (Grant and Grant, 1996).

Taking this powerful perspective systematically beyond fauna and flora, and without delving into its use as a metaphor shorn of material content (as occurs so readily also with the notion of island) is a fairly recent undertaking (e.g. Pugh, 2013; Stratford et al., 2011; Stratford, 2013). It is now a core concern of the international law of the sea, where the island members of an archipelago are located in such proximity to each other that they can naturally be seen as a unit, assigning them specific rights and obligations, such as designating sea lanes (Sand, 2012). Marrou (2005) deploys an archipelagic imagination to analyse the politics of the Azores, Portugal. Still in political geography, an archipelagic lens adds fresh insights to such complex jurisdictions as Taiwan (Baldacchino and Tsai, 2014), and the United Kingdom (Pocock, 2005: 29); as well as to Australia's shifting identity as island, continent, nation and archipelago (Perera, 2009); and to the consciousness of the Japanese state as a *shimaguni* (island nation) and its possible bearing on how it tackles the escalating tensions in the China Sea (Suwa, 2012).

Returning to Butler's four-point typology, we can sense that, if what appear to be single islands are mostly and actually archipelagos, then physical separation does not just separate them from mainlands but from each other; thus, inter-island crossings between (especially inhabited) islands, often at levels of demand that preclude profitability, will be hot items on the local political agenda. Cultural differences between islanders within the same island cluster may be enhanced and exaggerated, even invented, in order to appeal to specific tourist niches; a stretch of water can make a world of difference. In an archipelago, the ability to attract tourists may need to stretch to include the ability to share and spread the tourist dollar to the far-flung corners of the island group. And its political establishment would need to reconcile the need to offer a sharp, strong consistent and clearly identifiable brand as a single destination with the need to allow each of the islands within the archipelago to develop and sound its own voice and identity. The expression of a plurality of voices and interests, often in competition for scarce fiscal resources, may not exactly align with notions of an earthy island paradise, although the tourist may be quite immune to this cacophony and complexity.

Definition

> They know nothing and they've never heard of the archipelago as a whole or any one of its innumerable islands (Solzhenitsyn, 1973, p. 3).

The most common definition of an archipelago is simply as 'a group of islands'. This construct is simple, yet powerful: archipelagic formations are common: the world is one such. The significance of the assemblage goes beyond that of a simple gathering, collection or composition of things that are believed to fit together. Much like the thinking behind systems theory, assemblages act in concert: they actively map out, select, piece together, and allow for the conception and conduct of individual units as members of a group. Just like constellations: assemblages of heavenly bodies that, like Orion the Hunter, take on one (or more) recognisable forms only when their wholeness arises out of a process of articulating multiple elements by establishing connections amongst them. An archipelago is similar: its framing as 'such and such an assemblage' draws our attention to the ways in which practices, representations, experiences, and affects articulate to take a particular dynamic form. Archipelagos are fluid cultural processes, sites of abstract and material relations of movement and rest, dependent on changing conditions of articulation or connection (Stratford et al., 2011, *passim*).

Three Major Attributes

Referring to the archipelago as a 'societal sub-type' in a short contribution, LaFlamme (1983) offers a more nuanced definition; he proposes 'four major attributes' of the archipelago state, and all but one of these insights – that component islands are small and underdeveloped; they do not have to be either of these – are what largely drive the conceptual framework of this book. The first of these tenets is that an archipelago consists of a large number of islands: Bahamas, Fiji, Indonesia, Japan and the Philippines are suitable examples. In our case, we argue that a unit as small as a two-island group is also an archipelago, albeit the simplest imaginable, and the analysis that follows in the pages below is just as applicable to these.

Second, an archipelago state considers the waters surrounding its component islands as being within its boundaries and an integral part of its heritage: these notions of an inner or territorial sea, if disputed, can escalate tensions and precipitate armed conflict, with recent events involving China and Japan squabbling over the Daioyu/Senkaku islands being cases in point (Nyman, 2013b). Many of the world's flashpoints have been located on or around islands (Anderson and Owen, 1993); and islands continue to serve as geo-strategic platforms to the world's major powers, and particularly to the United States (Bartmann, 2007).

Thirdly and finally, every archipelago has a centrifugal tendency: 'in an archipelago, the temptation is always great, at worst to secede and at best to disregard the political jurisdiction of the centre' (LaFlamme, 1983, p. 361). This intra-archipelago dynamic of uneven island-island politics strikes at the very heart of the central *problematique* addressed by this book: how do multi-island jurisdictions, often run by democratically elected politicians, balance the wishes of their various island publics and constituencies with the rationale of hub-and-spoke transport logistics (versus costly repetitive infrastructure), tourism differentiation (versus repetition), complimentary (rather than similar) and cooperative (rather than competitive) economic development trajectories? All islanders know that they experience tense relations with their island neighbours; often made fun of in popular idiom, these tensions and rivalries may find expression in discriminatory practices of various kinds, official or otherwise; and these become more likely if specific islands claim, or are represented as claiming, a linguistic, ethnic, religious, historical, occupational and/or economic status that is distinct from that pertaining to other islands. Island nationalism knows no limits, as various attempts at secession demonstrate: for example, Mayotte (resident population: about 212,000) did not join the other Comoros islands to independence and is now an integral part of France, although the Comoros continue to claim the island (Muller, 2012); Tuvalu (population: 10,000) successfully engineered its separation from Kiribati (population: 100,000) before becoming an independent state in 1978 (McIntyre, 2012); Nevis (population: 12,000), failed by a whisker to pass a referendum in 1998 that would have seen it secede from St. Kitts (population: 32,000) (Premdas, 2000).

One needs to be wary of the extent to which 20th century ethno-nationalism in particular (Smith, 2009), has given scope to an acceleration of constructed identities, justifying why some islands should be run autonomously or independently of other islands, or of contiguous mainlands. This 'fission effect' remains very strong, with secessionist and independence parties and movements still active in many islands (and also in some mainland countries) around the world, from Åland to Greenland, and from New Caledonia to Bermuda (Hepburn and Baldacchino, 2013). Tourism marketing has also encouraged a similar development, with even the islands grouped within the same archipelago seeking to rise above the competitive noise of their island neighbours and seeking to lure tourists to their particular space, in what is often construed as a 'zero-sum' game: the Canary Islands (Spain), the Azores (Portugal), and the Caribbean region as a whole – where inter-island state rivalry extends well beyond cricket – are suitable examples (Baldacchino and Ferreira, 2013; Fraser and Wresch, 2005).

This Book

> Multi-destination travel in island chains may be an added attraction for tourists ... Cooperative marketing and complementary product development is important for archipelago islands. This will create a diverse touristic experience giving archipelagos an advantage over single islands, particularly if they are small (Sheldon, 2005, p. 2).

This book explores the conceptual insights provided by the archipelagic 'twist' in the specific context of tourism principles, policies and practices. *Archipelago tourism* is the term being proposed here to describe tourism experiences to multiple and contiguous island destinations in the same holiday. There is a growing practice of 'island hopping' and inter-island travel, by small plane, small yacht or pleasure craft, regular ferry or cruise ship; but there is hardly any academic literature or tourism management 'best practices' in this field.

Should one trawl the world wide web with the term 'archipelago tourism', many sites would come up, from Mergui (in Myanmar) to Tuamotu (in French Polynesia); also suggestive, by the way, of the potential market for this book. Yet, these sites are descriptive, touristy and place-specific; and the archipelago is just backdrop or context. This book allows for the pioneering exploration of the archipelago as tourism study *focus* (and not just *locus*); a heuristic device for rendering islands as sites of different tourism practices, industries and policies, but also challenges and possibilities. Few academic studies have so far specifically and systematically adopted an archipelagic outlook towards the critical understanding of tourism branding, marketing and management (exceptions include Baldacchino and Ferreira, 2013; Bardolet and Sheldon, 2008; Bethel, 2000).

Five Attributes of Archipelagos Specific to Tourism

> Every constituent of an archipelago is an island that can seem isolated in and by itself, and it is only in analysing how currents move between and among them, by locating vantage points that give one a wider horizon, that the pattern that suggests an archipelago reveals itself (Sengupta, n.d., p. 1).

Butler's island typology thus needs to be enriched and nuanced with a distinct archipelagic layering to take note of the multi-island reality within which island tourism typically unfolds. We propose here five distinct attributes of archipelagos that have a strong bearing on how they behave as tourism destinations.

The first is *visibility*. This is the most basic principle of marketing, since no one will contemplate travelling to a place unless one knows that such a place exists. Maps already misplace various archipelagos that form part of larger states, consigning them to the tragedy of the inset: for example, the far-flung French overseas island departments of Martinique, Guadeloupe, Réunion and Mayotte (along with non-island French Guyana), may be integral to the French state; yet they must contend with hovering at the edges of maps of continental France. But this can get even worse, since various maps of 'France' completely exclude these territories, only portraying the island of Corsica as an inset, if at all. Alderney in relation to Guernsey, Union in relation to St. Vincent, Barbuda in relation to Antigua, Azores and Madeira in relation to Portugal, Hawai'i (and non-island Alaska) in relation to the United States, Rotuma in relation to Fiji, and Aldabra in relation to Seychelles are suitable examples. Shetland is home to the 'box people': those that inhabit the box in the sea usually to be found off the Northeast coast of Scotland (e.g. School Atlas of 1852; Map Shop, 2014). Indeed, all locales that could appear as insets risk elimination from pictorial representation and thus can get consigned to visual exclusion. The smaller the island within an archipelago, the further away from the archipelago's centre of gravity and the smaller its resident population, the more likely that its presence, let alone its location, will be summarily dismissed as insignificant; the loss of a minor detail that is amply justified by the resulting larger scale rendition of the main (is)land(s).

Additional, deliberate acts of invisibility occur when neighbouring islands may belong to different states. The islands in the Aegean, the world's first archipelago, belong mainly to Greece and Turkey; and various Greek islands exist within a few miles of the Turkish mainland; yet, a representation of the Greek state, or of the ferry services that serve its islands, tend to make no visual reference to mainland Turkey, or to any of its own islands; as if that neighbour simply does not exist (Greece Aegean Maps, 2014). National pride and state territoriality, with some doses of wish fulfilment, act in concert to excise a looming, contiguous jurisdiction. This occurs even in situations like that of the world's only ten inhabited islands shared between two or more countries (Borneo, Hispaniola, Ireland, New Guinea, Timor …): politics trumps geography, with maps which would show just that part of the island that represents the state in question, rather than the whole island (Hepburn and Baldacchino, 2013).

The key advantage of invisibility may lie in those situations where a small island deliberately wishes to stay off the tourist map. Thus, a raised coral atoll like Aldabra, a UNESCO World Heritage Site that is within reach to only a few visitors (mainly scientists) annually, may prefer not to proclaim its existence; invisibility here aligns nicely with a jealously guarded inaccessibility (e.g. Šúr et al., 2013). In much the same way, the tourist map of the Hawaiian islands, available on the official tourism website, purposely excludes Nihau (a private island) and Kaho'olawe (a sacred island), both of which are taboo to tourists (Go Hawaii, 2014).

The second attribute, following deftly on the first, is that of *tweaked representation*: this involves the physical rendering of island/s that is *not* in conformity to geo-physical size, location, proximity or proportionality. Thus, assuming that an island *does* appear on the map of its archipelago, it may do so in ways that do not strictly reflect one or more of its physical features. Typically, outlier islands are brought in closer to the centre of gravity of the archipelago; smaller islands are represented as if they were larger; and larger islands represented as if they were smaller, in relation to the other members of the island jurisdiction. This is presumably done to satisfy two objectives: first, to suggest that the archipelago as destination is more compact than it actually is, and therefore making it easier to travel from one island to another; second, to hint that the different constituents of an archipelago enjoy an equality that obliges a levelling out of geo-physical features (especially land size). Thus, the islands make a picture of a happier team, rubbing shoulders, and thus promoting island-hopping tourism. Where territorial flags carry symbols that represent the individual member islands of archipelagos, these symbols (stars for the Azores, Cape Verde, St. Kitts-Nevis and Tuvalu; island motifs for the Canary Islands) *are of equal size*, even though the constituent islands would have quite disparate land and population sizes. Perhaps these are deliberate centripetal acts that seek to balance out, at least visually, powerful centrifugal forces at work, about which we have commented above.

Indeed, the third thematic is *domination* and its corollary, *subordination*: it may not be self-evident on the flag, but there is always, even if subtle, a power inequality in the presentation and behaviour of (usually) one island in relation to other islands in the same cluster. Although all are islands in the assemblage, one of the islands may behave as the mainland to the others; indeed, some such islands are called mainland: Åland, Shetland, Orkney are suitable examples. In Japan, its four largest islands – Hokkaido, Honshu, Kyushu and Shikoku – are considered to be the country's mainland region. In archipelagic Fiji, Vanua Levu and Viti Levu constitute the mainland.

This situation creates a core-periphery relationship within the archipelago, irrespective of size. Even small island groups are not exempt from dependency dynamics that unfold elsewhere. Urbanisation, migration, gross fixed capital formation, investment … these are manifest as flows of labour, talent and resources away from the periphery and towards the core of the archipelago. Thus, some islands – or perhaps just one – would grow their populations at the expense of all the others, kicking in a vicious cycle of decline; while adding to the strain of the infrastructure of the receiving island.

From a tourism perspective, the ascendancy of the main island would also be reflected in its status as a gateway to the whole archipelago. With its (usually considerably better) transport infrastructure, the main island – think New Providence/Nassau in the Bahamas, Viti Levu in Fiji, South Tarawa in Kiribati, Majuro in the Marshall Islands, Mahé in the Seychelles, or Tongatapu in Tonga – would usually be the main port of call for incoming air or sea passengers. Most such visitors may choose to stay on this island, depriving the other members of the archipelago of tourism-related economic benefits. In tourism promotional material, this hierarchy may be visible in the very logo of the archipelago. Thus, the logo of the Guernsey tourism organisation has 'Guernsey' on the top line, with Herm – Sark – Alderney laid out below (Visit Guernsey, 2014). The pecking order is obvious (see Plate 6.1). In the Maltese case, a flexibility in which island name comes on top of the listing of the component members of the archipelago is just as telling, and presents itself as a smart compromise (see Plate 2.1).

Of course, the inhabitants of most small islands will not take this situation lightly. Sensing that tourism may be the solution to their economic misfortunes, they will lobby vigorously – and, in democratic contexts, often successfully, sooner or later – to have their own airports, ferry / cruise ship terminals, or connecting bridges/tunnels, in order to share in the spoils. The politico-economic elites of these smaller islands will expect such transport infrastructure to be in place and operating, even if it may not be profitable, citing social welfare needs and a chronic vulnerability where connectivity is sheer survival and the key to any economic competitiveness (e.g. CPMR, 2002). Thus, on the official tourism website for the Canary Islands, one finds the names of all its seven main islands prominently displayed, and in fonts of equal size; one is also invited to 'get to know each island' (Turismo de Canarias, 2014).

Some idea of the replication of infrastructure and services that these dynamics engender have been calculated for the South Aegean, consisting of some 40 inhabited islands spread over the Cyclades and Dodecanese island groups. If the region's population was living on just one island, a maximum of three ports would be sufficient, while now there are 50, along with 14 airports instead of one, 21 power production plants instead of one, five hospitals instead of one, 211 primary schools instead of 90, 35 waste water treatment units instead of eight, and so on (ESPON, 2011; Spilanis et al., 2012, p. 211).

The fourth feature in the archipelago puzzle is *liminality* or *layering*: a reminder that an island could be the mainland of another island, which could itself be the mainland of yet another island …. Without delving into the fine details of computer science (e.g. Mandelbrot, 1982; Royle, 2007), geographers remind us of the fractal nature of islands: switch magnification, and what may have been a small island off a mainland itself becomes 'the mainland' for even smaller islands (Depraetere and Dahl, 2007, p. 64). Thus, El Hierro, the smallest of the Canary Islands, is also the site of some intense volcanic activity of late; an eruption could force masses of rock to the surface, creating a new island (Mail Online, 2014). In such a scenario, El Hierro may find itself as the default mainland to this new islet. The scientists who can be expected to come and investigate this new island would probably use El Hierro as their base.

This is a reminder that the definition of an archipelago is pliant enough to generate multiple identities; an island may feel at the wrong end of the stick in relation to a bigger island; and yet push its weight around in relation to even smaller neighbours. This relativity can extend up or down multiple scales.

Take the volcanic finger-like rock of La Canna, a nature reserve which arises about 74 metres above the sea, as an example. It lies off the island of Filicudi (population: 235), its mainland. Yet Filicudi is an administrative subdivision of Lipari (population: 11,000) which is the largest of the Aeolian Islands. Lipari, in turn, is quite small compared to neighbouring Sicily (population: 5 million), the largest island in the Mediterranean sea, but itself a province of Italy (Wish Sicily, 2014).

The further down an island lies on a measure of size and centrality, the more likely that its inhabitants will experience 'multiple peripherality' (Spilanis, et al., 2012, p. 202); their lines of dependence become longer and flimsier, needing to navigate multiple access points, and dependent on monopoly transport providers to reach those points. There may be,

> … different destinations that island residents may have to travel to in order to have access to a number of vital services; [considerations include] the type of available transportation, the frequency of connections and the cost in time and money that this access may involve (ibid.).

These access points may also translate as multiple journeys (probably by sea): two or more trips, with ample down time, including overnight stops, may be required to get from one's island home to a critical service node (such as a passport office, tax bureau, job centre, university campus, or international airport).

The fifth and final feature to present here is the *nature and expression of differentiation between islands.* Having established the pressures that keep, or present, a group of islands together, and yet that also work to unpack them as separate destinations, at different scales, one now needs to delve into the characterisations of such a dissimilarity. Here, one often faces a contrast: one between official/top-down attempts at 'ordering' an archipelago to appeal to multi-island visitations, and a more authentic yet chaotic and complex relationality that is competitive and grounded in other, inter-island relations.

Official representations of such places as the North Aegean in Greece, The Bahamas, Indonesia, the Maldives and the Philippines gush with a kaleidoscope of warm and appealing colours (Bahamas Tourism Office, 2014; Indonesia Travel, 2014; Tourism Philippines, 2014) (e.g. Plate 12.1). Their visual tones suggest diverse attractive and somehow complimentary destinations that exude an alluring synergy; many, or perhaps all, islands need to be visited to flavour the full experience of the archipelago (e.g., Plate 1.1). The signal is one of an intricate patchwork quilt, rainbow or bouquet of island experiences that beckon visitors to practise 'island hopping' (Bahamas Promotion, 2010), and come and sample as many islands as possible. After all, 'every island has its own character, its own atmosphere and subtle differences in culture' (ibid.).

And yet, there are other narratives in play. The multiple geographies of archipelagic spaces need not be rendered in that coy artificiality concocted by branding consultants. The cultural nuances of islander lives can also be expressed in more authentic, inter-island rivalries that have a long history. And the nuances can be themselves consequences of the different ways in which tourism practice has unfolded on the different components of the same archipelago, as noted with Norderney versus Spiekeroog in Germany's East Frisian Islands (Mose, 1997, pp. 109–10). It thus becomes important to explore more critically how this plurality of narratives intersects, aligns or jars with any official rhetoric(s) of representation. Marketing strategies speak highly of brand consolidation; yet, the analysis of praxis suggests that brand consolidation may unfold at the expense of either showcasing diversity, or presenting its fake, fairy tale rendition (e.g. Baldacchino and Ferreira, 2013).

These are the five overarching characteristics of archipelagic tourism that foreground the case studies that follow. A multi-disciplinary team of scholars, researchers and practitioners – and including engineers, anthropologists and land use planners – have come together in this volume to give global critical expression to the policies and practices of archipelago tourism. They were allowed free rein to deploy the archipelagic imagination in a specific regional (e.g. Caribbean, Mascarenes), national (e.g. Bahamas, Malta), or sub-national (e.g. Sardinia, Yasawa) context. But all authors were urged to address these three key questions:

> *Logistics* – how best to organise travel to and among the constituent members of an archipelago? What considerations need to be made in determining the siting and coordination of expensive airport and sea terminal infrastructure and operations?
>
> *Marketing* – how best to present island destinations to prospective tourists and visitors such that they display their unique cultural and bio-geographical attributes but also in a manner than complements the attributes held by neighbouring islands (which may be competing for the same tourist market segment)?
>
> *Branding* – how are visual and other promotional and identity discourses used to locate and position separate neighbouring islands as a 'natural' cluster or assemblage whose constituent, separate and multiple island units deserve being experienced? How do the constituent parts sacrifice their visibility for the sake of the whole (and vice versa)?

The outcome is a rich documentation of the workings of archipelago tourism, organised in terms of the four aquatic zones where the world's major island tourist destinations are located: the Mediterranean Sea, the Atlantic, Pacific and Indian Oceans. This case material, which comes in eleven distinct contributions, is then book-ended by more conceptual and generic reflections by specialists in the field of tourism (Richard W. Butler, Dimitri Ioannides and Evangelia Petridou) as well as by a geographer who happens to be a seasoned island traveller (Stephen A. Royle).

Finally, a personal note. The book's inspiration arises also from my own experience. Born and bred in the small island state of Malta, I did not think much at first of the way in which the main island (also called Malta; population: 380,000) overshadows the second, much smaller island (Gozo, population: 30,000), including in touristic representations. (More on this in the chapter by Theuma and Chaperon below.) I am now much more cognisant and critical of how Gozo is portrayed as a strikingly different destination from 'mainland' Malta, encouraging tourists who arrive in Malta's international airport to take the 5-mile (8 km) ferry ride to Gozo for at least a day trip. The distance between the two islands may be small: and yet, even a small stretch of water can and does make a world of a difference. Debate and controversy rage on as to whether Gozo should have its own airfield, a tunnel/bridge connecting it to Malta, and its own tourism authority (e.g. Macdonald, 2007). (So far, it has none of these).

Conclusion

> In an archipelago, the temptation is always great, at worst, to secede, and at best to disregard the political jurisdiction of the centre (Lewis, 1974, p. 136).

Tourism remains the world's largest service industry. Since it deals with such intangibles as 'experiences' which have no weight and occupy no physical space, it is an industry especially favourable to small islands; these would otherwise be seriously challenged to secure and maintain competitiveness in dealing with alternative, tangible products that must be exported to, and sold in, overseas markets. All the more reason then to recognise that most islands are actually archipelagos which may need to more effectively acknowledge and incorporate this geo-physical condition into their branding initiatives, tourism marketing plans, and tourism infrastructure blueprints. From the policies and practices that it showcases, this book, one hopes, provides some evidence, reflection and inspiration towards this (often overdue) recognition.

Acknowledgements

I am indebted to many colleagues and friends for the journey that has led to the conceptualisation and production of this book. I walked into Elaine Stratford's office at the University of Tasmania (UTAS), Hobart Campus, Australia, in February 2011, proposing that we should really do something with the idea of the archipelago. She ran away with the inspiration – more like a hunch at that point – and spurred me on to explore it more widely and deeply. A day-long workshop in Hobart, in April 2011, involving Dr Stratford with Elizabeth McMahon (University of New South Wales), Carol Farbotko (Commonwealth Scientific and Industrial Research Organisation) and Andrew Harwood (PhD candidate at UTAS), kept the juices flowing. I then presented papers based on these evolving ideas-in-progress during conferences and workshops in Ponta Delgada (Azores, Portugal), Tortola (British Virgin Islands), Valletta (Malta) and Sydney (NS, Canada). In the Azores, I had the privilege of working with Eduardo Costa Duarte Ferreira, and a paper based on our joint research there was presented as part of a day-long island studies panel – aptly titled 'reframing islandness' – at the 2012 annual meeting of the American Association of Geographers (AAG), in New York City. Elaine Stratford (again: where would I be without her?) helped put this powerful panel together, along with Joseph Palis, at North Carolina State University, USA. Select papers from this panel were revised, edited, reviewed and published in a special section of *Island Studies Journal*, 8(1), May 2013. By December 2013, I could organise a workshop specifically on archipelago tourism with a selection of manuscripts being prepared for this book, as part of an international conference held in Maspalomas, Gran Canaria, Canary Islands, Spain. Thank you Richard Butler, Rita Cannas, Fathimath Amira, Ernestina Giudici, Sophia Karampela, Sophia Rolle and Stephen Royle for joining me in Gran Canaria to discuss and refine our work. And to these, and all the other authors in this book, my sincere thanks for believing in the basic hypothesis, and running away with it. All the maps in the book have been meticulously prepared by Nikoleta Koukourouvli, Department of Geography, University of the Aegean, Greece, who I also thank. Finally, I also acknowledge the support of my publisher, Ashgate. My commissioning editor, Katy Crossan, was always there to guide and mentor me every step of the way, making this a satisfying editorial experience. May it prove to be a just-as-pleasant one for the readers of this volume: they should find various nuggets to drive insights into the archipelagic, surprisingly under-acknowledged, feature of island tourism.

References

Anderson, E.W., and Owen, G. (1993). *An atlas of world political flashpoints: A sourcebook of geopolitical crisis.* London: Burns & Oates.

Apostoulopoulos, Y., and Gayle, D.J. (eds) (2002). *Island tourism and sustainable development: Caribbean, Pacific and Mediterranean experiences.* Westport CT: Praeger.

Bahamas Promotion. (2010). Island hopping. Retrieved from http://www.bahamas.co.uk/home/island-hopping

Bahamas Tourism Office. (2014). Official website of the Bahamas Tourist Office. Retrieved from http://www.bahamas.co.uk/

Baldacchino, A., and Baldacchino, G. (eds) (2012). *A taste of islands: 60 recipes and stories from our world of islands.* Charlottetown, Canada: Island Studies Press.

Baldacchino, G. (2006a). Islands, island studies, *Island Studies Journal*, 1(1), 3–18.

Baldacchino, G. (2006b). Innovative development strategies from non-sovereign island jurisdictions? A global review of economic policy and governance practices. *World Development*, 34(5), 852–67.

Baldacchino, G. (2007). *Bridging islands: The impact of fixed links.* Charlottetown, Canada: Acorn Press.

Baldacchino, G. (2010). *Island enclaves: Offshoring strategies, creative governance and subnational island jurisdictions.* Montreal, QC: McGill-Queen's University Press.

Baldacchino, G. (2011). *Island songs: A global repertoire.* Lanham, MD: Scarecrow Press.

Baldacchino, G., and Ferreira, E.C.D. (2013). Competing notions of diversity in archipelago tourism: transport logistics, official rhetoric and inter-island rivalry in the Azores. *Island Studies Journal*, 8(1), 84–104.

Baldacchino, G., and Tsai, H.-M. (2014). Contested enclave metageographies: the offshore islands of Taiwan. *Political Geography*, 40(1), 13–24.

Ballerino Cohen, C. (2010). *Take me to my paradise: Tourism and nationalism in the British Virgin Islands.* New Brunswick, NJ: Rutgers University Press.

Bardolet, E., and Sheldon, P.J. (2008). Tourism in archipelagos: Hawai'i and the Balearics. *Annals of Tourism Research*, 35(4), 900–923.

Bartmann, B. (2006). In or out: sub-national island jurisdictions and the antechamber of para-diplomacy. *The Round Table: Commonwealth Journal of International Affairs*, 95(386), 541–59.

Bartmann, B. (2007). War and security. In G. Baldacchino (ed.) *A world of islands: An island studies reader*, pp. 295–324. Charlottetown, Canada and Luqa, Malta: Institute of Island Studies, University of Prince Edward Island and Agenda Academic.

Baum, T.G. (1997). The fascination of islands: a tourist perspective. In D.G. Lockhart and D. Drakakis-Smith (eds) *Island tourism: Problems and perspectives*, pp. 21–35. London: Mansell.

Baum, T.G., with Hagen-Grant, L., Jolliffe, L., Lambert, S., and Sigurjonsson, B. (2000). Tourism and the cold water islands of the North Atlantic. In G. Baldacchino and D. Milne (eds) *Lessons from the political economy of small islands: The resourcefulness of jurisdiction*, pp. 214–29. Basingstoke: Macmillan.

Bethel, N. (2000). Navigations: Insularity versus cosmopolitanism in the Bahamas. Formality and informality in an archipelagic nation. Extract from PhD dissertation. Cambridge: University of Cambridge. Retrieved from http://www.nicobethel.net/nico-at-home/academia/forminformal.html

Briguglio, L., Archer, B., Jafari, J., and Wall, G. (eds) (1996a). *Sustainable tourism in islands and small states – Vol. 1: Issues and policies*. London: Pinter.

Briguglio, L., Butler, R., Harrison, D., and Leal Filho, W. (eds) (1996b). *Sustainable tourism in islands and small states – Vol. 2: Case studies*. London: Pinter.

Brown, M.P. (2003). *The Lindisfarne gospels: Society, spirituality and the scribe.* Toronto, ON: University of Toronto Press.

Butler, R.W. (1993). Tourism development in small islands: past influences and future directions. In D.G. Lockhart, D. Drakakis-Smith and J.A. Schembri (eds) *The development process in small island states*, pp. 71–91. London: Routledge.

Cameron, A, (2012). Splendid isolation: 'philosopher's islands' and the reimagination of space. *Geoforum*, 43(4), 741–9.

Conlin, M., and Baum, T.G. (eds) (1995*). Island tourism: Management principles and practices*. Chichester: John Wiley.

Connell, J. (2003). Island dreaming: the contemplation of Polynesian paradise. *Journal of Historical Geography*, 29(4), 554–81.

Connell, J. (2013). *Islands at risk? Environments, economies and contemporary change*. Cheltenham: Edward Elgar.

Convention on Biological Diversity (2010) *Island biodiversity*. Montreal, Canada: Secretariat of the Convention on Biological Diversity. Retrieved from http://www.cbd.int/iyb/doc/prints/factsheets/iyb-cbd-factsheet-island-en.pdf

CPMR (2002). *Off the coast of Europe: European construction and the problem of the islands*. Rennes, France: Eurisles on the initiative of the Islands Commission, Conference of Peripheral Maritime Regions.

Crouch, D., Jackson, R., and Thomson, F. (eds) (2005). *The media and the tourist imagination: Converging cultures.* London: Routledge.

Darwin, C. (1839). *Journal of researches into the geology and natural history of the various countries visited by H.M.S. Beagle*. London: Henry Colburn.

Delumeau, J. (1992). *Une histoire du paradis*. Paris, France: Fayard.

Depraetere, C. and Dahl, A.L. (2007). Island locations and classifications. In G. Baldacchino (ed.) *A world of islands: An island studies reader*, pp. 57–105. Charlottetown, Canada and Luqa, Malta: Institute of Island Studies, University of Prince Edward Island and Agenda Academic.

Dowling, R.K. (2006). *Cruise ship tourism*. Wallingford, UK: CABI.

ESPON (2011). The development of the islands: European islands and cohesion policy (EUROISLANDS). Targeted Analysis 2013/2/2. Retrieved from http://www.espon.eu

Fraser, S., and Wresch, W. (2005). National competitive advantage in e-commerce efforts: a report from five Caribbean nations. *Perspectives on Global Development and Technology*, 4(1), 27–44.

Galani-Moutafi, V. (2000). The self and the other: traveler, ethnographer, tourist. *Annals of Tourism Research*, 27(1), 203–24.

Gillis, J.R. (2004). *Islands of the mind: How the human imagination created the Atlantic world*. New York: Palgrave Macmillan.

Gillis, J.R., and Lowenthal, D. (2009). Islands. Special issue. *The Geographical Review*, 97(2).

Go Hawaii (2014). Hawaii geography and maps. http://www.gohawaii.com/statewide/travel-tips/geography

Gössling, S. (ed.) (2003). *Tourism and development in tropical islands: Political ecology perspectives*. Cheltenham: Edward Elgar.

Gössling, S., and Wall, G. (2007). Island Tourism. In G. Baldacchino (ed.) *A world of islands: An island studies reader*, pp. 429–54. Charlottetown, Canada and Luqa, Malta: Institute of Island Studies, University of Prince Edward Island and Agenda Academic.

Grant, P.R., and Grant, B.R. (1996). Speciation and hybridisation in island birds. *Philosophical Transactions of the Royal Society B*, 351, 765–72.

Greece Aegean Maps (2014). Retrieved from http://www.greeceathensaegeaninfo.com/a-presentational/blue-map-greece.gif

Gregory, J. (2008). The world's 10 best vacation islands. Rates-to-Go, 6 July. Retrieved from http://www.ratestogo.com/blog/10-best-vacation-islands/

Hay, P. (2006). A phenomenology of islands. *Island Studies Journal*, 1(1), 19–42.

Hepburn, E., and Baldacchino, G. (eds) (2013). *Independence movements in subnational island jurisdictions.* London, UK: Routledge.

Horn, W., White Marshall, J., and Rourke, G.D. (1990). *The forgotten hermitage of Skellig Michael.* Berkeley CA: University of California Press.

Indonesia Travel (2014). Indonesia's official tourism website. Retrieved from http://www.indonesia.travel/

Jackson, M., and Della Dora, V. (2009). 'Dreams so big only the sea can hold them': man-made islands as anxious spaces, cultural icons and travelling visions. *Environment and Planning A*, 41(9), 2086–2104.

LaFlamme, A.G. (1983). The archipelago state as a societal subtype. *Current Anthropology*, 24(3), 361–2.

Lanfant, M.F., Allcock, J.B., and Bruner, E.M. (1995). *International tourism: Identity and change.* London: Sage.

Larson, E.J. (2001). *Evolution's workshop: God and science on the Galápagos islands.* New York: Basic Books.

Lewis, V. (1974). The Bahamas in international politics. *Journal of Interamerican Studies and World Affairs*, 16(1), 131–52.

Lockhart, D.G. (1997). Tourism and islands: an overview. In D.G. Lockhart and D. Drakakis-Smith (eds), *Island tourism: Trends and prospects*, pp. 3–20. London: Pinter.

Lockhart, D.G., and Drakakis-Smith, D. (eds) (1997). Island tourism: Trends and prospects. London: Pinter.

Löfgren, O. (2002). *On holiday: A history of vacationing.* Berkeley CA: University of California Press.

Loxley, D. (1990). *Problematic shores: The literature of islands.* New York: St. Martin's Press.

Macdonald, V. (2007). The case for a Gozo Tourism Authority, 17 May. Retrieved from http://www.timesofmalta.com/articles/view/20070517/interview/the-case-for-a-gozo-tourism-authority.180009#.UsGJsLSmbYY

Mail Online (2014). Could the Canaries soon get a new island? 30 December. Retrieved from http://www.dailymail.co.uk/sciencetech/article-2531173/Could-Canaries-new-island-Recent-earthquakes-hint-imminent-underwater-eruption.html

Mandelbrot, B. (1982). *The fractal geometry of nature.* New York: W.H. Freeman & Co.

Map Shop (2014). Wall map of the British isles. Retrieved from http://www.themapshop.co.uk/images/OSButtons/comms.jpg

Marrou, L. (2005). Quand l'île cache l'archipel: l'inscription des îles-escales dans l'archipel des Açores. In L. Marrou, N. Bernardie and F. Taglioni (eds), *Les dynamiques contemporaines des petits espaces insulaires: De l'île-relais aux réseaux insulaires*, pp. 181–97. Paris: Kathala.

Mayr, E. (1942). *Systematics and the origin of species.* New York: Columbia University Press.

McElroy, J.L. (2003). Tourism development in small islands across the world. *Geografiska Annaler*, 85B(2), 231–42.

McElroy, J.L. (2006). Small island tourist economies across the lifecycle. *Asia Pacific Viewpoint*, 47(1): 61–77.

McElroy, J.L., and Hamma, P.E. (2010). SITEs revisited: socioeconomic and demographic contours of small island tourist economies. *Asia Pacific Viewpoint*, 51(1), 36–46.

McIntyre, W.D. (2012). The partition of the Gilbert and Ellice Islands. *Island Studies Journal*, 7(1), 135–46.

More, T. (1516/2005). *Utopia*. G.M. Logan and R.M. Adams (eds). Cambridge: Cambridge University Press.

Mose, I. (1997). Mass tourism versus eco-tourism? Tourism patterns on the East Frisian Islands, Germany. In D.G. Lockhart, and D. Drakakis-Smith (eds), *Island tourism: Trends and prospects*, pp. 102–17. London: Thomson Learning.

MTA (2014). Malta Tourism Authority. Official logos. Retrieved from http://www.mta.com.mt/official-logos

Muller, K. (2012). Mayotte: between Europe and Africa. In R. Adler-Nissen and U. Pram Gad (eds) *European integration and postcolonial sovereignty games*, pp. 187–202. London: Routledge.

Nyman, E. (2013a). The island as container: islands, archipelagos, and player movement in video games. *Island Studies Journal*, 8(2), 269–84.

Nyman, E. (2013b). Oceans of conflict: determining potential areas of maritime disputes. *SAIS Review of International Affairs*, 33(2), 5–14.

Pearce, D. (1989). *Tourist development*. 2nd edn. New York: Wiley.

Perera, S. (2009). *Australia and the insular imagination: Beaches, borders, boats and bodies*. New York: Palgrave Macmillan.

Picard, D. (2011). *Tourism, magic and modernity: Cultivating the human garden*. New York: Berghahn Books.

Pocock, J.G.A. (2005). *The discovery of islands*. Cambridge: Cambridge University Press.

Premdas, R. (2000) Self-determination and secession in the Caribbean: The case of Nevis. In R. Premdas (ed.), *Identity, ethnicity and culture in the Caribbean*, pp. 447–84. St. Augustine, Trinidad and Tobago: School of Continuing Studies, University of the West Indies.

Pugh, J. (2013). Island movements: thinking with the archipelago. *Island Studies Journal*, 8(1), 9–24.

Quammen, D. (1996). *The song of the dodo: Island biogeography in an age of extinctions*. New York: Random House.

Robertson, R. (1995). Glocalisation: time-space and homogeneity-heterogeneity. In M. Featherstone, S. Lash and R. Robertson (eds), *Global modernities*, pp. 25–44. London: Sage.

Royle, S.A. (2007). Definitions and typologies. In G. Baldacchino (ed.), *A world of islands: An island studies reader*, pp. 33–56. Charlottetown, Canada and Luqa, Malta: Institute of Island Studies, University of Prince Edward Island and Agenda Academic.

Royle, S.A. (2001). *A geography of islands: Small island insularity*. London: Routledge.

Sand, P.H. (2012). Fortress conservation trumps human rights? The 'marine protected area' in the Chagos archipelago. *The Journal of Environment and Development*, 21(1), 36–9.

Scafi, A. (2006). *Mapping paradise: A history of heaven on earth*. Chicago, IL: University of Chicago Press.

School Atlas of 1852. Map of the British isles. Rertrieved from http://www.hipkiss.org/
    data/maps/blackwood-and-sons_keith-johnsons-physical-school-atlas_1852_geology-
    the-mountains-of-the-british-isles_2362_3015_600.jpg

Schulz, R.K. (2011). The World Tourism Organisation studies and promotes global tourism, 10
    June. Retrieved from http://geography.about.com/od/culturalgeography/a/The-World-
    Tourism-Organization.htm

Sengupta, S. (no date). Notes for keynote conversation. The bigger picture: Crossing art
    forms and cultures in an international context. Retrieved from http://cms.unimelb.edu.
    au/_data/assets/pdf_file/0004/419638/ssengupta.pdf

Sheldon, P.J. (2005). The challenges to sustainability in island tourism. University of
    Hawai'i, USA. *Occasional Paper* 2005-01, October. Retrieved from http://www.tim.
    hawaii.edu/ctps/Sheldon_Challenges_to_Sustainability.pdf

Smith, A.D. (2009). *Ethno-symbolism and nationalism: A cultural approach.*
    London: Routledge.

Smith, V.L. (1989). *Hosts and guests: The anthropology of tourism.* 2nd edn. Philadelphia,
    PA: University of Pennsylvania Press.

Solzhenitsyn, A.I. (1973/2007). *The Gulag archipelago 1918–1956: An experiment in
    literary investigation, Parts I–II.* London: Harper Collins.

Spilanis, I., Kizos, T., and Petsioti, P. (2012). Accessibility of peripheral regions: evidence
    from Aegean islands (Greece). *Island Studies Journal*, 7(2), 199–214.

Stratford, E. (2013). The idea of the archipelago: contemplating island relations. *Island
    Studies Journal*, 8(1), 3–8.

Stratford, E., Baldacchino, G., McMahon, E., Farbotko, C., and Harwood, A. (2011).
    Envisioning the archipelago. *Island Studies Journal*, 6(2), 113–30.

Šúr, M., Bunbury, N., and van de Crommenacker, J. (2013). Frigatebirds on Aldabra
    Atoll: population census, recommended monitoring protocol and sustainable tourism
    guidelines. *Bird Conservation International*, 23(2), 214–20.

Suwa, J.C. (2012). Shima and aquapelagic assemblages. *Shima: The International Journal
    of Research into Island Cultures*, 6(1), 12–16.

Tourism Philippines. (2014). Tourism branding campaign. Retrieved from http://www.
    tourism.gov.ph/Pages/20120723CampaignGuidelinesforItsMorefuninthePhilippinesLo
    go.aspx

Turismo de Canarias. (2014). Retrieved from http://www.turismodecanarias.com/canary-
    islands-spain/

Turner, L., and Ash, J. (1975). *The golden hordes: International tourism and the pleasure
    periphery.* London: Constable.

UNESCO (2014). World heritage list. Paris, France: United Nations Scientific, Educational
    and Cultural Organisation. Retrieved from http://whc.unesco.org/en/list

Visit Guernsey (2014). Home page. Retrieved from http://www.visitguernsey.com/

Wagner, W.L., and Funk, V.A. (1995). *Hawaiian biogeography: Evolution on a hot spot
    archipelago.* Washington DC: Smithsonian Institution Press.

Whittaker, R.J., and Fernández-Palacios, J.M. (2007). *Island biogeography: Ecology,
    evolution and conservation*, 2nd edn. Oxford: Oxford University Press.

Wish Sicily. (2014). Filicudi and Alicudi. Retrieved from http://www.wishsicily.com/
    filicudi-and-alicudi/71

World Tourism Organisation (2005). *Making tourism work for small island developing
    states.* Madrid: World Tourism Organisation.

Young, L.B. (1999). *Islands Portraits of miniature worlds.* New York: Henry Holt & Co.

Review Essay
Navigating a World of Islands: A 767 Island Odyssey

Stephen A. Royle

Introduction: Developing Islophilia

I am a Professor of Island Geography; rather I am *the* Professor of Island Geography as I am not aware of any other person who holds the same title. The title maybe conveys more distinction than is merited. I was appointed as a Lecturer in Geography at Queen's University Belfast in Northern Ireland in 1975 and progressed through the various grades of the British academic system: Lecturer, Senior Lecturer, Reader and Professor. Professors at Queen's can choose their titles; I decided to be Professor of Island Geography. So there was not a contest to be appointed to a post of this name during which I beat off a stellar list of candidates; it is the title of my personal chair. However, given my long-standing interest in islands, my 132 (and counting) publications of all sorts on the topic, including the oft-cited *A Geography of Islands* (Royle, 2001) and the 767 (and counting) islands I have visited, my title is merited and I bear it with pride. Thus, I was pleased to be mentioned honourably in Godfrey Baldacchino's editorial, 'Five Years On' (2010) in the volume of *Island Studies Journal* in which my inaugural address was published (Royle, 2010). I also had the opportunity to publish an earlier account of my island odyssey in *Irish Geography* from my Presidential Address to the Geographical Society of Ireland (Royle, 1999).

It was on an island in the west of Ireland that I evinced an ambition to become a geographer of islands. Whilst on holiday in 1974, my wife and I drove to the cable car connecting Dursey to the mainland. We crossed to discover an island in decline with just a few elderly residents. I climbed into an abandoned property and found a newspaper reporting the loss of the airship R101, which had caught fire on its maiden voyage 44 years earlier, this dating the abandonment of the cottage. I recall saying to my wife that I found Dursey's decline to be fascinating and I would love to study why it had occurred.

The next year I was appointed to Queen's as an urban geographer. My research focus was urban historical geography and I sought a new research arena within Ireland. I had analysed English 19th century Census Enumerators' Books in my PhD and I assumed I could do the same in Ireland. However, the Irish equivalent from the late 19th century had not been preserved whilst manuscripts from the earlier censuses were destroyed when the Public Records Office was blown up during the Battle of Dublin in the Irish Civil War in 1922. Just a few fragments survived and here is further serendipity in my island odyssey, for these included a complete record of the 1821 census for the three Aran Islands, County Galway. I worked an analysis of these manuscripts into an article (Royle, 1983). Given I had already written about a French island (Royle, 1982), I became a published geographer of islands, although I continued to work on urban material, especially Belfast (e.g. Boal and Royle, 2006; Royle, 2011a). It is to the credit of our prized academic freedom that no barriers were erected to prevent the young urban geographer becoming the grizzled Professor of Island Geography and a Member of the Royal Irish Academy.

As hinted, I take every opportunity to add to my list of islands. There is a shallowness here; I have sometimes stepped onto the island side of a bridge, spun round and left, my one footprint being deemed sufficient for the island to be counted. Further, I am delighted to discover when places generally regarded as one island are made up of discrete insular units: 17 entries on my list are from the archipelago that is Bermuda. By contrast, there are deep studies such as books on historical development regarding St. Helena (Royle, 2007a) and Vancouver Island (Royle, 2011b) and I have researched on the Irish islands for decades. Further, I have a long record of interaction with island associations and attend their conferences held round the world. I have taught island studies courses in universities in Prince Edward Island and Taiwan as well as at my own university. I would like to think it was for contributions of that nature rather than for my numerical insular boasting that I was asked by Godfrey Baldacchino to contribute to this volume an expansive piece on observations from my odyssey: 'Have you ever written about your experiences as a navigator of the world's archipelago of islands?'

Baldacchino's question takes 'archipelago' beyond its normal geographical understanding as a group of neighbouring islands. And why not, for 'island' itself has long been used in a metaphorical sense, not just as a 'piece of land completely surrounded by water' to cite the Oxford English Dictionary's definition. Indeed, even that simple physical definition of an island has to be subject to interpretation. For it is only convention that sees the European/Asian/African landmass, which is surrounded by water thus fulfilling the basic characteristic of an island, as forming instead three separate continents. The island metaphor has been used for isolated terrestrial ecosystems including mountains (sometimes called 'sky islands'), patches of forest, even parks; also lakes. In his *Eccentric islands* (2000), Bill Holm used the metaphor imaginatively: he himself was enisled by pain when he became ill; he had a chapter on a piano as an island. So 'island' might represent anything that is isolated, the root of 'isolated' itself being traced by the Oxford English Dictionary via Italian and French (*isolato, isolé*) back to the Latin for island, *insula*. With a similarly relaxed approach, one can readily accept Baldacchino's reading of the earth's landmasses as a 'world archipelago' and the geographical norms regarding the usual use of archipelago will be loosened in this chapter.

Logistics

Travel to or from an island involves crossing that pesky stretch of water surrounding it. I was recently once more on Inishmaan (*Inis Meáin*) in the Aran Islands, site of my early study. Despite being an islophile I dislike sea travel, being prone to seasickness, so I arranged flights to and from Inishmaan's small airstrip at the Aran Islands' dedicated airport on the County Galway mainland. This is a journey of eight minutes in a 10-seater plane. It is old fashioned flying; you are not asked if you are carrying liquids, you are not searched, rather you are weighed so the load can be distributed optimally around the aircraft. The flight was fine as the weather was clear and after arrival, before my home cooked supper in the guesthouse, I leant against a wall by a mighty pre-Christian fort on the upland part of Inishmaan drinking in the magnificent view whilst being serenaded by birdsong, the loudest noise I could hear. This was island life at its best. The next day, when I was to return to Belfast, things could not have been more different for a major storm had scurried in overnight with driving rain and howling winds. Islanders issued dire warnings about my getting off; the guesthouse held my room in the expectation I would be staying. In the event my flight was indeed cancelled and perhaps so should have been the ferry into which I was decanted, for to say the voyage was awful does not get near to measuring its horror and, at times, fear. The logistics were fine; Inishmaan has two modes of transport to connect it to the outside world and one substituted for the other in a case of need, but the lived experience was dreadful: Galway Bay was a pesky stretch of water indeed.

Where the island journey is by boat, the water crossing then is a barrier. Ferries can be uncomfortable and, depending on distance and speed, the time spent aboard lengthy. No wonder ferry companies try to sell journeys as mini-cruises: 'eat, shop, enjoy, play' and 'enjoy more of what you love' are phrases found on the BC (British Columbia) Ferries website (BC Ferries, 2013). Sometimes the realities are different and more serious than seasickness. In August 2013 a ferry in the Philippines sank, the latest of at least nine recent sinkings in the archipelago including the world's worst maritime peacetime death toll in 1987 when 4,300 people died in the loss of the ferry *Donna Paz.* In short, travelling to islands or within archipelagos by boat can be not just uncomfortable, but risky, one reason why authorities try to build fixed links wherever practical (Baldacchino, 2007). Where this has not been done, having a regular and, hopefully, reliable ferry is key for island tourism. Even in places like the Balearic Islands where most tourists come by plane, ferries bring in goods and bulky items such as cars and there are sailings to this archipelago from four ports on the Spanish mainland as well as from Mallorca to the two smaller islands that flank it.

Regarding access by plane, the Mediterranean contains examples of islands where air travel has massively assisted and enabled their tourism, especially regarding visitors coming from some distance. Getting a flight in, say, Germany and stepping off in Mallorca, Cyprus or Malta is functionally the same for a German as flying on holiday to the Costa del Sol or a resort on the Black Sea; the water crossing to the island is not an additional barrier.

Without reliable transport links, matters can be difficult for visitors and, to continue sharing my 'experiences as a navigator', let me report again from my 'anecdotage'. I once visited Inishturk, County Mayo, Ireland. I parked my car at Roonagh Quay, also in County Mayo, and identified the boat for Inishturk. This was a small vessel used to carry supplies as well as passengers and I helped load groceries and fuel onto it before the bicycle I had brought with me was manhandled on and I was assisted onto the deck. I stayed on Inishturk for a couple of days, cycling round. I had been assured that the boat would be returning at a certain time on a stated day. I turned up to find that this boat was not sailing after all but another one would be going later on. I took that but was deposited not at Roonagh Quay, not in County Mayo at all but at a quayside in County Galway. Luckily – or given the effort it took to return to my car, perhaps unluckily – I did have a bicycle with me! Tourism cannot be expected to flourish in such circumstances. Visitors like to 'get away from it all' on an island trip, but they really need to be delivered efficiently and promptly back into their workaday world once the holiday is completed.

It is no wonder then that in the transformation of conditions including infrastructure that has taken place regarding the Irish islands since the late 1980s, regularising ferry services has been a priority. It wasn't just Inishturk that was difficult to reach; I recall waiting in vain for a boat to Tory Island that never turned up. The transformation mentioned can be set to a wide application of the concept of the archipelago. Mostly the inhabited Irish islands are distributed discretely around the coast of the island of Ireland itself. However, in the early 1980s there was a campaign to meld these dispersed bodies of land into what might be construed as an archipelago of interest. Led usually by officials from their producer co-operatives, islanders began to meet for discussions together: always on islands, despite the transport difficulties. There was a realization that their needs were similar, were shared, and that if they banded together maybe the conjoined voice could trumpet louder than their individual calls. At that time the islands were insignificant outliers of different county councils, their location keeping them out of sight of the council officials; their small populations keeping them out of mind. But once the islands started to work together to press for what they all needed, scaled up into a federation, *Comhdháil na nOileán*, they could be heard and seen. In a sense, sublimating the islands into this federated council was rather like archipelago branding: the individual is gathered into and supported by the collective (Royle, 1986). After some time the Irish government recognised the validity of the campaign, and responsibility for drawing up and operating a national policy and programme towards the islands became a ministerial duty. A mission document on the islands was published (Interdepartmental Co-ordinating Committee, 1996) and a recent statement from the relevant ministry claims success:

> In recent years, priority has been given to the development of island infrastructure as well as subsidising comprehensive access services. The quality of life of the island populations has improved significantly because of this (Department of Arts, Heritage and the Gaeltacht, 2013).

The scaling up, archipelago of interest, idea operated in that there are three situations where groups of neighbouring islands are now supplied by a single provider regarding cargo services, reducing costs by maximising economies of scale. Further, in 2010 the government of Ireland got together with the devolved UK administrations of Northern Ireland and Scotland to commission a report from the consultants, Grant Thornton (available through the Irish ministry's website) to investigate economies of scale and flexibility in the procurement and operation of five ferry services in Scotland; one in Northern Ireland and two in the Republic of Ireland. This further demonstrates the essential significance of reliable access, which eases life for islanders and helps tourism. My story of Inishturk is from the past. Now, O'Malley Ferries operate a dedicated service to this island with a published timetable; visitors know when the boats run and to where they are sailing! On the Department of Arts, Heritage and the Gaeltacht website is a document detailing the contracts to firms running ferries to the islands and the subsidies their services attract. That to O'Malley Ferries who connect to Inishturk once or twice per day throughout the year is over €315,000 p.a. Inishturk had 53 residents at the 2011 census, demonstrating that supporting access is expensive on a per capita basis, but it is necessary if island life is to be maintained. Ireland has over 200 islands that have lost their populations since the mid-19th century; state and European Union policy is now to support those that are left. Improving or sustaining and certainly subsidising their logistics are important elements of that support. For Tory Island, where once access was somewhat ad hoc, the sturdy ferry that now braves the rough seas of Tory Sound brings people to festivals, to hear the island music, to see the island's famous artists (the Tory School of Primitive Art), to experience its Gaelic culture and observe its extraordinary landscape. The visitors on that ferry, tying up at the improved, EU-funded harbour, are what keeps the island going, much more so now than the traditional pursuits of farming and fishing. Tory's population, having been as low as 119 in 1991, had risen to 144 by 2011.

Regarding true, geographical archipelagos, logistical arrangements can be uneven. Plane travel might well favour the main, often the capital, island of the group. For example, most travellers wanting to visit Gozo first arrive at the state of Malta's international airport at Luqa on the island of Malta and then travel up to the ferry port at Cirkewwa in the extreme northwest for the boat to Mgarr on Gozo. This adds expense and inconvenience to a Gozo holiday and also introduces intervening opportunities: why not just holiday on the island of Malta? Gozo can be seen on a day trip, after all. Many Gozitans, whose primary identity and loyalty would be to their home island in preference to their archipelagic state, would like Gozo to have its own airport at least partly to encourage long-stay holidaymakers. In small island developing states (SIDS), travel to the outer islands might not even be easily arranged. On a trip to the Marshall Islands I, of course, landed at the capital island, Majuro. In addition to studying this, the most commercialised island of the group, I wanted experience of the outer islands. On a similar mission in the much wealthier Bahamas I was able to take my pick of internal flights to what are there called the 'family islands' and chose to visit Abaco where there was a car rental service so I was able to see a great deal. In the Marshall Islands things proved not to be so easy. I was recommended by the Mayor of Wotje atoll, who lived on Majuro, to see his home island. I made enquiries. "There might be a plane going, contact us tomorrow and we should know" was the gist of the response. On the morrow I was told to come back the next day. Finally I ran out of days and never got to Wotje or any outer island. This lack of ready access handicaps any development or income that might be garnered through tourism.

As for travelling between archipelagos, I had to leave Majuro because my research programme was taking me to Tuvalu. I had been briefly on Funafuti, its capital atoll on my way north to Majuro from Fiji and there was a short wait between flights. I had not ventured outside the airstrip because I didn't wish to spoil my experience by rushing around for 30 minutes as I was coming back in a few weeks for an intensive research programme. I wish now that I had stepped into the settlement, for I never returned to Tuvalu. I quote from my contemporary journal:

> I am, quite literally, stranded on Tarawa Atoll in Kiribati, in a pleasant hotel, to be sure, but no less stranded for that. I had been frustrated by the fact the Air Marshall Islands' schedule gave me no time in Kiribati; now I have an indeterminate amount of it! What will happen to my trip to Tuvalu, though, is not yet known.
>
> I awoke on Majuro well before the alarm at 05.15 and bid a reasonably fond farewell to the Marshall Islands. I needn't have worried about getting the driver up early for the airport run, he clearly had not been to bed; so I looked for a seat belt but there was none. Nonetheless, I arrived safely at the airport in good time with lots of people and activity and stamping of passports and writing things down. The flight was delayed whilst the baggage was loaded, some sharing the passenger cabin. Once aboard, there were no problems until a bumpy landing at Bonriki International Airport, South Tarawa in Kiribati, a scheduled intermediate stop. Then there were problems! We were being herded back out to the plane, onwards to Funafuti, when the steward appeared atop its steps and waved us back. Then nothing happened for about 90 minutes, no word, nothing. We just sat in the transit shed or wandered about, the only excitement was watching an intra-archipelago plane arrive and depart. Then some of the passengers started to make enquiries. Rumours spread that there was no problem with the plane, but a navigation beacon to the south on one of the northern atolls of Tuvalu was down. (The rumour round the hotel later was that it has been down for weeks but the big chief from the regional Civil Aviation Authority was visiting

so it suddenly became important.) No beacon; no flight. Repair? Only shrugs came in answer. After much debate amongst Air Marshall Island people, a decision was made. Those joining the flight here at Tarawa were to return to home or hotel; those from Majuro were to be flown back there; it's only the Tarawa-Funafuti route that is forbidden. Back to Majuro, thinks Royle, when there is South Tarawa to be seen! Not on your life!

'I'll stay here', I announce to the airline representative.

'You have no hotel'.

'I have no hotel in Majuro. The only hotel I have is in Funafuti and you cannot take me there'.

'You cannot break your ticket'.

Now I expect that that was right but it just so happened that the travel company in the UK had issued me with a ticket not from Majuro to Funafuti, but one from Majuro to Tarawa and another from Tarawa to Funafuti. That meant I had a legitimate right to be in Tarawa, so I could stay and I was rushed out to be shovelled onto the minibus taking some frustrated Tarawa passengers back to their international hotel. What luck!

Eventually, after many days and frequent enquiries and changes of plans, once even having my baggage checked in for a mythical, ghost plane to Tuvalu that turned out not to exist, I was flown from South Tarawa direct to Nadi in Fiji. My research programme for Tuvalu had been adapted and was performed on Kiribati; island researchers have to be flexible!

Access is maximized by fixed links. In Scotland, the Western Isles are too distant for a link to the mainland, but efforts have been made to join up the various islands into three interconnected groups. Lewis is already joined to Harris, for these two 'islands', always regarded as separate and formerly in different counties, are actually part of the same landmass, whilst the outlying islands of Great Bernera and Scalpay were linked to it. To the south, North and South Uist are connected by a causeway across Benbecula with Eriskay and Berneray linked. Finally Barra was joined to Vatersay in 1991 (Royle, 1990) by a causeway, which has certainly supported Vatersay now a short journey from the principal settlement and service centre of Castlebay on Barra. Vatersay's population had fallen from 107 in 1981 to just 72 in 1991 when the causeway was built; it was 90 in 2011, so not yet back to its 1981 level but certainly more stable and without this link maybe Vatersay would have lost its population by now. In similar vein, it has been shown that, with regard to the Irish islands, building a fixed link helped to secure their future and population decline for islands with a fixed link has been less than for the true islands (Royle, 2007b).

Fixed links can transform tourism opportunities as with Prince Edward Island, Canada's smallest province. Before the 13km-long Confederation Bridge was opened in 1997, visitors and Islanders (convention gives an upper case to 'Island' and 'Islanders' regarding Prince Edward Island) alike had to queue for the ferry and in the brief but busy summer season these queues could be frustratingly long. Now one just drives across the Northumberland Strait from the New Brunswick shore of mainland Canada. Clever marketing helps in that the journey to Prince Edward Island is 'free'; the toll booths are on the Island and people are charged to leave. Tourist numbers to Prince Edward Island have risen since the bridge opened, but many stays are for shorter periods than before, including day trips, as ease of egress is, paying the toll apart, just as simple as the drive onto Prince Edward Island.

Some islands remain handicapped by their isolation. One example is St. Helena in the South Atlantic. St. Helena is far from being part of a geographical archipelago, its couple of offshore rocks notwithstanding. However, the wider, functional concept of the archipelago has been applied to ease matters including its isolation. At the time of writing, St. Helena has no airport; but Ascension Island, another British territory to its north does, a military facility used by the British and Americans. One way of reaching to St. Helena is to fly to Ascension to coincide with a visit of the government ship that serves St. Helena and take the two-day voyage south. Ascension is also the staging post for military flights to the Falkland Islands on which civilian passengers can book places if space allows. The string of British territories in the South Atlantic also includes Tristan da Cunha, which used to receive regular visits from the St. Helena government ship. The archipelago construct also operates insofar as St. Helenians form the reserve labour force for these British islands, taking the civilian jobs on Ascension and a wide range of occupations on the labour-short Falkland Islands. Construction of a functional archipelago in this fashion, however, can only go so far in easing the tyranny of absolute isolation. Isolation used to be a positive attribute for St. Helena. The island was truly discovered by Europeans, in this case Portuguese in 1501. It was not permanently settled, rather used as a way station for ships returning to Europe having been trading in Asia, given its strategic position in relation to the trade winds blowing up the Atlantic. Water was available and food could be obtained: goats and pigs released onto the island might be hunted. Only in 1659 was a permanent island base constructed after St. Helena was annexed by the English East India Company to serve as its exclusive property (Royle, 2007a). St. Helena's initial economic role, the servicing and resupplying of sailing ships, became obsolete nearly two centuries ago and apart from a spell producing flax for making string and – employing its isolation – occasional use as a prison, as for Napoleon and later for Boers in the South African War from 1900–02 (Royle, 1998), it has never had a sustainable economic role. Tourism would seem to be indicated: the island has a romantic history given its part in Napoleon's story and has fine historic fortifications and buildings if only because there has been insufficient economic vitality to replace them. The choke point is access. At the time of writing the island's visitors and St. Helena's c. 4,000 people are dependent upon the government ship or private yachts. The ship, RMS *St. Helena*, does bring some visitors in addition to catering for islanders who have been away usually for medical, educational or employment reasons. But there are only a few voyages per year; they are lengthy and expensive and the number and type of tourists who can reach St. Helena are restricted. The obvious if costly solution is to build an airport and there had been proposals for this since at least the 1980s. Only in 2013 was construction started. The aid money must have been found, the technical problems – St. Helena is mountainous – overcome as have been environmental issues such as the runway and terminal having to be in an area where the island's only surviving endemic bird, the now critically endangered wirebird (*Charadrius sanctaehelenae*) lives and breeds. A mitigation plan has been designed to relocate the wirebird to areas away from the airstrip. The remaining potential problem is one faced by other islands before: what will happen to the island's society when tourism increases? Presently the Saints are open and friendly to tourists when these usually elderly and wealthy beings are encountered. The airport and associated developments such as a golf resort will massively increase tourism from its present level of a few hundred per year. Whether this society will be able to stave off the pressures that will inevitably follow is a major concern. A socio-economic impact study has identified fears such as increased crime, introduction of disease including HIV/AIDS, drugs and the pressures that might be placed on the island's infrastructure, from roads to medical services (St. Helena Airport Project, 2013). However, without an airport, with access restricted to an ageing and often-unreliable government ship calling a few times per year and a dependent economy with few opportunities for growth, St. Helena's long term future might have been in doubt. As it is, the potential problems associated with the island developing a tourist economy can be anticipated and policies established to forestall them or at least mitigate their effects.

Marketing

Tourism, especially if properly marketed, can help islands insofar as it is a renewable resource; people seek holidays and trips regularly. Islands and archipelagos try to tap into this resource, aided by the positive feelings people now generally have towards islands: escape, exoticism, getting away from it all, *Treasure Island* fantasies, the word association between 'island' and 'paradise'. Sometimes such generalities, positive though they are, do not help an individual place, especially where there is competition. I mentioned above my latest trip to Inishmaan. From the mainland airport are flights to all three Aran Islands, usually two planes together to the largest, Inishmore (*Inis Mór*), and then one each to the smaller Inishmaan and Inisheer (*Inis Oírr*). The flights to the small islands were leaving at about the same time so the passengers had to be sorted. Passengers wait in the lounge and the clerk comes out to get you to be weighed. You don't need advance booking, you can turn up a few minutes before a flight and if there is room, on you get. The clerk approached a German woman and asked which island she was visiting. The woman did not know. Her husband was called over and declared they were for Inisheer. This illustrates a problem for island tourism within an archipelago: how do you make tourists choose your island especially in circumstances where access is uniform? In my example there were flights to both Inisheer and Inishmaan at the same time and for the same price. That the woman did not know where she was going implies that the choice of destination had been made on no very solid basis; she was just for a generic small Aran island. How does Inishmaan, which lost out in that competition, ensure that it would be chosen by others? More and better marketing is one answer. At the airport there were leaflets for various Aran Island attractions. Many were for Inishmore, the largest and most commercialised island with the most significant tourist honeypot in the archipelago, the mighty clifftop fort of Dun Aengus. Regarding the small islands, there was a leaflet for Inisheer as a whole but none for Inishmaan. Maybe it was as simple as that: the husband had seen the leaflet and chose Inisheer.

Another strategy for archipelagic islands is to co-operate with the others, to try to encourage visits to multiple islands. This can be facilitated by transport provision and one can indeed take ferries, if not (without special arrangements) planes, between the three Aran Islands. Joint marketing is another stratagem. A good example here comes from the Scottish Hebrides. Some of the most sought after Scotch whiskies come from these islands; their distilleries compete for sure, but there is also co-operation. I have a leaflet on the 'Islay and Jura Whisky Trail' and on the internet are other joint marketing ventures for the neighbouring islands of Islay with its nine distilleries and Jura with one: 'Islands with Spirit' is the tag line of VisitIslayJura.com. This is an example of not just co-operative archipelago tourism but of niche marketing. Islands, especially small islands, have limited scale for production. To produce standard goods competing in a wider off-island market puts island manufacturers at a disadvantage as they have to face the added costs of transport to and from the island for goods, services and their finished products. Matters can be eased if, rather than producing standard lines, the goods can be set to a niche market prepared to pay more for higher quality and/or the island romance. On Texel in the Netherlands, all sheep are the chubby Texels and their breeding is carefully controlled to maintain the quality of their notably lean meat; premium prices can be charged for carcases and wool. The small Islay and Jura distilleries manufacture expensive malt whiskies; cheaper, mass-market blended whiskies are usually produced in more industrial settings on the Scottish mainland. Take Laphroaig for example, 'the world's most richly flavoured Scotch whisky'. A statement on the distillery's home page does not gloss over the rigour of the island setting, rather uses this as a marketing device:

> Over the millennia, Islay's island geography and weather has shaped the communities that live and work here with us. We are a strong and uncompromising people, yet fiercely loyal and honest with a deep sense of community spirit. You can taste these qualities in every bottle of Laphroaig whisky (Laphroaig, 2013).

Another example comes from Inishmaan, which is intensely rural, with cattle and a few sheep populating its tiny walled fields but which must be, in terms of percentage of labour force employed, one of the world's most industrialised places for it has a textile factory employing 17 of its c. 150 people. The company, using the Irish name for the island, Inis Meáin Knitting Company, manufactures high end, expensive products making much of the island's traditions:

> The fabrics, the stone walls, the houses, the tiny gardens and the fishing boat or currach and of course the clothes and knitting. It is this tradition that inspires the clothes we make in Inis Meáin. We are constantly delving into the island's rich knitting traditions to find and reinterpret old stitches in new ways (Inis Meáin Knitting Company, 2013).

The company's products are exported across the world, whilst, of course, there is an outlet at the factory for tourists who do choose to visit this Aran island.

In terms of tourism, islands and archipelagos make use of what they have. This can be a magnificent, world class attraction: the wildlife of the Galápagos; the scenery of the Canaries. Sometimes the 'attraction' has unpleasant connotations, but dark or thano-tourism is still tourism. So, visit the Falkland Islands and in addition to the splendid landscape and magnificent wildlife especially the birds, including penguins, see the relics of the 1982 Conflict with Argentina. Most of the action and thus its impact stitched into the landscape took place on East Falkland; there are battlefield sites, crashed planes, memorials and markers, including headstones. There was less activity on West Falkland but I was once taken to the site where a British Special Forces officer was killed; a single bullet case was shown to me and then reverently replaced on the ground. Cultural heritage is marketable, too, such as the *moai* of Easter Island/Rapa Nui, the *dol hareubangs*, stone figures that protect buildings, on Jeju, South Korea or the wind lion lords of Kinmen, Taiwan, which were believed to ward off typhoons. Intangible cultural heritage is also marketable such as language, music, dance and singing. I have heard the throat singers of the Penghu Islands off Taiwan and I once walked away from a display of sega dancing in Mauritius because I thought the young girl performers were being put in inappropriate situations when joined by male tourists.

A final observation comes from the archipelago that is Singapore, which has several offshore islands. Brani Island is part of the harbour; Sentosa Island is a resort, although it also contains important historical sites such as Fort Siloso, the last remaining World

War II gun battery. Off the northeast coast lies Pulau Ubin, which remains still a fairly traditional Malay *kampung* or village, the last settlement of this nature in Singapore. As such Ubin attracts tourists, maybe not those who would favour the breathless activities of Sentosa, but people looking for quietude and rurality, an escape from the urgencies of the intensely urban main island. When I last visited (and I hope still today) trippers disembarking from their bumboat and exiting the dock area are confronted by bicycle hire outlets. One in particular stood out for me for it bore a sign saying 'We are islanders'. The message was clear: you have come to experience this island, so support its people, hire your bike from us for 'we are islanders': island marketing at a simple but effective level.

Branding

Branding in the context of this chapter and book maybe has two meanings, Archipelago branding is one interpretation. Certainly there are archipelagos that are known as such, not Bermuda or Singapore, but the Canary Islands, the Maldives, Tuvalu (whose name means 'eight standing together'), the Galápagos, the Caribbean as a whole and many others (as are profiled in this book). There might be a reputation for the archipelago brand; people will say they are going on holiday to the Canaries, the Azores, the Seychelles or the Maldives. By contrast, sometimes the archipelago is not known. People do not announce that they are vacationing in the Mascarene Archipelago; rather that they are going to Mauritius or Réunion or, much less likely, Rodrigues. However, even when the known archipelago is accessed, how many sample more than one island? Do not most tourists remain relatively immobile once they have arrived? And sometimes even if you try, you cannot experience the archipelago more fully – recall my failure to get to an off-island from Majuro. Rather than archipelagic branding having any real impact on behaviour, most tourists do not take full opportunity of making multiple island visits. We are back to the competition between Inishmaan and Inisheer for visitors seeking a generic Aran Island.

The term 'branding' might also relate to the branding of island goods. This has been touched upon under marketing: high end products from islands usually bear the name. 'Islay Single Malt' it says under the word Laphraoig on their whisky bottles; Inis Meáin Knitting Company's products are all badged with the company logo: three men carrying an upturned curragh with the island's name written boldly underneath. I have tasted Orkney cheese, Cape Breton beer (the brewery has since closed), Bornholmer akvavit, Corsican wine, Manx (Isle of Man) kippers and the alcoholic concoction Singapore Sling (which I didn't like). The whisky I drink comes from Islay. I have a Guernsey, an Aran sweater and a Shetland sweater, though not a true hand-knitted Fair Isle garment as these are out of my price range. I own a piece of Murano glass from the Venetian island factory. One final example of branding and the last, rather latest, stop in my island odyssey (my 767th island) is from the Italian island of Capri, which attracts those who could certainly afford Fair Isle sweaters – when I visited in September 2013 I noticed a couple of furriers doing business in the 40 degree heat. Despite the wealth, there is some production of humble crops, including lemons. Capri has become known for them and lemons from the island and surrounding mainland (Sorrento lemons with a protected geographical status) are used to make Capri-branded, value-added products such as sweets, biscuits and especially a liqueur, limoncello. This is made from the zest of the lemon steeped in grain alcohol, resulting in a bright yellow, sweet and very warming digestif. The bottle I brought back – for research purposes – bears the word 'Capri' as prominently as the word 'limoncello': island branding.

Pimples and Prisons

I went to Capri, which lies off Naples, whilst at a conference in Rome, given that I could justify taking a day out for the purpose and still claim to be working – being that Professor of Island Geography does have its benefits. Other than giving me a pleasant career, what has my experience of 767 islands taught me? That islands are easily defined but less easy to grasp, to encapsulate, to understand. Their common characteristic of being surrounded by water means that islands are always apart, cut off, also easy to dismiss. I could not have become a 'professor of insular geography' for 'insular' is not a neutral word; it has negative connotations of being circumscribed, provincial, narrow in outlook. This has always been the case: one Cummian wrote of the Christian, Columban community on Iona in the Scottish Hebrides around 632 AD that they were 'insignificant', they and their island were "but pimples on the face of the earth" (Walsh and Ó Cróinín, 1988, p. 75). Views have not changed. Russian President Vladimir Putin, through a spokesman in September 2013, put down remarks from the British Prime Minister by saying that David Cameron represented 'a small island no one pays any attention to' (Murphy, 2013). That the UK's principal island of Great Britain far from being small is the ninth largest island in the world is not so important; it was the ready association of islands with insignificance that is telling here. Furthermore, islands, especially if, unlike Great Britain, they are actually small, have been associated with problems with economic and social issues, with decline. Recall my Pauline conversion to island geography on Dursey, when I wanted to discover why the island community had decayed to the extent visible around us. But that was in 1974, many years ago. Since then, attitudes to islands have changed. One way in which this has been manifested is in the development of island studies as a respectable academic pursuit, expressed not least through the success of two dedicated journals, *Island Studies Journal* and *Shima* as well as books like this one. Another development, more central to the theme of this particular book, has been rather than seeing islands as places to leave, to avoid, there has been a growth of a more positive attitude to islands and island living, a regard for what islands have to offer. Even the water around islands might be seen now not so much as a barrier as a paddling pool. This attitude is perhaps more to be found amongst people who do not have to make a living directly from limited island resources. Tourists, retirees, second home owners, those who can work from distance, these are the sorts of people who have become attracted to islands. Some of the qualities that caused problems to traditional communities, particularly isolation, might now be valued. Rich people have been known to buy their own islands, the ultimate bounded, if not actually gated, dwelling space.

One final anecdote illustrates this welcome new regard for islands. In County Cork in the far south of Ireland, there is a series of islands in Cork Harbour, an almost enclosed water body. Some have always been in institutional use: Haulbowline Island, as its name implies, has been associated with shipping and is now the headquarters of the small Irish navy; Spike Island nearby was a prison. Spike has a fort erected by the British during the colonial era, a building important architecturally but also historically for some of the prisoners held there were significant in Ireland's struggles toward independence. The prison continued to be used by the Irish state until 2004 when it was declared that it no longer met modern standards. There was a proposal to build a new prison on Spike Island. An alternative use was put forward by a pressure group, which instead wanted Spike to become a heritage centre to be cherished for its role in Irish history. An event was organized; I was one of those invited to speak. We took a boat trip out to Spike in full knowledge that the security guards on the island would forbid our landing. This they duly did. But the publicity was invaluable: a local newspaper reported on "noted academics" being refused entry to Spike Island – how I gloried in being "noted". I still assumed the campaign would fail, for after all the island was already the property of the prison authorities and islands do make good prisons. Not so, the new regard for islands trumped the practical; Spike Island was saved, the prison service had to look elsewhere for new accommodation. The island was transferred free of charge to the local county council. Now ferries take visitors out there and Spike Island is marketed in an archipelagic way as part of the 'tourism and heritage infrastructure in Cork Harbour' (Spike Island, 2013). No longer banned, I must get down there to add it to my list.

References

Baldacchino, G. (ed.) (2007). *Bridging islands: The impact of fixed links*. Charlottetown, Canada: Acorn Press.

Baldacchino, G. (2010). Five years on. *Island Studies Journal*, 5(1), 3–4.

BC Ferries. (2013). Home page. Retrieved from http://www.bcferries.com

Boal, F.W., and Royle, S.A. (eds) (2006). *Enduring city: Belfast in the twentieth century*. Belfast, Northern Ireland: Blackstaff Press.

Department of Arts, Heritage and the Gaeltacht. (2013). The offshore islands. Retrieved from http://www.ahg.gov.ie/en/Islands

Holm, B. (2000). *Eccentric islands: Travels real and imaginary.* Minneapolis MN: Milkweed.

Inis Meáin Knitting Company. (2013). About. Retrieved from http://inismeain.ie/about

Interdepartmental Co-ordinating Committee. (1996). *Island development: A strategic framework for developing the offshore islands of Ireland*. Dublin: The Stationery Office.

Laphroaig (2013). Our Islay. Retrieved from http://www.laphroaig.com/our-islay

Murphy, J. (2013). G20 summit: isolated David Cameron is forced to shrug off Vladimir Putin 'small island snub' over Syria. *The Independent*, 6 September.

Royle, S.A. (1982). Tide mills: an example from Brittany. *Industrial Archaeology Review*, 6(3), 241–4.

Royle, S.A. (1983). The economy and society of the Aran Islands, Co Galway, in the early 19th century. *Irish Geography*, 26(1), 36–54.

Royle, S.A. (1986). A dispersed pressure group: *Comhdháil na nOileán*, the Federation of the Islands of Ireland. *Irish Geography*, 19(2), 92–5.

Royle, S.A., Robinson, J. and Smyth, B.L. (1990). Fixed links in the Western Isles: the Barra-Vatersay causeway. *Scottish Geographical Magazine*, 106(2), 17–20.

Royle, S.A. (1998). St. Helena as a Boer prisoner of war camp, 1900–1902: information from the Alice Stopford Green papers. *Journal of Historical Geography*, 24(1), 53–68.

Royle, S.A. (1999). From Dursey to Darrit-Uliga-Delap: an insular odyssey. Presidential Address to the Geographical Society of Ireland. *Irish Geography*, 32(1), 1–8.

Royle, S.A. (2001). *A geography of islands: Small island insularity*. London: Routledge.

Royle, S.A. (2007a). *The Company's Island: St. Helena, company colonies and the colonial endeavour*. London: I.B. Tauris.

Royle, S.A. (2007b). Islands off the Irish coast and the 'bridging effect'. in G. Baldacchino (ed.), *Bridging islands: The impact of fixed links*, pp. 203–18. Charlottetown, Canada: Acorn Press.

Royle, S.A. (2010). 'Small places like St. Helena have big questions to ask': The inaugural lecture of a Professor of Island Geography. *Island Studies Journal*, 5(1), 5–24.

Royle, S.A. (2011a). *Portrait of an industrial city: 'Clanging Belfast', 1750–1914.* Belfast, Northern Ireland: Ulster Historical Foundation.

Royle, S.A. (2011b). *Company, crown and colony: The Hudson's Bay Company and territorial endeavour in Western Canada.* London: I.B. Tauris.

St. Helena Airport Project. (2013). Environmental statement. Retrieved from http://www.sainthelenaaccess.com/application/documents/Environmental-Statement/Volume_6_Socioeconomic_Report

Spike Island. (2013). Welcome to Spike Island. Retrieved from http://www.spikeislandcork.ie

Walsh, D., and Ó Cróinín, D. (eds) (1988). Cummian's Letter: *De Controversia Paschali. Pontifical Institute of Medieval Studies, Studies and Texts*, 86.

PART I
Mediterranean Sea

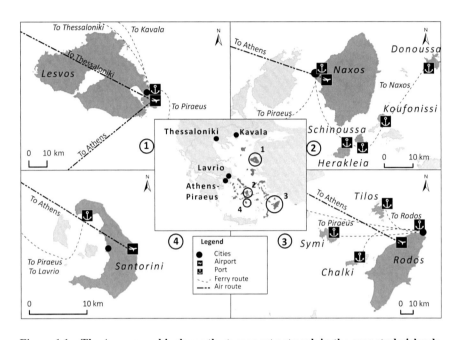

Figure 1.1   The Aegean archipelago: the transport network in the case study islands

Chapter 1

Patterns of Transportation for Tourists and Residents in the Aegean Archipelago, Greece

Sofia Karampela, Thanasis Kizos and Andreas Papatheodorou

Introduction

The word archipelago is an international geographical term that characterizes a geological formation consisting of a chain or cluster of islands. Essentially it means "first sea", from the two Greek words *archon* (leader / first) and *pelagos* (sea). Typically, archipelago is defined as either a large group of islands, or a sea containing a large number of scattered islands. Some definitions consider the distance from the mainland and suggest that the islands need to be far away from the mainland coast. Many of the world's islands are part of archipelagos (Bardolet and Sheldon, 2008). For the purpose of this chapter, an archipelago is defined as a cluster of islands in a common area of water.

Transportation for Tourists and Residents

Travel, and hence transportation, is an integral part of tourism. All definitions of tourism involve some aspect of travel, because all definitions of tourists include the fact that the individuals travel to a different location from the one they habitually reside on. While travel, and hence transportation, is important to varying degrees to all tourists, it is also of great importance to the destination areas themselves (Butler, 1996). The relative accessibility or inaccessibility of a destination is normally a major factor in determining not only the number of tourists who are likely to visit the destination, but also the types of tourists, the duration of their stay, their behaviour (Butler, 1996), and as a result of these factors, their impact on the destination.

Island destinations are, by definition, pieces of land surrounded by water, and so can only be reached by boat and airplane. Their accessibility to both residents and tourists is typically more limited than mainland destinations, and this, in turn, makes them more vulnerable to changes in transportation (Papatheodorou, 2001). Such changes may occur through developments in transportation technology and physical infrastructure (including fixed links such as bridges, causeways and tunnels), political developments, and changes in economic conditions. These can occur singly or in combination, and tend to have major impacts on island tourism.

Inter-island transportation in an archipelago is much more problematic than transportation between islands and the mainland because many such archipelago islands – especially smaller ones – face problems of "multiple insularity" for movement of people, goods and other economic activities vital for the quality of life on the island and the performance of its economy (Spilanis et al., 2012). These smaller islands are almost always highly dependent on larger nearby islands, which function as local service centres.

This chapter explores the link between accessibility and tourism development for island destinations and analyse patterns of transportation for tourists and residents via ferry and airplane for a number of Aegean Greek islands and groups of islands. The reason behind this choice of case material is the exploration of internal differences inside an archipelago: as the scale changes, these differences become more apparent and yielding a number of smaller archipelagos in the end. Transportation patterns reveal a number of finer strokes in a bigger archipelago canvas.

The research methods used in this study are presented in the next section, followed by a presentation and discussion of the findings, and a conclusion.

Methods and Data

In Greece, four insular administrative NUTS II[1] regions are found, two of which comprise the majority of the Greek Aegean archipelago (some islands lying close to continental Greece are parts of continental NUTS II level regions). Geographically, the Aegean Islands are a complex of 3,053 islands in a space defined by Crete in the South, continental Greece in the North and West, and continental Turkey in the East, with a total land area of 19,076 km[2]. In the two regions of the North Aegean and South Aegean, there are 64 inhabited islands (Hellenic Statistical Authority, 2013).

Historically, geographically, politically and economically, islands are very important for Greece. Their distinctive geographical features (many islands of various sizes, many at considerable distances from the Greek mainland and scattered in space) and the important but unequal tourism development, make the Aegean islands well-suited to study patterns of transportation for tourists and residents via ferry and airplane. Overall, the transportation needs of more than 200 inhabited islands are today served by a network of 24 airports and 90 seaports. Demand for transport services is highly seasonal, with the summer-time peak period, fuelled mainly by leisure tourism, being significantly higher than that for the rest of the year (Rigas et al., 2011). It is ironic that transportation services can render islands difficult places to access, even as marketing and branding initiatives premised on complementarity encourage tourists to visit more than one island: witness, for example, the case of the nine islands of the North Aegean (Plate 1.1).

In this chapter, we select four distinct cases of islands in the Aegean archipelago, differing in terms of accessibility and tourism recognition: (a) one very popular international destination, Santorini; (b) one case of an international destination with a number of satellite islands: Rodos [Rhodes] with Chalki, Symi and Tilos; and (c) two cases that are less important in terms of international tourism: Lesvos, and Naxos with its satellites: Donoussa, Schinoussa, Herakleia and Koufonissi. The selection is based on two criteria: (i) tourism development, selecting two cases with high and two cases with low development; (ii) "satellite" islands: that is, islands depending on a larger island for

---

1   The NUTS classification (Nomenclature of Territorial Units for Statistics) is a hierarchical system for dividing up the economic territory of the EU for the purpose of: (a) the collection, development and harmonisation of EU regional statistics, (b) socio-economic analyses of the regions (NUTS I: major socio-economic regions, NUTS II: basic regions for the application of regional policies, NUTS III: small regions for specific diagnoses) and (c) framing of EU regional policies. The latest NUTS classification (2012–2014) lists 97 regions at NUTS I, 270 regions at NUTS II, and 1,294 regions at NUTS III level (Eurostat, 2014).

services and economic activity, with two cases of single islands and two cases of islands with satellites.

Until the administrative reforms of 2011, the smaller islands were separate municipalities, while in the larger ones more than one municipality was found. Since the reforms, larger and smaller islands form a single municipality, except for the satellites of Naxos, which belong to the municipality of Naxos and Lesser Cyclades. Santorini, Naxos (with its satellites) and Rodos (with its satellites) belong to the South Aegean region; while Lesvos belongs to the North Aegean region (both NUTS II level).

For the analysis of accessibility and tourism development, various secondary data sources are used: these include published official data such as population censuses and annual statistical surveys, ferry and airplane schedules, types of ferries and passengers arrivals. The data is drawn from the most recently available official statistics, obtainable from the Hellenic Statistical Authority and the Civil Aviation Authority. The calculation of tourist arrivals by air and sea was based on annual statistics data of disembarked passengers, obtained from the Civil Aviation Authority and the Hellenic Statistical Authority, with the assumption that residents (and not tourists) travel mostly during February, which is one of the months with the lowest peak seasonality of tourism activity. These figures were subtracted by the number of passengers from each month to provide an indication of the number of tourist arrivals, assuming that the number of residents traveling is roughly the same the whole year round. For matters of convenience, ferry routes to Athens stop at the port of Piraeus in the greater Athens metropolitan area, while in the case of air routes to Athens, the landing point is the Eleftherios Venizelos airport in Spata (the largest airport in Greece).

Findings

Population

As shown in Table 1.1, the population of the case study islands has dropped significantly as a result of economic decline from 1951 to 1991, with 9 of the 11 islands losing population, the two exceptions being Santorini (an increase of 0.3%) and Rodos (a staggering rise of 66.6%). The mean population decline is of 27.6%, with three cases reporting over 50%: Chalki, Tilos and Donoussa. In 1991–2001, the trend was reversed and the population increased on all islands, with a mean increase of 35.1%. It continued to increase at a more modest rate (a mean of 25.7%) in the following decade (2001–11), with the exceptions of Lesvos (a decline of 4.8%) and Herakleia (a decline of 0.7%). Remarkably, on Rodos and Santorini, the population increased throughout this whole period. Overall, 54.4% of the total Aegean island population lives on Rodos, and 85% lives on Rodos and Lesvos. Population and area size are strongly correlated (Pearson's $r=0.9^{**}$, $p<0.01$, $N=11$).

The average population density of the case study islands is currently 59 inhabitants/km^2, but this conceals important differences: Santorini has the highest density with an average of 234 inhabitants/ km^2 followed by Rodos (109 inhabitants/km^2) and Koufonissi, Naxos' satellite, with 72 inhabitants/km^2. Lesvos and Symi have a density of 53 inhabitants/km^2, Naxos 43 inhabitants/km^2, Chalki and Schinoussa roughly 25 inhabitants/km^2. Finally, Tilos, Donoussa and Herakleia are the most sparsely populated, with under 13 inhabitants/km^2.

Table 1.1 Area size, population change and population density for case study islands 1951–2011

	Islands	Area size (km²)	Population							Change of Population (%)			Population Density (inhabitants/ km²)
			1951	1961	1971	1981	1991	2001	2011	1951–1991	1991–2001	2001–2011	2011
1	Lesvos	1,630	126,928	117,379	97,013	88,603	87,151	90,643	86,312	-31.3%	4.0%	-4.8%	52.9
2	Santorini	76	9,332	7,651	6,199	7,083	9,360	13,670	17,752	0.3%	46.0%	29.9%	234.2
3	Rodos	1,398	58,946	63,934	66,609	87,833	98,181	117,007	152,538	66.6%	19.2%	30.4%	109.1
	Chalki	28	580	523	387	334	281	313	702	-51.6%	11.4%	124.3%	25.0
	Symi	58	3,978	3,126	2,497	2,273	2,332	2,606	3,070	-41.4%	11.7%	17.8%	52.8
	Tilos	63	1,052	789	349	301	279	533	829	-73.5%	91.0%	55.5%	13.2
4	Naxos	428	18,593	16,703	14,196	14,037	14,838	18,188	18,340	-20.2%	22.6%	0.8%	42.8
	Donoussa	13	272	210	149	116	111	163	176	-59.2%	46.8%	8.0%	13.1
	Schinoussa	8	226	196	197	140	122	206	225	-46.0%	68.9%	9.2%	28.9
	Herakleia	18	189	155	129	95	115	151	150	-39.2%	31.3%	-0.7%	8.5
	Koufonissi	6	300	300	251	237	275	366	412	-8.3%	33.1%	12.6%	72.3

Source: Hellenic Statistical Authority, processed by the authors.

Table 1.2   Transport connections of case study islands, February 2013

a/a	From	To	Weekly Frequency of Routes		Average Travel Duration (hh:mm)	
			by sea	by air	by sea	by air
1	Mytilene (capital of Lesvos)	Athens	10	23	12:27	0:50
		Kavala	2		10:45	
		Thessaloniki	1	6	15:00	0:55
2	Santorini	Athens	10	12	8:23	0:47
		Lavrio	1		14:30	
3	Rodos	Athens	8	44	18:26	1:00
		Thessaloniki		7		1:17
	Chalki	Athens	2		23:22	
		Rodos	9		1:22	
	Symi	Athens	2		16:45	
		Rodos	4		1:05	
	Tilos	Athens	2		15:15	
		Rodos	4		2:18	
4	Naxos	Athens	13	6	5:27	0:40
		Lavrio	1		8:20	
	Donoussa	Athens	2		7:10	
		Naxos	5		2:40	
	Schinoussa	Athens	3		7:20	
		Naxos	9		1:36	
	Herakleia	Athens	3		7:00	
		Naxos	9		1:16	
	Koufonissi	Athens	3		8:05	
		Naxos	9		2:20	

Source: Greek Travel Pages, processed by the authors.

Transportation Supply and Accessibility

Transportation patterns for tourists and residents and information of transportation supply characteristics for the case study islands are provided in Table 1.2. There, the average weekly frequency of routes is presented from the islands to the mainland, by sea and air for the month of February, along with the routes from the small satellite islands, to the main islands.

Four international airports operate in the case study islands, on Lesvos, Santorini, Rodos and Naxos, and at least one port on each island. Air traffic is of higher frequency than ferry traffic and therefore more alternatives are offered in air travel for the passengers, on the islands where airports are located (Rigas, 2012). Taking into account the total weekly frequency routes by sea and air, the classification of the main islands in descending order is: Rodos (44 weekly routes by air) Lesvos, Santorini, Naxos. The Athens–Lesvos, Athens–Rodos and Athens–Santorini air services are run as commercial operations; while the Athens–Naxos route has been granted a Public Service Obligation (PSO) status being effectively subsidized by the Greek state. Only on Naxos are the frequency of sea routes almost twice as frequent as air routes, mostly due to the proximity to Athens (a 5-hour ferry trip away, compared to 12.5 hours for Lesvos and 18 hours for Rodos).

On the main islands, connection by sea with Piraeus exists from eight times a week for Rodos, to thirteen times a week for Naxos. Also, a connection with North Greece (to Kavala and Thessaloniki) is offered to Lesvos by sea and air and to Rodos only by air.

As previously mentioned, none of the satellite islands has an airport. At the same time, weekly frequencies of ferries to the mainland are particularly rare: two ferry arrivals/departures per week in the case of Rodos' satellites and Donoussa; and three for the remaining satellites of Naxos. Their connection with the main island in each case ranges from four weekly routes for Symi and Tilos, to nine for Chalki, Schinoussa, Herakleia and Koufonissi, with an average travel time of about one hour to two and a half hours. In the case of Rodos' satellites, with just two weekly routes to Piraeus, the average travel duration is from 15 to 23 hours. Figure 1.1 provides a graphical representation of the connections in question. The actual routes of the ferry schedules are very important for smaller islands and groups of islands, as the example of Donousa reveals: the ferry trip to Naxos and Athens lasts less than that of Koufonissi, due to one weekly route that links only Donousa with Naxos and Athens (and Amorgos), while the rest of the routes stop at all the islands from Herakleia to Donousa (Figure 1.1). The example of the Rodos satellites also demonstrates that proximity and accessibility are not always direct functions of distance but also of the ferry schedule and routes: thus, the distances of Symi and Tilos are comparable (approx. 45 km and 70 km respectively), but the durations are very different (1:05 hours and 2:18 hours respectively) because the ferry stops at Chalki first (distance 65 km, duration 1:22 hours) and then takes another hour to get to Tilos.

Quality of Ferry Transportation

Sea transport is the dominant mode of transportation for all case study islands. This renders critical a number of quantitative (e.g. the frequency of the ferry schedule) and qualitative (e.g. the time that the ferries arrive and leave, the quality and capacity of boats) characteristics (Kizos, 2007). Therefore, the coastal passenger fleet is presented and analysed in this section. This analysis is performed with a number of indicators such as: the average age of the ferries serving each island, travel speed, carrying capacity and "transport power", which is a measure of the fleet's capability to perform transport work in unit time. The ship's transport capacity is calculated by multiplying number of passengers by the ship's speed in knots (Tzanatos, 2005).

Furthermore, the coastal lines of Piraeus (Athens), Lavrio and North Greece (Kavala, Thessaloniki) are presented and analysed in terms of passenger transport supply, quantitative and qualitative involvement of the fleet and network complexity and coverage. There are five main ferry companies: NEL Lines, Hellenic Seaways, Blue Star Ferries, Anek Lines and Lane Lines. All are subsidized for at least one of their routes, but not for all. They offer connections between the islands and Piraeus; but only one of these companies offers connections between the islands and Lavrio and Thessaloniki. On the main islands of Lesvos and Santorini, three companies operate routes, while two companies operate routes in the case of Rodos. In the cases of Naxos and its satellites as well as of Rodos' satellites, only one company operates routes, a fact that identifies the vulnerability of the transportation pattern, should this company financially collapse or decide to remove this route from its schedule.

Table 1.3   Coastal passenger fleet for case study islands, February 2013

a/a	Islands	Destination	No of operating companies on route	Mean Age of vessel (years)	Mean Speed of vessel (knots)	Mean Transport Capacity (Passengers per vessel)	Mean "Transport Power" (mean speed x mean transport capacity)
1	Lesvos (port of Mytilene)	Athens	3	21	15.6	1,594	24,863
		Kavala	1	38.5	11.4	1,330	15,096
		Thessaloniki	1	38	5.2	1,660	8,632
2	Santorini	Athens	3	27	17.3	1,188	20,558
		Lavrio	1	13	15.9	1,675	26,633
3	Rodos	Athens	2	23	18.3	1,436	26,321
	Chalki	Athens	1	33	16.9	991	16,748
	Symi	Athens	1	23	17.3	1,462	25,293
	Tilos	Athens	1	23	17.3	1,462	25,293
4	Naxos	Athens	1	11	21.7	1,474	31,912
		Lavrio	1	13	15.9	1,675	26,633
	Donoussa	Athens	1	11	22.0	1,474	32,428
	Schinoussa	Athens	1	11	22.0	1,474	32,428
	Herakleia	Athens	1	11	22.0	1,474	32,428
	Koufonissi	Athens	1	11	22.0	1,474	32,428

Source: Greek Travel Pages and www.marinetraffic.com, processed by the authors.

The number of companies serving the case study islands is never more than three as shown in Table 1.3. In most destinations, just one ferry company monopolizes transport, which is typical across the whole Aegean (Rigas, 2012). Although economic orthodoxy in coastal maritime transport claims that a competitive transport environment is expected to improve the quality of transport services (e.g. Rigas, 2012, Hernandez Luis, 2002), for many of the smaller islands this is not the case, as the transport potential is very low for commercial interest and competition, a fact recognized by the Greek State that subsidizes the so-called "non-profitable lines".

All vessels operating in the case study area are of the Ro-ro/passenger type, allowing the transport of passengers and vehicles. Service levels cannot be considered as homogenized across the market, as the technical characteristics of the vessels are not uniform (Rigas, 2009). The information provided in Table 1.3 reveals that Naxos and its satellites have the "best quality" ferries on average, according to their age, speed and capacity. In contrast, the case study islands of Lesvos and Chalki seem to have the "worst quality" transport, when taking into consideration these transport supply characteristics. "Transport power", as already mentioned, is calculated for coastal passenger ships and the high average values are mostly based on the high average speed rather than on the fleets' mean carrying capacity (Tzanatos, 2005, Lekakou, 2007).

Transportation Demand of Tourists and Residents

For transportation demand, the main difficulties deal with the proper identification of who the 'tourist' is (Baldacchino and Ferreira, 2013). First, not all passengers on flights and ferries are tourists; many are local residents. We use February as a benchmark, assuming that all passengers then are residents and they represent the average number of residents that travel in a typical month. Results are presented in Table 1.4 for the year 2011. Number of tourists is negative in the case of Tilos because it is serviced by smaller boats from Rodos usually for day trips and this data is not recorded.

Significant disparities exist in terms of recorded arrivals among the case study islands but also regarding the mode of travel (sea and air). The most noticeable difference is Rodos, with more tourist air arrivals than all the other islands combined. Differences for residents are smaller but indicate the limitations of our assumption and higher mobility propensity for larger islands. For example, on Lesvos and Rodos, each resident travels three times on average per year either by sea and air; while on Santorini, a resident travels off island almost nine times per year, on average. As may be expected, the residents of smaller islands travel off island more often, given that the small island scale can sustain only limited urban amenities including hospitals, higher education institutions and banks.

An indication of the significance of tourism can be observed when comparing the number of tourist arrivals to the resident population. This is because, as for most small islands, tourist arrivals exceed the size of the resident population, sometimes many times over (Papatheodorou and Arvanitis, 2009; Rigas, 2012). Also, the ratio of visitors to the local population is the most common indirect measure of tourism's socio-cultural impact (McElroy, 2003, Coccosis, 2002). In the Aegean, tourist numbers to Lesvos are over twice as large as that island's population, those to Rodos and Naxos are over ten times as larger, and those to Santorini almost forty times larger. Extreme cases are the satellites of Naxos, with tourists arrivals ranging from one hundred times larger than the resident population (in Koufonissi) to over two hundred times (in Herakleia and Donoussa). These

Table 1.4 Transportation demand of tourists and residents by sea and air and real distance for the case study islands, 2011

a/a	Islands	Tourists		Residents		Total Passengers (tourists and residents)		Tourist arrivals / population	Resident arrivals / population	Tourist arrivals / area size	Real distance (km) from Athens
		by sea	by air	by sea	by air	by sea	by air				
1	Lesvos	97,972	108,083	115,748	122,928	213,720	231,011	2.4	2.8	126	285
2	Santorini	455,302	332,747	116,044	42,888	571,346	375,635	44.4	9.0	10,398	237
3	Rodos	139,401	1,813,003	162,736	253,920	302,137	2,066,923	12.8	2.7	1,396	439
	Chalki	3,475	n/a	2,496	n/a	5,971	n/a	5.0	3.6	124	399
	Symi	79,807	n/a	26,000	n/a	105,807	n/a	26.0	8.5	1,374	398
	Tilos	-1,366	n/a	2,844	n/a	4,210	n/a	-1.7	3.4	-22	368
4	Naxos	199,455	7,857	133,304	4,416	332,759	12,273	11.3	7.5	484	181
	Donoussa	37,525	n/a	1,984	n/a	39,509	n/a	213.2	11.3	2,784	213
	Schinoussa	9,598	n/a	2,700	n/a	12,298	n/a	42.7	12.0	1,234	206
	Herakleia	29,149	n/a	2,260	n/a	31,409	n/a	194.3	15.1	1,656	203
	Koufonissi	43,098	n/a	4,204	n/a	47,302	n/a	104.6	10.2	7,561	208

Sources: Hellenic Statistical Authority and Hellenic Civil Aviation Authority, processed by the authors.

ratios are extremely high during peak season especially in August; however absolute numbers of tourist arrivals and resident population are relatively small.

Another important index is tourism's environmental impact, i.e. the ratio of visitors to the area size. Figures for Santorini (10,398) and Koufonissi (7,561) are very high, while even though Rodos receives the highest number of tourists, (1.95 million), the island has a relatively low index value because of the size of its land area (1,398 km^2) and finally having almost the same index value with Symi (1,374) instead of their different absolute numbers. On the other hand, Donoussa, with its low number of tourists (37,525) has a relatively high index value because of its small area size (13.48 km^2).

Real distance expressed in this case study in kilometres, emerges as another factor affecting the mode of travel. The ferry appears to be the mode of choice for destinations closer to Piraeus (Rigas, 2011). Rodos being the most distant island from Piraeus had a high air transportation percentage which in all categories (for both tourists and residents) exceeds 60%; while Naxos, being the least distant island, had a low air transportation percentage in all categories (on average 3.5%). Lesvos and Santorini have equal distribution of percentages for tourists and residents by sea and air, except for the residents of Santorini, many of whom prefer to travel by sea (73%).

Seasonality of Tourism Demand

Tourism in the Aegean islands is mostly a summer activity peaking in July and August as holidays are predominantly related to warm water, sea, sand, sun and relaxation. Most islands have at least one of these characteristics, many have more than one and some have them all (Kizos, 2007). Given that demand for traveling to islands is mainly associated with leisure tourism, a high seasonality effect is expected in tourism arrivals. Table 1.5 demonstrates this seasonality by comparing tourism demand levels in July and August as a share of total tourism flows in 2011.

From the total number of disembarked tourists at the ports (1,093,416), 25% visit the case study islands in July and August, compared to 44% disembarked tourists at the airports (total tourists by air: 2,261,690). However, a more detailed examination of both air and sea arrivals reveals a fundamental difference: air arrivals during these months are mostly international (38.8%, with domestic at 5.2%), while sea arrivals are only domestic (all the 25%). Schinoussa, Herakleia and Donoussa, which are Naxos' satellites, present a high seasonality demand ranging from 46% to 64% respectively; while Koufonnisi and Naxos present low seasonality demand due to arrivals being dispersed throughout the whole year.

Discussion

The transportation network of the Aegean Sea displays a virtually mono-hub structure based upon the Port of Piraeus and the Athens International Airport (Tzanatos, 2005). Theoretically, the hub and spoke model is a system which makes transportation much more efficient by greatly simplifying a network of routes (Lekakou, 2007; Stabler et al., 2010). It is extensively used in commercial aviation for both passengers and freight, and the model has also been adopted in the technology sector. The model is named after a bicycle wheel, which has a strong central hub with a series of connecting spokes.

In archipelagos, the "central" island is typically the one where public services are based and the bulk of the population resides. It is often the only island with an international airport

Table 1.5   **Tourist arrivals by sea and air for case study islands, July–August 2011**

a/a	Islands	Tourists in July and August	% Tourists in July and August/ Total	Tourists in July and August			% Tourists in July and August/ Total
		by sea		by air			
				Domestic	International	Total	
1	Lesvos	31,638	32.3	18,143	27,340	45,483	42.0
2	Santorini	107,759	23.7	52,725	107,559	160,284	48.0
3	Rodos	25,885	18.6	44,524	724,782	769,306	42.0
	Chalki	919	26.5	n/a	n/a	n/a	n/a
	Symi	7,158	9.0	n/a	n/a	n/a	n/a
	Tilos	42	-3.1	n/a	n/a	n/a	n/a
4	Naxos	48,083	24.1	2,404	384	2,788	35.0
	Donoussa	24,132	64.3	n/a	n/a	n/a	n/a
	Schinoussa	4,501	46.9	n/a	n/a	n/a	n/a
	Herakleia	13,681	46.9	n/a	n/a	n/a	n/a
	Koufonissi	5,543	12.9	n/a	n/a	n/a	n/a

Source: Hellenic Statistical Authority and Civil Aviation Authority, processed by the authors.

or seaport: all visitors on commercial flights or sea trips to central islands must then transit the hub alongside. Inter-island links that do not involve the central hub are rare or non-existent, or else not advertised or communicated to visitors (Baldacchino and Ferreira, 2013). In the case study islands, several smaller hub and spoke systems (mini-archipelagos unto themselves) emerge, with small sea companies that inter-connect these spokes, all of them included into a larger canvas: the Aegean archipelago. There are, of course, disadvantages to a hub and spoke model. Any disruption at the hub, such as bad weather or a security problem, can create delays throughout the system. The overall operating efficiency is also limited by, and dependent on, the capacity of the hub (Lekakou, 2007; Stabler, et al., 2010).

This network of hubs and spokes is served mainly by ferries. In the late 1990s and early 2000s, an attempt to replace older vessels by new ones was supported by a bullish stock market. But, with its collapse, many of the ferries that service the islands are now aged (a number of them were built in the 1970s). In spite of some modernization attempts, low service levels remain, especially in network coverage and frequency of services. In 2004, more than 300 vessels of various types were serving the entire Greek network, with almost 70% of them operating in the Aegean (Rigas, 2011). According to Tzanatos (2005), this fleet is continually improving on the basis of the transport power index, mainly based upon the increase in the fleet's average speed. But this finding reflects only larger island lines, or the popular central Cyclades lines (i.e. Siros, Paros, Naxos and Mykonos islands). At the same time, the situation for many of the smaller and remote islands has worsened significantly, with old vessels and lower frequencies, especially since the companies complain about increasing fuel prices (which, they claim, account for over 60% of their total operating costs) along with crew restrictions. An improvement in commercially viable lines took place mostly through an increase of travel speed and only partially through increasing vessel size (Tzanatos, 2005).

Another interesting finding for the case study islands in transportation demand by both tourists and residents is that the ferry appears to be the mode of choice for destinations closer to the Piraeus hub. It has to be noted, however, that ferry and air service frequencies play a major role here as well, since the ferry connection to and from Naxos is one of the best in the Aegean, with relatively new and fast ferries that make the trip to Piraeus comfortable and fast.

With respect to tourism demand, transportation patterns demonstrate that the existence of direct air flights to a large island such as Rodos, increases the possibility for tourists to visit, compared to smaller, satellite islands that do not benefit from these flights directly. This issue is of course related to the "image" of the island, as Rodos can be considered an island with a distinctive character, as well as within the overall 'Aegean islands' framework. Meanwhile, smaller islands struggle to differentiate themselves and stand above the noise of their larger competitors, especially since after 2009 many of them are part of larger municipalities. This is typically the case of a "periphery within a periphery" (Papatheodorou, 2004).

The case studies presented here have served to explore the transport practices of different types of islands and island clusters within a broader and larger archipelago. The differences observed are not surprising; larger islands and islands with a developed tourism sector are served better (Bardolet and Sheldon, 2008). The findings also demonstrate that the spill-over of this link of the larger islands to their satellites remains rather limited, especially in the case of Naxos' satellite islands. These cases seem to represent different archipelagos within the broader archipelago, presenting on a smaller scale features similar to those of the greater system: high spatial differences and high degrees of dependency (Papatheodorou, 2004).

In archipelagos, the potential exists for both collaboration and competition (i.e. co-opetition) between the islands of the same archipelago (Bardolet and Sheldon, 2008). Prideaux and Cooper (2002) argue that the destination brand is the tangible and positive outcome of the achievement of unity and collaboration amongst the stakeholders of a tourism destination. The conceptualization of destination branding as a collaborative process can be considered as the central theme that characterizes how tourism literature has described the interrelationships amongst stakeholders in the process of branding a tourism destination (Marzano and Scott, 2009). For the Aegean Islands in general, an international image and brand already exists, as an archipelago. But, despite historical, geographical, climatic, linguistic, landscape and other similarities, there remain considerable differences in perception, representation and imagination within this ancient archipelago. For example, Santorini is a well-known international "brand" in itself, at the same time within and outside of the Aegean Islands brand.

Another point worth mentioning that does not emerge directly from the transportation data is related to the difference in transport links between residents and tourists, especially for smaller, satellite islands. Tourists and residents have diverging needs in terms of the timing of transport. For example, for a resident of Tilos, it is important for the local ferry to leave in the morning *from* Tilos and return some time in the afternoon, in order to use the public and private services of Rodos. But, for a tourist in Rodos, this timing is not convenient as it means that s/he would arrive on Tilos late in the afternoon and have to leave early in the morning, obliging at least an overnight stop; a morning ferry *to* Tilos would be preferred for day trippers. Such qualitative aspects of transportation are hard to depict in statistical tables, but are nevertheless of great significance (e.g. Vannini, 2012).

Conclusion

How can the actual differences observed in archipelagos be used to cover or improve issues of access and tourism planning? The findings of the case studies suggest at least two important observations:

A number of different spatial configurations emerge as the scale increases or decreases. A number of archipelagos emerge, or are merged into broader spatial entities. The scale where finer spatial configurations are more evident, that of small islands, appears to be the most suitable to handle dependence and transportation issues. This is inevitably related to the concepts of liminality and fractality in space (Thomassen, 2009) as most islands play the role of a mainland to smaller islands; whereas those smaller islands play equally the role of a mainland to even smaller islands, and so on. As discussed by Papatheodorou (2004), the tourism landscape is characterized by a notable dualism in market and spatial structures: core tourism areas have adequate transport accessibility and accommodation infrastructure, occasionally due to the operations of transnational companies; whereas peripheral resorts are served poorly and usually host small, traditional tourism establishments. Core resorts may cast an "agglomeration shadow" on smaller, peripheral ones. This would be the case of Rodos vis-à-vis Chalki, Symi and Tylos, which are denied autonomous development and have a relationship of substantial dependency with Rodos. In any case, however, each territorial area may simultaneously play the role of a core in a lower spatial order and the role of a periphery in a higher one. For example, Rodos is clearly the business and administrative centre of the Dodecanese Islands and a core tourism resort of the Aegean Archipelago. At a wider Greek level, however, Rodos plays only a modest role as a business centre, while its role in the global tourism map is noteworthy but certainly not core.

On these grounds, within the archipelago, the image of smaller islands is overshadowed by that of larger ones or of the archipelago itself. Of course, to consider that *all* small islands could have their own, distinctive and unique image is perhaps impossible (Baldacchino and Ferreira, 2013). The exploitation of existing differences within the archipelago needs to be carefully managed within a simple but effective marketing strategy that puts the focus on the Aegean and on smaller archipelagos inside it, *as a whole*, and as the provider of a multiple tourism product. Local island councils, where they exist, not surprisingly, disagree: these have their own tourism strategic plans, and archipelago issues do not feature prominently (Baldacchino and Ferreira, 2013). In fact, the Aegean Archipelago is administratively divided in only two regions: the North and South. Had these regions been granted the necessary powers by the state not only *de jure* but also *de facto* (i.e. in terms of financial means), a self-regulated and unified island governance framework could have gradually emerged. At present, nonetheless, the regions are overwhelmed by local micro-politics (at an island level) whereas they remain strongly financially dependent on the central government.

In the case of the Aegean, the image of the archipelago is very powerful despite the existence of islands such as Santorini (an international 'brand') and Lesvos (a regional 'brand') that manage to stand out on their own. The question of how neighbouring or satellite islands can benefit from these brands is a complex one, but also of great importance for smaller islands in the Aegean. A possible solution would have to consider benefits for both sides: larger islands would benefit by offering an opportunity to tourists to experience something different compared to their satellite islands; and smaller islands have an opportunity to receive some of these tourists, even if only for day trips.

Acknowledgements

Part of this work is supported by the project: The Integrated Programme for Insularity Research (IPIR) of the programme 'The University of the Aegean, the prominent and driving factor for the economic and social growth of the wide Aegean area' of the Operational Programme 'Education and Lifelong Learning', which is co-funded by European Union (European Social Fund) and National Resources. An earlier draft of this paper was presented at an island tourism conference held in Maspalomas, Gran Canaria, Spain, in December 2013. The usual disclaimers apply.

References

Baldacchino, G., and Ferreira, E.C.D. (2013). Competing notions of diversity in archipelago tourism: transport logistics, official rhetoric and inter-island rivalry in the Azores. *Island Studies Journal*, 8(1), 84–104.

Bardolet, E., and Sheldon, P.J. (2008). Tourism in archipelagos: Hawai'i and the Balearics. *Annals of Tourism Research*, 35(4), 900–923.

Butler R. (1996). Transportation innovations and island tourism. In D.G. Lockhart and D. Drakakis-Smith (eds), *Island tourism: Trends and prospects*, pp. 36–56. London: Pinter.

Coccosis, H. (2002). Island tourism development and carrying capacity. In Y. Apostolopoulos and D.J. Gayle (eds), *Island tourism and sustainable development: Caribbean, Pacific and Mediterranean experiences*, pp. 131–44. Westport CT: Praeger.

Eurostat (2014). Introduction to the NUTS Classification. Retrieved from http://epp. eurostat.ec.europa.eu/portal/page/portal/nuts_nomenclature/introduction

Greek Travel Pages. (2013). Various reports. Retrieved from http://www.gtp.gr

Hellenic Civil Aviation Authority. (2013). Various reports. Retrieved from http://www. hcaa.gr

Hellenic Statistical Authority. (2013). Various reports. Retrieved from http://www.statistics. gr/portal/page/portal/ESYE

Hernandez, L.J.A. (2002). Temporal accessibility in archipelagos: inter-island shipping in the Canary Islands. *Journal of Transport Geography*, 10(3), 231–9.

Kizos, T. (2007). Island lifestyles in the Aegean islands, Greece: heaven in summer, hell in winter? In H. Palang, H. Sooväli and A. Printsmann (eds), *Seasonal landscapes*, pp. 127–49. New York: Springer.

Lekakou, M.B. (2007). The eternal conundrum of Greek coastal shipping. In T. Pallis (ed.) *Maritime transport: The Greek paradigm*, pp. 257–96. Oxford: Elsevier Science.

Marine Traffic (2013). Various data. Retrieved from http://www.marinetraffic.com

Marzano, G., and Scott, N., (2009). Power in destination branding. *Annals of Tourism Research*, 36(2), 247–67.

McElroy, J.L. (2003). Tourism development in small islands across the world. *Geografiska Annaler*, 85B(4), 231–42.

Papatheodorou, A. (2001). Tourism, transport geography and industrial economics: a synthesis in the context of Mediterranean islands. *Anatolia*, 12(1), 23–34.

Papatheodorou, A. (2004). Exploring the evolution of tourism resorts. *Annals of Tourism Research*, 31(1): 219–37.

Papatheodorou, A., and Arvanitis, P. (2009). Spatial evolution of airport traffic and air transport liberalization: the case of Greece. *Journal of Transport Geography*, 17(5): 402–12.

Rigas, K. (2009). Boat or aeroplane? Passengers' perceptions of transport services to islands: the example of the Greek domestic leisure market. *Journal of Transport Geography*, 17(5), 396–401.

Rigas, K. (2012). Connecting island regions: a qualitative approach to the European experience. *SPOUDAI Journal*, 62(3–4), 30–53.

Rigas, K., Sambracos, E., and Gatzoli, A. (2011). Air and sea transport: competition strategies under normal and economic crisis environments. *SPOUDAI Journal*, 61(3–4), 65–84.

Spilanis, I., Kizos, T., Vaitis, M., and Koukourouvli, N. (2012). Measuring the economic, social and environmental performance of European island regions: emerging issues for European and regional policy. *European Planning Studies*, 1(1), 1–22.

Stabler, M.J., Papatheodorou, A., and Sinclair, M.T. (2010). *The economics of tourism*, 2nd edn. London: Routledge.

Thomassen, B. (2009). The uses and meaning of liminality. *International Political Anthropology*, 2(1), 5–28.

Tzanatos, E.S. (2005). Technical reliability of the Greek coastal passenger fleet. *Marine Policy*, 29(1), 85–92.

Vannini, P. (2012). *Ferry tales: Mobility, place and time on Canada's west coast*. New York: Routledge.

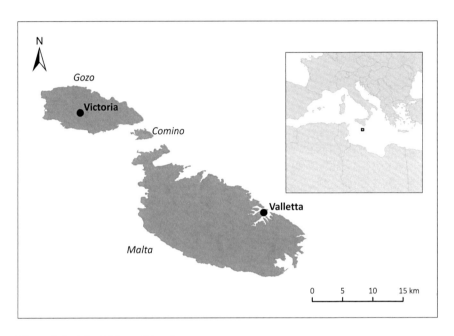

Figure 2.1   The Maltese Islands

Chapter 2

The Malta-Gozo-Comino Story: Implications of a Malta-Gozo Fixed Link on Tourism Activity

Samantha Chaperon and Nadia Theuma

Introduction: Tourism and Peripherality

A 'periphery' represents a boundary, the edge of a defined space, or the outer-limits of an area (Hall, Harrison, Weaver and Wall, 2013), but an area's peripherality can be perceived in different ways. For example, it can refer to a place that is geographically located a long distance from a capital city, other centres or core population; or it can be a long way from a spatial concentration of wealth or power. A region can also be described as peripheral, if geographically distant from main gateways or arrival points. Alternatively, peripherality can refer to people's subjective perceptions of a place as peripheral. For instance, a destination with excellent motorway or rail links may be more accessible to a centre than closer destinations without such links. Journey time and cost, frequency of service and the necessity for interchange between services are all potentially important measures of accessibility and subsequently can influence perceptions of peripherality. However, it is reasonable to accept that "no matter how the region's peripherality is assessed, it will invariably involve the very real fact that the location is relatively difficult to get to" (Nash and Martin, 2003, p. 163).

Tourism in Peripheral Areas

Numerous peripheral regions actively seek to attract tourism, and many are well placed to do so because they possess destination features demanded by the tourism industry. Although peripheral locations, by their very nature, can have major problems in terms of accessibility, there is a potential contradiction in that there are also tourism advantages associated with wild, remote and natural environments (Hall and Page, 2006). The appeal of peripheral places is based on their power to signify to the visitor the unspoilt, the pristine and the traditional. This is in contrast to the symbolic associations of the centre (and increasingly of mass tourism resorts in the pleasure periphery) with the inauthentic, the spoilt, the jaded and the modern (Scott, 2000). There has been a notable shift in demand from holidaying in built-up resort areas to less developed coastal and rural locations, which coincides with a general increased interest in the environment. As traditional destinations become crowded, travellers search for regions that are more peripheral and off the beaten path (Timothy, 2001). The attributes of peripherality, long viewed as disadvantageous, are now seen as providing tourism marketing advantages and the opportunities to create destination distinctiveness.

However, tourism development in peripheral areas is not without its challenges. For example, these areas tend to lack infrastructure; this may be a lack of basic infrastructure such as energy and water, but they are also likely to be deficient in transport infrastructure, and this proves to be the most problematic (Buhalis and Diamantis, 2001). Peripheral regions are distant from core spheres of activity, and therefore they may have poor access to and from tourist generating markets (Khadaroo and Seetanah, 2007). Many tourists will choose not to visit a peripheral area because of the greater travel time involved and necessity for interchange. Poor weather conditions in peripheral areas may compound this inconvenience. Further, weather conditions will often dictate the length of the tourist season in a peripheral tourist destination, and this can lead to extreme seasonality in the tourism industry.

Peripheral areas clearly face significant challenges in terms of accessibility, but they possess product strengths in terms of their strong natural environment and remoteness, and these destination features are increasing in popularity. However, if the demand proves too great or is inadequately managed, then the peripheral destinations that begin to prosper economically may become overcrowded, environmentally degraded or subject to pressure to modernise, thereby losing the very characteristics that encouraged their success. Peripheries are not static phenomena destined never to change, even if some tourists would prefer that (Brown and Hall, 2000); and Hall et al. (2013) question whether peripheral areas are valued for their intrinsic properties or mainly as sites of tourist consumption.

Tourism in Islands

Many island characteristics are similar to those of peripheral areas. The potential for (and seemingly inevitability of) tourism development in islands also mirrors that of peripheral regions. However, islands have an extra dimension: the impediment of a marine barrier. The fact that tourists have to complete their journey by making a crossing between the mainland and the island adds inconvenience, time and cost (Royle and Scott, 1996). However, the marine barrier is not seen by everyone as an inconvenience, and the perception – and, in the case of islands, the geo-physicality – of isolation and remoteness can be of great appeal to tourists. The physical separation from the mainland creates a feeling of visiting somewhere different (Butler, 1993), even exotic. Baum (1997, p. 21) suggests that there is something distinctive about taking a boat or plane to reach a destination, as opposed to land-based driving or taking a train. He states that 'the feeling of separateness, of being cut off from the mainland, is an important physical and psychological attribute of the successful vacation'. Whereas islanders may see aquatic borders as symbolising confinement, the same features can appeal to tourists seeking escape and relaxation (Gössling and Wall, 2007).

The small size of many islands also gives tourists the perception that these destinations are likely to be less developed and more 'authentic' than larger places. They may exhibit quaintness, cultural difference, political separateness, and 'otherness', these being features that often have a greater tourist appeal than larger, more metropolitan locations. There is the perception of island life as being slower paced, and perhaps a little further back in time. Even islands with little to offer by way of natural and cultural attractions may capitalize on the inherent attributes of smallness, foreignness and islandness (Conlin and Baum, 1995).

There is an apparent irony in that the appeal of isolation for tourists only becomes functional when islands become accessible, and islands with the best connections generally attract the most visitors. Air and sea transport are crucial to link islands with the outside world, and advances in air and sea transport have assisted previously inaccessible islands to establish themselves in tourism markets (Andriotis, 2004).

Core-periphery Relations in Archipelagos

The Core-periphery Context

There are many common experiences for islands that go beyond their position as land masses surrounded by water. Because of their relatively small size and limited political clout, small islands which lie offshore a much larger island state (as in many archipelagos) or continental mainland are particularly liable to demonstrate dependency. Small island economies are often vulnerable to external forces, and will usually experience external economic and political dependency, often in inverse proportion to their size and population. Some have referred to this phenomenon as the 'core-periphery' conflict (Britton, 1982; Weaver, 1998; Chaperon and Bramwell, 2013).

One of the defining features of the core-periphery relationship is the idea of domination of the periphery by the core (Jordan, 2004). 'Core-periphery' is most closely associated with dependency theory, and sometimes with a modernisation perspective, and it provides a fundamentally geographical framework to comprehend spatial disparities in power and levels of development (Weaver, 1998).

Based on his research on Trinidad and Tobago and Antigua and Barbuda, Weaver (1998) constructed a core-periphery model to demonstrate the economic and political interactions between islands. In this context, he explains that there is a subordinate island or peripheral area, a dominant island (or country), and an external core. He suggests that the interaction between the subordinate island(s), the dominant island, and the external core may be perceived as a series of nested core-periphery relationships. The dominant island (i.e. Trinidad, Antigua) is a core with respect to the subordinate island, but a periphery with reference to the external core. The subordinate island (Tobago, Barbuda) is a periphery with respect to both the dominant island and the external core. Weaver identifies two main channels of influence in this scenario: the external core faces constraints in dealing with the dominant island, mainly due to the prerogatives of sovereignty. The external core, in dealing with the subordinate island, is still subject to the same filtering process which moderates its influence over the dominant island; therefore any projects, imports or exports, travel, etc., relating to the subordinate island have to be approved by central government agencies based on the main island. However, the dominant island faces few substantive barriers in dealing with the subordinate island. The subordinate island is thus faced with a sort of 'double exploitation'.

It is perhaps unsurprising that a centrifugal, internal core-periphery relationship emerges, given that islands are distinctive cultural, economic and political entities, where the power and benefits seem to be held by the larger islands at the expense of the smaller. Moreover, Weaver (1998) suggests that central government, while not hesitant to emphasize its own perceived status as a periphery oppressed by an external core, often appears unable to acknowledge the possibly exploitative nature of its own relationships with its small island partners; all the more so since, in many cases, the latter enjoy a theoretically significant degree of autonomy.

Tourism and Core-periphery Relations

Governance in archipelagos is often a shared and multi-tiered affair. Tourism development policies must negotiate the complexity of hierarchical government structures (mainland, archipelago, island), potentially causing conflict and political difficulties not faced in individual islands (Trousdale, 1999). Because island government is often located off-island and can frequently have different priorities and policies to those of the island population, local involvement in tourism policy-making can be limited. Island residents may lack political 'clout' in decision-making (Chaperon and Bramwell, 2011; 2013).

Islands in archipelagos, especially warm water islands, have a considerable economic dependence on tourism (Baldacchino, 2013), yet the small economies of some islands mean that it can be difficult to raise local capital for investment in tourism. Much of the required investment in island tourism may come from elsewhere; thus control over tourism and its benefits can end up in the hands of outsiders who may not have local or national interests at heart, and this often leads to high economic leakages (Andriotis, 2004; Scheyvens and Momsen, 2008). As a result, many islands have little economic choice other than to accept as inevitable the expansion of conventional tourism, which is characterised by mass tourist arrivals, control by external actors, and large scale facilities (Bramwell, 2003).

Different cultural and community interests on each island may make stakeholder involvement in any centralized tourism planning challenging (Sheehan and Ritchie, 2005). Views held about tourism development from community and tourism stakeholders in a peripheral island may be markedly different from those held at the core. Actors in positions of power (i.e. on the dominant island) may see the subordinate island mainly as a place where tourism can maximise short-term financial or economic returns on capital investment. Indeed, the earlier discussion of core-periphery relations describes a situation of economic exploitation and dependency. Conversely, there may be at least some actors at the core who prefer to protect the environmentally and culturally distinct assets of the subordinate island (Chaperon and Bramwell, 2011). For long term success, balancing the opinions of each island's community as the archipelago develops tourism is necessary. In a sense, each island becomes a stakeholder in the archipelago's development and each must be heard (Bardolet and Sheldon, 2008).

In terms of logistics for tourism in archipelagos, its governance is often characterised by a top-down, core-periphery relationship. This means that the central (or dominant) island – usually the location of the capital city and largest population – is often the one with an international airport or seaport. All visitors to the 'offshore' (or subordinate) islands must first arrive at, and transit through, the main central island (Baldacchino and Ferreira, 2013). Travel between islands in an archipelago is critical to their tourism development. The distances between islands and the modes and schedules of transportation linking the islands are a vital part of the archipelago's tourism policies. Inter-island links that do not involve the central hub are rare or non-existent, or hardly ever advertised or communicated to visitors (Baldacchino and Ferreira, 2013). If most visitors stay on one island, different issues will surface than if significant multi-island travel occurs (Bardolet and Sheldon, 2008). For this reason, islands can be completely dependent on the services of airlines and shipping/ferry companies, and these companies may make decisions in the interests of their stakeholders rather than of the islanders (Conlin and Baum, 1995).

The research for this chapter involved detailed content analysis of news items, commentaries and letters about tourism in Maltese daily and weekly newspapers, notably the daily English-language *Times of Malta* and *Malta Independent*, starting from 1999. This information was complemented by a few select interviews with stakeholder representatives, as well as the insider knowledge of the co-authors, one of whom is Maltese and the other a frequent visitor to Malta.

Case Study: The Maltese Islands

Geography

The Maltese Islands are situated in the central Mediterranean, 93 km distant from Sicily and 290 km distant from Libya (NSO, 2013). The archipelago consists of: Malta (the main island), Gozo, Comino, Cominotto, Filfla and St. Paul's islands, with the latter three being uninhabited. With a total area of 316 km² and a population of around 420,000 (NSO, 2012) the Maltese archipelago is the most densely populated country in Europe and the third in the world. Malta is the largest of the islands, with a total area of 246 km² and a population of about 390,000. Gozo lies to the north-west of Malta and is much smaller, with a total area of 67 km² and a resident population of around 30,000. Comino is the smallest of the three with a total area of 3 km² and a resident population of 2 persons; the latter, however, is also a summer resort and is more active during the months of April and October. The three main islands are separated by a small channel (*il-fliegu*) that can be crossed by a ferry journey of 30 minutes. Ferry boats between Malta and Gozo operate on a daily basis throughout the day, whilst small boats carry people between Malta and Comino and Gozo and Comino, mainly during the summer months.

Malta, the main island, is the hub for administrative activity, with the capital city, parliament and main administrative bodies being located here. Gozo is for many reasons considered to be the periphery of Malta. During the British era (1800–1964), Gozo had it own Council; however, post-independence Gozo was administered from Malta. Since 1987, Gozo has had its own minister; the responsibilities of the Ministry for Gozo include tourism, education, health and transport.

The three islands have quite distinct characteristics. Malta, bearing over 90% of the country's resident population, is mainly built up, with a hive of tourism activity around the capital city of Valletta, the nearby seaside towns of Sliema and St. Julian's, and the night-life hub of Paceville. Gozo is less built up and has a much lower population density. With a more rural, rustic setting, Gozo has also attracted interest from foreign European visitors during the Romantic period, especially because of its possible association to the Isle of Calypso as featured in Homer (Freller, 1997). In the past years, the Maltese Government has committed itself to retain Gozo's special characteristics by promoting it as an ecological island (Ministry for Gozo, 2009); but this has hardly stemmed the rate of property construction on the island. Comino is nearly barren, except for one hotel-and-bungalow tourist complex operating between May and October each year (Comino Hotels, 2014).

Malta is the main access point to the islands: the sole international airport and cruise liner terminal are both located there. Accessibility to Gozo occurs via the state-owned company Gozo Channel that operates a ferry service between Cirkewwa in the North of Malta and Mġarr in Gozo. This is predominantly used by cars, passengers and day trippers and some freight. There is a dedicated freight service that operates once daily from Pieta (near Valletta) to Mgarr Harbour in Gozo. This is a longer trip that takes over 1.5 hrs to complete. The service has for a long time been deemed inefficient and unable to meet the needs of Gozitans, especially the business community (Theuma and Theuma, 2006). Moreover, the 30 minute ferry ride, for many Gozitans who need to commute to work and to study (as with those reading for a university degree),[1] takes an

---

1   The University of Malta has a main campus in Msida, Malta; another one in Valletta, Malta; and a campus in Gozo which offers only limited part-time courses. Most students from Gozo who want

"average of two hours" when waiting times and additional road transportation times are factored in (personal communication).

As part of its plans for EU membership in 2004 and in the subsequent programming period of 2007–2013, the Maltese government addressed the issue of transport and Gozo-Malta links as well as the road network (NSRF, 2007). Investments have been made both on the TEN-T road network that links the Freeport and Airport in the south and eastern parts of Malta with Grand Harbour and Cirkewwa Harbour, as well as in the upgrading of the Mġarr and Cirkewwa harbour facilities to better accommodate commuters between the two islands.

Tourism

Three sectors are especially significant to the economy of the archipelago: tourism (responsible for some 25% of direct and indirect economic activity); manufacturing (14%); and financial services, including banking and insurance (8%) (Sant, 2012). Tourism arrivals for 2012 reached 1.4 million, logging 12.6 million tourist nights, and the average length of visitor stay of 8.7 nights (MTA, 2014). Tourism arrivals in Malta have increased steadily since the mass tourism boom of the 1960s until the late 1990s, when decline in tourism numbers urged the tourism authorities to address the product offer. Tourism figures continued to oscillate in subsequent years until 2009 when figures started to increase steadily once again. Low cost carriers had a positive impact on tourism figures and have brought about a mix of nationalities to the islands. However, Malta still depends mainly on the UK market for tourist arrivals. The Italian market represents the second largest share, recently overtaking the German's share (Ministry for Tourism, Culture and the Environment, 2012, p. 5).

The situation in Gozo is quite different. Gozo receives four types of visitors: (1) foreigners who spend their entire or part of their holiday in Gozo; (2) Maltese who spend one night or more in Gozo; (3) foreign day trippers; and (4) Maltese day trippers (Muscat, 2006).

Table 2.1 compares tourist data for Malta (the main island only) and for Gozo separately. In 2012, over 1 million vehicle trips and 4 million person trips between the two islands were made (inclusive of all Gozitans, Maltese and foreigners). These include an estimated 600,000 foreign day trippers, meaning that around half of the tourists who visited Malta got to visit Gozo. However, just 36,739 Maltese and 37,046 foreigners visited Gozo for more than 1 day during 2012.

Hotels represent the backbone of the Maltese accommodation sector, with 33,234 bed places, while other collective accommodation such as aparthotels, guesthouses and hostels, comprise the remaining 6,262 bed places (NSO, 2012). Moreover, considering the spatial distribution of hotels and resorts, there are areas characterised by heavy concentration of accommodation facilities and consequently of tourists. In Gozo, the picture is different. There are just ten hotels; the accommodation sector is heavily skewed towards farmhouses, with circa 1,434 beds in collective accommodation and circa 1,679 beds in registered farmhouses, guesthouses and apartments.

Maltese visitors tend to increase their visits to Gozo on long weekends, Carnival weekend (when the Maltese travel to Gozo specifically to enjoy the traditional Nadur Carnival), and

---

to follow a full time degree course commute to Malta. Some do so daily; others rent an apartment and live in Malta during the week and commute during the weekend.

Table 2.1   Comparative tourist data for the islands of Malta and Gozo (2012)

	Malta	Gozo
Staying arrivals	1,277,536	73,585
Number of guest nights	7,561,367	270,220
Number of hotels	108	10
Number of tourist villages/ aparthotels	30	2
Number of guest houses / hostels	55	8
Tourist accommodation capacity (Number of beds)	44,570	4,591
Average length of stay (nights)	5.9	3.7
Occupancy rates (%)	56.7	45.0
Cruise passengers	562,812	3,546

Source: MTA (2014, p. 7).

during the mid-August holiday break of the feast of St. Mary (the week of 15 August). Other major cultural events during the year also lead to an increase in visitor crossings between the two islands. These include the Opera festivals in October and the Nativity village in the locality of Ghajnsielem, which was visited by some 74,000 people over the Christmas period of 17 December 2013 to 5 January 2014 (*Times of Malta*, 2014).

Over the years, Gozo has successfully developed its tourism product offer: this includes scuba diving, cultural tourism (especially the visual arts), and in more recent times eco/ rural tourism.

Core-periphery Relations and Tourism

The Maltese Islands exhibit the hallmark characteristics of Weaver's (1998) nested core-periphery relations. Malta became a member of the European Union (EU) in May 2004, but it remains on the socio-economic and political margins of Europe (or external core). It is also geographically peripheral, being located on the southern edge of Europe. Malta is peripheral with respect to its external core, but is the dominant island with respect to its smaller, sister island of Gozo. Tourism-related policy, marketing and development decisions for Gozo are often made in mainland Malta. This is because the seat of government is located here, and it is also where key tourism organisations such as the Malta Tourism Authority and the Malta Environment and Planning Authority (MEPA) are located. The subordinate island is geographically, economically and politically peripheral to Malta; this puts Gozo on the periphery of the periphery, and thus it faces especially difficult core-periphery relations (Chaperon and Bramwell, 2013).

Core-periphery relations are exhibited, and the dependence of Gozo on Malta is highlighted, where there are discussions related to improving accessibility. All visitors to the Maltese Islands must first arrive into Malta by air or sea and then continue their journey to Gozo. Thus, Malta is the main gateway to the Maltese Islands. It is argued by Gozo tourism businesses, and others, that a frequent and reliable transport link between Malta and Gozo is vital for both the tourism industry and the large number of Gozitans that commute to Malta for work or to pursue higher education.

The Malta-Gozo Link: Proposed Runway Development

A runway development for Gozo, to allow for fixed-wing aircraft to operate to and from the island, has been discussed and debated for many years. It has been described as "one of those skeletons in the cupboard which simply refuses to go away" (Deidun, 2005). It was in the late 1960s when a private businessman first proposed to provide a fixed-wing air service between Gozo and Malta if the Maltese Government agreed to provide an airstrip (Pisani, 2005). A site was earmarked for its development at Ta' Lambert in Xewkija, but the plans were abandoned. Then, in 1990, the Nationalist Party decided to use the land for the construction of a heliport. A regular helicopter service between Malta International Airport and Gozo was consequently started by Malta Air Charter, a subsidiary of the national airline Air Malta. The service was state subsidised, reflecting the significance of the service to Gozo as a necessity. The helicopter service provided a vital link between the islands, and was used by both tourists and business people, and in 2003 over 60,000 people used the service (Castelain, 2004a).

However, in October 2004 the service ceased to operate. The helicopters did not meet EU safety requirements, and the company was operating the service at a loss, notwithstanding the subsidy (Bonello, 2003). After considering proposals from private businesses to operate fixed-wing, helicopter and seaplane services, the Maltese Government decided to re-introduce a helicopter service, but this time without subsidy. In March 2005, Helisureste, a Spanish company, commenced a helicopter service operation between Malta and Gozo (Cini, 2005). The new helicopter carried only 13 passengers, which was half as many as the previous type, and the fares almost doubled. On 29 October 2006, this service was also terminated because it had been incurring losses (Zammit, 2006).

Whilst the Maltese government was deciding which new transport service to introduce, Gozo was left for several months with only the ferry service to rely on for travel between the islands. There were occasions during this time when poor weather conditions forced sailings to be cancelled, and Gozo was left isolated from the main island. The Gozo Business Chamber, the Gozo Tourist Association and the Malta Labour Party all deplored the cessation of the helicopter service for this length of time, since "to leave the island without a helicopter service was a blow to the tourism industry and to the Gozitan economy" (Castelain, 2004b). It was at this time that the idea of a fixed-wing air service re-emerged as a hot topic for discussion, and was proposed at the same site in Xewkija that had been allocated for a runway some 40 years before. The development that was most frequently discussed in local newspapers was an extension to the existing Gozo runway by about 270 metres. The Gozo heliport currently has a runway which is 230 metres long, and it is commonly believed that short take-off and landing aircraft, by definition, need only 500 metres of tarmac. The terminal building, fire station, and other necessary infrastructure are already in place. The development of a runway to allow for a fixed-wing air service was claimed by many to be the solution to Gozo's accessibility problems, one which would encourage tourists to visit the island, and prevent Gozitans from being isolated again in the future.

In 2007, a Maltese-Canadian consortium started a seaplane operation between the Valletta Waterfront and Sliema to Gozo. The sea plane, which had a seating capacity for 14 passengers, also operated daily scenic flights around Malta and Gozo. The sea plane was in operation on a daily basis; however it did not operate during the night and on the days where the sea was rough. Moreover, it presented certain difficulties to foreign visitors as they had to be inconveniently transferred twice: from the airport in Luqa to

Valletta Waterfront and then from Mgarr harbour to their hotel in Gozo (Barry, 2012). The service was halted 'temporarily' on August 2012 and has not been resumed since (ibid.); no other air-link has been made available.

Meanwhile, other proposals for linking the two islands have been put forward. In 2012, the Maltese government commissioned a feasibility study to explore other possible fixed links between the two islands, with one being an underwater tunnel that would link the two islands without impacting on Comino (MacDonald, 2012). This document outlines proposals as well as socio-economic impacts for sea tunnel options (bored tunnels or immersed tube tunnels). The tunnel, which would take 5–7 years to build, has a cost estimated between €156m and €492m. Besides the cost, which is proposed to be funded through EU funds and private-public partnerships, the project has other major environmental impacts on the coast, the fauna and flora, land and sea Natura 2000 sites, as well as areas of ecological and high landscape value in both in Malta and Gozo. The tunnel could reduce the average journey by a minimum of 40 minutes, and increase traffic towards the island of Gozo, implying that there will be an increase of socio-economic benefits to the island of Gozo.

In June 2013, the newly-elected Labour Government announced that it had commissioned a study for a bridge between the two islands. This study is expected to be completed by November 2014 (Sansone, 2013). The airstrip is "now a priority in Labour's plans for Gozo", as declared by a spokesperson for the Minister for Gozo (Debono, 2013a). The connectivity saga continues.

Attitudes to the Intra-island Permanent Link Projects

Accessibility has been central to the Malta-Gozo relationship. All the more so when the debate reflects on the core-periphery dynamic between the two islands.

In a survey conducted in July 2013 with a random sample of 400 respondents by *Malta Today*, a local newspaper, it transpired that 37% of respondents would prefer better sea transport between Malta and Gozo, 34% would prefer a bridge, 16% prefer no change, and 12% would prefer a tunnel. Older and more educated respondents were the most in support of the status quo (Debono, 2013b). See Table 2.2.

The Gozitan economic community is at the forefront of the campaign for a permanent link between the islands. This view contrasts with that of non-business persons, foreign visitors and the Maltese. Many foreign visitors feel that any form of permanent structure will affect Gozo negatively whilst at the same time spoil the tranquil nature of Gozo (e.g. Kreupl, 2009). A similar claim is also sustained by some Gozitan people who argue that physical structures such as bridges or tunnels that will link Gozo to Malta will lead to a decline in their quality of life, because the links will increase the number of people travelling to the island[2] and hence lead to environmental pollution and adverse social impacts.

Although visitor numbers have increased, with the Gozo ferry claiming to have increased its services (Gozo News, 2014a), Gozo tourism operators claim that low cost air carriers operating to and from Malta have now encouraged many Maltese to travel abroad rather than visiting Gozo; hence strengthening the case for a more stable, reliable and viable

---

2   Until 2013, Gozo Channel carried circa 1,700 cars per day. MacDonald (2012) claims that the proposed Malta-Gozo tunnel would be used by some 6,000 vehicles per day. No usage projections are yet available for an eventual bridge. In both cases, actual use would depend on the price of a bridge or tunnel toll, if any.

Table 2.2 **Preferred options for travelling between Malta and Gozo (by %)**
N=400 (Margin of error: +/- 4.9%)

Preference	18–34	35–54	55+	All
Bridge	28.6	37.2	36.5	33.7
Tunnel	14.3	15.3	6.7	12.1
Better Sea Transport	40	38	31.3	36.6
Same as Today	14.3	7.7	24.5	15.5
Don't Know	2.8	1.8	1.0	2.1

Source: Debono (2013b).

means of transport between the two islands (GTA, personal communication). This view is supported by non-business Gozitans and young people who claim that "Gozo deserves better" (e.g. GUG, 2011).

From a tourism perspective, The Gozo Tourism Association (GTA) and the Gozo Business Chamber (GBC) have been leading the debate on the need for Gozo to have better accessibility and more permanent structures that link the two islands. The main argument is that, due to the double insularity factor, goods and services are more costly leading to greater dependency on Malta. The decline in economic activity on the island due to increased energy and transport costs have also led to the current situation.

Over the years, GTA has launched a number of initiatives to promote more visits to Gozo and hence to increase its accessibility, these included special weekend packages, rebates on ferry tickets during the winter months for people travelling during the weekend, and even free travel over weekends (Gozo News, 2013b). These initiatives have led to increases in visitor numbers and spikes in economic activity.

One of the main arguments sustained by Gozo business representatives over the past 20 years has been that Gozo can and should be marketed as a separate destination from Malta (e.g. Briguglio, 2008; Gozo News, 2014b). Due to its special rural characteristics, Gozo can attract a different type of visitor than Malta (Ministry for Tourism, Culture and the Environment, 2012; ICER 2012). This distinctiveness can be further sustained by the fact that, apart from specialising in niche markets, Malta ironically uses 'Gozitan attractions' to market itself. A television spot for National Geographic – titled *'Malta: Truly Mediterranean'* – uses no less than 15 snapshots of Gozo (National Geographic, 2009). A recent copy of Air Malta's in-flight magazine mentions 20 "things to do in Malta", of which five are actually in Gozo, and one in Comino (Air Malta, 2014). Gozitan operators use this fact to further drive the point home that Gozo does not need Malta for its tourist base but can attract a market on its own steam, provided that Gozo is more accessible. However, there are divergent views since discussions with tourism operators in Gozo also indicate that some operators are inclined to see a tourism product that mirrors that of Malta, namely mass market based arrivals, cruise tourism, and a tourism product that attracts younger people.

An argument that as yet has to be properly addressed is that, should Malta and Gozo be permanently linked by a bridge or tunnel, then Gozo would most probably have to denounce the 'special status' that it has fought for and secured on accession to the EU (e.g. Malta Today, 2013).

In 2003, prior to Malta's entry into the EU, Gozo prepared a study to argue that, as a regional island, it enjoys NUTS III status and as such has special requirements that need to be addressed. The EU criteria that were used at the time to reinforce Gozo's special island status were that Gozo is: (1) *not linked to the mainland by permanent structures such as bridges or tunnels;* (2) distant at least 1 km from mainland; (3) inhabited by more than 50 permanent residents; and (4) did not host the capital of an EU state (Debono, 2003) (our emphasis). This argument was reiterated in the negotiations for the new tranche of funding, that is 2014–20, leading to the Maltese islands retaining their NUTS II status and hence able to benefit from additional EU funding given to 'developing European Regions'.

Thus, accessibility to Gozo, especially that in the form of a more permanent structure, may jeopardise the Gozitan identity in that it could lead to the situation where Gozo becomes part of Malta: something that, although deemed essential for the business community, may in the long run not be acceptable to the general population, and may even prove counter-productive in the longer term. While recognising the difficulties and costs of their physical separation from the main island of Malta, many Gozitans also think that a fixed link could prove more harmful than beneficial to Gozo.

Conclusion

The less developed, natural, and remote nature of peripheral islands tends to make them more attractive tourist destinations; but, ironically, and unless they can tap an upscale niche tourist market, it is only when accessibility to these places is improved that they can truly benefit from sufficient visitor numbers and the economic impacts that such visitors bring. For islands like Gozo, characterised by a 'double insularity and peripherality' (e.g. Saliba, 2012), without their own proper 'gateway' to international tourism, the issues and challenges associated with accessibility are poignant. There is a general acceptance that, if Gozo is to be competitive as an international tourist destination, accessibility to the island must be improved.

The difficulty lies in deciding how permanent the link between the islands should be. Various options – ranging from a more frequent ferry service, a helicopter service, and an air link, to a bridge and a tunnel – have been considered. This is where opinions diverge: some Gozitans (mainly tourism-related stakeholders) believe that a permanent link is a necessity if the dependence on Malta is to be reduced; yet, other Gozo residents believe that a fixed link would encourage too many visitors and too much tourism-associated development.

This debate is rendered more complex due to the core-periphery context of the Maltese Islands. Many political and economic decisions about Gozo, and not just those related to tourism, are taken in Malta. There are no regional (let alone secessionist) political parties or factions in Gozo; Gozitan politics now mirror those unfolding on the larger island. Hence, there is no political danger of a Malta-centric government losing out to a Gozo party (Baldacchino, 2007). The Maltese Government has moreover expressed a commitment to retain Gozo's special characteristics and to ensure environmental sustainability in the island; a policy of limited accessibility would seem to support this policy stance. The Maltese are also an important domestic tourist market for Gozo; as such, they may prefer to keep Gozo less developed in order to enjoy and consume it as their 'pleasure periphery' (Turner and Ash, 1975). The debate is influenced further by the relationship Gozo has established with the EU (its external core) which would not allow Gozo to maintain its special island status if it went along with a fixed link solution to bridging the 8km Gozo Channel, effectively erasing Gozo's status as an island in the eyes of the EU (e.g. Hache, 2007).

Powerful centrifugal forces remain at work. The creation of a coordinating Ministry for Gozo in 1987 was one such acknowledgement. Malta and Gozo now take it in turns as to which comes on top, in larger font, in the official tourism marketing logo, depending largely on context (see Plate 2.1) in this way, the Malta Tourism Authority's logo for the Maltese islands can now also position and present Gozo as a main destination within the archipelago. A recent announcement has declared that Gozo will start having "its own tourism policy" (Gozo News, 2014b). The National Statistics Office has opened a Gozo Office and is now producing Gozo-specific statistics (Gozo News, 2014c). Key exponents of Malta's political elite, including a former prime minister, seem to be coming round to admitting that it could be also in Malta's interest to peddle Gozo as a subnational jurisdiction, "with its own structures of governance" (The Malta Independent, 2014). Watch this space.

References

Air Malta (2014). Things to do in Malta. *Il-Bizzilla*. In-Flight Magazine, June, pp. 18–19.

Andriotis, K. (2004). Problems of island tourism development: the Greek insular regions. In B. Bramwell (ed.), *Coastal mass tourism: Diversification and sustainable development in Southern Europe*, pp. 114–32. Clevedon: Channel View.

Baldacchino, G. (2007). Jurisdictional capacity and landscape heritage: a case study of Malta and Gozo. *Journal of Mediterranean Studies*, 17(1), 95–114.

Baldacchino, G. (2013). Island tourism. In A. Holden and D. Fennell (eds), *The Routledge handbook of tourism and the environment*, pp. 200–208. New York: Routledge.

Baldacchino, G. and Ferreira, E.C.D. (2013). Competing notions of diversity in archipelago tourism: transport logistics, official rhetoric and inter-island rivalry in the Azores. *Island Studies Journal*, 8(1), 84–104.

Bardolet, E., and Sheldon, P. J. (2008). Tourism in archipelagos: Hawai'i and the Balearics. *Annals of Tourism Research*, 35(4), 900–923.

Barry, D. (2012). Harbour Air halted sea plane service for the summer. *Malta Today*, 16 August. Retrieved from: http://www.maltatoday.com.mt/en/businessdetails/business/businessnews/Harbour-Air-halted-seaplane-service-for-the-summer-20120816

Baum, T.G. (1997). The fascination of islands: a tourism perspective. In D.G. Lockhart and D. Drakakis-Smith (eds), *Island tourism: Trends and prospects*, pp. 21–35. London: Pinter.

Bonello, J. (2003). 'Options open' on helicopter or fixed wing aircraft service to Gozo. *Times of Malta*, 8 December.

Bramwell, B. (2003). Maltese responses to tourism. *Annals of Tourism Research*, 30(3), 581–605.

Briguglio, L. (2008). Sustainable Tourism on the small island of Gozo. *Occasional Paper Series*, No. 5, Msida, Malta: University of Malta, Islands and Small States Institute. Retrieved from http://www.um.edu.mt/__data/assets/pdf_file/0007/121579/2008_5.pdf

Britton, S. G. (1982). The political economy of tourism in the Third World. *Annals of Tourism Research*, 9(3), 331–58.

Brown, F., and Hall, D. (2000). *Tourism in peripheral areas.* Clevedon: Channel View.

Buhalis, D., and Diamantis, D. (2001). Tourism development in Greek archipelagos. In D. Ionnides, Y. Apostolopoulos and S. Sonmez (eds), *Mediterranean islands and sustainable tourism development: Practices, management and policies*, pp. 143–70. London: Continuum.

Butler, R.W. (1993). Tourism development in small islands: past influences and future directions. In D.G. Lockhart, D. Drakakis-Smith and J.A. Schembri (eds), *The development process in small island states*, pp. 71–91. London: Routledge.

Castelain. (2004a). Requiem for a service. *Sunday Times of Malta*, 31 October. Retrieved from http://www.timesofmalta.com/articles/view/20041031/gozo/commentary.108392

Castelain. (2004b). Gozo Chamber and GTA on suspension of helicopter service. *Sunday Times of Malta*, 7 November. Retrieved from http://www.timesofmalta.com/articles/view/20041107/gozo/gozo-chamber-and-gta-on-suspension-of-helicopter-service.107783

Chaperon, S., and Bramwell, B. (2011). Views on the scale and types of tourism development in the rural periphery: the case of Gozo. In D. Macleod and S. Gillespie, (eds), *Sustainable tourism in rural Europe: Approaches to development*, pp. 151–65. London: Routledge.

Chaperon, S., and Bramwell, B. (2013). Dependency and agency in peripheral tourism development. *Annals of Tourism Research*, 40(1), 132–54.

Cini, G. (2005). Gozo-Malta helicopter company eyes other destinations. *Times of Malta*, 23 March. Retrieved from http://www.timesofmalta.com/articles/view/20050323/local/gozo-malta-helicopter-company-eyes-other-destinations.95525

Comino Hotels. (2014). Home page. Retrieved from http://www.cominohotel.com/page.asp?n=homeandl=1

Conlin, M.V., and Baum, T.G. (eds) (1995). *Island tourism: Management, principles and practices.* Chichester: Wiley.

Debono, G. (2003). Gozo in Malta's negotiations with the EU. *Times of Malta*, 16 February. Retrieved from http://www.timesofmalta.com/articles/view/20030216/opinion/gozo-in-maltas-negotiations-with-the-eu.156520

Debono, J. (2013a). Gozo airstrip back on Labour's agenda. *Malta Today*, 24 October. Retrieved from http://www.maltatoday.com.mt/news/national/30909/gozo-airstrip-back-on-labour-s-agenda-20131023#.U6XYabHc06I

Debono, J. (2013b). A bridge too far? *Malta Today*, 16 July. Retrieved from http://maltatoday.com.mt/en/newsdetails/news/data/Majority-against-spring-hunting-Armier-shantytown-and-Gozo-bridge-20130715

Deidun, A. (2005). The green whistleblower: anti-golfing momentum. *Times of Malta*, 30 September. Retrieved from http://www.timesofmalta.com/articles/view/20051030/environment/the-green-whistleblower.73566

Freller, T. (1997). *Gozo: The island of joy.* Malta: Colour Image.

Gössling, S., and Wall, G. (2007). Island tourism. In G. Baldacchino (ed.), *A world of islands: An island studies reader*, pp. 429–54. Luqa, Malta and Charlottetown, Canada: Agenda Academic and Institute of Island Studies, University of Prince Edward Island.

Gozo News. (2013a). Gozo being marketed as a distinct tourism destination, 15 February. Retrieved from http://gozonews.com/36915/gozo-being-marketed-as-a-distinct-tourism-destination/

Gozo News. (2013b). 'Free travel to Gozo' weekend gets underway from Friday evening, 9 November. Retrieved from http://gozonews.com/42067/free-travel-to-gozo-weekend-gets-underway-from-friday-evening/

Gozo News. (2014a). Gozo ferry trips, vehicles and commuters all increase in Q4 of 2013. 10 January Retrieved from http://gozonews.com/43222/gozo-ferry-trips-vehicles-commuters-all-increased-in-q4-of-2013/

Gozo News. (2014b). Gozo to have separate policy on tourism; accessibility being looked at, 22 February. Retrieved from http://gozonews.com/43987/gozo-to-have-separate-policy-on-tourism-accessibilty-being-looked-at/

Gozo News. (2014c). Gozo branch of NSO opens next month: 'Gozo in Figures 2014' launched, 25 May. Retrieved from http://gozonews.com/50358/gozo-branch-of-nso-opens-next-month-gozo-in-figures-2014-launched/

GTA. (2013). Gozo Tourism Association laments low-cost airlines effect domestic tourism. *Malta Today*. 7 January. Retrieved from http://www.maltatoday.com.mt/en/newsdetails/news/elections2013/Gozo-Tourism-Association-laments-low-cost-airlines-effects-20130107

GUG. (2011). Gozo deserves better: Gozo University Group. *Gozo News*, 1 December. Retrieved from http://gozonews.com/20191/gozitans-deserve-better-gozo-deserves-better-gug/

Hache, J.D. (2007). Islands, fixed links and the European Union. In G. Baldacchino (ed.), *Bridging islands: The impact of fixed links*, pp. 161–84. Charlottetown, Canada: Acorn Press.

Hall, C.M., and Page, S.J. (2006). *The geography of tourism and recreation.* 3rd edn. London: Routledge.

Hall, C.M., Harrison, D., Weaver, D., and Wall, G. (2013). Vanishing peripheries: does tourism consume places? *Tourism Recreation Research*, 38(1), 71–92.

ICER. (2012). ICER conference in Gozo: Malta's smaller island promoting environmentally sustainable tourism. San Lawrenz, Gozo: Innovative Concept of Eco-Accommodation Approach in Rural Regions (ICER), February. Retrieved from: http://icerproject.eu/pages/index.jsf?p=2andid=7459

Jordan, L.-A. (2004). Institutional arrangements for tourism in small twin-island states of the Caribbean. In D.T. Duval (ed.), *Tourism in the Caribbean: Trends, development, prospects*, pp. 99–118. London: Routledge.

Khadaroo, J., and Seetanah, B. (2007). Transport infrastructure and tourism development. *Annals of Tourism Research*, 34(4), 1021–32.

Kreupl, L. (2009). The pros and cons of an airstrip in Gozo. *Gozo News*, 18 February. Retrieved from http://gozonews.com/7774/the-pros-and-cons-of-an-airstrip-in-gozo-lesley-kreupl/comment-page-1/

MacDonald, M. (2012). *Preliminary analysis: Assessment of road tunnel options between Malta and Gozo*. Retrieved from http://www.transport.gov.mt/transport-strategies/strategies-policies-actions/transport-strategies-in-development/malta-gozo-fixed-link

Malta Today. (2013). Gozo debates focus on identity, need for a holistic strategy for the island, 29 October. Retrieved from http://www.maltatoday.com.mt/news/national/30817/gozo-debates-focus-on-identity-need-for-a-holistic-strategy-for-the-island-20131020#.U6Xp_bHc06I

Ministry for Gozo. (2009). *Eco-Gozo, A better Gozo: Proposed action plan 2010–2012.* 29pp. Retrieved from http://www.eco-gozo.com/docs/Eco-Gozo_proposed_action%20 2010_2012.pdf

Ministry for Tourism, Culture and the Environment. (2012). *Malta tourism policy: 2012–2016.* Valletta, Malta. Retrieved from https://secure2.gov.mt/tsdu/downloads/tp12-16.pdf

MTA. (2014). *Tourism in Malta: 2013 edition.* Valletta, Malta: Malta Tourism Authority. Retrieved from http://www.mta.com.mt/loadfile.ashx?id=5765fb87-8702-4bd1-a4c9-ff44f03a372e

Muscat, J. (2006). *The Gozo tourism scenario*. Paper presented at the European Union of Tourist Officers. Malta Meeting, 26 October. Retrieved from http://www.euto.org/pages/news_story_downloadfile.asp?ID=178

Nash, R., and Martin, A. (2003). Tourism in peripheral areas: the challenges for Northeast Scotland. *International Journal of Tourism Research*, 5(3), 161–81.

National Geographic. (2009). *Malta: Truly Mediterranean.* Retrieved from http://www.youtube.com/watch?v=cxO_iMBmprw

NSO. (2012). *Census of Population and Housing 2011.* Preliminary report. Valletta, Malta: National Statistics Office. Retrieved from http://www.nso.gov.mt/statdoc/document_file.aspx?id=3424

NSO. (2013). Sea transport between Malta and Gozo Q2/2013. News release, 18 July. Retrieved from http://www.nso.gov.mt/statdoc/document_file.aspx?id=3643

NSRF. (2007). *National Strategic Reference Framework: Malta 2007–2013.* Malta: Office of the Deputy Prime Minister, Planning and Priorities Coordination Division. Retrieved from http://www.ppcd.gov.mt/07_13?l=1

Pisani, V. (2005). An airstrip for Gozo. *Times of Malta,* 1 February. Retrieved from http://www.timesofmalta.com/articles/view/20050201/letters/an-airstrip-for-gozo.100479

Royle, S.A., and Scott, A. (1996). Accessibility and the Irish islands. *Geography,* 8(12), 111–19.

Saliba, N. (2012). Addressing Gozo's double insularity. *The Malta Independent,* 8 June. Retrieved from http://www.independent.com.mt/articles/2012-06-08/opinions/addressing-gozos-double-insularity-311243/

Sansone, K. (2013). Chinese company to study Malta-Gozo bridge option, 14 June. Retrieved from http://www.timesofmalta.com/articles/view/20130614/local/chinese-giant-to-study-malta-gozo-bridge-option.473893

Sant, P. J. (2012). *Malta and the Maltese economy.* Bank of Valletta presentation. Retrieved from https://www.bov.com/filebank/documents/2_Peter%20James%20Sant%20Bank%20of%20Valletta_Malta%20and%20the%20Maltese%20Economy.pdf

Scheyvens, R., and Momsen, J.H. (2008), Tourism and poverty reduction: issues for small island states. *Tourism Geographies,* 10(1), 22–41.

Scott, J. (2000). Peripheries, artificial peripheries and centres. In F. Brown and D. Hall (eds), *Tourism in peripheral areas,* pp. 58–73. Clevedon: Channel View.

Sheehan, L., and Ritchie, B. (2005). Destination stakeholders: exploring identity and salience. *Annals of Tourism Research,* 32(3), 711–34.

The Malta Independent (2014). Sant says Gozo should operate as region with own structures and governance, 22 February. Retrieved from http://www.independent.com.mt/articles/2014-02-22/news/sant-says-gozo-should-operate-as-regionwith-own-structures-and-governance-4030005248/

Theuma, A., and Theuma, N. (2006). *Gozo business community: A way forward.* Report on workshop conducted for Gozo Business Chamber. Reported in *Isle Link,* No. 25, p. 6. Retrieved from http://www.gozobusinesschamber.org/images/pdfs/isle_link/isle_link_25.pdf

Times of Malta. (2014). 74,000 visit Bethlehem f'Għajnsielem. 6 January. Retrieved from http://www.timesofmalta.com/articles/view/20140106/local/74000-visit.501614

Timothy, D.J. (2001). Benefits and costs of smallness and peripheral location in tourism: St-Pierre et Miquelon (France). *Tourism Recreation Research,* 26(3), 63–70.

Trousdale, W. (1999). Governance in context: Boracay island, Philippines. *Annals of Tourism Research,* 26(4), 840–67.

Turner, L., and Ash, J. (1975). *The golden hordes: International tourism and the pleasure periphery.* London: Constable.

Weaver, D.B. (1998). Peripheries of the periphery: tourism in Tobago and Barbuda. *Annals of Tourism Research,* 25(2), 292–313.

Zammit, R. (2006). 'Wet lease' suggestion for Gozo heliservice. *Times of Malta,* 12 November. Retrieved from http://www.timesofmalta.com/articles/view/20061112/local/wet-lease-suggestion-for-gozo-heliservice.35577

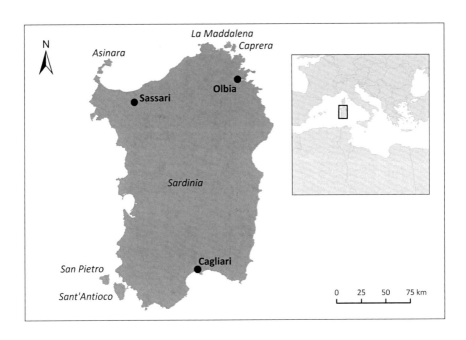

Figure 3.1   Sardinia and its four main islands

Chapter 3

Tourism Relationships between Sardinia and its Islands: Collaborative or Conflicting?

Rita Cannas and Ernestina Giudici

Introduction

This chapter focuses on the Italian island of Sardinia and its smaller offshore islands, located in the middle of Western Mediterranean Sea, and which can be considered as an archipelago, a group of islands in which there are "... fluid cultural processes, sites of abstract and material relations of movement and rest, dependent on changing conditions of articulation or connections" (Stratford, Baldacchino, Farbotko, Harwood and McMahon, 2011, p. 122). It explores the tourism consumption relationships that exist between the mainland of Sardinia, and its four so-called 'minor' islands of Asinara, the La Maddalena archipelago (itself made up of various islands, islets and shoals), Sant'Antioco and San Pietro. The Sardinian archipelago also includes some 50 other small islands, including Tavolara, Cavoli, Serpentara and Mal di Ventre; but these are not taken into consideration in this chapter, given time and word length constraints.

The research which supports this chapter seeks to highlight collaborative and/ or conflicting relationships within the Sardinian archipelago, in terms of tourism analysis, social representation and self-identity. The contribution first outlines the main characteristics of the Sardinian tourism sector, referring also to the dynamics between the main island of Sardinia and the Italian peninsula. It then explores the touristic assets of the Sardinian small islands: by critically comparing the tourism relationships between the two "archipelagos" of the mother island and its 'minor' islands, we seek to offer alternative interpretations for conceptualising the Sardinian experience.

This chapter is developed through a desk analysis of tourism demand and supply side statistics, legislation, technical reports, and research on Sardinian tourism, and a set of in-depth interviews with representatives of the main public and private tourism organisations, giving specific attention to the small islands. The research adopts a methodological design based on a qualitative approach, using interviews with key informants, and, as mentioned above, in-depth interviews with representatives of the small islands.

Island Tourism and Sustainable Development

The Sardinian archipelago shares similar tourism characteristics with other islands of the Mediterranean Sea (Cannas and Theuma, 2013). In fact, the islands and coastal areas of Mediterranean have been attracting international mass tourism since the 1950s, especially from northern Europe (Bramwell, 2004). Although mass tourism is prominently "a quantitative notion based on the proportion of the population participating in tourism or on the volume of tourist activity" (Bukart and Medlik, 1974, p. 42), this phenomenon has changed over time. Nevertheless, what remains evident in mass tourism is its strong spatio-temporal concentration in destinations, a characteristic that has been usually related to the effects of seasonality (Butler and Mao, 1997; Lundtorp, Rassing and Wanhill, 1999; Goulding, 2006; Cannas, 2010; Cannas, 2012). Such characteristics depend on the fact that the coastal areas of the Mediterranean still largely cater for a 'sun, sea and sand' tourism, mainly during the summer months.

Analysing mass tourism as the main component of tourism development in island destinations through the lens of sustainability (WCED, 1987) reveals challenges and problems in terms of environmental, economic and social distortions on a large scale (Lockhart and Drakakis-Smith, 1993). From an environmental perspective, mass tourism is responsible for the irreversible destruction and erosion of marine, coastal and terrestrial ecosystems, as well as for species extinction (Carlsen and Butler, 2011c). From an economic point of view, mass tourism in small island destinations impacts on a limited and finite resources base, a small domestic market, the absence of economies of scale, and a dependency on various external inputs, such as foreign air carriers, imported food and external investment finance (Lockhart and Drakakis-Smith, 1993; Ioannides, Apostolopoulos and Sonmez, 2001; Robinson, 2004). From a social perspective, mass tourism can also have a pervasive impact on island communities, including cultural commodification, and a swamping of local culture by global imports and habits (Robinson, 2004; Kokkranical, MacLellan and Baum, 2004; Baldacchino, 2008). Carlsen and Butler (2011a, p. 2) argue that "the irony is that sun, sand and sea (plus a fourth 's': sex) are probably the main experiences on islands that are sustainable, if properly managed".

Various configurations of tourism development can be found in the Mediterranean islands. For instance, tourism development can be seen along two main stages of maturity (Ruggieri, 2011): on the one hand, islands such as Majorca, Mykonos, and Rhodes have experienced fast and massive tourism inflows and score high values on the territorial exploitation index and tourism pressure index (OTIE, 2008). In particular is the development of coastal fringes achieved through rapid and often unplanned building development, along with a marginalisation of interior spaces, which occurred in Balearic Islands in the 1960s, and is a process now called *balearisation* (Selwyn, 2000; 2004). On the other hand, Sardinia scores low on the tourism impact index (OTIE, 2008), although it is the second largest island in the Mediterranean (after Sicily).The explanation might lie in the still low contribution of tourism to its economy, and where "issues of sustainable development, even though significant, seem to be less urgent" (Ruggieri, 2011, p. 194).

Literature on tourism seasonality shows a substantial failure in the reduction of tourism flows in the peak season while the most popular aim is to increase tourists during the shoulder months (Bar-On, 1975; Butler, 1994). Managing and modifying the effects of mass tourism in coastal areas and islands is still a tricky issue, especially because there is a fourth pillar of sustainability called "politics": the 'triple bottom line' – an accounting framework that deploys social, environmental (or ecological) and financial dimensions for measuring sustainabiity – is meaningless unless it enjoys political support (Carlsen and Butler, 2011b, p. 232). The main challenge for some coastal areas and islands of the Mediterranean is how to make current mass tourism less unsustainable in terms of social and environmental aspects, whereas, in other areas such as Sardinia, increasing economic returns from tourism while maintaining sustainable practices appears to be the crucial contemporary challenge. However, the concept of sustainable tourism in Sardinia needs to be analysed more deeply, in accordance to the specific features of how tourism 'plays out' in its archipelago, as explained below.

The Sardinian Archipelago: The Mainland

Sardinia has a land area of 24,100 km², and a resident population of 1,640,000, resulting in a low population density of 68 inhabitants per km². Politically and administratively, Sardinia is one of the 20 regions of Italy; but it has its own culture, identity, traditions and languages which mark a substantial difference from other regions (such as Sicily). The smaller Sardinian islands have their own history and traditions too, and each one feels a world apart and unto itself, about which more below. Looking at its geographical characteristics, Sardinia contains a coastline more than 1,800 km long, rich in long and white sandy beaches, fertile flats, impressive mountains, and large forests covering more than 1.6 million hectares. Sardinia is also different from the rest of Italy because of a unique civilisation. Between 1800 and 300 BC, the Nuraghic culture dominated the Sardinian mainland, building a complex system of villages around majestic stone towers, known as *i Nuraghi*. The scale, complexity and territorial spread of these buildings, which number about 7,000, testify to the high level of technical competence of the Nuraghic people, in which women had the same status as men. Sardinia was a crucial network of several commercial routes providing precious metals, utensils and votive bronze statuettes traded in Europe, North Africa and the Middle East. The strong interconnections between Sardinians and other civilisations, as well as their ancient origins, are testified in the presence of Sardinian DNA within the 'Man of Özti', a well-preserved mummy found in the Alps in 1991 (Callaway, 2012). According to the well-documented investigation reported by Frau (2002) about the effective location of the legendary Pillars of Hercules, Sardinia could even have been the ancient Atlantis. That investigation, which located the Column of Hercules in the Strait of Sicily, has garnered international interest, as shown in the exhibition "Atlantikà: Sardinia, Mythical Island" supported by UNESCO (2005). Some members of the prestigious scientific board of Italy, the Accademia Nazionale dei Lincei, have supported the hypothesis of Sardinia as Atlantis (e.g. Puddu, 2014); this idea has, however, not been largely recognized among archaeologists and historians and further investigations beckon.

Another peculiar phase of Sardinian's history occurred after the decline of the Roman Empire and the Byzantine age. Between 900–1400 AD, Sardinians were organised in four autonomous districts. Each of them was a separate state, led by a judge and administered through a sophisticated system of rules and regulations. Amongst these, Judge Eleonora D'Arborea emerged as an outstanding ruler who signed an innovative charter (called *Carta de Logu*) recognising the collective ownership of village lands.

The old districts still persist, in some way, in the present ones shaped under the Italian administrative structure. In fact, on the mainland of Sardinia there are four main districts: Cagliari, which is also the capital of Sardinia, situated in the South; Oristano located in the Central West; Nuoro in the Central East, and Sassari in the North. Particularly in the Northern district, there is the sub-area of Olbia, with its high concentration of accommodation facilities and tourist visitations.

Sardinia has been defined as a "continent" (Serra, 1970) in which manifold islands coexist. This concept has two meanings: one is referred to the high level of biodiversity of flora and fauna spread in the whole Sardinia; the second regards the way in which Sardinian people perceive and feel their own place. In fact, due to historical events during the centuries, territories have been shaped by several sub areas, each of them shows specific characters, in terms of different dialect, foods, folklore and so on, that determine the Sardinian image such as "islands within islands". For instance, Barbagia, the mountainous area situated in the Central East side of Sardinia, is characterised by the traditional presence of shepherds and farmers that historically live in a wild environment. During the Roman period, Barbagia remained the wildest and consequently least colonised area of Sardinia. The sense of diversity is still a trait of the local communities. A Sardinian novelist (Fois, 2008) provocatively states that the sea does not exist in Sardinia, stressing that the Sardinian multifaceted collective consciousness is shaped around the coexistence of many lands, each one a separate universe, according to the concept of island singularity reported in Stratford et al. (2011). The interconnections within the plurality of these lands do not include the existence of the sea. The inhabitants of the inner and mountainous areas discover the sea, which means that they become aware that they are islanders, only when they physically cross the sea.

Features of Tourism

According to ISTAT (2012), tourist arrivals in Sardinia in 2011 amounted to 2.1 million, generating 10.8 million bed nights; with an average length of visitor stay of 5.1 nights. In 2011, the domestic (Italian) market was responsible for 57% of these tourist arrivals, although the share of foreign tourism is increasing, from 24% in 2000 to 43% in 2012. The seasonal nature of the industry is evident, with 85% of all nights secured between the four months of June and September. Sardinia boasted 913 hotels with a capacity of just over 100,000 beds; while 4,100 other accommodation units offered an additional 104,000 beds.

Seasonality and coastal concentration are key features of Sardinian tourism, characterised by sunbathing on the beach (Sistu, 2007; Cannas, 2010; Cannas and Theuma, 2013): bed nights in July and August 2011 accounted for 53% of the total bed nights that year (Brandano and Biagi, 2013). The tourism pre-eminence of Olbia is due to the massive investment of international entrepreneurs in a luxury location, called the Emerald Coast that has been developing since the 1960s. Another area of attraction includes the city of Alghero and the coastal area of Sassari, on the Northern West coast of the mainland. Another key attraction of the Northern coast is the availability of travel infrastructure, such as the airports at Alghero and Olbia-Emerald Coast, as well as the harbours in Porto Torres and Olbia. The South coast is served by the airport and the harbour of Cagliari and the accommodation facilities are spread along the Eastern and Western coast of the South. The Western coast is the least impacted by tourism: it has been historically affected by massive mineral processing, and nowadays it represents the least economic developed area of the Sardinian mainland.

The rural and inner areas of Sardinia play a secondary role in tourism. Although local groups linked to the LEADER Programme of the European Union have helped to develop new tourism models in the rural areas – such as agritourism facilities, rural lodgings and wine trails – the results are not comparable to the performance of the coastal areas, whether in terms of tourist flows, level of employment or revenue generation. One such model, called the "diffuse hospitality" (Paniccia, 2012), or "spread hotel" (Tagliabue, Leonforte and Compostella, 2012) is based on the re-use of real estate that has been abandoned by people who left villages and resettled in the main Sardinian cities or went abroad, or on the re-use of the central areas of the rural towns. Thanks to EU funds, some such buildings have been restored and transformed into the rooms of rural hotels. The case of Santulussurgiu, a small and typical rural village of Sardinia, is considered as a good practice for sustainable tourism given that tourism entrepreneurs are local; they provide accommodation and homemade food to tourists in traditional settings; tourism is slow and follows the rhythm of the local community; and the village has maintained its own peculiarities in terms of planning and its own cultural traditions. The diffuse hospitality model is spread in some areas of the Sardinian mainland; but questions remain for policy makers and tourism entrepreneurs (Cannas, 2010): how should the main Sardinian tourism season be extended, and how can a larger part of the non-coastal space, so rich in amazing landscapes, archaeological heritage, visual anthropology, cultural traditions and handicraft, be better engaged in the tourism industry (e.g. Morelli, 1993)?

Sardinia, as a mainland, looks like a kaleidoscope by which its multiple characteristics may be perceived by tourists during their experience: for example, the hospitality of the people of coastal areas is different from that of the people of inner areas such as Barbagia for the way in which tourists are welcomed, the food that is offered, and the degree of tourist involvement in the local community. The Emerald Coast, in the North-east, is an artificial tourism system built by the Prince Aga Khan who considers this area of Sardinia as an exclusive alternative to the crowded Côte d'Azur in France (Bausenhart, 1995). The Emerald Coast, defined as a "Disneyland at sea" by Facaros and Pauls (2006), is a perfect example of a 'world apart' which has become simply a playground for the rich. The Emerald Coast has been seen by some authors (Roggio, 2002; Cannas, 2010) as an external model, an exclave in which local people work in the less prestigious jobs such as waiters and kitchen hands, while directors and managers of hotels come from the rest of Italy or abroad. There seems to be a social and economic asymmetry in the allocation of local work and revenue that smacks of social unsustainability. The high level of revenue provided by the Emerald Coast's tourism system makes it the subject of fascination by tourism businesses and politicians, who are tempted to replicate the economic model elsewhere; yet, many locals consider it a Sardinian non-place.

Looking into tourism relationships between the mainland of Sardinia and the Italian peninsula, a model of dependency from island-to-mainland, or a model of the island as a periphery and mainland as the centre, comes clearly across. These asymmetric relationships deriving from a dependency model, explained as a top down approach (Onnis, Perra, Sanna and Dibeltulo, 2009), unfolds, for instance, in the extant transport policy. According to ISTAT between 2010–2011 there has been a doubling in the cost of ferry tickets, +52.8%, as quoted by de Fourcade (2011). Among the causes of such boost may be considered the corporate restructuring of Tirrenia SpA, the public ferry company that has led to a monopolistic cartel run by private ferry companies (Moby SpA, Grandi Navi Veloci SpA, SNAV SpA, Marinvest Srl), for which the European Commission has opened an antitrust investigation, as mentioned by Comenale Pinto (2012). The change occurred in the ferry transport policy has affected the tourism sector: in the three harbours of Northern Sardinia, along the period 2010–2013, the ferry passengers have decreased by 41%, losing 1,880,000 passengers (Autorità Portuale Nord Sardegna, 2013).

It seems that the Sardinian archipelago is Italian only in so far as the central Government's intent to maintain its presence and use of military facilities, which occupy a large section of Sardinian territory: Italy's largest military facility, the test range at Salto di Quirra, is located in Sardinia (e.g., Cristaldi, Foschi, Szpunar, Brini, Marinelli and Triolo, 2013). However, Sardinian communities, politicians, and entrepreneurs bear their own responsibility by validating and perpetrating such dependency. The fact that the Sardinian archipelago attracts the same number of tourism overnights as the Maltese archipelago (Cannas and Theuma, 2013) although Sardinia is 70 times larger than Malta by land area, can be explained in part by the top-down approach to economic policy planning in Sardinia, as much as "... a desire to "normalise" a region that was deemed as being too different and distinct by the political elites" (Onnis, et al., 2009, p. 1332).

Bramwell and Lane (2011) state that innovations associated with sustainable tourism are dependent on, and affected by, trends in wider socio-economic and societal processes. This statement also pertains to the Sardinian tourism framework. The lack of a Sardinian tourism policy plan is strictly linked to the absence of a clear economic development vision for the whole region. Consequently, Sardinian regional policy lacks of an effective strategy for marketing cultural, sports and enogastronomic tourism' niches (the Sardinian Marketing Plan is dated at 2008 (RAS, 2008), as well as in branding strategy for promoting Sardinia as a whole. Similar critical issues involve the Italian tourism system which is affected by "... a lack of integration at level of governance, laws, statistics; disparities in development between the North and the South, with regions of the South appearing poorer in terms of transport infrastructures and quality of services; a fragmented promotion of Italian tourism attractions" (Angeloni, 2013, p. 137).

Tourism and Multifaceted Representations in Four Sardinian Small Islands

A constellation of different identities and peculiar histories emerge from an analysis of the four 'minor' islands that form part of the Sardinian archipelago. These are reviewed in turn below.

Asinara

Starting from the northern side, Asinara, (a name which is etymologically derived from the endemic presence of the white asinine, a donkey breed) looks like a world unto itself. Populated since the Neolithic age, in the last two centuries Asinara is known for three unsettling reasons: it has served as a *lazaretto* (quarantine site), a deportation site and a maximum security prison. All three events are redolent of the island's constructed sense of separation and alienation. In 1885, the island became a property of the Italian state; its 100 families were summarily deported, following a top-down order of the Italian government. A *lazaretto* was built at Cala Reale and an agricultural penal colony was established at Cala d'Oliva, by order of the King of Italy. During the First and the Second World Wars, the small island was the detention centre for various prisoners of war. By the 1970s, Asinara had gained a reputation as Italy's Alcatraz: the prisons on the island were restructured to become high-security facilities, where some of the most dangerous criminals were detained, including members of the *Brigate Rosse* (Red Brigades) and the Mafia, the most infamous of whom was Sicilian godfather Totò Riina (Sanna, 2010). For more than a century, Asinara had the status of a forbidden territory. The natural and built environment was shaped to serve a unique purpose: being a separate geographical area for the housing of unwanted individuals.

Only in 2002 was Asinara recognised as a National Park, and returned to open access to neighbouring people and tourists. Currently, Asinara may be visited only through Park's guide service, and some authorised operators. The lack of a residential community is seen as a social and environmental problem which affects the sustainability of the island. In summer, the population consists of tourists on day visits, tourism company staff, and public employees; during winter, the only 'visitors' are public employees who maintain the roads and public buildings. The real and only 'islanders' seem to be the white donkeys, wild horses and plenty of wild boars. From an administrative perspective, Asinara belongs to Porto Torres, a small industrial town located on the Sardinian mainland, and whose local community feels no a sense of belonging to Asinara, due to the historical inaccessibility of the prison-island. Since 2014, the local council of Porto Torres provides a weekly ferry to the island in wintertime in order to facilitate new connections between mainland residents and the island.

According to data provided by the Asinara National Park, there are some 70,000 day visitors annually who support a local economy of more than 200 small green businesses, and within them female entrepreneurs offer guide and transport service in Land Rovers along 25 km of paved roads. Such a cash injection is significant to the local economy of Porto Torres, which is suffering from the decommissioning of its chemical industry and the resulting high levels of unemployment and social distress, as stated by local interviewees. In Asinara, angling, sailing and diving are the most common tourism activities delivered by private operators, and supported by hostel accommodation, a restaurant and four bars. The National Park provides cultural facilities through a marine museum and botanical and wildlife observatories. The main challenge is to extend visits to include overnight stays, but this is unlikely as long as there are no suitable facilities and no permanent island community.

The attraction of Asinara depends upon its legendary story of inaccessibility which fascinates visitors, and the relative remoteness, which also plays an important role in protecting and preserving the natural environment. This combination of factors leads to a mix of positive emotions that impact on the feelings of tourists, who live unique experiences on the island.

La Maddalena Archipelago

The Archipelago of La Maddalena, situated in the Strait of Bonifacio between the Sardinian mainland and Corsica, is composed of seven main islands (La Maddalena, Caprera, Spargi, Santo Stefano, Santa Maria, Budelli and Razzoli), plus more than 60 islets. La Maddalena and Caprera, the biggest islands and the closest to mainland Sardinia, are linked together by a bridge; they are the only inhabited islands in the cluster and are accessible by car. The island of La Maddalena has some 11,000 inhabitants and has its own local council, the only one in the whole archipelago. La Maddalena has a harbour that connects the island to the Sardinian mainland through two ferry companies and it is easily reachable by tourists arriving by plane at Olbia international airport on the Emerald Coast, a 1.5 hour drive away. Caprera, noted for its wild terrain and a small population, is best known for housing Giuseppe Garibaldi, the hero of the unification of Italy, during his retirement; the island boasts a museum dedicated to him. The other, smaller islands are accessible only by private boat and the navigation is regulated by the La Maddalena National Park Service, established in 1994.

Historically, La Maddalena looks like a melting pot of people coming from the Italian peninsula and the Sardinian mainland. The islanders speak a dialect that is quite different from other Sardinian languages; they consider themselves *maddalenini* (people of La Maddalena) rather than Sardinians. The story of La Maddalena is tightly linked to geopolitical events: the young Napoleon Bonaparte saw his first military action there, in a failed attempt to wrest the islands from the Kingdom of Sardinia in 1793. Due to the strategic position of the La Maddalena Archipelago firstly the Royal Military Marine of the kingdom of Sardinia (since the eighteenth century) and then NATO (since 1972) established their own naval and military bases. The military presence has shaped the life of the archipelago's community, fostering an economy dependent on military-related expenditures. Tourism was not encouraged or promoted locally; the presence of some 2,000 US military personnel and their visiting relatives generated a satisfactory flow of revenue. Moreover, some other islands (such as Santo Stefano) were mostly inaccessible because of the presence of US nuclear-powered submarines. The US military base was closed down in 2008. The Italian government had planned a civil renaissance of La Maddalena by renewing the ex-military structures (including the Marine Arsenal) to host the 35th G8 summit in 2009. However, this G8 summit took place in L'Aquila, an Italian city on the peninsula, as part of an attempt to redistribute disaster funds after a major earthquake there. The renewal of the arsenal and surrounding area cost €327 million, most of them funded by the Sardinian Region (De Zeen Magazine, 2009); the result is a stock of modern but empty buildings which look like a "cathedral in a desert", by adopting the same expression that Hospers (2003) referred to the Sardinian industrial poles. The conversion of La Maddalena's economy from military expenditure to tourism has proved to be an unsustainable, top-down project which still shows its negative effects: the area is inaccessible and the supposed five star hotel and the 5,000-bed resort have yet to materialise.

The La Maddalena archipelago attracts marine tourists during summer. The island of La Maddalena offers accommodation facilities and restaurants, and various hotels and 'bed and breakfast' facilities are located in the main town. Caprera attracts only day trippers, thanks to its beaches and the museum, after the closure of a Club Med facility (Club Med Planet, 2014). In Santo Stefano, there is a four-star tourist village built by the Valtour Group and currently managed by ClubViaggi. In Santa Maria, a small luxury hotel offers exclusive holidays and private transport. The empty lighthouse of Razzoli may be converted into an accommodation facility, but it requires steady maintenance. A case apart is represented by the island of Budelli which has been recently bought by La Maddalena National Park for three million euros. The protected and inaccessible Budelli island is internationally well known for a natural treasure: a pink sand beach (Vladi Private Islands, 2014).

The archipelago of La Maddalena is characterised by different types of tourism: sailing, sunbathing, and natural tourism. Key informants state that La Maddalena's Archipelago attracts its tourists by completely bypassing the Sardinian mainland, especially in the case of sailors and VIP tourists who land directly in La Maddalena's heliport. The biggest share of tourists comes from the Sardinian mainland by ferry. Within Sardinia's small islands, La Maddalena's tourism looks like the most international, due to the presence of foreign tourists. Traditionally, August is peak holiday time for many Italians, and especially in the beginning and end of summer foreign tourists coming from Northern Europe choose La Maddalena for opening or closing their Sardinian holiday. Local key informants state that the main weaknesses regarding the hospitality offerings of La Maddalena archipelago are three: the high cost of the ferry, especially for tourists; the scant presence of beach services; and the lack of entrepreneurship, particularly amongst tourism operators. The absence of a waterfront in La Maddalena is a critical bottleneck to further development, as stated by a key informant: "La Maddalena is the only seaside town who hosts a parking area in the harbour rather than entertainment facilities", whereas these could be useful attractions for extending the tourist season.

Sant'Antioco

The island of Sant'Antioco (who bears the name of Saint Antiochus, evangeliser of the area and who was martyred in 125 AD) is the largest island of the Sardinian archipelago (except for the mainland), covering a land area of more than 100 km². Sant'Antioco is also the name of the largest town on the island. Since Roman times, Sant'Antioco island has been linked to the mainland with a bridge across the lagoon, over shallow waters. For this reason, Sant'Antioco may be considered the least remote island within the Sardinian archipelago. It was settled from at least the 5th millennium BC. Typical tombs (called *domus de janas*) and menhirs have been found. The island was also part of the Nuraghic civilisation. The town of Sant'Antioco was founded in the 8th century BC by the Phoenicians, with the name of Solki. Later, it became a Carthaginian colony. The Punic domination ended in the 2nd century BC, when Solki was conquered by the Romans. The island of Sant'Antioco was also an important fortified centre during the Byzantine period and along the centuries it has played a significant role in the history of Sardinia.

The town of Sant'Antioco has more than 12,000 inhabitants, whereas the second town, Calasetta, located on the northern side, boasts less than 3,000. Here is a rare phenomenon: these two communities on the same island practise different languages, cuisine, culture and tradition. The residents of Sant'Antioco are descendants of a Neolitic culture as well as of the mentioned Nuraghi settlers; today they speak Sardo; whereas the people of Calasetta came originally from Liguria, on the Italian peninsula, in the 18th century, and speak a Genoese dialect.

From a tourism point of view, the island used to be an inbound destination for lower-medium Sardinian tourists as well as for domestic visitors. In recent years, the socio-economic crisis has significantly affected the island economy as well as the whole Sardinian archipelago. As stated by key informants, on Sant'Antioco island, the tourism flow has dramatically decreased and the short tourist season has become even shorter. Tourism entrepreneurs blame the relatively high cost of transport between the Sardinian archipelago and the Italian peninsula, which has exponentially increased in the last three years.

Sant'Antioco is an island rich in culture. The high concentration of extraordinary historical heritage testifies its importance throughout the ages. Nevertheless, there are emergent weaknesses in the Sant'Antioco' tourism offerings. There is an absence of public transport. The two local councils of Sant'Antioco and Calasetta do not share a common tourism strategy; instead, they peddle separate and competitive policies. Cultural differences seem to work for dividing people, rather than to help them come up with a common plan to react against the effects of the economic crisis that have impacted on peripheral communities such as the island of Sant'Antioco so badly.

San Pietro

Finally, San Pietro presents its own unique picture. The island, with a land area of 51 km², hosts around 6,000 inhabitants who are mostly concentrated in the fishing town of Carloforte, the only town (and local council) on the island. San Pietro is connected by regular ferry to Portovesme (on the Sardinian mainland) and Calasetta (on the island of Sant'Antioco). San Pietro has been known to exist since ancient times. According to legend, the island is so named because St. Peter was supposed to have been a visitor. In 1738, San Pietro was colonized by settlers from Liguria (which is now a region on the Italian peninsula), coming from the Republic of Genoa's colony at Tabarka, in Tunisia.

They requested the King of Sardinia, Charles Emmanuel III, to settle on San Pietro Island. The name Carloforte (Charles the Strong, but also the Fort of Carlo) was given in honour of the king. Nowadays, Carloforte still maintains cultural ties with Genoa and Pegli, its suburb, and San Pietro islanders still speak a variant of Liguria's dialect called *tabarkìn*, completely different from Sardinian languages. The same dialect is also spoken in the closer Calasetta. The inhabitants of San Pietro are proud of their identity and do not feel Sardinian. The peculiar cultural roots of San Pietro's inhabitants makes the island an attractive destination to visitors and tourists coming from the Sardinian mainland. Carloforte is also known within the Italian tourism market and recently has also increased its popularity abroad (e.g. Kington, 2008).

In San Pietro's economy, fishing and tourism services play a significant role. Carloforte enjoys a long-standing tradition of wooden boat-building. The industry has being kept alive thanks to highly-skilled local craftspersons. Traditional sail fishing boats can be seen along the harbour. The town hosts a nautical high school, which reinforces the maritime character of the island. Tuna fishing and tuna farming are traditional activities, which have been engaging the local community since at least 1738. On the northern side of the island, there are historical buildings traditionally linked to the tuna fishing industry. Some of these buildings have been restored and currently host a wind-surfing school and a new privately-owned tuna processing business. Although the tuna capture industry has changed with time, it is still a peculiar characteristic of the San Pietro community. Since 2002, the event called *Girotonno* based on assisting local fishers in tuna capture, and involving participation in an international culinary festival, has been attracting local and international visitors: around 200,000 during a long week end (Girotonno, 2014). This happening hosts international chefs expert in serving tuna, and is well marketed and promoted amongst food lovers: an interesting tourism niche, especially in Southern Italy (Trunfio, Petruzzellis and Nigro, 2006). Enogastronomy (the matching of wine and food) is also an important tourism niche because of a higher multiplier effect in comparison to both cultural and beach tourism (Deandreis, 2013).

Several boat chartering, diving, and tourist businesses are based in Carloforte. They can be found out along its waterfront. The town offers different types of accommodation facilities, as well as top quality restaurants. San Pietro attracts tourists both from Sardinia – many summer residences of the people of Cagliari can be fund there – and from abroad. A peculiar feature of Carloforte is that tourists perceive it as a visit to another island which is different from the Sardinian mainland. Even for *i Sardi* who live on the biggest island of the archipelago, Carloforte represent 'another island' with its own specific identity. Since 2007, San Pietro has been piloted as an "ecological island in the Mediterranean" by the Italian Ministry of the Environment (e.g. Carloforte Green Workshop, 2011). The pilot project aims to reduce carbon emissions and to promote the integrated use of local resources for reaching a sustainable tourism model. In reaching that goal, San Pietro would become the first carbon-neutral Italian community, and a good practice model for other localities to emulate.

Conclusion

The co-authors of this chapter are both Sardinian islanders; this chapter illustrates their first encounter with the concept of the 'archipelago' and its application to Sardinia and its tourism industry. As Sardinian people who live in the second largest island in the

Mediterranean Sea, we usually perceive Sardinia as a whole, with its many smaller islands lost in the biggest one.

We now know better: by deploying the perspective of Sardinia as an archipelago composed of more than one island, we have revised our point of view and we have been forced to acknowledge our bias. We used to unwittingly consider Sardinia's small islands in the same way in which Italians consider the Sardinian mainland: a small, perhaps less important part of a bigger territory. This means that, in spite of implicitly adopting a hierarchical perspective to our study, we effectively embraced a more horizontal and dialogical epistemology, thanks to the concept of the archipelago which considers Sardinia as it is: a group of islands who share so much – history, culture, vision, tourists – but where each island still has its own peculiarities, with rich tourism implications.

Our contribution has highlighted the richness of each island, as well as the complementary interactions amongst the Sardinian islands; throughout, we have proposed two challenging perspectives for promoting the Sardinian archipelago as a tourism destination: on the one hand, by assuming and communicating Sardinia as an archipelago rather than a single island, the Sardinian archipelago may reinforce its tourism attractiveness and competitiveness. This perspective is based on the need to provide a systemic tourism policy for the Sardinian archipelago through a broad engagement with tourism stakeholders to counteract the fragmentation of the tourism product, as well as of the Sardinian archipelago's tourism promotion. On the other hand, by coming to appreciate the potential of such varied environmental treasures in the Sardinian archipelago, we suggest that this may become a sustainable Mediterranean destination. Rather than boosting the island of San Pietro as the more sustainable candidate in the Mediterranean, or applying the European Tourism Indicator System (European Commission, 2013) as a sustainable tool only in the Southern coasts of the mainland (Modica, 2014), the whole Sardinian archipelago could and should be shaped through this distinctive and strategic intent.

Indeed, we argue that sustainable tourism development where multi-island offerings complement each other is the enviable scenario towards which current policies and strategies must navigate in order to tackle the negative impacts of mass tourism in the coastal areas of the tourism-dense islands of Mediterranean, and beyond. Although mass tourism can be seen as a category unto itself, it should be adapted to the specific aspects of particular destinations. In Sardinia, the critical points seem related to the low contribution of tourism to economic development (Ruggieri, 2011); the lack of a coherent tourism vision and policy by policy makers; the lack of cooperation among tourism businesses (e.g., through networks that can help in promoting tourism services in a more profitable way); and the lack of "business acumen" within Sardinian citizens who do not recognise the value and the role of private enterprise.

Transport policy does not facilitate incoming tourism and the *massification* – a high concentration of services and tourists – of coastal areas remains a critical issue. In contrast, a more effective product policy would develop tourism in the inner areas of the island, especially in the shoulder season. Branding strategies can work better, considering that Sardinia is still relatively unknown in many markets such as Northern Europe, which represents the main share of Mediterranean tourism (Bramwell, 2004). Indeed, Sardinia is sometimes even physically absent from maps of Italy (e.g. Facebook, 2014); an invisibility that has psychological and political parallels. The case of Sardinia shows that, despite various attempts to develop sustainable island tourism, tourism practices are far from sustainable. Unless politicians back up their policies with measures that promote the actual implementation of sustainable tourism practices (Carlsen and Butler, 2011c; Jovicic, 2013; Cannas and Theuma, 2013), tourism sustainability in the Sardinian archipelago will remain elusive.

References

Angeloni, S. (2013). The competitiveness of Italy as a tourism destination. *Economia Aziendale Online*, 4(2), 125–41.
Autorità Portuale Nord Sardegna. [Northern Sardinia Harbour Authority] (2013). Piano Operativo Triennale Nord Sardegna 2014–2016. Retrieved from http://www. gazzettaamministrativa.it/opencms/export/sites/default/_gazzetta_amministrativa/ amministrazione_trasparente/_sardegna/_autorita_portuale_di_olbia_e_golfo_ aranci/180_ope_pub/2014/Documenti_1396254163838/1396254166528_pot_14_16_ per_invio.pdf
Baldacchino, G. (2008). Island tourism. In M. Luck (ed.) *Encyclopaedia of tourism and recreation in marine environments*, pp. 254–5. Wallingford: CABI.
Bar-On, R.V. (1975). *Seasonality in tourism.* London: Economist Intelligence Unit.
Bausenhart, H. (1995). *Sardinien.* Ostfildern: Mars Geographischer Verlag.
Bramwell, B. (2004). Introduction. In B. Bramwell (ed.), *Coastal mass tourism: Diversification and sustainable development in Southern Europe*, pp. 1–31. Clevedon: Channel View.
Bramwell, B., and Lane, B. (2011). Towards innovation in sustainable tourism research? *Journal of Sustainable Tourism*, 20(1), 1–7.
Brandano, M.G. and Biagi, B. (2013). Il sistema turistico. [The tourism system.] In CRENoS, *Economia della Sardegna, 20° Rapporto 2013*, pp. 75–85. Cagliari, Italy: Centre for North-South Economic Research.
Bukart, J., and Medlik, R. (1974). *Tourism: Past, present and future*. London: Heinemann.
Butler R. W. (1994). Seasonality in tourism: issues and problems. In A.V. Seaton (ed.), *Tourism: The state of the art*, pp. 332–9. Chichester: Wiley & Sons.
Butler, R.W., and Mao, B. (1997). Seasonality in tourism: problems and measurement. In P. Murphy (ed.), *Quality management in urban tourism*, pp. 9–24. Chichester: Wiley & Sons.
Callaway, E. (2012). Iceman's DNA reveals health risks and relations. *Nature*, 28 February. Retrieved from http://www.nature.com/news/iceman-s-dna-reveals-health-risks-and-relations-1.10130
Cannas, R. (2010). *Politiche pubbliche per la destagionalizzazione del turismo da una prospettiva territoriale. Casi di studio in Scozia e in Sardegna.* [Public policies for the removal of seasonality in tourism using a regional perspective: the cases of Scotland and Sardinia.] PhD Thesis, Bologna: University of Bologna.
Cannas, R. (2012). An overview of tourism seasonality: key concepts and policies. *AlmaTourism*, 5, 40–58.
Cannas R., and Theuma, N. (2013). Models for sustainable coastal tourism development in the Mediterranean destinations: exploring new insights in Malta and Sardinia. Paper presented at ATLAS Annual Conference on Environments of Exchange: Leisure and Tourism. Book of abstracts and extended abstracts, pp. 94–8.

Carloforte Green Workshop. (2011). S. Pietro: prima isola ecologica del Mediterraneo. [San Pietro: first ecological island in the Mediterranean.] 11 October. Retrieved from http://www.rinnovabili.it/categoria-eventi/s-pietro-prima-isola-ecologica-del-mediterraneo/

Carlsen, J., and Butler, R.W. (2011a). Introducing sustainable perspectives of island tourism. In J. Carlsen and R.W. Butler (eds), *Island tourism: Sustainability perspectives*, pp. 1–7. Wallingford: CABI.

Carlsen, J., and Butler, R.W. (2011b). Conclusion. In J. Carlsen and R.W. Butler (eds), *Island tourism: Sustainability perspectives*, pp. 220–29. Wallingford: CABI.

Carlsen, J., and Butler, R.W. (eds) (2011c). *Island tourism: Sustainability perspectives*. Wallingford: CABI.

Comenale Pinto, M.M. (2012) Dalla continuità territoriale nel trasporto aereo alla continuità territoriale nel trasporto marittimo. *Diritto@Storia*, Rivista internazionale di scienze giuridiche e tradizione romana, 10, 2011–12. Retrieved from http://eprints.uniss.it/8444/1/ComenalePinto_M_Dalla_continuita_territoriale_nel.pdf

Club Med Planet. (2014). Home page. Retrieved from http://www.clubmedplanet.com/resort.asp?cntnt=info&vilcode=CAPR

Cristaldi, M., Foschi, C., Szpunar, G., Brini, C., Marinelli, F., and Triolo, L. (2013). Toxic emissions from a military test site in the territory of Sardinia, Italy. *International Journal of Environmental Research and Public Health*, 10(4), 1631–46.

Deandreis, M. (2013). *L'impatto economico attuale e potenziale del turismo in Italia.* [The actual and potential economic impact of tourism in Italy.] Directorate-General, Intesa San Paolo Bank, 30 May. Powerpoint slides retrieved from http://www.federturismo.it/component/docman/doc_download/7843-presentazione-deandreis-srm-sessione-mattina-ventennale?Itemid=

de Fourcade, R. (2011). Caos-traghetti per la Sardegna, prenotazioni in calo. *Il Sole 24 Ore*, 5 July. Retrieved from http://www.ilsole24ore.com/art/economia/2011-07-05/caostraghetti-sardegna-prenotazioni-calo-082013.shtml?uuid=AadoAOlD

De Zeen Magazine. (2009). Ex Arsenale at Maddalena by Stefano Boeri Architetti, 1 July. Retrieved from http://www.dezeen.com/2009/07/01/ex-arsenale-at-maddalena-by-stefano-boeri-architetti/

European Commission (2013). *The European Tourism Indicator System. Toolkit for sustainable destinations.* Luxembourg: Publication Office of the European Union.

Facaros, D., and Pauls, M. (2006). *Sardinia*. London: New Holland Publishers.

Facebook. (2014). Little Italy. Retrieved from https://www.facebook.com/50338886841/photos/a.127529466841.103604.50338886841/10151338160936842/?type=1&ref=nf

Fois, M. (2008). *In Sardegna non c'è il mare.* [There is no sea in Sardinia.] Rome, Italy: Laterza.

Frau, S. (2002). *Le Colonne d'Ercole: Un'inchiesta, come, quando e perché la frontiera di Herakles/Milqart, dio dell'Occidente slittò per sempre a Gibilterra.* [The Pillars of Hercules: An inquiry as to when and why the border of Hercules/Melqart migrated for good to Gibraltar.] Rome, Italy: Nur Neon.

Girotonno. (2014). Home page. Retrieved from http://www.girotonno.it/

Goulding, P.J. (2006). Conceptualising supply-side seasonality in tourism: a study of the temporal trading behaviours for small tourism businesses in Scotland. PhD Thesis, Glasgow, Scotland: Strathclyde University.

Hospers, G.J. (2003). Localisation in Europe's periphery: tourism development in Sardinia. *European Planning Studies*, 11(6), 629–45.

Ioannides, D., Apostolopoulos, Y., and Sonmez, S.F. (2001). *Mediterranean islands and sustainable tourism development: Practice, management and policies.* London: Pinter.

ISTAT (Istituto Nazionale di Statistica, Italy) (2013a). *Capacità degli esercizi ricettivi 2012.* Rome, Italy: ISTAT.

ISTAT (Istituto Nazionale di Statistica, Italy) (2013b). *Movimento negli esercizi ricettivi 2012.* Rome, Italy: ISTAT.

Jovicic, D.Z. (2013). Key issues in the implementation of sustainable tourism. *Current Issues in Tourism*, 17(4), 297–302.

Kington, T. (2008). Caught in the spell of San Pietro. *The Guardian/The Observer*, 15 June. Retrieved from http://www.theguardian.com/travel/2008/jun/15/italy.europe

Kokkranical, J., MacLellan, R.L., and Baum, T.G. (2003). Island tourism and sustainability: a case study in the Lakshadweep islands. *Journal of Sustainable Tourism*, 11(5), 426–47.

Lockhart, D.G., and Drakakis-Smith, D. (1993). *The development process in small island states.* London: Routledge.

Lundtorp, S., Rassing, C.R., and Wanhill, S.R.C. (1999). The off-season is 'no season': the case of the Danish island of Bornholm. *Tourism Economics*, 5(1), 49–68.

Modica, P. (2014). The results of the first pilot testing phase: exchanges of experiences. Powerpoint presentation at the Workshop in European Tourism Indicator System, Brussels: European Commission, DG Enterprise and Industry, 4 July.

Morelli, R. (1993). Su concordu: antropologia visiva e canto liturgico popolare a Santulussurgiu. [In concert: visual anthropology and popular liturgical chants in Santulussurgiu.] In T. Magrini (ed.), *Antropologia della musica nelle culture mediterranee*, pp. 225–43. Rome, Italy: Il Mulino.

Onnis, O., Perra, O. Sanna, F., and Dibeltulo, M. (2009). Localisation in Sardinia and its obstacles: a reply to Hospers' 'Localisation in Europe's periphery: tourism development in Sardinia'. *European Planning Studies*, 17(9), 1323–33.

OTIE (Observatory on Tourism in the European Islands) (2008). *First focus on tourism in the European islands.* Palermo, Italy: Logos.

Paniccia, P. (2012). Nuovi fermenti di sviluppo sostenibile nel turismo: l'esempio dell' "albergo diffuso". Tra borghi storici, residenze d'epoca e antichi casali rurali. *Impresa Progetto – Electronic Journal of Management*, 1, 1–26. Retrieved from http://www.impresaprogetto.it/sites/impresaprogetto.it/files/articles/1-2012_wp_paniccia.pdf

Puddu, D. (2014). La Sardegna era Atlantide? [Was Sardinia Atlantis?]. *Sardegna in Blog*, 13 March. Retrieved from http://sardegnainblog.it/808/la-sardegna-era-atlantide-video/

Regione Autonoma della Sardegna. (RAS) (2008). *Piano di Marketing Turistico 2008–2009.*

Robinson, M. (2004). *Tourism, globalisation and cultural change: An island community perspective.* Clevedon: Channel View.

Roggio, A. (2002). Costa Smeralda: un luogo, un evento, un paradigma. In A. Mazzette (ed.), *Modelli di turismo in Sardegna: Tra sviluppo locale e processi di globalizzazione*, pp. 224–45. Milano: Franco Angeli.

Ruggieri, G. (2011). Tourism in Mediterranean islands: a comparative analysis. In J. Carlsen and R.W. Butler (eds), *Island tourism: Sustainable perspectives*, pp. 186–96. Wallingford: CABI.

Sanna, M. (2010). Il carcere dell'Asinara:gli anni del supercarcere. [The Asinara prison: the years of the maximum security prison.] *Diacronie: Studi di Storia Contemporanea*, 2(1).

Retrieved from http://www.studistorici.com/wp-content/uploads/2010/04/SANNA_ Dossier_2.pdf

Selwyn, T. (2004). Privatising the Mediterranean coastline. In J. Boissevain and T. Selwyn (eds), *Contesting the foreshore: Tourism, society and politics on the coast*, pp. 35–60. Amsterdam, The Netherlands: Amsterdam University Press.

Selwyn, T. (2000). The de-Mediterraneanisation of the Mediterranean? *Current Issues in Tourism*, 3(3), 226–45.

Serra, M. (1970). *Sardegna quasi un continente*. [Sardinia almost a continent.] Cagliari, Italy: Editrice Sarda Fossataro

Sistu, G. (2007). *Vagamondo: Turismo e turisti in Sardegna.* [Around the world: Tourism and tourists in Sardinia.] Cagliari, Italy: Centre for North-South Economic Research.

Stratford, E., Baldacchino, G., Farbotko, C., Harwood, A., and McMahon, E. (2011). Envisioning the archipelago. *Island Studies Journal*, 6(2), 113–30.

Tagliabue, L.C., Leonforte, F., and Compostella, J. (2012). Renovation of an UNESCO heritage settlement in southern Italy: ASHP and BIPV for a "spread hotel" project. *Energy Procedia*, 30, 1060–68.

Trunfio, M., Petruzzellis, L., and Nigro, C. (2006). Tour operators and alternative tourism in Italy: exploiting niche markets to increase international competitiveness. *International Journal of Contemporary Hospitality Management*, 18(5), 426–438.

UNESCO (United Nations Educational, Scientific and Cultural Organisation) (2005). Atlantika: Sardinia, Mythical Island. Retrieved from http://portal.unesco.org/en/ ev.phpURL_ID=26682&URL_DO=DO_TOPIC&URL_SECTION=201.html

Vladi Private Islands. (2014). Isola Budelli: enjoy Seychellois sophistication on a magical Mediterranean private island. Retrieved from http://www.vladi-private-islands.de/en/ objects/europe-mediterranean-sea/italy/buy/isola-budelli/

WCED (World Commission on Environment and Development) (1987). *Our common future*. Brundtland Commission. Oxford: Oxford University Press.

PART II
Atlantic Ocean

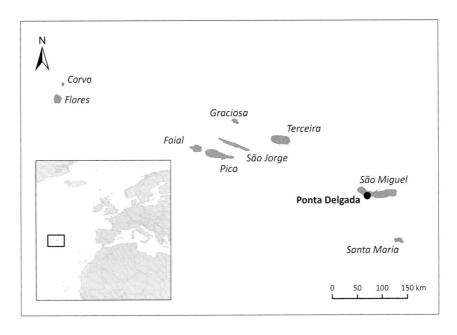

Figure 4.1   The Azores archipelago, Portugal

Chapter 4

Contrived Complementarity: Transport Logistics, Official Rhetoric and Inter-island Rivalry in the Azorean Archipelago

Godfrey Baldacchino and Eduardo Costa Duarte Ferreira

Introduction

At face value, the invitation looks fairly simple and straightforward: with multiple island destinations to choose from, and given enough inducement, a tourist may easily be swayed to sample them all. Island hopping is a growing sub-set of tourism practices, well established among yachters and cruise ship passengers; and with cyclists, as well as ferry, boat and air passengers following behind. Destination plurality is, in a sense, itself an alluring frontier that is being discovered by mainstream tourists (Keller, 1970; Sinclair, 1984; The Independent, 2011; Thorpe, 2009). One should not judge a book by its cover; indeed, one needs to dive into all its different chapters to enjoy, and get a proper sense of, the whole thing.

And yet, the practice could not be further from the principle. "Islands and archipelagos pose unique challenges for tourism policy" (Bardolet and Sheldon, 2008, p. 900). In this chapter, we explore the way in which the typically top-down marketing representations of 'diversity within unity' of an archipelago can jar and appear contrived, particularly in relation to other socio-cultural characteristics of the islands and their peoples. And yet, the pressures of democratic polities demand an investment in airport infrastructure, tourism marketing and branding exercises whose goal is to attract tourists to other and more islands (beyond the main island/s). We resort to the concept of contrived complementarity, as developed in the context of a critique of colonialism, to explain these dynamics in the context of the archipelago of the Azores.

Contrived Complementarity: The Power of Words

Fanon (1967, p. 14) claims that "what is called black soul is a white man's artefact." It is by the construction of an essential other that power manifests itself. This is an outcome of contrived complementarity, a rampant terminology of control. The construction of apparent opposites (as male and female; white and black; Christian and Muslim; West and East) operate as a split or dichotomy against which those who call themselves men, or white, or Christian, or Western, can make themselves whole (also Said, 1985).

We contend that a similar dynamic is at work even beyond binaries, in the construction of neat multiplicities that fit in the context of a harmonious and unified whole, as when comparing the islands of an archipelago to a patchwork quilt, or the colours of a rainbow. Borrowing from the exact natural science and physics of light refraction, or the precision and craft of quilting, branding agents and marketers undertake what tourism operators call "product differentiation": they present their multiple (actual or potential) island destinations as the comfortable participants of a precise as well as a natural synergy. Precise, because the diversity is neatly complementary, no island being like any other, and each displaying a suite of touristic experiences that are presumably unique and specific to itself. "Each island, however small, tends to have a distinct history, certain unique cultural characteristics, and often its own language or dialect" (Hamilton-Jones, 1992, p. 200). Natural, because this endowment is packaged, camouflaged and presented as if it were authentic, local and territorially rooted. The result is a lush kaleidoscope of neatly engineered colours and hues; a feast for the senses, hoping to appeal to island hopping, but also to attract different tourist types, and to suit different pockets. This strategy is intended mainly to boost the tourism experience, while maximizing visitations and length of stay, contributing to enhanced revenue generation. The focus here is on the management of diversity, and on how this condition can be expected to expand the impact, flavour and appeal of a particular tourist destination.

And yet, the plurality of an archipelago can be elusive; it may not easily lend itself to control and profiling; it may not fit submissively into tight historical, cultural or colour compartments; it could defy coordination and organization; and it could express itself via a cacophony of voices, aspirations and identities that clash with the 'official', smart logo, brand, *identity* and *history* – rather than *identities* and *histories* – of the island group. Nor is the differentiation that exists within an archipelago necessarily and inherently island based: we err by essentialising islands if we assume so. Difference could rather be region, theme or product based, involving sub-island and/or multi-island units of analysis, with clubs or clusters, each with their own specific marketing strategies, combining and separating islands at will (e.g. Edwards, 2004, contrasting the north and south of Tenerife, Canary Islands).

These difficulties can be camouflaged in official narratives about these island spaces, including those presented in attractive visual tones. Marketing agencies can do some aesthetically wonderful work in celebrating island differences in complementary pitches. The signal is one of synergy, a pleasant bouquet of island experiences that beckon visitors to visit one island, then the other. The more visited, the better. After all, "every island has its own character, its own atmosphere and subtle differences in culture" (Bahamas Promotion, 2010).

In this chapter, we ask ourselves to what extent are such discourses, and the harmony they infer, constructed and hyped versions of an altogether different practice: one driven by intense inter-island rivalries, characterized by too similar island destinations competing for the same tourists, where there are other differences *between* and *within* islands which may be socially and historically more relevant than what is officially portrayed, but which are dismissed as not appropriate or 'incorrect' for branding and marketing purposes.

The notion of an archipelago, or 'island-island' relationality, is a welcome alternative to both the 'land-sea' and 'mainland-island' approaches that have tended to dominate (in) island studies (Stratford, Baldacchino, McMahon, Farbotko and Harwood, 2011). There is a felt and growing need "to explore alternative cultural geographies and alternative performances, representations and experiences of islands" (ibid., p. 114). These alternative geographies and performances include the multiple ways in which 'diversity' can be represented, and managed in a particular archipelagic setting; and embrace the manner in which such representations align, or fail to align, with both techno-economic considerations of transport logistics as well as the socio-cultural understandings of islanders of their own internal status images, divisions and hierarchies. While diversity could be packaged as a form of comprehensive yet contrived complementarity for branding purposes, it can clash rudely with both alternative home-grown conceptualizations of the life world, and with technoscapes deemed necessary to bring marketing strategies to fruition.

Methodology

This chapter developed after we had exchanged various e-mails in the run-up to a week-long international migration conference held in São Miguel, Azores, in September 2011. At that point, Godfrey Baldacchino (GB) was exploring the potential use of the concept of the archipelago as a heuristic device, offering an approach to island studies that privileged island-island relationalities. In the course of a week of conversations, this interest met the enthusiasm of Eduardo Costa Duarte Ferreira (EF): a PhD candidate looking at migration in the context of the Azorean archipelago. Together, they were quick to realize that this 'archipelagic turn' could help shed some critical light on tourism policy in the Azores. GB, who had twice been to the Azores before, was aware of some inter-island rivalries; thanks to EF, they were able to recognize these as symptomatic of a certain type of enduring inter-island difference: one that did not feature in the official positioning of the Azores as a diverse destination. The island identity was clearly significant: even the Azorean communities in the diaspora would tend to organize themselves around their island of origin, just as they would be most likely to return again to their island of origin should they decide to resettle home (for example, Rocha, Ferreira, and Mendes, 2011; Teixeira, 2006; Teixeira and Murdie, 2009).

This chapter follows from various conversations between its two authors, a focused literature scan of archipelago tourism (practically all of it in relation to specific islands or jurisdictions), information solicited from other colleagues working or based on archipelagos that are tourism destinations, and a set of six semi-structured interviews that EF conducted with stakeholders in the Azorean tourism industry during 2012 (see Appendix 1). The interviews (conducted in Portuguese) elicited respondent opinions about tourism policy of the Azores, the extent to which this was sensitive to both inter-island differences and similarities, and how these sensitivities (or lack thereof) impacted on the long-term sustainability of the industry for the island region.

Forms of Archipelago Tourism

Organizing archipelago tourism is an important economic activity, and especially so for warm water islands which, unlike their cold water cousins, have a considerable economic dependence on tourism (Baldacchino, 2006; 2013). This dependence however often conceals a tightly coordinated, top-down, centre-periphery logistic relationship. The typical and simplest state of affairs is the hub-and-spoke network model, found in several sectors of modern society, including road transportation, telecommunication, and aviation logistics (Horner and O'Kelly, 2011). In this scenario, as it applies to archipelagos, the central island (usually, the one with the location of the capital city and the bulk of the resident population) is often the only one with an international airport, or seaport: all visitors on commercial flights to 'offshore' islands must then transit through the main island or transit hub alongside. Inter-island links that do not involve the central hub are rare or non-existent, or rarely if ever advertised or communicated to visitors (see Figure 4.2).

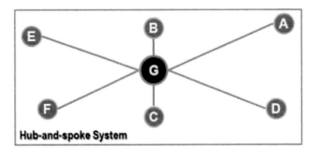

Figure 4.2   Schematic model of a hub-and-spoke systemic approach to transport management

Source: From Coyle, Bardi and Novak (1994, p. 402). © Brooks/Cole, a part of Cengage Learning, Inc. Reproduced with permission. www.cengage.com/permissions

This model has inherent advantages: it concentrates traffic, grouping passengers with the same travel origin but possibly different final destinations in 'feeder flights'. It also concentrates the required infrastructure to/from one location, reaping economies of scale, and avoiding costly duplication. However, hubs potentially increase bottlenecks, such as arrival and departure delays and traffic congestion. Moreover, most visitors would then tend to spend their time, and money, in that same location, or use it as their base if and when they venture to other islands (Costa, Lohmann, and Oliveira, 2010). Ironically, in this business model the branding of the offshore islands (and the vigorous affirmation of how different they are from the main island) is an exercise accomplished by *central* tourism agencies or state departments, and rarely by the offshore islands themselves or their representatives. Thus, the self-evident logistical and infrastructural dominance of the centre vis-à-vis the outer island(s) suggests a similar but more nuanced imposition by the centre/main island of the grand narrative that plays out for tourists about the different islands in the group. Archipelagic diversity yes; but on whose terms, and in whose words? After all, "narrative *constructs* … language has the capacity to make politics" (Hajer, 2006, pp. 66–7, emphasis in original).

There is another set of pressures that tends to drive what may initially have been a classical 'hub and spoke' model into one where the different island constituents each develop their airport and/or seaport infrastructure. In democratic island societies, where representatives are elected from multiple island constituencies, and where the smallest islands may have a disproportionately large influence on regional decision making, a series of policy decisions may come into play whose outcomes slowly but surely act to reproduce transport infrastructure, and develop direct flight and/or ferry connections to key national and international destinations, bypassing the erstwhile central island hub.

Enter the Azores

The Azores is a Portuguese subnational island jurisdiction in the mid-Atlantic Ocean with some 247,000 inhabitants, spread over 600 km of ocean along a general WNW-ESE strip; it presents itself as an even more diverse archipelagic configuration. The islands, an overseas region of the European Union, were ranked second out of 111 world island destinations for sustainable tourism. This report card states that "locals are very sophisticated" (National

Geographic, 2007, p. 110). We argue that the depth and sophistication of Azorean culture is more than meets the eye, and certainly more than the official narratives suggest.

Except for Bardolet and Sheldon (2008) and Marrou (2005), we are not aware of academic studies that have specifically adopted an archipelagic outlook towards the understanding of tourism among the several islands of the Azores: in fact, not a single entry for 'archipelago' appears in the keyword index for all 38 volumes of the *Annals of Tourism Research* – a leading scholarly tourism journal – published during 1973–2011 (Xiao, 2012).

All the Azorean 'great green ships' (after Updike, 1964), or the nine populated islands – each represented by an equally-sized star on the region's flag, and equidistant from one other (Plate 4.1) – have airports, but three are main international exemplars: the main one just outside Ponta Delgada, on the island of São Miguel; the other two at Lajes, on the island of Terceira, and at Horta, on the island of Faial. Explaining part of this different archipelagic character are long running tensions between the two main cities of the archipelago – Ponta Delgada, the capital, and, on Terceira, Angra do Heroísmo, a UNESCO world heritage city, closer to the centre of physical gravity of the scattered island group. In the Azores, Ponta Delgada may be the administrative capital, but the Regional Assembly and Regional Tourist Board are located in Horta; the judiciary and the Roman Catholic diocese are located in Angra do Heroísmo.

We are thus faced with a three-way/ three-island political decentralization (Ponta Delgada-Angra do Heroísmo-Horta) that is however not matched by the demographic data. Ponta Delgada by itself contains around 25% of the total resident population of the Azores, reflecting the region's scattered population; São Miguel over 50%. Four of the nine islands boast less than 10,000 residents each, with the smallest, Corvo, having less than 500 (Table 4.1).

Table 4.1   Azorean population distribution by island: 1981–2011

Island	1981	1991	2001	2011
Santa Maria	6,500	5,922	5,578	5,552
São Miguel	131,908	125,915	131,609	137,856
Terceira	53,570	55,706	55,833	56,437
Graciosa	5,377	5,189	4,780	4,391
São Jorge	10,361	10,219	9,674	9,171
Pico	15,483	15,202	14,806	14,148
Faial	15,489	14,920	15,063	14,994
Flores	4,352	4,329	3,995	3,793
Corvo	370	393	425	430
AZORES	243,410	237,795	241,763	246,772

Source: Instituto Nacional de Estatística, *Censos*, 1981, 1991, 2001, 2011.

The location of the three main international airports corresponds to the islands with the three largest capacity for tourist accommodation: Sao Miguel, Terceira and Faial (Moniz, 2009, p. 324). This pattern of unequal distribution of hotels and other accommodation facilities is further skewed by its urban bias: more than half of all beds in the Azores are to be found in just Ponta Delgada (49%) and Angra do Heroísmo (11%) (Serviço Regional de Estatística dos Açores, 2011).

In any case, what is clear is that demographic statistics, hotel stock and tourism visitation numbers (about which more below) present a picture of diversity and inequality that official discourse seeks to camouflage and tone down. It is not just the flag that suggests that each of the nine islands is of about the same size.

Data and its Challenges

One of the difficulties in undertaking any empirical studies to assess the nature and dynamics of archipelago tourism concerns the quality of available data. Island states and subnational island jurisdictions at least have a state or sub-state regional identity; this means that authorities regularly measure tourist arrivals (and departures), which are then reported in regional statistics. Visitation statistics per island may also be available. If the data collecting methodologies do not change over time, then such trend data is comparable across various years.

The main difficulties arise with the proper identification of who is the 'tourist'. First of all, not all passengers on international flights are tourists. Many could be local residents, which could include expatriates with non-Portuguese passports returning home from trips abroad. Second, and typical for small island territories, there is a significant overseas Azorean diaspora, which visits its homeland regularly – indeed, this is one of the main reasons that there are direct international flights to the Azores from Boston, Oakland and Providence (USA), Toronto (Canada), Frankfurt and Munich (Germany), London (United Kingdom) and Amsterdam (The Netherlands) (Azores Web, 2012). Many Azorean émigrés may live overseas and maintain a Portuguese/European Union passport: they would easily remain excluded from tourism statistics. Third, there are many international passengers travelling on domestic flights, arriving in the Azores from Porto or Lisbon, on the Portuguese mainland. Fourth, the Azores benefits from considerable domestic tourism: mainland Portuguese or Madeirans visit the islands. Fifth, various international flights transit in the Azores, coming, say, from Canada or the USA and heading on to Lisbon or to Porto as their final destination. Their passengers are not necessarily visiting the Azores. Finally, the status of passengers does not disclose the purpose of their visit: not all may be tourists in the narrow sense of the word: some may be students, or workers, or traveling on business. Mainly for these reasons, we have decided against collating data based on airplane passenger arrival statistics.

We have instead looked more closely at the statistics pertaining to foreign visitors (non-nationals) staying in Azorean hotels (Table 4.2). This approach eliminates the inclusion of tourists who may have family and/or friends in the Azores, perhaps even a second home, and would therefore be tourists but not lodged in hotels. In any case, these visitors are much more likely to be Portuguese nationals or members of the Portuguese overseas diaspora. Moreover, anonymous accommodation statistics do not reveal if tourists are engaging in inter-island travel. Nevertheless, our approach likely provides a valid indicator of the spread of international tourist arrivals over time; and the extent to which this sheds light on the nature of Azorean tourism. The data presented as Table 4.2 allows some interesting observations. First, the 'hub-and-spoke' model remains dominant: international tourist traffic to São Miguel dwarfs that to all the other islands. Second, the situation in the four other 'gateway' islands suggests a vague convergence: but Pico has been steadily losing

Table 4.2 Number of foreign visitors (non-nationals) staying in Azorean hotels, by island with a gateway: 2001–2011

	2001	2002	2003	2004	2005	2006	2007	2008	2009	2010	2011
São Miguel	56,329	53,820	58,671	74,751	103,886	104,403	99,784	96,442	93,099	98,835	100,382
Terceira	8,381	8,925	10,807	12,567	14,829	13,912	16,233	15,001	13,768	12,028	18,743
Faial	8,268	7,610	6,990	9,720	10,136	12,235	11,534	11,230	10,926	12,199	16,423
Pico	6,213	6,054	5,879	5,524	5,290	6,014	4,701	4,223	3,745	4,638	9,345
Santa Maria	1,199	910	1,035	1,545	1,474	1,890	1,778	2,064	2,349	2,701	3,974

Source: Servicio Nacional de Estatística de Açores, http://estatistica.azores.gov.pt

Table 4.3 Number of islands visited by tourists in the Azores, during summer of 2007 (N=916) and the winter of 2007–8 (N=998) (by %).

	Number of Azorean islands visited by tourists (%)									
	1	2	3	4	5	6	7	8	9	Total
Winter 2007–2008	75.8	14.6	4.0	3.9	1.0	0.6	-	0.1	-	100% N=916
Summer 2007	63.8	14.1	10.9	8.8	1.7	0.2	-	0.1	0.4	100% N=998

Source: Observatório Regional do Turismo (2008a, 2008b).

visitors until 2009; Terceira is only recently recovering after a peak in 2007; Faial has been doing well since 2003; and Santa Maria, because it is starting from a very low base, is gaining tourist visitors fastest of all.

Now, to what extent do these figures suggest that the Azorean archipelago is living up to its name and welcoming multi-island visitations? The Regional Government has been making a pitch in favour of such a practice:

> One of the greatest assets is the archipelagic condition ... a touristic experience ... on the basis of two or more islands is generally a richer and more satisfying experience than a tourist experience based on one island. Our mystique is more evident when we are understood in our insular plurality and archipelagic dimension (Autonomous Regional Government of the Azores, 2008, p. 169).

Limited data is available; but a sample tourist satisfaction survey undertaken during two successive seasons – the summer of 2007 and the winter of 2007–8 – sheds some interesting light on the matter (Observatório Regional do Turismo, 2008a, 2008b). Thirty-three per cent of the respondents sampled were Portuguese. Despite a discernible seasonal variation, a large number of tourists to the Azores still visit only one island (Table 4.3).

What these figures suggest is that inter-island circulation in the Azores remains highly restricted. The 'gateway' island remains the locus and focus of the tourists' visit, more so in winter than in summer. This situation is partly a function of the geographical separation between the islands, and the financial and temporal costs of inter-island transport, specifics which are very unequal within the archipelago.

The weather is another major obstacle to timely inter-island connections, especially during the autumn and winter. An 'Azorean Circuit' package deal was being sold a few years ago to the main European markets, and including the Netherlands. This package offered tourists the possibility of visiting the three main islands (São Miguel, Terceira and Faial) during the same week; however, this offer proved most impractical since bad weather, and the cancellation and delay of inter-island flights, put at risk the tourists' ability to catch their flight back to the country of origin (e.g. Circuito Açores 8 Dias, 2007). During summer, when the weather is more favourable, tourists arriving in Faial have an easier opportunity to visit Pico and Sao Jorge by boat; for visitors arriving in São Miguel, it is similarly easier to visit Santa Maria.

Even so, these examples come across as the exceptions that justify the rule. It appears that Graciosa, Flores, and Corvo – all non-gateway islands – are the least visited: by less than 5% of all visitors to the Azores. São Miguel stands out as the main island visited: four out of every five visitors to the Azores has been to this island, in summer as much as in winter; this is followed by Terceira, Faial, and Pico. Indeed, São Miguel is often the only island visited by tourists to the Azores (Observatório Regional do Turismo, 2008a; 2008b).

And so, this data begs two observations. First, the strategy to sell the diversity of the Azorean archipelago has so far not been very successful. The evidence suggests that most tourists who come to the Azores return to their country of origin having visited only one island (usually São Miguel). They remain unable to compare the specificities of that island to any other or with what is inferred or officially announced about them. The plurality and diversity of the Azorean archipelago – not only, but including, that diversity which is island based – thus remains a virtual and unfamiliar detail, to be glimpsed and consumed from a website, brochure or internet blog, if at all.

The second observation is a sober reflection on the extent to which it is worth continuing to drive the local economy of the less visited islands in the direction of a general type of (mass) tourism. Official encouragement for the construction of (even if small) hotel units, support for small businesses to sell arts and crafts and local products, and investment in the training of waiters needed to serve the 'regular tourist', are initiatives that end up not having the expected economic and social return within this framework. Presently, this official discourse may already be seen as a deception to many economic agents and stakeholders in the hospitality industries of the 'small five' (Santa Maia, São Jorge, Graciosa, Flores and Corvo); it may eventually even be interpreted by them as a kind of deliberate trick or deception coming from the authorities. Is São Miguel really committed to help other islands upgrade their tourist numbers, in what could be a zero sum game where São Miguel would stand to lose?

The Nature of Rivalry

In an archipelago, the temptation is always great, at worst, to secede, and at best to disregard the political jurisdiction of the centre (Lewis, 1974, p. 136). As with other island territories (Baldacchino, 2000, p. 27), on the Azores, relations between the various settlements – parishes, municipalities, islands and/or groups of islands (the extinct *distritos*) – are affected by ancestral rivalries and 'parochial tensions' (Da Cunha, Raposo, Estevão, and Enes, 1970).

> The geography alone embodies isolation – and then the isolation delves farther into a bag of tricks. It surprises people that the nine islands … are not exactly cheek by jowl … Inter- and intra-island rivalries seem inherent (De Melo, 1991, p. iii).

Such rivalries have historically been manifest in the oral tradition of the Azorean people; they remain alive mainly in various forms of folklore, including a specific type of Azorean popular music (*cantorias ao desafio*). This style involves a repertoire of anecdotes about each place or island, and brings to light several stereotypes about the Azorean people distinguished by island or community of belonging (Almeida, 1991, 1992; Dias, 2011).

Here are some examples of these anecdotes, as elicited mainly by ECDF thanks to his status and knowledge as an Azorean insider, his various local contacts, and a resident of São Miguel. They are indicative of the main stereotypes that circulate among islanders of the Azores archipelago. They permit a brief analysis of how these inter-island tensions are socially constructed and articulated.

In general terms, the inhabitants of Terceira and Santa Maria have tended to look at the inhabitants of São Miguel as snobbish and pretentious because of the latter's geographical size, its relatively large population, or its relative degree of development. On the other hand, *Micaelenses*, the people of São Miguel, are likely to accept condescendingly the jokes coming from the neighbouring island of Santa Maria – the latter call the *Micaelenses* 'Japanese' because of their accent, and their rural folk *'faquistas'* (people who brandish knives during fights), because of their short temper. The *Micaelenses*, on their part, never miss an opportunity to respond to the jaunts and jibes of islanders from Terceira. Part of their retaliation repertoire has been to refer to the inhabitants of Terceira as lazy and envious, only interested in having fun, and coveting all that already exists in São Miguel: from hotels and marinas to car races. Meanwhile, São Miguel and neighbouring Santa Maria maintain a special relationship; but Santa Maria still looks to São Miguel with a feeling of suspicion.

The reverse is not true; sitting on the top perch, São Miguel can afford not to feel threatened by any community.

The rivalry between Faial and Pico is historically based on a vertical and almost feudal relationship, involving the rich and landowner class from Horta, capital of Faial, and the poor peasants from Pico. The island of Pico is known for its traditional knowledge of viticulture and wine production. For more than two centuries, the moneyed class of Faial owned land and vineyards on Pico, employing many local peasants, and establishing a dependency relationship over time. The outcome: the inhabitants of Faial do not hide a fear of vendetta to be exacted on them by the people of Pico, whom they do not trust. On the other hand, the response of the islanders from Pico underlies two aspects: the fact that Faial always depended economically on Pico; and its 'geographical inferiority'. Pico may be a small island but it lies at the foot of a majestic volcanic peak, the highest mountain in Portugal (at an altitude of 2,341 metres). These tensions and strategies are well presented in some popular sayings from either of the two islands. A popular saying from Faial goes: 'We cannot trust those from Pico, whether by the spoken or the written word'. But then, in quick repartee, a witty and popular saying from Pico advises: 'The best thing on Faial is the boat that sails towards Pico'.

These tensions are part of a hierarchical system, where a relative preponderance of tourist traffic rides side by side with jurisdictional clout, whether the islands are considered either singly or each as a member of one of three sub-regional island groups. An island's 'ranking' would also depend on the size of its resident population, its land area, and geographical location, all of which are material criteria. Within this system, and at any one of these two levels, there are both *dominant islands* and *satellite islands*. Island inter-visibility helps to ensure that neighbouring islanders have strong, and not usually complimentary, opinions about each other. But ranking is also a function of the status that an island may have enjoyed during specific historical periods. The nine Azorean islands are a permeable and dynamic system, consisting of a core and internally hierarchical sub-system of three islands (São Miguel, Terceira and Faial) with political, economic, religious, and cultural dominance throughout a history of settlement of almost eight centuries (Martins, 1992; 1999). During this time, these three contenders for the top spot have jockeyed for position, brandishing different assets: economic muscle in the case of Sao Miguel; religious and cultural functions on the part of Terceira; or the intimate connection with the ocean and navigation in the case of Faial. Such descriptors have functioned as markers of difference between these three and the other islands, paradoxically helping to forge and ensure the rich mosaic of the whole archipelagic social system. There is a tendency for the intensity of rivalry to manifest unequally, being richer on those islands where there is a greater subjective sense of inferiority and peripherality (Da Cunha, et al., 1970, p. 142); in contrast, in places like São Miguel today, a certain complacency in the face of such tensions suggests a position of comfortable dominance.

Following the last point, there is a tendency for the intensity of rivalry to also manifest unequally, being concentrated mainly on the island where there is a greater subjective sense of "inferiority", resulting from that perception, and after the evaluation and comparison between different statuses. Thus, and according to a system of binomial tensions proposed (ibid.), it is possible to structure the rivalries between the islands as a subconscious pecking order, as follows (Figure 4.3). We do not think that these rivalries and tensions are either amusing social quirks or geographical pathologies. On the contrary, they are deep-seated political and emotional geographies, whose interrogation is essential to a more thorough

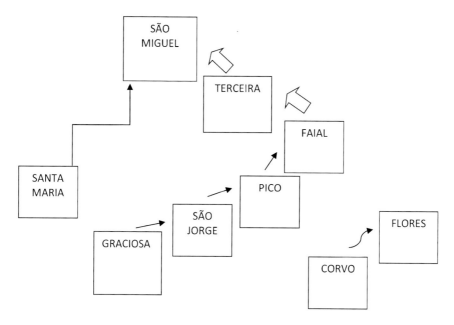

Figure 4.3   Representing the social hierarchy of Azorean islands in the local imaginary. © 2014, the authors

Source: The authors.

understanding of the Azorean condition and its historical antecedents. And yet, ever since the region's autonomy status was put in place in 1976, successive governments have sought to remove the basis for such tensions. The political strategy followed has been to make every effort to level the playing field; carefully distribute the various functions of government between the main islands; build equally strong infrastructure across the archipelago; and equip every island with similar and adequate sources of revenue, particularly through tourism.

Why a Multi-centric Approach to Tourism?

In the Azores, the distribution of tourist flows along five current 'centres of gravity' – five international airports to date, the latest ones being constructed on Santa Maria and Pico – is the result of a deliberate economic policy being pursued by successive regional governments, with different political persuasions, since the early 1990s, and at accelerated pace since 2004 (Moniz, 1996, p. 71). These political efforts are being carried out in accordance to what official sources refer to as a *policy of regional cohesion*; a political principle that strives to respond to the large demographic, social, and economic asymmetries and differences that exist between the different islands of the Azores by seeking to achieve a condition of convergence. The objective of the cohesion policy is to provide similar opportunities to each of the nine island communities of the Azores, opening the way to the equable and harmonious development throughout the archipelago. Of course, what this policy also means is that any socio-economic or geographic differences must not stand in the way of 'development': all Azorean islands and islanders deserve the same (large scale) tourism infrastructure in order to benefit from the same, successful type of tourism.

There is a political sub-text to these development plans and their emphasis on parity. Each of the nine islands, irrespective of its size, is guaranteed the election of at least two deputies, plus additional ones for every 6,000 voters, on a 57-member Regional Assembly. This level of representation privileges the smallest islands, and exercises considerable pressure on elected deputies to accept and satisfy the desires and wishes (rather than needs) that are expressed and articulated primarily by the main lobbies of their specific island constituency, institutionalized in nine island advisory councils. These tend to dig up old rivalries and jealousies between the different islands. A 'one size fits all' economic policy, therefore, comes across as an effective response by the political centre to such competitive parochial grassroots, and improves the likelihood of re-election.

Recognising the Problems of a Cohesion Policy

And yet, this strategy of appeasement brings its own challenges. First, is the uncritical acceptance of the cohesion policy, and of its implications. After all, the nine islands may share some characteristics but not others: they differ in size, population, landscape, even history and culture, as well as what can be described as 'tourism products': Graciosa has fabulous thermal springs; Santa Maria offers unique opportunities for diving and big game fishing activities; Flores presents exceptional natural conditions for birdwatchers and botanists; Pico has its volcano and its lava-fed vines and wines; and so on. Moreover, all six least-populated islands except Corvo (Flores, Graciosa, Pico, São Jorge, Santa Maria) face falling populations (Table 4.1) and all six have a serious shortage of young and qualified personnel with which to ensure the effective functioning of any infrastructure and services aligned to the tourism industry. Within this six-island sub-group, different types of service cultures come to play in dealing with visitors: this is largely a function of the historical experience of each island population in welcoming and socializing with the *estrangeiro*. Due to their proximity to Faial (long known for its international sailboat port), people in Pico and São Jorge have considerable experience playing hosts to visitors from all over the world. In contrast, islanders elsewhere among the six have remained more isolated, with fewer and less regular contacts with the outside world.

Encouraging people on each of the nine islands to improve their capacity to host more tourists may not necessarily foster development; it may even threaten their future viability and attractiveness. Such a gross model of economic growth predicated on convergence does not acknowledge or respect that a different set of physical and cultural attributes could be put to better use if they appeal to a different type of tourist and tourist niche. Such complementarity, should tourists be or become aware of its existence, offers a more likely form of sustainable tourism; is better aligned to local resources; encourages more visitors to visit more than one Azorean island; and is a much more robust strategy in the face of eventual tourism downturns and crises, as is the current fiscal situation in Portugal (Wise, 2012).

Second, the character of diversity of the constituents of the archipelago is constructed, driven, coordinated, and decided from the centre. Of course, 'brand consolidation' is important: potential tourists, tour operators, and travel agents need to receive uncompromising and non-conflicting market signals about specific places (Baldacchino, 2010). So, for example, in the Azores each of nine colours represents what each of the nine Azorean islands is purported to offer: green for São Miguel and its pastures; brown for São Jorge for its rocks, and so on (e.g. Metropolis Conference 2011, p. 116):

São Miguel known as the green island due to its pastures and fields.

Flores known as the pink island due to the great profusion of wild flowers especially hydrangeas, which have large blue or pink petals.

Santa Maria known as the yellow island due to the abundance of yellow broom on the island.

Faial known as the blue island due to the different colours of blue that decorate the houses ad that divide the fields and line the roadsides.

Corvo known as the black island due to the lava walls that divide its fields and pastures.

Graciosa know as the white island due to its landscape and names given to certain places like "Pedras Brancas" or White Stones, "Serra Branca" or White Mountains, and "Barro Branco" or White Clay.

São Jorge known as the brown island due to its rocks.

Terceira known as the purple island due to its lilac grape bunches.

Pico known as the grey island due to its outstanding mountain, the highest point in Portugal. (Metropolis Conference, 2011, p. 116).

But to what extent do these markers of difference and complementarity, constructed by marketing professionals and endorsed by politicians, dovetail with local sentiments and meet local approval? Or do they rather act as fabricated tourist bait, providing a very particular and peculiar rainbow of concocted diversity? In some cases, the unnatural feature of the colour and its rationale is even more explicit, and verges on the ludicrous, the trite, and the banal: take Graciosa which, we are told, is known as the white island due to its landscape "… and the names given to certain places"; Terceira, with its world heritage city status, is supposed to be known as the purple island "due to its lilac grape bunches".

What alternative narratives and dimensions of diversity are unacknowledged, stifled, or muted? Does it not make more sense to recover other, culturally engrained – dare one say more authentic – aspects of identity from the different islands and, at the very least, align these with the existing brand? As things stand, the brand is somewhat contrived: could it not, should it not, be aligned more closely to geographically, sociologically and historically actual features, traits and tensions?

We offered these key questions to six stakeholders from the Azorean travel and tourism industry (and who hail from different islands). Their responses largely confirm an alignment with the specific island brand; but at least two respondents are critical enough to recognize that the island characteristics showcased for tourist purposes are consequences of 'marketability' rather than 'authenticity': official concoctions created and based, for instance, on stereotypes and seasonable events: as in the case of Santa Maria, known as the 'Island of the Sun' and where, during the summer, several music festivals are held. One respondent insightfully questions whether this very island–specific approach carries much merit, since it underplays the proximity of islands to each other:

> The authorities forget that, apart from any endogenous features and advantages of Santa Maria, the island is very close to São Miguel. This fact should be taken into account; it should be seen an advantage, but no one sees it from this angle.

Why not appreciate and acknowledge that an island may also be attractive based on its historic relations with another island or islands?

Conclusion

Recognizing that language constructs as much as it reflects politics, this chapter has sought to flesh out some of the contending and competing geographical representations involved in the archipelagic space of the Azores. It has done so by probing into the cultural nuances of (albeit overly essentialised) Azorean island lives, as expressed in inter-island rivalries and tourism marketing pitches, and the all-too-glaring gaps, differences, and inconsistencies between these practices. We contend that this approach is an important tool with which to consider the plurality of archipelagic narratives and to explore more critically how these narratives cut across, align, or jar with any official rhetoric(s) of representation and of routings made available through transport logistics. Marketing strategies speak highly of brand consolidation; yet, the analysis of praxis, at least in the case of the Azores, suggests that brand consolidation may unfold at the expense of either showcasing diversity, or presenting its fake, fairy tale, rainbow rendition. In this sense, we suggest a strong parallelism with the concept of contrived complementarity as emergent from critical theories of (neo)-colonialism.

Inter-island rivalry does not seem to interfere with the promotion of the Azores as a tourist locale. The implicit understanding here is that rivalry is unattractive, shatters the more harmonious profile of the islands presented by tourism discourse and official representations of the islands – uncompromisingly united and equal, like the nine stars on the flag – and should anyway not feature in tourism promotion. We beg to differ: there is certainly scope and potential in recognizing other forms of inter (and intra) archipelagic diversity beyond the official paraphernalia and glossy brochures; especially those that resonate more closely with political history and socio-cultural praxis. The Azores may stand a better chance of holding on to, and even perhaps reinforcing, its reputation as a premier tourism destination if it integrates less sham and contrived, multiple voices into its representation.

Of course, *how* this integration could be effectively accomplished remains an interesting question for further consideration. Like Grydehøj (2008), we suggest that, if archipelagos wish to promote their diversity more faithfully and effectively, then the unity within that diversity needs to become more anthropologically sensitive to actual and historically valid forms of difference.

Such observations offer what may be a fresh perspective to tourism marketing in other archipelagos, and particularly for archipelagic states, often with centralized government agencies (including tourism departments) that venture and apply their own representation of the diversity of their territory, including the definition of that territory's diversity. This is a task that states may undertake with some urgency, especially in large archipelagic and decolonizing territories such as Indonesia or the Philippines, with a keen eye towards nation building and the enhancing of the polity's credentials as a unitary state, in control of its own representation.

Acknowledgements

This chapter is based on material that appeared in Baldacchino and Ferreira (2013). © Institute of Island Studies, University of Prince Edward Island, Canada. Reproduced with permission.

References

Almeida, O.T. (1991). *Ah! Mónim dum corisco*. Azores: Eurosigno.

Almeida, O.T. (1992). *No seio desse amargo mar*. Lisbon: Edições Salamandra.

Autonomous Regional Government of the Azores (2013). Retrieved from www.azores.gov.pt

Azores Web (2012). *Fly to the Azores*. Retrieved from http://www.azoresweb.com/travel. html

Bahamas Promotion (2010). *Island hopping*. Retrieved from http://www.bahamas.co.uk/ home/island-hopping

Baldacchino, G. (2013). Island tourism. In A. Holden and D. Fennell (eds), *The Routledge handbook of tourism and the environment*, pp. 200–208. New York: Routledge.

Baldacchino, G. (2010). Islands, brands and 'the island' as a brand: insights from immigrant entrepreneurs on Prince Edward Island. *International Journal of Entrepreneurship and Small Business*, 9(4), 378–93.

Baldacchino, G. (ed.) (2006). *Extreme tourism: Lessons from the world's cold water islands*. Amsterdam: Elsevier.

Baldacchino, G. (2000). 'Gozo's social structure: issues and implications'. In: *Improving the Employability of the Workforce in Gozo*, pp. 15–27. San Lawrenz, Gozo, Malta: Bank of Valletta Gozo Conference.

Baldacchino, G., and Ferreira, E.C.D. (2013). Competing notions of diversity in archipelago tourism: transport logistics, official rhetoric and inter-island rivalry in the Azores. *Island Studies Journal*, 8(1), 84–104.

Bardolet, E., and Sheldon, P.J. (2008). Tourism in archipelagos: Hawai'i and the Balearics. *Annals of Tourism Research*, 35(4), 900–923.

Circuito Açores 8 Dias (2007). Retrieved from www.aerohorta.com/viagenselazer/index. php?option=com_content&task=view&id=85&Itemid=2

Costa, T.F.G., Lohmann, G., and Oliveira, A.V.M. (2010). A model to identify airport hubs and their importance to tourism in Brazil. *Research in Transportation Economics*, 26(1), 3–11.

Coyle, J.J., Bardi, E.J., and Novack, R.A. (1994). *Transportation systems*, 4th edition. New York: West Publishing.

Da Cunha, J.C., Raposo, J.R., Estevão, M.L., and Enes, J. (1970). *A agricultura açoriana: A realidade e perspectivas*. Lisbon: Secretaria de Estado da Agricultura/Junta de Colonização Interna (mimeo).

De Melo, J. (1991). *My world is not of this kingdom*. Translated by G. Labassa. Lisbon: Círculo dos Leitores.

Dias, F.S. (2011). *Dicionário sentimental da ilha de São Miguel: De A a Z*. Azores: Publiçor.

Edwards, L. (2004). Canary islands: it's not so grim up north. *The Guardian (UK).* 12 December. Retrieved from http://www.guardian.co.uk/travel/2004/dec/12/canaryislands.observerescapesection1

Fanon, F. (1967). *Black skin, white masks.* Translated by C. Len Markmann. New York: Grove.

Grydehøj, A. (2008). Branding from above: generic cultural branding in Shetland and other islands. *Island Studies Journal*, 3(2), 175–98.

Hajer, M.A. (2006). Doing discourse analysis: coalitions, practices, meaning. In M. van den Brink and T. Metze (eds) *Words matter in policy and planning*, pp. 65–74. Utrecht: Netherlands Graduate School of Urban and Regional Research.

Hamilton-Jones, D. (1992). Problems of inter-island shipping in archipelagic small island countries: Fiji and Cook Islands. In H.M. Hintjens and M. D. Newitt (eds), *The political economy of small tropical islands*, pp. 200–222. Exeter: University of Exeter Press.

Horner, M.W., and O'Kelly, M.E. (2001). Embedding economies of scale concepts for hub network design. *Journal of Transport Geography*, 9(4), 255–65.

Instituto Nacional de Estatística. *Censos* (various). Retrieved from http://censos.ine.pt/xportal/xmain?xpid=CENSOS&xpgid=censos2011_apresentacao

Keller, A. (1970). Tourists never take the mail boat: that clinched it. *New York Times*, 24 May. Section 10.

Lewis, V. (1974). The Bahamas in international politics. *Journal of Interamerican Studies and World Affairs*, 16(1), 131–52.

Marrou, L. (2005). La mer en réseau, de nouvelles voies pour la mise en mouvement des territoires. Vivre en archipel: le service public de transport au Açores. Retrieved from http://archives-fig-st-die.cndp.fr/actes/actes_2005/marrou/article.htm

Martins, R. de S. (1999). *A cerâmica modelada feminina dos Açores: Sistemas produtivos, formas de articulação e processos de mudança.* Cascais, Portugal: Patrimonia.

Martins, R. de S. (1992). Etnomuseologia no arquipélago dos Açores. *Património e museus locais*, Nos. 1–2, pp. 133–5. Lisbon, Instituto Rainha D. Leonor.

Metropolis Conference (2011). *16th International Metropolis Conference*, Ponta Delgada, Azores. General Information. Retrieved from http://www.metropolis2011.org/images/stories/metropolis.pdf

Moniz, A.I. (1996). *O turismo nos Açores: Estudo sobre a oferta de alojamento turístico.* Ponta Delgada, Azores: Jornal de Cultura.

Moniz, A.I. (2009). *A sustentabilidade do turismo em ilhas de pequena dimensão.* Ponta Delgada, Azores: Centro de Estudos de Economia Aplicada do Atlântico.

National Geographic (2007). A report card for the world's islands. *National Geographic Traveller*, November-December, 110–27.

Observatório Regional do Turismo (2008a). *Inquérito à satisfação do rurista nos Açores: Verão 2007.* PowerPoint presentation. Retrieved from http://www.observatorioturismoacores.com/data/1207156938.zip

Observatório Regional do Turismo (2008b). *Inquérito à satisfação do turista nos Açores: Inverno 2007/8.* Retrieved from http://www.observatorioturismoacores.com/data/1216133942.pdf

Rocha, G.P.N., Ferreira, E.C.D., and Mendes, D. (2011). *Between two worlds: Emigration and return to the Azores.* Azores, Portugal: Government of the Azores.

Said, E. (1979/1994). *Orientalism.* New York: Vintage.

Serviço Regional de Estatística dos Açores (2011). *Statistical Yearbook, Azores Region 2010.* Retrieved from http://estatistica.azores.gov.pt/upl/%7B82fc3ed6-4580-4261-90b6-5d803bf62b78%7D.pdf

Sinclair, M. (ed.) (1994). *Scottish island hopping.* Edinburgh, Scotland: Polygon.

Stratford, E., Baldacchino, G., McMahon, E., Farbotko, C., and Harwood, A. (2011). Envisioning the archipelago. *Island Studies Journal*, 6(2), 113–30.

Teixeira, C. (2006). Comparative study of Portuguese homebuyer suburbanization in Toronto and Montreal Areas/Étude comparée de la suburbanisation des nouveaux propriétaires portugais à Montréal et Toronto. *Espace, Populations, Sociétés*, 1, 121–35.

Teixeira, C. and Murdie, R. (2009). On the move: the Portuguese in Toronto. In C. Teixeira and V. da Rosa (eds), *The Portuguese in Canada: Diasporic challenges and adjustment*, pp. 191–208. Toronto, ON: University of Toronto Press.

The Independent. (2011). Island hopping on two wheels, 3 August. Retrieved from http://www.independent.co.uk/travel/uk/island-hopping-on-two-wheels-2330686.html

Thorpe, A. (2009). Island-hopping in Croatia. *The Guardian.* Retrieved from http://www.theguardian.com/travel/2009/jun/21/croatia-island-hopping-europe-ferry

Updike, J. (1964). Azores: a poem. *Harper's Magazine*, January, p. 37. Retrieved from http://harpers.org/archive/1964/01/azores/

Wise, P. (2012). Portugal braced for 'fiscal earthquake.' *Financial Times* (UK). December 30. Retrieved from http://www.ft.com/cms/s/0/39985d42-50d7-11e2-b287-00144feab49a.html

Xiao, H. (2012). *Annals Index: Vols. 1–38 (1973–2011).* Retrieved from http://www.elsevier.com/framework_products/promis_misc/ANNALS-INDEX1-38_2011.pdf

Appendix

Interviews were conducted by EF with the following:

Catarina Cymbron, travel agent, Melo Travel Agency (São Miguel Island).

Humberto Pavão, owner of Plátano Hotels (São Miguel), and regional delegate for Hotels Association of Portugal in the Azores.

José Pacheco de Almeida, former Regional Secretary for Transport and Tourism, and former Chief Executive Officer of SATA Airlines.

Laurinda Sousa, director and board member of the Association for Tourism in Rural Areas, and owner of a cottage/house for rent (Santa Maria and São Miguel).

Lizete Albuquerque, tour guide (Graciosa).

Pierluigi Bragaglia, owner and manager of a private lodging unit, and author of several Azorean tourist guide books (Flores).

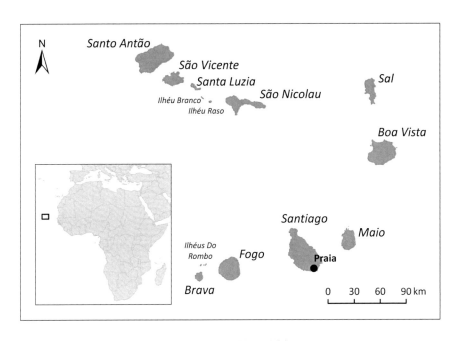

Figure 5.1 The archipelago of Cape Verde, West Africa

Chapter 5
Cape Verde 2.0: Branding and Tourism Development Across the Archipelago

Pedro F. Marcelino and Luzia Oca González

Introduction

The archipelago of Cape Verde consists of ten volcanic islands located 500 km west of Dakar, nine of which are inhabited: St. Anthony (Santo Antão), St. Vincent (São Vicente), St. Nicholas (São Nicolau), Sal and Boavista in the Windward (Barlavento) group; Brava, Fogo, Santiago and Maio in the Leeward (Sotavento) group. The country covers a total land area of 4,033 km² on the outskirts of the Sahelian climate zone. Most islands are mountainous, except for the three easternmost (Sal, Boavista and Maio), which are generally flat and sandy. For a total of 491,683 local inhabitants (INE, 2010), twice as many are estimated to live overseas, as an extensive and engaged diaspora. Santiago is the largest and most populous, followed in size by St. Anthony and St. Vincent in number of inhabitants.

After obtaining its independence from Portugal in 1975, Cape Verde went through fifteen years of single party rule led by the politico-military force of the anticolonial struggle, the PAIGC. This period was marked by an outstanding nation-building effort, despite the partly unfounded fatalistic prophecies of international experts that deemed the newly independent country economically 'unviable'. From 1991 onwards, the various governments consistently banked on opening up the economy and attracting foreign capital and private investment to industries such as tourism, fisheries, energy, transportation, and telecommunications (Piñeira, Oca and Furtado, 2011). In 2007, Cape Verde graduated from the ranks of the Least Developed Countries to the ranks of developing economies, or Middle Income Countries (MIC). While the islands remained largely dependent on external aid, its economy boomed and the income *per capita* rose to US$3,438, three times higher than in 2000. The 2013 Mo Ibrahim Index of African Governance for the first time placed the country 3rd overall (ahead of South Africa), 6th in terms of economic opportunity, and 5th in terms of human development (MIF, 2013).

Services – commerce, new businesses, air transportation, and tourism – are nowadays the main employers, representing 66% of the GDP in 2008 (BCV, 2014), constituting the backbone of the Cape Verdean economy. Tourism contributed with 60.8% of all services in 2008 (INE, 2010). The share of tourism in the GDP grew exponentially, from a mere 2% in 1995 to 10% in 2003 and 19.4% in 2008 (BCV, 2014), matching an 11.4% overall growth in tourism intakes between 2000 and 2008 (INE, 2010). This growth was mostly based on the 'sun and sand' business model aimed at key foreign markets, and attracting particularly British, Portuguese and Italian visitors. Domestic tourism was at 13% of the total in 2009 (INE, 2010). As an emerging destination the residential option plays a significant role in attracting private foreign investment, focused primarily on Sal and Boavista (Romero-Girón, 2010).[1]

In spite of the accelerated economic growth since independence, the country exhibits a number of core fragilities. Examples thereof are the excessive dependence on imports, and the logistical difficulties inherent to its territorial discontinuity. Despite the astounding progress in human development over the last few decades, Cape Verdeans also remain inadequately qualified for and mismatched with the job market; the tourism and service industries demand skills and training that are in short supply (Piñeira, Oca, and Furtado, 2011).

The country markets itself as a tourism destination by showcasing its archipelagic diversity and, as is common with other multi-island jurisdictions (e.g. Baldacchino and Ferreira, 2013), each of the inhabited ten islands appears to share the same stature and lure as the other nine on the official logo (Plate 5.1). On the identity front, however, and notwithstanding a clear socio-political consistency across the country, a degree of differentiation beyond petty regional rivalries separates Santiago from the other islands. This cultural/identity split establishes it as the centre against which the periphery is measured and defined. Santiago is the most African of the bunch, in light of its early colonisation and centuries of intense slave trade history. Its *mestizo* inhabitants gradually moved on to Fogo and Brava, and would only later (1800–1900s) reach the northern islands, by then still receiving slave workers. Societies with diverse socio-economic bases resulted from these distinct settlement processes: whereas the earlier wave of colonisation was based on a large-property model, the smaller properties of later settlements resulted in a reduced social distance between slaves and slave owners. In some islands, a *mestizo* commercial elite would eventually emerge, educate itself and start defining and reflecting upon Capeverdeanness as neither African nor European, but somewhere in-between. In contrast, by this stage, Santiago was seen as the refuge of runaway slaves and their descendants, devoid of markers of modernity and urbanity, and closer to its African roots (Fikes, 2006).

These ancient tropes manifest themselves through an ongoing rivalry between Praia (in Santiago), and Mindelo (in St. Vincent), the two largest cities. While the former was made national capital after the abandonment of the settlement of Ribeira Grande (also known as Cidade Velha, 'Old City'), the latter was for decades the islands' thriving cultural capital. After independence, Praia boomed, becoming the principal centre of political, administrative, economic and cultural life, despite recent decentralising efforts (Piñeira et al., 2011).

Marketing 1+10 Brands from the Ground Up: Entangled Much?

Tourism was not embodied as a national priority immediately after independence, but would become a strategic sector after the regime change of the 1990s. This process starts with that archipelago's fast-paced embrace of direct foreign investment over the course of that decade. Little more than twenty years down the road, tourism came to be defined

---

1   According to the Cape Verdean Touristic Observatory's data, 95% of the tourist inflow is concentrated in only four islands: Sal (57%), Santiago (20%), Boavista (10%) and St. Vincent (8%). This is connected to available bed space: 50% of the country's beds are in Sal, 23% in Boavista, 11% in Santiago (Romero-Girón, 2010).

as a key economic pillar that had to be designed from scratch. The first Tourism Act (*Lei Básica do Turismo*) was passed in 1991 (dos Santos, 2012). Two years later, the government created the Special Tourist Zones (*Zonas Turísticas Especiais*, or ZTEs), then considered the foundation for all the policies in the sector. These areas were defined on the basis of their importance for the development of a national tourism industry, and may have two statuses (Romero-Girón, 2010).

The first is that of the Integrated Tourist Development Zones (*Zonas de Desenvolvimento Turístico Integrado* or ZDTIs), which are spaces slotted for the development of tourist centres of national import. These lands may be subject to territorial expropriation, and severely restrict any constructive or extractive activities. The ZDTIs are currently located in Boavista (3), Maio (3), Sal (4), Santiago (8) and St. Vincent (7). Eighteen of the twenty-five ZDTIs listed in 2009 were created early on, in the 1990s. Some of the most important among them were reconfigured and expanded in the 2000s, when eight additional areas were defined.

The second is that of the Tourist Reserve and Protection Zones (*Zonas de Reserva e Protecção Turística*, or ZRPTs), located in areas with significant scenic or natural value. They may or may not be contiguous areas to existing ZDTIs, and may also simply be reserved zones pruned for future ZDTI redevelopment. At present, this typology can be found in the islands of St. Vincent, Sal, Boavista, Maio, St. Nicholas and Fogo.

The making of Cape Verde as a 'sun and sand' destination was from the onset premised on the orography of Sal and Boavista, two islands characterised by expansive sandy beaches and sparsely uninhabited spaces. Their populations increased dramatically between 1990 and 2010: Sal skyrocketed from 7,715 to 25,779 inhabitants, fuelled partly by the only international airport in the country for much of the 1990s; Boavista went from 3,452 to 9,162 in the same period. Efforts to diversify the tourist offer over the last decade were anchored in the creation of products with historical, cultural and natural value, the overhaul of airport infrastructures (currently four international and three domestic airports), and the extension of the tourism portfolio to Santiago and St. Vincent.

In 2010, the Tourism Act was redesigned to accommodate planning and execution instruments, among which the four-year *Strategic Plan for Tourism Development*, reinforced by planning frameworks for each of the ZDTIs. That same year, the government-backed *Marketing Plan 2010/2011* sought to brand the archipelago as a global destination composed of multiple island spaces with diverse offerings under the 'one country, ten destinations' umbrella brand. However, by highlighting people, sun, Creole culture, safety, proximity, sports, history, nature and cuisine, the plan effectively fires in every direction, and fails to define real priorities. Nonetheless, it grouped islands together based on their potential for individual promotion. Sal, Boavista, Santiago and St. Vincent are defined as possible individual brands, but simultaneously part of the three strategic groups of islands defined according to market niches.

The 'Sunny Islands' group bundles up Sal, Boavista and Maio, focusing on sun and sand offerings complemented by nautical sports. Its marketing strategy targets current and potential regional markets: mainly Germany, Italy, United Kingdom, Portugal, Spain, France, Scandinavia, and the Netherlands. The sub-market segments focus on family and couples.

The 'Essence Islands' group includes Santiago and St. Vincent, which are associated with business/leisure packages and events, complemented by cultural products (history, music, dance and cuisine). It identifies Portugal, France and Cape Verde as current markets, and countries such as Switzerland, Germany, Spain or Italy as potential ones, across four market segments.

The 'Senses Islands' group lumps together every other island, including uninhabited Santa Luzia. This heterogeneous group focuses on a promotional strategy of 'unusual nature', culture and non-aquatic sports. Its three market segments are more limited, and aimed primarily at the French and domestic tourists.

Santiago, an Insular Mainland

Santiago has always been in centre stage, partly because it hosted both the old and the new national capitals. Nonetheless, the island itself occupied a subordinated mental space for most Cape Verdeans up until independence, mostly for its connotation with characteristics perceived as African, rude and uncultured. Throughout its history, the island was used as a labour reserve feeding the colonial system (Fikes, 2006). In fact, whilst from the mid-19th century onwards – that is, after the abolition of slavery – outmigration was allowed from other islands, in Santiago the authorities supressed it, redirecting population overflows as indentured labourers in extensive plantations in São Tomé and Angola. Upon independence, however, Santiago became the undisputed centre of the archipelago, often growing at the expense of the remaining islands, and indeed playing the role of 'mainland' to them.

Unlike the sun and sand islands to the northeast, at 273,919 inhabitants spread over 991 km^2 (INE, 2010) Santiago is densely populated. Most of these live in the southern coastal plateau around the capital, and the rest in valleys and plateaus further inland.

Praia, the capital, has undergone a hurried process of urbanisation, its population trebling since 1970 and peaking at 132,317 inhabitants in 2010 (INE, 2010). Its growing pains of social inequality and exclusion have started to translate into growing security concerns. Home to many internal migrants from the interior and from other islands, the capital also accommodates a large contingent of foreigners, notably mainland Africans, Chinese, and expats linked to international institutions and companies.

Santiago's tourism identity remained mostly undefined until the 1990s, when the island started to be promoted as a cultural destination, with growing event and business market segments in Praia. The most significant product in the cultural segment is Cidade Velha, particularly since being listed as a UNESCO World Heritage site in 2009 (UNESCO, 2014), although this remains largely unexplored insofar as domestic tourism is concerned, and as a roots/genealogy tourism segment tapping into Cape Verde's extensive diaspora, and west African middle classes (Agunias and Newland, 2012; Holsey, 2004). A calendar of music festivals (KriolJazz, Gamboa) and international meetings and fairs attempts to create demand for the event and business segments, but for the time being appear insufficient to deliver on the image promoted through official channels. However, the island's status as the 'core' of Cape Verde, home to its institutions, company HQs and half of its population, nonetheless make it a mandatory point of passage.

Although the island's extensive coastline also has manifest tourist potential, it is generally degraded for both environmental and social reasons. Sand and gravel extraction is particularly notable in this regard, as an income activity common to the poorest households in the country, which are often women-led. The construction boom from the 1980s onwards aggravated the situation, as a newly independent country was constructed, with Praia at its heart (Oca, 2009). Three decades later, most beaches have virtually disappeared beyond any engineered regeneration. A few – Ribeira das Pratas, Pedra Badejo, Praia Baxu, São Francisco – have escaped under the authorities' watchful eye, and at least Tarrafal is promoted as a beach destination (which has seen better days).

Santiago's eco-tourism and rural tourism potential is obvious, since the island is home to one of the few National Parks (Serra Malagueta) and one of the country's highest peaks (Pico d'Antónia). In recent years, some businesses associated with these market segments have mushroomed across the island, but its overall expression is minimal and poorly articulated. On the contrary, despite an official discourse for the promotion of integrated and sustainable tourism in Santiago, a handful of planned projects suggest the very opposite.[2] Over the last decade, numerous construction projects aimed at urbanising vast swaths of land in the vicinity of the capital fashioned a mirage of hotels, time-share apartments, golf courses, marinas, artificial beaches and other pharaonic leisure facilities aimed at attracting foreign investors, particularly from the British Isles. Most failed due to their excessive ambition, legal problems related to expropriations and land rights, and the suspension of works following planning infractions. The global economic crisis took care of the few projects that persisted, stymieing construction and leaving a scared landscape of flattened soil and ghost concrete structures.

This haphazard brand and territorial (mis)management creates the impression that Santiago has been sacrificed for the sake of immediate economic growth, seemingly repeating the failed experiences of the Canary Islands, where the collapse of lower quality tourism has already shown how wrong the model was.

Tourism, Heritage and Community in Cidade Velha

As mentioned above, Cidade Velha occupies a special place in Santiago's (and Cape Verde's) product portfolio. Its marketability was boosted in 2009 when UNESCO declared it World Heritage, following a decade of architectural interventions. Founded in 1462 as Ribeira Grande of Santiago, it was the site of the colony's earliest settlement, its main slaving entrepôt, the administrative centre for the Guinea Coast, and for a little over two centuries the national capital. The vast collection of ruins and heritage buildings attests to the site's importance within the colonial system.[3] The significance of the site was initially recognised by the colonial state in the 1960s, when Portugal repaired some of the crumbling structures as it struggled to hold on to the colonies by glorifying its 'civilising' mission. In 1990, the Cape Verdean government designated the Historic Site as National Heritage, and in 1993 a municipal bylaw established strict local construction guidelines, kick-starting a series of conflicts with the population, who by then lived *in and around* the heritage grounds; an old convent was used by then as a pigsty.[4]

---

2   For example, a large development is projected for the coastal ZDTI of Achada Rincão, contiguous to the fishing village of Porto Rincão (population 2,000). This currently uninhabited area would receive a housing complex for thousands of tourists, built with Norwegian funds (Piñeira et al., 2011).

3   Architectural gems include the first church built in Africa (1495), the Pillory (1512), the Fortress of São Filipe (1591), a convent (1640) and the ruins of the old cathedral (1700) (UNESCO, 2014).

4   Until 2005, the town and its rural surroundings was under the jurisdiction of the capital, Praia, 15 km away. Cidade Velha is now the seat of a new municipality.

Figure 5.2   Cidade Velha's everyday life: fishers on Calhau beach © Luzia Oca.

Figure 5.3   Cidade Velha: Pelourinho Square. © Luzia Oca.

Figure 5.4   Cidade Velha: Washing in the street © Luzia Oca.

In the late 1990s, both the Portuguese[5] and Spanish[6] cooperation agencies (IPAD and AECID respectively) were brought in to implement heritage protection and restoration projects, after which the government began preparing an application package to UNESCO, following a pre-recovery failed attempt in the mid-1990s. These efforts continued after the 2001 government change and the creation of the Research Institute for Cultural Heritage (IIPC). Its local branch spearheaded an international competition for the recovery of public spaces and historic buildings, in partnership with AECID, who funded the projects. Predictably, a Spanish company (INYPSA) was awarded the contract and conducted the restoration works between 2001 and 2006. The interventions focused on the recovery of built heritage and the development of tourism, particularly in the lower area of the town. An inn designed by the Portuguese star-architect Álvaro de Siza was built in the valley, and a restaurant/bar was opened in Pelourinho Square (pillory).[7]

---

5   In 1998, via IPAD, the Government of Cape Verde designated the Portuguese architect Álvaro de Siza as coordinator of the *Plan for the Protection and Restoration of Monuments* in Cidade Velha. IPAD's efforts focused on the consolidation and restoration of the Cathedral.

6   In 1999, AECID launched the *Recovery Program for Architectural Heritage and the Development of Tourism and Agriculture in Cidade Velha*, through INYPSA. Its intervention began in the Fortress of São Filipe.

7   This caused an immediate conflict with a family who operated a local bar, and who for years complained publically in posters around the square. The same space now accommodates two seafront bars, ten metres from each other: a local dig attracts Cape Verdeans, while tourists tend to flock to the 'Spanish bar' next door.

In 2006, when the restoration process had been finalised, the Ministry of Culture launched a public tender for the management of the town's tourism resources. Again unsurprisingly, a company with Spanish capital (Proim-Tur) won the contract. Almost unoriginally, one of Proim-Tur shareholders was found to be a leading architect with INYPSA, hinting at insider dealing. This case led to expressions of discontent by much of the local and national population, who felt that their public space had been privatised and handed over to "the Spaniards", now considered "the new owners of Cidade Velha" (De olho na Praia, 2007). In 2007, AECID opened a Technical Cooperation Office in Praia, and would thereafter implement most of its projects either directly or through NGOs, in collaboration with the IIPC and the municipality. According to its own assessment, their earlier interventions had resulted in few benefits for the local population, due to the lack of a participatory methodology (AECID, 2004). In 2008, as the new UNESCO application package was finalised, the population was for the first time formally heard and taken into account (Gov.CV, 2008). It would have a voice in the future management body, through the site's Ombudsman.

In short, Cidade Velha has been the subject of interventions by various local and exogenous actors, both institutional and private, pursuing different objectives and interests, often at odds with each other. The authors' assessment, based on a decade of community work in Cidade Velha, is that up until 2009 successive projects failed to take the local population into account, resulting in conflicts related to the use of public space, and to building restrictions. The local population did not feel like participants or beneficiaries of the asset recovery process, and often considered the new building standards as unwanted impositions.[8] An example of this was the resistance of residents of Banana Street to having their roofs traditionally re-thatched, rather than keeping their modern roofs. In another prominent case, the residents of Calhau Street, a row of seafront houses, harshly critiqued the construction of a traditional stone wall over their façades: a cosmetic intervention that made no attempt at improving the residents' lives, even though several houses had no sewage or running water.

Unlike many other World Heritage sites, Cidade Velha is densely populated. The 1,214 inhabitants are clustered around the historic site, occupying a third of the overall protected area (209ha). The town has a high incidence of poverty (38.9%), unemployment (8%), and illiteracy (30%) (INE, 2007). The building restrictions prevented the construction of new houses to households that didn't even have access to buildable land until recently (and only in the upper town). Ironically, the land contiguous to the Historic Site as been allotted to the ZDTI Santiago Resort to the east, and to the ZDTI Achada Santa Marta to the west, both limiting the alternatives for local families, and endangering the visual integrity of the site. In the latter case, real estate speculation resulted in the sale of plots almost exclusively to people and companies with a high purchasing power: national elites, diaspora buyers, and foreigners. As a response, the population often contravened the law, expanding their houses or even building new ones, in the hope that finalised structures would be allowed to stand. The municipality's cautious reaction has been to impound any construction sites, but never demolishing structures. Nonetheless, the process has been frayed with allegations of partisanship: since 2008 the main opposition party holds the local municipality, putting it at odds with central authorities sharing jurisdiction over municipal lands. In 2013, the municipality presented the Atxada Forte New Town (Cidade Nova) project (Semana, 2013)

---

8   As featured in the documentary *The Architect and the City*, directed by Catarina Alves Costa (2004).

to meet the need for land. Its location has been contested, and the population shrewdly questions the existence of the necessary funds. While we cannot refer to a 'space war' *just yet*, it should be pondered that the arrival of new actors (mostly tourists, but also the capital's urban elites, entrepreneurs and returned migrants) does increase social pressure, leading to the loss of space for native residents' everyday life.

But the lack of local participation was not limited to urban planning. A major flaw has been the inability (or unwillingness) to prepare the local population, which inhabits the tourist space, to run activities that allow them to benefit from the inflow of tourists. Proim-Tur, the concessionary, limits training activity to the personnel required to operate its own circuit and its own supporting businesses. In fact, with few exceptions, no training activity was held for the general population until 2011. Capacity building projects funded by various partners have ensued. But this is too little, too late, since most business licenses already lie with out-of-towners. The rare economic links between the local populations and touristic activity mean locals watch busloads of tourists pass by, barely impacting their lives.

Since 2005, the influx of tourists has increased dramatically: from 1,000 foreigners per year in 2007, to over 30,000 in 2012 and an astounding 15,000 in the first quarter of 2013, according to the Ombudsman (Sapo, 2013). The inclusion of Cidade Velha on UNESCO routes has quadrupled the figures of previous years, although the statistical hike may also be related to a new market segment: cruise ships.[9] Unfortunately, bus tours are organised by Proim-Tur, who also levies charges for 'its' historic circuit, and preferably directs tourists to its own facilities. Cape Verdeans are charged the same price to visit these national heritage sites as any other visitor (exception is made to the inhabitants of Cidade Velha, after much debate). Ultimately, and sadly, Santiago's cultural tourism brand can only be seen as a missed opportunity and a social-economic flop.

Imposing a Mass Tourism Model in Small Island Communities

In densely populated Santiago, the by-products of accelerated growth have been the commodification, institutionalisation and privatisation of its (in)tangible cultural heritage. Meanwhile, in St. Vincent, Sal, Boavista, Maio and, to a lesser extent, Fogo, the core issues appear to be gentrification, land tenure, and the dilution of identity – and thus weaker branding. This is, at the end of the day, part of a process that islands, archipelagos, and large cities around the world have undergone, are undergoing, or will undergo, and in which paradises are discovered, occupied, developed, possibilities realised but in which something is necessarily lost (Clark et al., 2007).

European tourists certainly pose a set of challenges to a country undergoing profound social-economic change. The real estate boom has led to large portions of prime land being sold to foreign investors for the construction of gated communities and tourist resorts, at times through allegedly unlawful land seizure by the authorities. These properties—found on, or projected for, almost every island—are owned, marketed, and sold mostly to foreigners, and sometimes to the diaspora, for a premium, which has pushed the prices of land and housing to levels untenable for average Cape Verdeans. This is not only the case with new constructions unaffordable to the middle class, but in some cases already extends

---

9   In 2013, the Port of Praia received 39 ships totaling 26,585 passengers, most of whom spent a few hours in Cidade Velha. See: http://goo.gl/QlrkBM

to the customary colonial-style housing used by many locals,[10] and now also out of reach because it has been deemed 'typical', 'picturesque', and thus so desirable that it can be sold for a premium to a foreigner. As a result, much of the prime real estate in Boavista and Sal, and a handful of large colonial properties in the cities of Mindelo (St. Vincent) and São Filipe (Fogo) are increasingly in the hands of foreigners or non-residents whose priority is the valuation of an investment.

Although Cape Verde has never been a "cheap" country in which to live, because of its island nature and import dependency, it has become considerably more expensive with the growth of the tourist industry and the arrival of European residents over the last few years. Cape Verdeans are now coping with ramping inflation, often absurdly priced real estate and inflated commodities, utilities, telecommunications, and air travel prices, and find themselves increasingly out-of-pocket or out of stock.[11]

Foreigners have been part of the national fabric from the early colonial days. While the Portuguese returned right after 1975, it was not until after the 1991 election that the new climate of economic liberalisation and the pro-business atmosphere attracted a significant number of other Europeans: at first adventurous tourists, then investors, and eventually hordes of tourists in search of the newest 'untouched' paradise. As Cape Verde's economy took off to what appeared to be a future promising growth in the real estate and tourism services markets, their numbers skyrocketed. By 2009, thousands were arriving for charter holidays, fewer for tailored travel (eco, solidarity and cultural tourism), and hundreds more had moved from all over Europe to every island. Communities of Europeans are now found in all major cities and towns, and even in the most remote corners of the mountainous island of St. Anthony.[12] In Sal and Boavista, two islands with relatively few inhabitants but extensive tourist infrastructure, the permanent or seasonal communities of Europeans account for a large slice of the local population. Not necessarily the largest local minorities, they are, however, the most influential, and are perceived as the wealthiest. Many Europeans acquired second homes routinely used for one or two seasons every year. As tourists, Europeans can easily purchase a visa upon arrival; as temporary residents they are allowed to be in the country for six months.

Initially, investors and tourists arrived from Portugal, but were very soon followed by others: Spanish, due to the proximity to the Canaries; Italian, exploring historical connections with Sal and Boavista, and bypassing the northern European markets that had saturated other islands; French, whose interest spanned from the huge cultural capital of a sizeable Cape Verdean community in Paris, including musical icons such as Cesária Évora; and Dutch and German, who sought off-the-beaten-track adventurous high-mountain thrills in St. Anthony or Fogo. By 2005, the country's reputation had grown across continental Europe, finally reaching the mass market in the United Kingdom when a national travel industry award identified Cape Verde "as one of the few safe and secure holiday destinations in Africa [...] located close enough to Europe to sustain charter tourism," and dubbing it

---

10   E.g.: Mindelo's colonial houses, known as *caza ingles*, or 'English house', small but solid street-level constructions, painted with bright colours and often located in the inner city.

11   In a country where goods have to be shipped in, produce is often simply unavailable. Eggs will typically run out just before Christmas, when many emigrants come back on holiday, the coveted Fogo white wine will seldom reach markets outside the capital and Mindelo, and many other products disappear from the shelves weeks at a time. Specific examples would include the scarcity of the local favourites (tuna and swordfish) from the city's fish market, as luxury hotels and restaurants pre-order whatever little stock is available.

12   Many have invested in small businesses servicing the island's booming eco-tourism industry.

an up-and-coming holiday and second home destination. A number of business missions resulted in significant English, Irish, and Scottish capital being invested in multiple real estate projects in several islands. Although the holiday property market boomed, fuelling the Cape Verdean economy and attracting large quantities of migrant workers, it remains to be seen how the industry will recover from the post-2008 global economic crisis that severely depleted the portfolio of available buyers.

Of Gentrification, Space Wars and Non-places

The island of Sal, former jewel of the crown, has learned this the hard way. Mega-real estate projects both there and in St. Vincent have been hit hard by the global crisis and now stand empty, half-built. Every time a newer, more enthusing island is discovered, the previous is left to dwindle. Sal has lost its monopoly on transatlantic flights. Following this, a significant part of its tourist market simply moved – or moved on – to Boavista. There is little doubt tourists will keep moving until eventually Cape Verde runs out of islands and tourists move elsewhere, unless out-of-the-box marketing and retention strategies help the islands escape this vicious logic and proactively move toward differentiation and customer loyalty.

Meanwhile, on Sal, the tensions are palpable. Local merchants and hoteliers state that street sellers harass tourists to the point of exhaustion, and accuse them of establishing a "bad reputation" for the resort island, drastically reducing the return rate (Conde, 2008). Although there is an imposing presence of African mainlanders in Santa Maria, the island's sleepy main town, some of the accusations are not only unfounded, but may constitute scapegoating. The troubles of Sal may have been compounded by the global economic crisis, more so than in any other island. Gigantic mixed-use real estate projects lie half-abandoned across the island like concrete ghosts waiting for the real estate market to take off again, and leaving hundreds of migrants now unemployed (Expresso das Ilhas, 2009). More accurately, however, Sal's economic woes most likely lie in its own development model: basic, unoriginal resort tourism that appears to be in decline, just as Boavista – a prettier, wilder island with an edge – ascends to a similar, and higher quality, position. It does not help Sal's case that Boavista now has its own international airport (for charters loaded with wealthy foreigners), while most business traffic was diverted to the capital's revamped Nelson Mandela International Airport (Marcelino, 2013).

Meanwhile, in Boavista, the dire consequences are visible. Here, paradisiacal luxury hotels and affluent residential developments are surrounded by pristine sand dunes peppered with date trees and a 6km-long insular extension of the Sahara Desert. Once paraded as the country's pearl, Boavista today boasts one of the highest costs of living in the country fuelled by its bourgeoning tourism industry, and is beginning to exhibit the growing pains of social conflict. Nowhere in the archipelago is the disparity between rich and poor as shocking as in this large and sparsely populated island. While Cape Verdeans lived in simplicity before the touristic boom, their living conditions are now in stark contrast with the über-luxury of the mega-resorts. Not far away, African migrants attracted by construction jobs in the Boavista ZDTI live segregated in the outlying Barraca, a community rife with unemployment, malnourishment, infectious diseases, alcoholism, drug abuse, drug trafficking, as well as petty and violent criminality (Marcelino, 2013). Worryingly, and predictably, as the economic crisis settles in, violent criminality is overflowing from the boundaries of this isolated ghetto to the islands' main urban centre, the sleepy town of Sal Rei, "risking spoiling Boavista's positive image and damaging its tourism potential"

(Expresso das Ilhas, 2009). While municipal authorities confess to not having the capability to resolve this urban time bomb – a flagship case for workforce mismanagement – much of the public discourse on Barraca to date seems to revolve around the negative projections to the exterior rather than focus on integration processes.

Yet, the island's woes extend much further. From nary any population just a few years back, Boavista swelled to over 6,000 inhabitants in 2010 (INE, 2010), out of which an estimated 2,800 live in the degraded shantytowns in Salinas and Barraca (Frederico, 2010), and almost all the rest in Sal Rei, the island's main town. In the high season, the island's population spills over the 10,000 mark. Notwithstanding, several resorts are either under construction or have been approved, to accommodate thousands of additional guests. Slowly, but surely, the Boavista ZDTI has transformed the most sparsely populated island in the country into a large sandy resort where Cape Verdeans provide services with limited added value, receive little in the way of community benefits, are themselves subject to European price-points, and have become a vague and exotic background to someone else's holiday pictures. Bizarre examples of this can be found in the Viana Desert, where a small Portuguese company offers 'culture-hungry' tourists the chance to taste the true hospitality of 'Cape Verdean Berber tents' and the exhilarating experience of partaking in a camel caravan led by real 'Cape Verdean Touaregs'. These are, in fact, Senegalese migrants clad in the traditional cyan garments and *sheshes* (turbans) of their Mauritanian and Malian neighbours and are a symptomatic sign of visual politics and problematic tourist representations (Wildman, 2004).

As if this wasn't surreal enough, two mega-resorts owned by the Spanish multinational Riu reinforce the theme: Riu Touareg is a tacky pastiche of a typical southern Moroccan sand palace, surrounded by booze-fuelled swimming pools, while in Riu Karamboa, nested between the sea and protected sand dunes, Tatooine chic meets Abu Dhabi grandeur meets the iconic roofs of Timbouktou. Not content with transforming Boavista into an *Anywhere, Cape Verde*, or what the sociologist Marc Augé (2006) would call a *non-place*, these architectural gems have taken the island by storm: Timbouktou-inspired domes now deck buildings in Sal Rei (Moassab, 2012).

A few exceptions offer a glimmer of hope that policy makers will wake up and smell the beans: the smart, culturally-sensitive Italian Guesthouse Migrante in downtown Sal Rei is a rare case of quality accommodation set amid local life, and is part of AITR, the Italian Association of Responsible Tourism (Migrante, 2014). Two hours off-roading away, the Spinguera Resort, another Italian hotel, is a low-impact premium eco-lodge built on the ruins of an abandoned village on the rocky side of the island. Service is thoughtful, cultural heritage patent in every detail, water sourced from new wells. A discrete 500-metre path leads down to a pebbly beach where sharks are said to roam. Reading on a hammock is, therefore, encouraged (Boutique Travel Blog, 2013).

From the coast, the hotel is all but invisible. Water sports are available… back at the mega hotels. Both companies are based locally, reinvest locally, and try hard to remain local. But, in a market that favours multinational-owned resorts benefitting from endless tax breaks, directly importing all their supplies and directly exporting all their profits, competition is fierce. At first glance, the Boavista ZDTI fails to value local customs and thus seems both a social failure, and a serious lack of vision.

Right next door, the island of Maio deserves at least a brief note. Up until the early 2000s, it was probably the only one that still felt like Cape Verde in the 1980s: quiet, quaint, 57 km of uninterrupted beachfront reached by the occasional airplane. This was too good to be left untouched. Rather than leveraging its identity, the government insisted in bunching Maio with Boavista, and slotting it for similar development. In just a few years, half-built luxury villas peppered the cliffs outside Vila do Maio, abandoned during the 2009 economic bust; downtown, a gigantic row of 3–4 storey condos have been built right on the pristine beach stretching between the pier and the salt marshes (read: swamp). Within months, predictably, water had to be pumped continuously to prevent them from sinking. Less than 2 km past the marshes, a fenced-in megalomaniac seafront project also lies abandoned. Straw roofed huts reminiscent of French Polynesia and Kenyan-style wall decorations are visible from the beach. Despite these flops, the population of the tiny island rose from 6,754 in 1990 (INE, 1990) to 8,303 in 2000 (INE, 2010). Thousands more are expected to fill new beds over the next decade. The high added-value tourism patent in quality guest houses, a handful of world-class restaurants (owned by dreamy French, Spanish and Kiwi expats), and even in a colony of a peaceful and mysterious sect (whose members wear white garments reminiscent of the Holy Land circa 10AD), all hint at a missed opportunity to reinforce eco- and cultural tourism alternatives.

Appadurai (2006, p. 83) notes that "majorities can always be mobilised to think that they are in danger of becoming *minor* (culturally or numerically) and to fear that minorities, conversely, can easily become major ..." This fear of dilution of identity is perhaps best illustrated by the situation of Boavista and Maio, often pointed out within Cape Verde as examples of places where the local population has been surpassed by tourists and foreign residents, transforming locals into service providers rather than native residents. According to Appadurai (2006, p. 83) "globalisation intensifies the possibility of this volatile morphing," but the fear of socio-economic loss helps maintain the status quo, at least in the most vulnerable islands.

Meanwhile, and notwithstanding the logistical, marketing, and branding difficulties facing either of them, St. Vincent, St. Anthony (Santo Antão), and Fogo are carving their own niches, cementing a reputation for high quality, diversified tourism alternatives, namely sports and adventure travel, rural and mountain tourism, cultural immersion tourism, responsible and 'solidarity' tourism, or eco-tourism, among other initiatives.

The least developed of this group is Fogo, a poor and emigration-prone island with the second oldest human settlement in the country. The stunning colonial manors and black sandy beaches of the city of São Filipe attract tourists for a day or two, usually on their way to a short trip up to the national park, revolving around a 2,829-metre active volcano. Cultural immersion, community tourism and mountain sports have increased exponentially in the island, but full island circuits are scarce. Few independent travellers ever venture there, with most arriving as part of organised hiking groups, often flying with a private air charter company. The tendency, however, is for the development of an integrated, community-relevant tourist model, to which the neighbouring island of Brava might be better attached if ferry connectivity is streamlined.[13]

St. Vincent, which is vaguely a synonym for Mindelo – the country's second largest city – can easily be a stand-alone destination, much in the way Zanzibar is. With 150 years of a cosmopolitan harbour city history, a unique architectural heritage, and a literary,

---

13   In mid-November 2014, for the first time since 1995, the Fogo volcano erupted. By the time this book went to press, the communities within the perimeter of the crater had been completely erased from the map. This included the local winery, most of the touristic and communal infrastructure, and the iconic Fogo Natural Park HQ building, inaugurated to international acclaim only eight months before. The memory of that site has been captured on photos by Fernando Guerra, a Portuguese architecture photographer (Guerra, 2014). This is a major setback to the prominence of eco- and community tourism in Cape Verde, but plans are already afoot to start reconstruction.

theatrical and musical tradition spearheaded by internationally renowned Cesária Évora, the Barefoot Diva, it attracts a more interested tourist who stays in local guesthouses, wanders the streets, and engages with the locals in the ubiquitous cafés. S/he might even come across one of Mindelo's most colourful characters: the *secretário*, the shrewd, unsolicited and often quirky guides, interpreters and facilitators who have been following foreigners around since the time of the steamship. Late each year, yachts crossing the Atlantic also berth in the city's circular harbour.

Like the locals, tourists often pack up and head to St. Anthony, a short ferry ride away, for a few days of Alpine hiking and a trip back in time. Although a couple of resorts have popped up in the island, the majority of the available accommodation is culturally sensitive, focusing on eco- and responsible tourism. Community stays are also popular with hikers, particularly in the most remote areas. Hiker groups will often pay €20/head to sleep under the stars on the flat roof of a family dwelling. A couple of community-led cultural villages (Lagedos, Monte Trigo) have thrived in recent years, and local guides are trained in languages, mountaineering and natural heritage. The development of this market niche has been fuelled by infrastructural projects, notably the international airport in St. Vincent, and improved ferry connections to St. Anthony. The rapport between the two islands works perfectly for the market niche they serve, and they complement each other to create an offer adequate to that type of tourist.

Yet, opposite forces collude to offset these gains, entice some of the local businesses, and annoy the more involved tourists. Cruise ships the size of several city blocks have started to routinely dock at Mindelo. A few dozen tourists will typically stream out into the streets, swarm handcraft stores and invariably end up at the local beach, with the level of interest and cultural sensitiveness that would be expected. Most, however, are loaded into dozens of mini-buses at the port and ferried straight across the island to a beach where they are greeted by sweet cocktails, serenades and 'traditional' dancers wearing Hawaiian-style grass skirts. A single local company monopolises the bus, entertainment and restaurant services, outsourcing whatever it cannot provide. A few hours later, as the ship honks twice for the traditional send off, Mindelo life goes back to normal. In recent years, a handful of cruise ships have started to make incursions to the remote west side of St. Anthony, remaining offshore and ferrying a few tourists to the island each time.

These are, thus, very diverse circumstances facing a variety of islands, creating opportunities and threats, but mostly unmatched by the state's manicured but inflexible development plans, zoning and policies. As Clark and his colleagues note in their study of conflicts over island space; which they call "space wars":

> Gentrification is an inherently conflict-ridden process characterised by two outstanding features: a marked shift in occupancy upward in terms of class/socio-economic position, and, reinvestment in the built environment (Clark, Johnson, Lundholm and Malmberg, 2007, p. 506).

As a direct consequence of this process, those who cannot afford the new spaces are excluded, dislodged and relegated to the outskirts/peripheries. Gentrification is arguably underway in several Cape Verdean islands, bringing about fundamental conflicts over space, encouraging corruption and creating a degree of animosity toward tourists and investors, seen as hoarders pricing everyone else out (with the connivance of speculating Cape Verdean property holders).

By not tackling the distinct needs and identities of the islands on a case by case basis (with the possible exceptions of the duos Fogo-Brava and St. Vincent–St. Anthony), the government's development plans not only fail to tap into existing resources and high value added niche markets, but also set some of them up with the phenomenon of gentrification (Sal, Boavista, St. Vincent, and Fogo), space wars (Boavista, St. Vincent), and the construction of non-descript destinations joining the rank-and-file of non-places scattered around the world (Sal, Boavista, Maio). And non-places, unfortunately, are the places few upscale tourists return to.

The Bottom Line: Lack of Strategic Foresight or Chronic Misbranding?

The current competing touristic development models in Cape Verde were defined over a period of nearly two decades in a stop-gap fashion, more responses to immediate needs rather than components of a master-strategy and a clear direction for the industry. For much of that period, the country faced chronic socio-economic and infrastructural challenges that distinguished it from more developed tourist destinations. Unfortunately, instead of proactively plotting an upgrade by studying and adopting the successful international models of specialised, high value added places such as the Seychelles, The Bahamas or Tobago, Cape Verde buckled under pressure. By the time sustainable tourism ideas took hold, the 'sun and sand' mass tourism model was already grandfathered. The confused (and confusing) branding attempts that followed were, therefore, designed on a flawed basis, sacrificing some of the islands to this kind of tourism, and stopping short of forcing a different kind of investment.

At its most pernicious, this is replicating botched mass tourism models, mutilating the landscape and failing to create a distinctive brand identity. No one knows what defines the Cape Verde brand (or any of its islands and sub-brands, for the matter). In too many cases, the islands were centrally bunched together with others, irrespective of what local aspirations might have been. Most concerning, however, are the social consequences of this centralised approach: while many of the national tourism development projects theoretically contemplate the population, it is necessary to reflect upon the obvious lack of foresight vis-à-vis the real impacts of large residential complexes in islands with a couple thousand inhabitants, or the social tensions derived from space disputes in established urban centres.

From a developmental point of view, training people to serve mass tourism feeds the industry's aspirations, but it does not empower citizens, nor does it prepare communities to own or benefit from it. In the long run, whether it is the remarkable unremarkableness of Sal, or the social conflict in Cidade Velha, imposed tourism models without proper local consultation and socio-economic adjustments have little chance at being sustainable. Misguided branding efforts, unfortunately, are just the tip of the iceberg. National policies cannot bypass nine distinctive island identities for the sake of growth; nor can island identities circumvent existing policies and practices that make a dog's dinner of their individual brands.

References

AECID (2004). Evaluación del Programa para la Recuperación del Patrimonio Histórico-Arquitectónico y para el Desarrollo Turístico y Agrícola de Cidade-Velha en la República de Cabo Verde. Madrid, Spain: Ministerio de Asuntos Exteriores y Cooperación.

Agunias, D.R., and Newland, K. (2012). *Developing a road map for engaging diasporas in development: A handbook for policymakers and practitioners in home and host countries.* Washington, DC: IOM and Migration Policy Institute.

Appadurai, A. (2006). *Fear of small numbers: An essay on the geography of anger.* Durham NC: Duke University Press.

Augé, M. (2006). *Non-places: An introduction to supermodernity.* New York: Verso.

BCV (2014). Home page. Retrieved from http://www.bcv.cv. Praia: Banco Central de Cabo Verde.

Boutique Travel Blog. (2013). Cape Verdean Paradise at Spinguera Ecolodge, 4 June. Retrieved from http://boutiquetravelblog.com/2013/06/04/cape-verdean-paradie-at-spinguera-ecolodge/

Clark, E., Johnson, K., Lundholm, E. and Malmberg, G. (2007). Island gentrification and space wars. In G. Baldacchino (ed.) *A world of islands: An island studies reader,* pp. 483–505. Charlottetown, Canada and Luqa, Malta: Institute of Island Studies, University of Prince Edward Island and Agenda Academic.

Conde, M. (2008). Comerciantes do Sal descontentes com excesso de Senegaleses: 'Eles extorquem dinheiro às pessoas'. *Expresso das Ilhas,* 8 July.

De olho na Praia. (2007). 18 August. Retrieved from http://deolhonapraia.blogspot.com.es/2007/08/proim-tur-os-novos-donos-da-cidade.html

DGT (2010). Plano Estratégico para o Desenvolvimento do Turismo em Cabo Verde (2010/2013). Praia: Direção Geral do Turismo, Ministério de Economia, Crescimento e Competitividade,

Expresso das Ilhas (2009). Assédio e Insegurança Ensombram Turismo. *Expresso das Ilhas,* 2 September.

Frederico, S. (2010). Boa Vista: estudo desmistifica o Bairro da Barraca. *A Semana Online,* 26 February.

Fikes, K. (2006). Emigration and the spatial production of difference from Cape Verde. In K. Clarke and D. Thomas (eds), *Globalisation and race,* pp. 97–118. Durham NC: Duke University Press.

Gov.CV (2008). Plano de Gestão da Cidade Velha 2008–2012, Centro Histórico de Ribeira Grande. Praia: Government of Cape Verde, p. 76. Retrieved from http://www.cidadevelha-pm.cv/documentos/planopt.pdf?phpMyAdmin=bfed44982b3d4d9ce26de a372944ceca

Guerra, F. (2014) *Cabo Verde: Ilha de Fogo.* Retrieved from https://fernandoguerra.exposure.co/caboverde.

Holsey, B. (2004). *Transatlantic Dreaming: Slavery, Tourism, and Diasporic Encounters.* In F. Markowitz and A.H. Stefanson (eds), *Homecomings: Unsettling paths of return,* pp. 166–82. Lanham MD: Lexington Books.

INE (1990). Censo da População. Praia: Instituto Nacional de Estatística. Retrieved from http://www.ine.cv/dadostats/dados.aspx?d=1

INE (2007). Questionário Unificado de Indicadores Básicos de Bem-Estar. Praia: Instituto Nacional de Estatística. Retrieved from http://catalog.ihsn.org/index.php/catalog/102

INE (2010). Censo da População. Praia: Instituto Nacional de Estatística. Retrieved from http://www.ine.cv.

IPDT (2010). Plano de marketing para o turismo de Cabo Verde (2011–2013). Praia: Instituto de Turismo, Direção Geral do Turismo, Ministério do Turismo, Indústria e Energia,

Marcelino, P. (2013). *O novo paradigma migratório dos espaços de trânsito africanos: Inclusão, exclusão, vidas precárias e competição por recursos escassos em países tampão: o caso de Cabo Verde*. Praia and Bissau: Ilhéu Editora and Corubal Editora.

Migrante. (2014). Migrante Guesthouse. Retrieved from.http://www.migrante-guesthouse. com/en/

Moassab, A. (2012). Território e identidade em Cabo Verde: debate sobre a (frágil) construção identitária em contextos recém independentes no mundo globalizado. Republished by Buala.org. Retrieved from http://www.buala.org/pt/cidade/territorio-e-identidade-em-cabo-verde-debate-sobre-a-fragil-construcao-identitaria-em-context.

Mo Ibrahim Foundation. (2013). 2013 Ibrahim Index of African Governance: Summary. London: Mo Ibrahim Foundation. Retrieved from http://www.moibrahimfoundation. org/downloads/2013/2013-IIAG-summary-report.pdf

Observatório do Turismo de Cabo Verde. (2010). *Revista*, 3. Instituto de Planeamento e Desenvolvimento do Turismo. Retrieved from https://portoncv.gov.cv/dhub/porton. por_global.open_file?p_doc_id=810

Oca, L. (2009). Informe: Investigación acción participativa. Fortalecimiento de las Capacidades humanas, sociales e institucionales. Madrid: Asociación para la Integración del Menor PAIDEIA, ACCVE, AECID.

Piñeira, M.J., Oca., L. and Furtado, C. (2011). Cabo Verde, um país insular de diáspora na confluência entre a Europa e África. In R. Lois (ed.), *Ordenamento e planejamento territorial na África occidental: Cabo Verde, Senegal e Mali*, pp. 65–115. Santiago de Compostela: Lóstrego.

Romero-Girón, V. (2010). *Informe: Guia Práctica – El Sector del Turismo en Cabo Verde*. Praia: Oficina Camaras Canarias/Proexca en Cabo Verde. Retrieved from http://aws2. nivaria.com/proexca/de/Estudios_de_Mercado/Cabo_Verde/2010/Guia_Practica_-_ PROEXCA.pdf.

Dos Santos, F.L. (2012). Cidade Velha, património mundial e medidas arquitectónicas. *Revista de Estudos Cabo-verdianos*, 4, pp. 41–57.

Sapo (2013). Quatro anos depois, Cidade Velha Património da Humanidade quer ser destino turístico de eleição. Retrieved from http://noticias.sapo.cv/vida/noticias/ artigo/1321144.html.

Semana (2013). Cidade Jardim nasce em Ribeira Grande Santiago. Retrieved from http:// asemana.publ.cv/spip.php?article85520&ak=1.

UNESCO (2014). Global strategy. Paris: UNESCO. Retrieved from http://whc.unesco.org/ en/globalstrategy/

Wildman, K. (2004). Picturing Coffee Bay: the visual politics of tourist representations. *Postamble*, 1(1), 2–10.

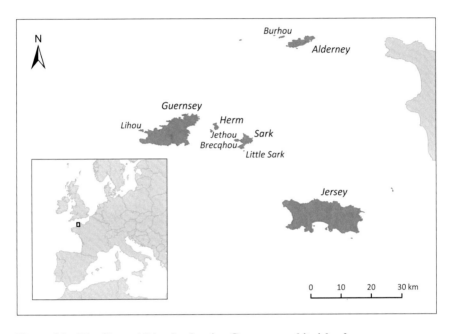

Figure 6.1 The Channel Islands, showing Guernsey and its islands

Chapter 6
A Tale of Two Guernseys: Tourism Branding and Island Hopping in an Archipelagic Context

Henry Johnson

Introduction

Guernsey offers a unique location for the study of tourism branding in an archipelagic context. First, as an island, Guernsey is the second largest of the Channel Islands, but it also administers several smaller islands and islets within its jurisdiction. Second, as part of an archipelago, the Bailiwick of Guernsey comprises the main islands of Guernsey, Alderney, Sark and Herm, with the first three being separate jurisdictions. Each of the islands within the Bailiwick are within easy reach of one another, whether by sea or air (when possible), while the island of Lihou can be reached on foot at low tide for visitors to walk to via a short causeway. In this archipelagic setting, island hopping can be an inherent part of the itinerary for any visitor, and is sometimes an option offered by the tourist industry.

This chapter discusses tourism branding and island hopping in archipelagic context in connection with both the island of Guernsey and the Bailiwick of Guernsey. The island context of this case study necessarily extends to embrace all the Channel Islands, where the other jurisdiction, the Bailiwick of Jersey (Jersey is the largest of the Channel Islands), adds an additional zone of interconnectivity on the one hand, and competitiveness to gain the tourist pound on the other. Moreover, travel to and from most of Guernsey's smaller islands is often via Guernsey or sometimes Jersey, both of which act as hubs for travel between the islands and beyond, especially to the UK and France, and sometimes further afield.

Two main areas of visual and textual marketing within archipelagic tourism branding in this island region are critically examined below: (1) the island of Guernsey branding itself along with the Bailiwick's smaller islands; and (2) the Bailiwick's smaller islands branding themselves along with the island of Guernsey (focus is given to Sark as a case study). The distinction between these two spheres is not always so well defined, and this chapter offers a content analysis of promotional materials in the islands' tourist industry (i.e., website marketing) as a way of comprehending symbiotic relationships, whether real or imaginary, between the islands.

The packaging of the archipelago as a site for touristic experience, whether from the perspective of mainland Guernsey outward, or from the Bailiwick's smaller islands inward, must reconcile itself to the actual modes of transport that are available to and from each of the Channel Islands. While focusing on these points in this web of islands, offshore islands, mainlands and jurisdictions, this chapter shows how the two layers of island marketing in Guernsey sometimes act collectively and sometimes separately, but with each, interconnections between islands are often foregrounded as an essential part of reinforcing a sense of island and archipelagic identity. With the number of tourists visiting Guernsey each year being in excess of 192,000 (States of Guernsey, 2013c, para. 1), and with the Bailiwick having smaller islands within easy reach of one another, there is much potential for marketing Guernsey either in connection with the island context, or with a focus on the other islands either in their own right or with the potential of island hopping.

This research builds on previous studies of island branding in the tourism sector more broadly (Baldacchino, 2005; 2010a; 2012; Grydehøj, 2008; 2010; Hayward and Kuwahara, 2013; Kelman, 2007; Khamis, 2010; 2011; Leseure, 2010; Lichrou, O'Malley and Patterson, 2010; Pounder, 2010; Reddy and Singh, 2010). Such studies contribute to scholarly discourse on the importance of islands, tourism and branding, where it has been noted that "islands – especially small ones – are now, unwittingly, the objects of what may be the most lavish, global and consistent branding exercise in human history" (Baldacchino, 2012, p. 55). Indeed, it is such a branding exercise that forms the focus of this discussion. While many of these and other studies focus on island brands in terms of products and places (Askegaard and Kjeldgaard, 2007; Baldacchino, 2010b; Johnson, 2012), the topic of archipelagic branding as part of the tourism industry offers a further level of analysis and critical reflection for the field of Island Studies.

Central to this chapter is the study of tourism in archipelagos. Moreover, just as the importance of "cultural heritage assets" (Ivanovic, 2008, p. 215) has been noted in connection with specific places, so too can islands be seen as "assets" for the tourist industry. That is, islands are often branded as places in their own right, along with tourist attractions on the island, and thus might be viewed as cultural heritage themselves. However, this chapter contributes a further level of study in terms of extending the lure of islands to archipelagos and the branding of an island group as part of a tourist attraction where visitors can include island hopping as part of their island experience (Baldacchino and Ferreira, 2013; Butler, 1993; Guthunz and von Krosigk, 1996; Topsø, 2012). That is, "while tourism development in islands is well studied, little attention has been given to archipelagos and their special challenges" (Bardolet and Sheldon, 2008, p. 900). In connection with the emergence of the notion of island hopping as a phenomenon in the field of Island Studies, as pointed out by Baldacchino and Ferreira (2013, p. 84), "it is a specific tourism experience not yet recognized as a specific policy area or field of academic inquiry". Also, as Kavaratzis (2008, p. 51) comments, "the conscious attempt of governments to shape a specifically designed place identity and promote it to identified markets, whether external or internal, is almost as old as civic government itself". But when archipelagos are branded in one touristic package as part of a territorialization of island space, the dynamics of inter-island relationships are challenged. At the same time, as islands promote themselves along with their unique touristic trappings, when an island includes other islands as part of the marketing exercise, it is both extending its branding domain and challenging others, whether part of the same jurisdiction or not (cf. Baldacchino and Ferreira, 2013, p. 89). Moreover, as DeLoughrey (2001, p. 23) argues, "no island is an isolated isle and that a system of archipelagraphy – that is, a historiography that considers chains of islands in fluctuating relationship to their surrounding seas, islands and continents – provides a more appropriate metaphor for reading island cultures". This stance is particularly applicable to Guernsey, which is an island, an archipelagic jurisdiction and part of a larger archipelago.

The methods used in acquiring data for this discussion have been through first-hand knowledge and fieldwork experience on the islands under study, secondary sources, as well as critical interpretation of branding materials publicly available from official websites of tourism organisations, which have a purpose of encouraging visitors to these island and archipelagic locations. This approach to textual and visual analysis frames Guernsey's government-funded tourism agency in terms of its publicity materials (especially its website) for critical analysis. As 'text', such data provide information for media interpretation, and my approach to this takes a form of content analysis based on the existence of pertinent terms that reinforce a sense of archipelagic tourism, rather than on any form of quantitative analysis. Such a topic builds on qualitative communication research methods as summarised by Lindlof and Taylor (2002), and is especially relevant for the research emphasis of this particular study.

As a way of showing two types of island branding within one island group, this chapter is divided into three main parts. The first of these explores the location of the Bailiwick of Guernsey and its constituent island tourist destinations in geographic context. As well as providing information on the islands' geography, a succinct background on history and politics is included as a way of setting the scene for the islands as destinations within the tourist industry. The following two parts of the chapter are case studies and a discusssion. The first focuses on Guernsey as a central location where island hopping is part of a potential tourist attraction, and the second is a short case study on one of the Bailiwick's smaller islands where it becomes the centre in an archipelagic setting. Within these two case studies, two touristic portals are analysed in terms of offering a critique of how island hopping is branded and marketed with two contrasting yet interconnected settings.

Location and Dislocation

The Channel Islands are located just off the north coast of France in the Bay of St. Malo (see Figure 6.1). The islands are British, but not part of the United Kingdom, nor are they a part of the European Union. The Channel Islands comprise two bailiwicks: the Bailiwick of Jersey and the Bailiwick of Guernsey. The former has one main island, Jersey, along with several uninhabited reefs and small islets; and the latter includes the island of Guernsey along with several smaller islands, two of which have their own jurisdiction within the Bailiwick: Alderney and Sark.

The Bailiwick of Jersey is the most southern of the jurisdictions, and the island of Alderney (part of the Bailiwick of Guernsey) is the most northerly island and closest to both England and France. A further group of small islands called Chausey is also located to the southwest of the Channel Islands, although Chausey belongs to France; there are no direct commercial crossings to Chausey from the Channel Islands; one marine adventure business occasionally visits the location.

The Bailiwick of Guernsey comprises several islands. From large to small, the islands are Guernsey, Alderney, Sark, Herm, Brecqhou, Jethou and Lihou. Each of the islands is populated, except for Lihou, although it does have accommodation for special groups of visitors such as school students. There are also several uninhabited small islets and reefs, some of which are also included as tourist destinations (e.g., Burhou, where birdwatchers can view puffins and either stay in a small hut with very basic facilities, or take a cruise around the island). Each of the Bailiwick's populated islands is visible from Guernsey. Lihou is the closest to Guernsey and it takes just several minutes to cross the causeway to reach it at low tide. From Guernsey's capital, St. Peter Port, the islands of Herm and Jethou are the next closest, and it takes just a few minutes to make the 4.8 km journey by ferry to Herm (Jethou is privately leased). A short distance further are the islands of Sark and Brecqhou (the islands form the fief of Sark), which are only accessible by boat (tourists must travel to Brecqhou from Sark), except for the owners of the Brecqhou island tenement (landholding) who travel to and from the island by helicopter. Much further away is Alderney, which is accessible by air or boat from Guernsey.

The Channel Islands belonged to the Duchy of Normandy at the time of the Norman conquest of England in 1066. In 1204, the Channel Islands maintained their allegiance to their "Norman" ruler, King John of England, even though he lost the Duchy of Normandy to King Philip II of France. Thereafter, the Channel Islands developed their own unique system of government, were divided into two Bailiwicks, and are nowadays referred to as British Crown Dependencies. Due to their very close proximity to France, they were the only part of the British Isles to have been occupied by German forces from 1940 to 1945 during World War II.

As British Crown Dependencies, the Bailiwicks of Jersey and Guernsey have a Lieutenant Governor for each bailiwick, who is Her Majesty's personal representative. Three of the main islands in the Bailiwick of Guernsey are administered by Guernsey: Lihou, Herm and Jethou. Of these islands, Herm and Jethou are leased, and only Lihou and Herm are open to visitors. Two of the Bailiwick's islands have their own administration: Alderney and Sark.

The centrality of the island of Guernsey, as represented by the island's size and population (Table 6.1), as well as being a political and administrative hub for the Bailiwick, is reflected by the location of its "sister islands". That is, from Guernsey there are views of all the other main Channel Islands, and some are particularly visible from Guernsey's capital, St. Peter Port. While some of the most distant islands can be seen on a clear day, most visible are Herm, Jethou and Sark (Brecqhou is in front of Sark and difficult to discern). Alderney and Jersey, while much further away, are also visible from Guernsey on clear days. Such views offer the tourist a visual reminder that Guernsey is at the heart of the Channel Islands, and that the other islands are within easy reach. Moreover, while the main Channel Islands have been mentioned already, the island-hopping tourist is also able to visit several other smaller Channel Islands and islets, which include Green Island (Jersey), Mont Saint Michel (France) and Burhou (Alderney). There are also several forts built on rocks and islets around Jersey, Guernsey and Alderney, and even Castle Cornet in St. Peter Port in Guernsey was once an islet until a harbour wall was built connecting it to the mainland.

Table 6.1   Population of the Bailiwick of Guernsey, 2011

Population Count	Number
Guernsey (including Herm, Jethou and Lihou)	62,915
Alderney	2,111
Sark (including Brecqhou)	591
Total	65, 617

Source: International Covenant on Civil and Political Rights (2012, p. 35).

Island Hopping and Guernsey

"VisitGuernsey" is the brand name of Guernsey's government-supported tourism agency. VisitGuernsey is physically located in St. Peter Port, Guernsey's capital, within the island's Information Centre, but much of its promotional activities are undertaken through its comprehensive website and print media. While the Information Centre is the responsibility of the Department of Culture and Leisure (within the States of Guernsey: the island's legislative assembly), VisitGuernsey and tourism are the responsibility of the Department of Commerce and Employment (States of Guernsey, 2013a; 2013b).

The VisitGuernsey brand was launched in 2004 (TravelMole, 2004), and has since led the promotion of Guernsey's tourism industry. The brand's online portal offers freely available information and resources that provide much information on visiting Guernsey as well as promoting the island's tourist industry more broadly, whether through web pages, downloadable files or print media (VisitGuernsey, 2012–13; 2013d). As noted by the Director of Marketing and Tourism, which is a part of the Department of Commerce and Employment, "VisitGuernsey is engaged in 'destination marketing': a method concerned with making people want to come to Guernsey, rather than promoting any one hotel or group. The States of Guernsey are not a tour operator, nor a hotelier. VisitGuernsey's job is to raise Guernsey's profile as a destination" (Elliott, 2011, para. 4). What is important in this profile of the agency is that VisitGuernsey's purpose is to market Guernsey as a "destination", and a study of its online marketing media offers insight into how the notion of island hopping is presented as an important part of Guernsey's top-down tourism promotion endeavour.

At the time of writing this chapter, VisitGuernsey offered some data on performance figures for 2012 and the year to date in 2013, as shown in Table 6.2 (VisitGuernsey, 2013c). With a resident Bailiwick population of about 66,000, the number of visitors to Guernsey across a range of categories shows the island as a significant visitor destination, whether for leisure, business or private visitors. In connection with travel to Guernsey from within the Channel Islands, and showing an aspect of the island hopping theme, of the total number, 13% travelled from Jersey (VisitGuernsey, 2013c).

Table 6.2   Visitor economy performance in 2012

Staying Visitors	191,700	Down 2.2%
Staying Business Visitors	49,100	Down 3.9%
Leisure Day Visits	42,900	Down 10.3%
Visiting Friends and Relatives	49,300	Down 20%
Business Day Visits	33,900	Up 1.1%

Source: VisitGuernsey (2013c).

As part of its marketing exercise, VisitGuernsey has created a brand in several ways, including a name and a logo, and it is with these two facets of the organisation that the discussion now offers a critical analysis of island hopping from the Guernsey perspective. As Freire (2009) comments, "today it is argued that not only should products and services develop a system of brand management focused on their identity, which helps develop a coherent execution, but places should also develop a similar brand management system" (p. 420). Indeed, Guernsey does not rely on potential tourists finding the island and its neighbouring islands solely through the activities of professionals working in the tourist industry, but it has established a part of its governmental structure to ensure that the places it has to offer are marketed as destinations in ways that a single operator might not be able or willing to do. As part of this process, Guernsey has developed a brand for its tourism marketing, and as part of this publicity exercise, the notion of island and archipelagic destinations are revealed as pivotal tropes.

As a brand name, "VisitGuernsey" can be interpreted in several ways. The compound nature of the two words creates a blended term that is especially practical in the internet age where web addresses often comprise combined words and offer a new way of adding meaning to brands. The design of this linguistic marker, along with its component parts, gives the brand a distinct visual and semantic meaning. The first part of the term "VisitGuernsey" has tourism at its core. While the word "visit" denotes movement, the use of the term preceding an island location such as Guernsey, which has a long history of tourism, immediately implies a touristic meaning. Even if one were to think of "visiting" Guernsey for business or agricultural purposes, to name two of Guernsey's better-known industries, there might either be aspects of the visit that could be included within a broader touristic interpretation, or information offered by VisitGuernsey that might be of interest to such a visitor. "VisitGuernsey" is therefore a linguistic logo, a blended brand name and a phrase that stands for marketing tourism in Guernsey.

The brand name "VisitGuernsey" is visually and textually promoted with the addition of a brand logo (Plate 6.1), which VisitGuernsey has made available as a download for in-house and commercial use within the Guernsey tourist industry (Department of Commerce and Employment, 2007). The text of the VisitGuernsey logo offers several levels of meaning. There are four words, each using uppercase letters: Guernsey, Herm, Sark and Alderney. These are the names of the Bailiwick of Guernsey's four largest islands. On the logo, the word "Guernsey" is depicted in a larger size font than the names of the other three islands, and it is positioned on the top of two lines of text. The names of the other three islands are shown on the second (lower) line of text and are in a slightly smaller uppercase font. The logic for depicting the islands' names in this order is based on the signification of Guernsey as the Bailiwick's largest island, with Herm, Sark and Alderney being the next closest in distance to Guernsey respectively. Rather than listing the islands in order of size or alphabetically, the use of a textual logo that incorporates a symbolic representation of the geography of the four islands offers some recognition of the Bailiwick as an archipelago setting with the logo emulating its geographic location. Such visual representation would clearly be understood by those with prior knowledge of the geography of the islands; and for those who do not, it would help establish a sense of geographic location between the islands as part of the brand. VisitGuernsey, therefore, promotes not only the Bailiwick's largest island, as emphasised in the logo by its dominant position, but also the other main islands in the Bailiwick of Guernsey. In this context, island hopping is an inherent trope of VisitGuernsey's branding exercise, and reinforced linguistically through the use of island names, and visually by representing island locations symbolically in a logo. While "visual stimuli are a critical part of any branding strategy", and "may be effective because they are learned faster and remembered significantly longer than verbal stimuli" (Henderson, Cote, Leong and Schmitt, 2003, pp. 297–98; also Erdelyi and Kleinbard, 1978), what is particularly distinct about the VisitGuernsey logo is that it offers a calculated blending of text and design. As such, Guernsey has developed a logo "that project[s] key elements of the destination's image" (Blain, Levy and Ritchie 2005, p. 328). In other words, the island of Guernsey is seen as a hub in close proximity to several other islands, which collectively comprise a political jurisdiction.

Herm, Sark and Alderney each have their own tourism marketing brands and web portals (see VisitChannelIslands, 2013), and VisitGuernsey offers a Bailiwick-wide promotion of the four main islands. Moreover, while the website focuses on Guernsey as a tourist destination, it does present the island as a hub for visiting its neighboring islands. For example, it promotes this trope with the following: "Discover Guernsey's 'sister islands' that make up the Bailiwick: Alderney, Sark and Herm, each Island has a very unique and special character, offering a variety of different environments to enjoy and in which to relax" (VisitGuernsey, 2013d, para. 2). Furthermore, the colour of the logo adds to the archipelagic branding. That is, while the text uses a white font, the background, when printed in colour, is light blue (for monochrome it is black). The use of blue as a background can be interpreted as signifying the sea that surrounds the islands and helps locate the Bailiwick of Guernsey as an archipelago.

The island hopping theme is embedded in VisitGuernsey's raison d'être. As well as being particularly visible in branding and marketing content, the organisation has published a *Travel agent training guide* (VisitGuernsey, 2006) in which it provides "tips on how to sell Guernsey and her islands of Sark, Herm and Alderney". In one section of the guide, the following points are especially relevant to this chapter and offer several themes that enmesh Guernsey as a destination of islands:

> "Because there is a flight or a sea journey, people feel that they have reached 'different shores' – quite literally."

> "Day trips or longer stays to our beautiful sister Islands of Herm (20 minutes away) and Sark (40 minutes away)."

> "Experience and learn of Guernsey's rich heritage from neolithic tombs, to the island's seafaring history over time; from WWII museums to the former residence of the writer Victor Hugo. So many things to see and do."

> "Children on holiday here have to suffer crabbing in rock pools, playing on the sands, boat trips to see the puffins parading off the coast of Herm island."

> "The islands of Herm and Sark are car-free" (VisitGuernsey, 2006).

The physicality of existing in an archipelagic setting is emphasized with various references to the sea and travel. This is especially significant for all visitors as they must travel by air or sea from their departure point to reach Guernsey. The sea trope is also evident in terms of making a journey to one of the "sister islands", two of which are "car-free". Furthermore, the activity of taking day-trips is mentioned in the guide as a way of promoting Guernsey in the broader context of the Bailiwick of Guernsey, the Channel Islands and France. Indeed, as noted in Table 6.3, nearly half of all visitors to the Bailiwick chose the destination because of the location's "sister islands".

Table 6.3   Reasons for choosing Guernsey

Feature	%
Natural beauty	81.2%
Walking	54.2%
Sister islands	45.8%
Food	44.2%

Source: VisitGuernsey (2013c).

The *Travel agent training guide* emphasises key island-centric tropes as a way of promoting the islands. The notion of travel is fundamental, not only to reach the islands themselves, but also to travel between them. Here, the notion of liminality is evident in the process of departing, traveling and arriving, which might be interpreted as not only offering a journey to a location "betwixt and between the categories of ordinary social life" (Turner, 1974, p. 53), but also as part of a ritual process.

In terms of actual tourist numbers, during the winter month of January 2012, passenger departures from Guernsey by sea were 5,800, about 10% of the 53,413 air departures; but, in the peak summer month of August, sea departures were recorded at 91,230 and air departures at 90,148 (VisitGuernsey, 2013c). The figures for air and sea departures during August are shown in Table 6.4 and Table 6.5, which also depict destinations. Such a difference in numbers helps show the importance of the summer months in travel, especially when some of the islands in the Bailiwick are only accessible by sea. Furthermore, in 2012, there were 39,299 air departures from Guernsey to Alderney, 143,908 air departures to Jersey, and 100,004 sea departures to Jersey (see Table 6.5 for the full figures for August) (VisitGuernsey, 2013c).

Table 6.4   Air departures from Guernsey during August 2012

Destination	Passengers
Birmingham	2,795
Bournemouth	5
Bristol	3,494
East Midlands	3,986
Exeter	2,257
Gatwick	35,008
Manchester	7,444
Norwich	319
Southampton	13,206
Stansted	2,925
Other UK	50
UK Total	**71,489**
Guernsey	140
Alderney	4,990
Jersey	11,612
Channel Island Total	**16,742**
Dinard	532
Geneva	2
Zurich	7
Other international	1,376
International Total	**1,917**
Total	**90,148**

Source: VisitGuernsey (2014).

Table 6.5   Sea departures from Guernsey during August 2012

Destination	Passengers
Dielette (Flamanville)	3,327
Herm	15,765
Sark	9,734
Jersey	19,265
St. Malo	15,889
Poole	25,028
Portsmouth	2,222
Total	**91,230**

Source: VisitGuernsey (2014).

The trope of island hopping is especially evident in the content of the VisitGuernsey website, which even includes a link to "Sister Islands and Day Trips" (VisitGuernsey, 2013b). The "sister islands" are noted with the following summary: "Guernsey is the perfect launch pad to explore neighbouring Bailiwick islands and beyond" (VisitGuernsey, 2013b, para. 1). Five locations are included with links to further information: Herm, Sark, Alderney, Jersey and France. Keeping with the layout of the brand's logo, the "sister islands" are introduced in order of proximity to Guernsey. The "beyond" locations are Jersey, the other Bailiwick in the Channel Islands, and France, both of which are introduced in order of proximity to Guernsey. The summary offered to describe these locations notes that:

> Herm and Sark offer a traffic-free paradise for those who long for the quiet life. Alderney will welcome you with open arms and Jersey is perfect if you want a more cosmopolitan day out. Further afield, France offers a whole host of opportunities. Explore ancient picturesque towns or just sit and watch the world go by in one of the many cafes and restaurants. (VisitGuernsey, 2013b, para. 2)

In industry terms, "travel between the islands in an archipelago is critical to their tourism development" (Bardolet and Sheldon, 2008, p. 902), and the promotion of Guernsey's neighbouring islands offers not only an obligation by VisitGuernsey to represent each of the Bailiwick's islands, but it also helps brand the location as an archipelago that might be visited for this very reason. Moreover, VisitGuernsey's website includes a link showing potential ways for tourists of getting to the Bailiwick, and the trope of island hopping is included in the promotional information: "As well as discovering what Guernsey has to offer, the island is also the gateway to its neighbouring Bailiwick islands Alderney, Sark and Herm as well as Jersey and the Normandy and Brittany coastlines of France" (VisitGuernsey, 2013a, para. 4). Here, the island of Guernsey is expressed as the hub for the Bailiwick's smaller islands, as well as a possible transit point for visiting Jersey and France. The information on the website is also available in French and German.

Each of the links to the "sister island" locations takes the reader to a wealth of information, resources and further links to official tourism websites. What this part of the VisitGuernsey website does is to offer the reader a further incentive for visiting Guernsey. While attracting visitors to Guernsey is clearly the main objective of VisitGuernsey, the additional level of attraction offered in the co-marketing of other islands in the Bailiwick and Jersey, as well as "mainland" France, creates a brand – a type of "territorial assemblage" (Deleuze and Guattari, 1987, p. 79) of islands – where the notion of islands is clearly a targeted level of attraction. Indeed, in such a context "visitors are encouraged to explore and sample different island constituents of the territory; there is often a deliberate attempt at product differentiation by the tourism authorities that seeks to appeal to different tourist types, and to suit different pockets" (Baldacchino and Ferreira, 2013, p. 85).

The focus of this part of the chapter now moves to the island of Sark. While the island hopping paradigm could be explored from any of the Channel Islands, and beyond, for the purpose of this discussion I will now focus on Sark as one "sister island" example. Sark has its own legislative assembly, as does Alderney, and it is also an island that must be accessed by sea (except in emergencies when the neighboring private island of Brecqhou has made a helicopter available if needed).

The word "Sark" has a double meaning in the Channel Islands in terms of what island or islands it refers to. Just as the word "Guernsey" can refer to different island locations, Sark too is both an island and an island binary that includes the neighbouring island of Brecqhou. As Brecqhou is a private island, it has not traditionally been a tourist destination, although from 2012 the owners, billionaire brothers David and Frederick Barclay, opened up the island to visitors who were staying at one of the four hotels that they own on Sark. Such visitors make the 15-minute trip between the islands during a three-hour excursion to visit its gardens. While the two islands are just metres apart, the journey is made by boat between the islands' harbours. A trip to Brecqhou offers visitors a final part of a potential island hopping tour. That is, visitors must travel to Guernsey in order to get a boat to Sark; and they must then travel by boat from Sark to Brecqhou in order to visit the latter island's gardens, but only if they have fulfilled the condition of staying for two nights or more at Sark Islands Hotels.

The official website for Sark offers a range of information on the island, including much about what is available for the visiting tourist (Isle of Sark, 2013b). Visitors to Sark must travel by sea, whether by the commercial boat that makes several trips each day, or by private boat. The closest commercial sea route between any of the other Channel Islands, with the exception of Brecqhou, is from Guernsey (St. Peter Port Harbour). With a journey time of about 55 minutes, there are multiple daily sailings during the summer, and a Monday to Saturday service operates during the winter months (Isle of Sark, 2013a). This route offers visitors the opportunity to stay on Guernsey before or after their trip to Sark, where Sark can be either the main destination or part of a visit to other islands nearby.

With Sark as a destination, there are several ways of getting to the island from another one of the Channel Islands, or from further afield. There is a weekly service to Sark from the most distant of the Channel Islands, Alderney, and between April and September there is a passenger service to Sark from Jersey, which takes about 50 minutes and originates in either Granville or Carteret in Normandy in the north of France. From this perspective, while Sark might at first be viewed as relatively isolated, its sea links to Guernsey, Alderney and Jersey offer a route to locations further afield. Visitors from the other Channel Islands may also travel by air to, from and between the islands of Jersey, Guernsey and Alderney, but in order to reach Sark they must finish their journey by sea.

A sea trope has already been discussed earlier in connection with VisitGuernsey marketing, and a similar theme also emerges in connection with Sark, especially when considering the process of having to travel by sea to and from Sark. As a small island, Sark has championed its lack of cars or planes as part of its potential appeal to visitors, which therefore necessitates travel to the island by boat: "There are no cars on Sark, only tractors, bikes or horses and carriages. The pace of life is leisurely and relaxed. The island provides a haven away from the noisy, everyday world; the perfect place to get away from it all. The views from the coastal headlands are magnificent" (Isle of Sark, 2013b, para. 4). As suggested in this quote, Sark treasures its unique lifestyle that is mostly a world away from some of the other tourist centres in the Channel Islands. But visitors must travel to the island by boat and the island makes much of the journey and other connections with the sea when it promotes itself:

> Sark is approached by boat. The visitors' first sight of the island is the towering cliffs topped by steeply sloping common land, called *cotils*, covered in bluebells, thrift and daisies in the spring, then turning green, and finally bronze in the Autumn. Seabirds wheel over the bays, and sometimes in late spring boat passengers are able to see puffins bobbing about on the surface of the sea. Dolphins may also make the occasional appearance. (Isle of Sark, 2013b, para. 2)

Indeed, the importance of the sea for Sarkese and visitors is remembered each year with a "Sea Service", which "reminds residents of the island's total dependency on the skill of those who man the vessels upon which Sark's very existence depends" (This is Guernsey, 2010, para. 3). Travel by sea, therefore, is part of the experience of visiting Sark, and it is an island where the sea is truly a part of island life. In this setting, travel by sea must be made via one of the other Channel Islands, although visitors have a choice of how long they stay in the other islands. The variety of different options available for sea transportation also offers visitors a choice of travelling to one or more of the other Channel Islands as part of the same island-hopping experience.

Discussion

Island hopping is a key part of government-sponsored tourism branding in Guernsey. However, closer analysis of the ways in which island hopping are included in tourism publicity offers examples of power and contestation. While offering a media-oriented approach to website analysis, and discussing several key themes that are at the heart of VisitGuernsey's marketing campaign, of particular concern for this chapter has been VisitGuernsey's branding exercise, which reveals an underpinning archipelagic-focused objective of marketing not only the island of Guernsey, but also the Bailiwick of Guernsey as a whole, which includes several smaller or 'sister' islands. This approach to branding the Bailiwick of Guernsey is especially evident in VisitGuernsey's logo in terms of its image and textual design that is symbolic of the Bailiwick's geography as an archipelagic jurisdiction within the Channel Islands.

The VisitGuernsey branding exercise necessarily includes themes that offer visitors further levels of island and archipelagic awareness, including day-trips or longer excursions to Guernsey's "sister islands", where the notion of travel and sea are expressed on many levels of marketing. This is all part of VisitGuernsey's vision in its destination marketing, where not only the island of Guernsey is celebrated in terms of what it has to offer visitors, but also the attraction of combining a visit to one or more of Guernsey's other islands, or even further afield to a neighbouring jurisdiction, Jersey, or to France. For example, Herm and Sark are not only branded as "car-free" and having a wealth of other natural and cultural attractions, but the other Channel Islands in general are marketed in terms of travel. That is, in order to reach the other islands, it is important to consider the modes of transport, which for Guernsey, Alderney and Jersey include travel by sea or plane, but for Herm, Sark and Brecqhou travel must be made by boat (visitors can walk to Lihou at low tide), the latter of which requires two boat journeys (from Guernsey and then from Sark). Hence, the key points included above have shown that much is made in tourism branding exercises in terms of stressing the interconnections between the islands, which reinforces a sense of archipelagic identity, primarily within the Bailiwick of Guernsey, but also including Jersey as a further option within the Channel Islands. This notion is strengthened when considering the fact that most of the Channel Islands are in view of one another, and from St. Peter Port in Guernsey there is a panoramic view of many "sister islands" that helps situate Guernsey as a location of islands.

VisitGuernsey includes the island of Guernsey and its 'sister islands' in its marketing as part of a Bailiwick-centred approach to tourism branding, which embraces the potential of island hopping options as part of the tourist experience. Yet, the content of its website dwells mainly on the island of Guernsey, presumably because it is the largest and most populated island in the Bailiwick. Just as the VisitGuernsey logo gives prominence to the island of Guernsey in terms of its visual representation of the archipelago by its graphic dominance, so does the content of its website, where the "sister islands" are introduced on a separate webpage and have much less content in comparison to Guernsey. The VisitGuernsey logo, therefore, reinforces a hierarchy of islands in terms of their political influence, distance from the island of Guernsey, and physical size.

The VisitGuernsey brand is an example of jurisdictional advertising on several territorial levels. The Bailiwick of Guernsey's main islands are promoted (Guernsey, Alderney, Sark and Herm), and within the brand there are three separate jurisdictions (Guernsey, Alderney and Sark). Herm is leased by the States of Guernsey, and while it too has its own tourism website (http://www.herm.com), it is included in the VisitGuernsey brand as an island that has tourism at its core and is administered by Guernsey. But while VisitGuernsey offers a "sister islands" component to its marketing, it actually gives equal attention to these islands as it does to Jersey (a neighbouring jurisdiction) and France (a neighbouring country). As part of a potential island hopping context, Jersey also has its own significant tourist industry. It seems, therefore, that island hopping is a key feature in VisitGuernsey's branding in that Jersey is just as important as Guernsey's "sister islands" themselves, but only in web content. The inclusion of France in the marketing drive offers a further day-trip option as part of a possible multiple destination experience.

Sark too has its own website marketing dedicated to tourism. From this viewpoint, Sark focuses on itself (of course), and the other islands in its Bailiwick. Jersey and France also receive some promotion, but not as tourism destinations. With Herm and Alderney also offering similar tourism promotion, the four islands that are included as part of the VisitGuernsey brand are actually in competition with each other. The notion of island hopping may, on one level of analysis, offer a degree of attraction to an archipelago; but, when an archipelago like the Channel Islands is divided into several jurisdictions, each with its own tourism industry, a sense of competition unfolds. As such, the Channel Islands are not usually branded collectively because they are politically separate, and while VisitGuernsey offers a degree of Bailiwick-wide publicity, the island of Guernsey and its politically separate "sister islands" (as well as Herm) are in actual fact in direct competition with each other, and as such the notion of island hopping is simultaneously celebrated and contested.

The diverse jurisdictional context of the Channel Islands allows each territory to market itself against each other, yet at the same time they embrace the notion of potential island hopping as a further way of attracting tourists to the islands. From the perspective of Jersey, just as VisitGuernsey includes this other Channel Island bailiwick as an option for an island hopping day trip, so does the Jersey Tourism website (http://www.jersey.com) include a page dedicated to day trips to the other Channel Islands and France. However, the information provided about the available day trip destinations shows only the means of transport (i.e., boat or airline) for traveling from Jersey.

Conclusion

The Channel Islands offer examples of potential island hopping within tourist publicity, but with travel across waters and between islands divided by geographies of space (land and sea), as well as governance (with the existence of different jurisdictions). Guernsey's political system has in part helped determine VisitGuernsey's branding exercise. Guernsey comprises two identities: the island and the Bailiwick. The States of Guernsey markets both entities through VisitGuernsey, and some of the Bailiwick's other islands market themselves through their own tourism marketing. There is clearly a symbiotic relationship between the islands, where Guernsey offers a focal point, yet the smaller islands are able to exert their own island identity in a process that both complements and competes with VisitGuernsey.

In this context, a study of the VisitGuernsey brand in a discussion of island hopping in touristic locations helps show not only the importance of marketing a collection of islands, but also how islands can become part of an island identity. For Guernsey, therefore, both the island and the Bailiwick, islands are part of its political history, heritage and contemporary cultural identity, and in this location, the tourism industry helps foreground some of the underpinning themes that make these locations so popular for visitors in the first place.

References

Askegaard, S., and Kjeldgaard, D. (2007). Here, there, and everywhere: place branding and gastronomical globalisation in a macro-marketing perspective. *Journal of Macromarketing*, 27(2), 138–47.

Baldacchino, G. (2005). Successful small-scale manufacturing from small islands: comparing firms benefiting from locally available raw material input. *Journal of Small Business and Entrepreneurship*, 18(1), 21–38.

Baldacchino, G. (2010a). Island brands and 'the island' as a brand: insights from immigrant entrepreneurs on Prince Edward Island. *International Journal of Entrepreneurship and Small Business*, 9(4), 378–93.

Baldacchino, G. (2010b). Islands and beers: toasting a discriminatory approach to small island manufacturing. *Asia Pacific Viewpoint*, 51(1), 61–72.

Baldacchino, G. (2012). The lure of the island: a spatial analysis of power relations. *Journal of Marine and Island Cultures*, 1(1), 55–62.

Baldacchino, G. and Ferreira, E.C.D. (2013). Competing notions of diversity in archipelago tourism: transport logistics, official rhetoric and inter-island rivalry in the Azores. *Island Studies Journal*, 8(1), 84–104.

Bardolet, E., and Sheldon, P.J. (2008). Tourism in archipelagos: Hawai'i and the Balearics. *Annals of Tourism Research*, 35(4), 900–23.

Blain, C., Levy, S.E., and Ritchie, J.R.B. (2005). Destination branding: insights and practices from destination management organisations. *Journal of Travel Research*, 43(4), 328–38.

Butler, R.W. (1993). Tourism development in small islands: past influences and future directions. In D. Lockhart, D. Drakakis-Smith and J. Schembri (eds), *The development process in small islands*, pp. 71–91. London: Routledge.

Deleuze, G., and Guattari, F. (1987). *A thousand plateaus*. New York: Continuum.

DeLoughrey, E. (2001). 'The litany of islands, the rosary of archipelagos': Caribbean and Pacific Archipelagraphy. *Ariel: Review of International English Literature*, 32(1), 21–51.

Department of Commerce and Employment. (2007). *Brand guidelines*. St. Peter Port: Department of Commerce and Employment. Retrieved from http://www.guernseytrademedia.com/files/managed/pdf/guidelines.pdf

Elliott, C. (2011). Tourism in Guernsey: a response. Retrieved from http://www.businesslife.co/Features.aspx?id=tourism-in-guernsey-a-response

Erdelyi, M.H., and Kleinbard, J. (1978). Has Ebbinghaus decayed with time? The growth of recall (hypermnesia) over days. *Journal of Experimental Psychology: Human Learning and Memory*, 4(4), 275–81.

Freire, J.R. (2009). 'Local people': a critical dimension for place brands. *Journal of Brand Management*, 16(7), 420–38.

Grydehøj, A. (2008). Branding from above: generic cultural branding in Shetland and other islands. *Island Studies Journal*, 3(2), 175–98.

Grydehøj, A. (2010). Uninherited heritage: tradition and heritage production in Shetland, Åland and Svalbard. *International Journal of Heritage Studies*, 16(1–2), pp. 77–89.

Guthunz, U., and von Krosigk, F. (1996). Tourism development in small islands states: from Mirab to Tourab. In L. Briguglio, B. Archer, J. Jafari, and G. Wall (eds), *Sustainable tourism in islands and small states: Issues and policies*, pp. 18–35. London: Pinter.

Hayward, P. and Kuwahara, S. (2013). Divergent trajectories: environment, heritage and tourism in Tanegashima, Mageshima and Yakushima. *Journal of Marine and Island Cultures*, 2(1), 29–38.

Henderson, P.W., Cote, J.A., Leong, S.M., and Schmitt, B. (2003). Building strong brands in Asia: selecting the visual components of image to maximize brand strength. *International Journal of Research in Marketing*, 20(4), 297–313.

International Covenant on Civil and Political Rights. (2012). Seventh periodic report from the United Kingdom, the British Overseas Territories, the Crown Dependencies. London: Ministry of Justice.

Isle of Sark. (2013a). How to get here. Retrieved from http://www.sark.co.uk/how-to-get-here

Isle of Sark. (2013b). Welcome to the beautiful island of Sark. Retrieved from http://www.sark.co.uk

Ivanovic, M. (2008). *Cultural tourism*. Cape Town: Juta.

Johnson, H. (2012). 'Genuine Jersey': branding and authenticity in a small island culture. *Island Studies Journal*, 7(2), 235–58.

Kavaratzis, M. (2007). From city marketing to city branding: an interdisciplinary analysis with reference to Amsterdam, Budapest and Athens. PhD thesis. Groningen: University of Groningen.

Kelman, I. (2007). Sustainable livelihoods from natural heritage on islands. *Island Studies Journal*, 2(1), 101–14.

Khamis, S. (2010). An image worth bottling: the branding of King Island cloud juice. *International Journal of Entrepreneurship and Small Business*, 9(4), 434–46.

Khamis, S. (2011). 'Lundy's hard work': branding, biodiversity and a 'unique island experience'. *Shima*, 5(1), 1–23.

Leseure, M. (2010). Exploitation versus exploration in island economies: a brand diagnostic perspective. *International Journal of Entrepreneurship and Small Business*, 9(4), pp. 463–80.

Lichrou, M, O'Malley, L., and Patterson, M. (2010). Narratives of a tourism destination: local particularities and their implications for place marketing and branding. *Place Branding and Public Diplomacy*, 6(2), 134–44.

Lindlof, T.R., and Taylor, B.C. (2002). *Qualitative communication research methods*. 3rd edn. Thousand Oaks CA: Sage.

Pounder, P. (2010). Branding: a Caribbean perspective on rum manufacturing competitiveness. *International Journal of Entrepreneurship and Small Business*, 9(4), 394–406.

Reddy, M., and Singh, G. (2010). Branding of Fiji's bottled water: edging into sustainable consumption. *International Journal of Entrepreneurship and Small Business*, 9(4), 447–62.

States of Guernsey. (2013a). Commerce and Employment. Retrieved from http://www.gov.gg/article/1709/Commerce-and-Employment

States of Guernsey. (2013b). Culture and leisure. Retrieved from http://www.gov.gg/cultureleisure

States of Guernsey. (2013c). VisitGuernsey. Retrieved from http://gov.gg/article/2328/VisitGuernsey

This is Guernsey. (2010). Sea service was so stirring. Retrieved from http://www.thisisguernsey.com/latest/2010/08/21/sea-service-was-so-stirring

Topsø, K.L. (Ed.) (2012). *From one island to another: a celebration of island connections*. Nexø, Denmark: Centre for Regional and Tourism Research.

TravelMole. (2004). VisitGuernsey to be officially launched. Retrieved from http://www.travelmole.com/news_feature.php?news_id=100457&c=setreg&region=2

Turner, V.W. (1974). *Dramas, fields and metaphors*. Ithaca NY: Cornell University Press.

VisitChannelIslands. (2013). The Channel Islands. Retrieved from http://www.visitchannelislands.com

VisitGuernsey. (2006). *Travel agent training guide*. St. Martin: VisitGuernsey. Retrieved from http://www.guernseytrademedia.com/files/managed/pdf/holidays20closer20to20home_no20partners.pdf

VisitGuernsey. (2012–13). *Guernsey: A visitor's guide for 2013*. Retrieved from http://ebrochure.submarine.gg/vg-en/files/assets/common/downloads/VisitGuernsey%202013.pdf

VisitGuernsey. (2013a). Getting here. Retrieved from http://www.visitguernsey.com/getting-here

VisitGuernsey. (2013b). Sister islands and day trips. Retrieved from http://www.visitguernsey.com/sister-islands-and-day-trips

VisitGuernsey. (2013c). Trade and media. Retrieved from http://www.guernseytrademedia.com/blog/file.axd?file=VISIT.GUERNSEY.MAY.SEMINAR.2013.pdf

VisitGuernsey. (2013d). Welcome to VisitGuernsey. Retrieved from http://www.visitguernsey.com

VisitGuernsey. (2014). Facts and figures. Retrieved from http://www.guernseytrademedia.com/marketing-guernsey/facts-figures/default.aspx

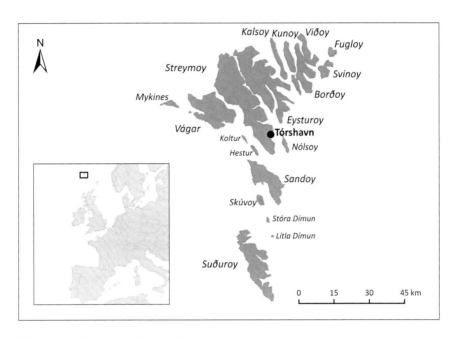

Figure 7.1   The Faroe Islands, Denmark

Chapter 7
Remote yet Close: The Question of Accessibility in the Faroe Islands

Rosemarie Ankre and Per-Åke Nilsson

Introduction

When approaching the Faroe Islands from the air, you are greeted by an amazing picture of a last outpost in the ocean. It is a lush, treeless, harshly cut archipelago, thousands of kilometres from the nearest mainland in the middle of the North Sea; northwest of Scotland and halfway between Iceland and Norway. Coming by boat from Denmark and Iceland, it is sometimes a turbulent and testing 44-hour sea voyage, interrupted only by a stop in Shetland. Occasionally, the sea offers a sunny leisure break where one can enjoy the views over the North Sea and its surging water, and eventually the horizon imagined contours of an exciting and inviting collection of rocky islands that shimmers in green and grey:

> Superb glaciated landscape with improbably steep slopes. Little flat land. Local society unified and resolutely Faroese, not Danish, with own language, etc. Built heritage, down to the grass roofs, reasonably protected, certainly cherished. Most tourists adventurous and well-informed … If the numbers of cruise ships continue to grow rapidly, there may be problems with island carrying capacity. Quite rightly, tourists are expected to be like the Faroese, such as taking choppy ferries and hiking through any weather. The future could bring severe social and environmental impacts, but the Faroese are aware of the dangers and are debating solutions (National Geographic Travel webpage, 24 September 2013).

Islands offer something special in comparison to the mainland because one has to travel by boat or airplane to reach the destination. Therefore, to be detached from the mainland gives an important physical and psychological aspect to an island visit (Baum, 1998).

The Faroe Islands is an archipelago composed by eighteen islands with 1,100 km (687 miles) of coastline. At no time is one more than 5 km (3 miles) away from the ocean which of course has a major influence on the landscape (with its distinct lack of trees). But the sea is also the element which separates the islands from each other and creates different challenges regarding accessibility. The airport is, for example, located on one island while seaports are situated in another islands. How to get to the Faroe Islands is one issue, however, when one finally arrives at this particular destination, one has to consider how to access different parts of this 18-island archipelago.

Due to the recent development of various bridges and tunnels, some of the islands have been physically connected to each other and are thereby more accessible, while others can still be considered remote. This infrastructural development has basically transformed the archipelago into almost one sprawling, inter-connected land mass which raises questions how this change of accessibility may have transformed the Faroes as a tourist destination, how some islands are viewed as more distant than others, as well as how the lack of accessibility may be an asset (and not a hindrance) in tourism development. For example, Nordin (2005) suggests that transportation to and from islands in an archipelago is viewed differently by the permanent population, the representatives of tourism and recreation, and the representatives of conservation. Often, the interests of conserving different areas from human influence are opposed to the interests of decreasing isolation, getting access to attractive areas, and getting merchandise transported. Some areas of an archipelago may be easier to reach than others, depending on the presence, cost and frequency of ferries or bridges.

The aim of this chapter is to outline the possibilities and challenges of accessibility for the Faroe Islands, as witnessed in inter-island travel and the relationships to the neighbouring cluster of other islands. In the case of the Faroes, inter-island travel is mainly by car since most islands in the archipelago are connected to each other by a tunnel or a bridge. To some extent, inter-island travel also includes transportation by car-ferries. This situation is partly due to a conscious decentralisation policy in a territory where inter-island travel has become quite a necessity for the inhabitants, but also creates an appreciated experience for visitors.

Another challenge is the position of the Faroe Islands; the archipelago is relatively physically close to neighbouring countries (Iceland, Norway and Scotland), but mentally remote due to culture, traditions and to some extent language issues. According to Sandell (2001), social and cultural relationships (founded on childhood, experiences of school and associations, self-contemplation and upbringing) have an effect on how the individual perceives accessibility in the context of tourism and outdoor recreation. Hall and Boyd (2005) discuss how accessibility is constructed by social and physical dimensions. These include socio-cultural sanctions and legal ability to travel as well as the physical landscape and infrastructure, which also have influence on the ability to travel i.e. accessibility.

The Faroe Islands

The population of the Faroe Islands currently consists of about 48,000 people, of whom some 20,000 live in the metropolitan area surrounding the capital Torshavn on the island of Streymoy. Another 4,600 people live in Klaksvik, which is the second largest town in the Faroe Islands, located on the island of Bordoy. Since the financial crisis in the 1990s, almost 10,000 Faroese have migrated to Denmark (leading to a deficit of 2,200 women). In 2008, another financial crisis struck the Faroe Islands, and this has affected population growth negatively ever since. Long-term commuting to Norway for work (mostly by men) is common from 2–3 weeks up to 12–14 weeks. This is mainly within the oil and building industries, but also among seafarers and fishers; this has caused a skill shortage on the Faroe Islands. Every recent year, the Faroese population has decreased marginally by around 100 people, but the Government is concerned to make emigrant Faroese return, appealing to place identity and the landscape as important pull factors (Jennissen, 2007; Holm et al., 2012). According to Faroese politicians, the number one challenge is to urge young people to move back home after studying abroad. It is also possible to pursue tertiary education in Torshavn at the University of the Faroe Islands, which consists of two faculties and about 700 students.

Since 1948, the Faroe Islands have, together with Greenland, been a self-governing region of the Commonwealth of Denmark. It has its own Parliament (*Lagtinget*) and its own flag, stamps, anthem as well as banknotes, but uses Danish currency. The relationship to the outer world is sometimes labelled as both between and betwixt; there is a department of foreign affairs but no foreign policy. The Faroe Islands has no military force, but is a member of the military alliance NATO since foreign policy is managed by Denmark (Gaini, 2013). However, even though the Faroe Islands has established a fishing and trade agreement with the European Union, it is not (like Denmark) an EU member state (Ackrén, 2006).

The fishing industry is the most important source of income, followed by tourism and woolen garments. Nature-based tourism consists of trekking and bird- and whale watching. The peak tourism season is June to September. However, thanks to the tempering effect of the Gulf Stream, the harbours never freeze and the temperature in winter is moderate considering the high latitude; snowfall occurs, but is short-lived. The bird fauna of the Faroe Islands is dominated by birds attracted to open land and seabirds, where the Faroese puffins are significant and also part of the local food tradition. Only a few species of wild land mammals (e.g. hare, brown rat and the house mouse) are found in the Faroe Islands today, all introduced by humans. Grey seals are often seen around the shorelines, as well as various species of whale. Best known are the long-finned pilot whales (*grindval*) which are still hunted on the Faroe Islands. They are forced to the coast, and then driven up on land where the final killing causes public events almost similar to festivals (Proctor, 2013).

Accessibility of the Faroe Islands

To airborne visitors, the airport on the island of Vágar is the first contact with the Faroese archipelago. Even though the beauty of the surroundings is striking, the airport has an image of being very dangerous to land on, given its rather short runway (even though in 2011 it was extended from a frightening length of 1,250m to 1,799m). Once, then Danish Prime Minister, Anders Fogh Rasmussen, nearly crashed during a landing at this airport. The Faroese, however, do not accept the image of danger, as stated by representatives of the organisation Visit Faroe Islands: "The airport requires special pilots, not because of the runway but the weather and the surrounding mountains".

The airport, however, was not deliberately located at Vágar, with its fickle weather situation. It was the considerable distance to the city of Torshavn that convinced the occupying British troops to build the airbase on Vágar during World War II. In case of an attack, the location of the airport would decrease the impact. It was also a good place for the development of amphibious vehicles for use in the surrounding waters. When the United Kingdom finally withdrew its troops, the airport was mostly used by aero enthusiasts. Eventually, Vágar became a state-owned regular airport in 1963, run by the Atlantic Air Company which offers various regular (and mainly summer) flights to destinations including Billund, Bergen, London, Milan, Barcelona and Aalborg (Visit Torshavn webpage, 24 Oct. 2013).

Flights to Norway are normally not for visitors but for long-term commuting workers. However, international travel has developed to include an increasing tourism market: "Previously, the air company flew Faroese to Denmark, now they fly visitors to the Faroes", remembers Skuvdal (entrepreneur, Vestmanna Bird Watching). There are also regular daily flights to Kastrup Airport in Copenhagen, Denmark, and weekly regular flights to Reykjavik, Iceland, and optional flights to different places in Europe, most of them outgoing.

In 2011, a total of 124,856 passengers arrived to the Faroe Islands, 23,786 of them by boat (Figure 7.2). There are no figures about the share of visitors, but during the peak summer season the number of ferry passengers (roughly measured in an ocular way) is

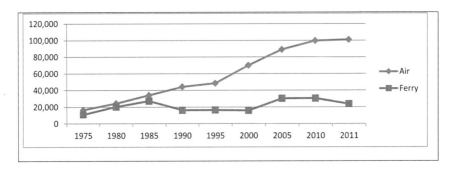

Figure 7.2   Arrivals to the Faroe Islands by air and ferry

Source: Statistics Faroe Islands (2014).

large. Of note, cruise tourism has increased and there are now about fifty ship calls during the peak season, mostly for Torshavn but also for Klaksvik and Runarvik (on the island of Eysturoy). For example, the cruise company P&O Cruises includes Torshavn as a port of call for tours to Iceland, the Faroes and Ireland in its *Cool Tours*. Also, Norwegian Cruise Line includes the port of Torshavn in its *North Sea Tour* which travels from Copenhagen to Great Britain, Shetlands, the Faroes, Iceland and Norway.

Only 19% of arrivals to the Faroes are by sea. Just like the situation at the airport, there is only one operator for outbound ferry transport: *Smyril Line*. The company has, apart from its home harbour in Torshavn, two ports to call: Hirtshals in northern Denmark, and Siglifjörður on the east coast of Iceland. Tours by ferry are bound for Iceland with a return the week after, thereby allowing for a 7-day stopover in Torshavn. During peak season, there are two tour stops a week. For those just heading for Iceland, there is an eight-hour stop in Torshavn on the north sailing and a six-hour stop on the south sailing (Smyril Line webpage, 2014). During peak season, it is not allowed to disembark, since the stops are much shorter.

During the stops at Torshavn harbour by *Smyril Line* when sailing north to Iceland, bus tours are arranged for one or two-hour tours, mostly to Eysturoy. Not far from the famous site of Kirkjubøur on Streymoy, there are a few organised boat trips to Hestur island, but only on request. There are also 5–7 daily departures from Torshavn to Runarvik on Nólsoy, and up to 7 daily departures from Klaksvik to Kalsoy. Moreover, there are boat tours (mostly for visitors) from the island Viðoy to the outermost islands to the north-east, Svínoy and Fugloy. Mykines Island, perhaps the most frequented island by visitors due to its puffin colony, is reached in summertime from the island Vágar. Also, helicopter tours can be arranged from twelve different departure points, managed by *Atlantic Helicopters* together with *Atlantic Airways*. There are regular helicopter tours three days a week to some of the islands, including transport of goods hooked underneath the helicopter. The company has 11 pilots and flies all the year round.

The islands (that are not connected by bridges, land or underwater tunnels) are connected by seven different ferry links, operated by the nationally owned transport company SSL. Thereby the islands Suduroy and Sandoy can be reached by car ferries while smaller boats operate the routes to the small islands. The longest route is between Torshavn and the southernmost island of Suduroy, with about 5,000 inhabitants. A big car ferry operates the trip, which takes over two hours. This meant periods of waiting, or in order to avoid that, good planning. The islands which only are accessible by ferries are also linked by means of small vessels, suitable for visitors during summer. SSL also runs bus routes between the populated villages in the Faroe Islands that are accessible with a motor vehicle (Faroese infrastructure webpage, 2014).

However, in summertime, most passengers are visitors with their own vehicles. With the improved roads and the extended tunnel system, it has become increasingly popular to visit and explore the Faroe Islands by car, either one's own with a camper or mobile home, but also by hiring a vehicle. It is often said that, due to the road facilities, the islands should be experienced by car. For example, the hotels in Torshavn and Klaksvik cooperate with the tourist information office tours by car from the airport. The landscape along the tour is magnificent and best appreciated in clear weather, which gives most visitors an unforgettable souvenir. This means that the location of the airport on a rather distant island has almost turned into a blessing. The information office, together with the hotels, arranges excursions by boat, bus or car for the airborne passengers. Since most visitors arrive by air, this is the most common way for the visitors to travel around. When marketing the Faroe Islands as a tourist destination, short distances have become an asset instead of a menace. Actually, the only complaint visitors may express is that the distances between the assets are too short, a complaint which may also be taken as a complement.

Domestic logistics of the Faroe Islands are dominated by an excellent road network (Visit Faroe Islands, 2014). Thereby 90% of the inhabitants can reach another island by car, and all islands (except for Streymoy and Eysturoy) are connected by a total of seventeen land tunnels. However, there is a bridge between Streymoy and Eysturoy, consequently called the 'Bridge over the Atlantic'. In the beginning, it was a small wooden bridge but today it is an impressive steel construction permitting vessels to pass. There are also two underwater tunnels, in addition to three bridges and seven ferry lines. In 1963, the first tunnel was completed to be followed by several more tunnels dispersed on seven of the eighteen islands. The tunnels vary in length from 220 to 3,240 meters where the most trafficked tunnels have two lanes. The island with the most tunnels is Kalsoy, which despite its small population of about 100 people, has a total of five single-laned tunnels. Except for land tunnels, there are two underwater tunnels; the first connects the islands of Vágoy and Stremoy, while the second connects the island of Bordoy (where Klaksvik is located) with Eysturoy. Naturally, the developed infrastructure is of great significance to local businesses and local population since accessibility has increased (Faroese infrastructure webpage, 2014). After the 5,000 meter connecting tunnel between the islands Vágar and Streymoy was built in 2002, the distance from Vágar to Torshavn decreased from 62 km to 45 km. However, the underwater tunnels are subject to tolls which imply that there are also costs to consider as a user of the road network.

Interestingly, like other small archipelago jurisdictions (e.g. Baldacchino and Ferreira, 2013), personal votes make it possible for candidates from small places to get into the Parliament of the Faroe Islands, since local people can be elected as representatives for the home island, not for a party. This has underpinned the establishment of the good road network and the numerous tunnels. Most of the unconnected islands are very small with a limited number of inhabitants; it may very well be, however, that they too will make and win the case for a fixed connection. For example, it has now been decided to start a pre-study for a tunnel from Streymoy to Sandoy with its 20 inhabitants. There are also future plans to connect the southern end of Eysturoy to Torshavn (Faroese Main Road Authority webpage, 2013).

Cold Water Tourism: A Cold Case?

"Why the Faroe Islands?" is a fair question to be asked by the tourism industry. In a 2001 survey, the answer to this question was 'once-in-a-lifetime' and that is probably still relevant (Rassing and Sørensen, 2001). Moreover, the tourist information officer confirms that visitors always mention *nature* when asked about their experience of the archipelago. Often, they also add *exotic* or *different*. The marketing also focuses on semi-tangible assets like *culture, cuisine, film, music, Faroese identity, friendly people,* or simply *unknown.* Yet, to be an archipelago in cold water is not a tourist magnet for most people (Butler, 2006; Nilsson, 2008). It lacks the sun and fun concept, and to get to the destination is often time-consuming and inconvenient. The present representatives of the Faroe Islands tourism industry identify several challenges. There is a high seasonality with very short shoulder seasons, tourism establishments are small-scale, and facilities are not limited in absolute terms. Also, accommodation costs at hotels and living costs are high. Local residents are not always prepared to see the benefits of tourism, even if they do not feel disturbed by the visitors. In the case of the Faroe Islands, local involvement can be both intense and ignorable (Nilsson, 2007).

Even if the shores of the remote 18 islands are not surrounded by warm water, where sun and fun normally turn to rain and pain, the people are still warm and welcoming. In peripheries, and especially on cold water islands, an organic social solidarity is often the norm, where all are involved in most processes of life, labour and recreation (Martin, 2001). At the University of the Faroe Islands, it is a commonly thought that the archipelago will stand up against globalization, because global needs and local culture can combine and draw strength from each other in a reflexive process. "The Faroese are typical sailors, at home everywhere but always longing for their native place", a researcher sums up the perception of his compatriots (Hovgaard, 1998). He has, like most of the academic people on the islands, got his academic degree at a Danish university and after a research career abroad, decided to return home.

Conclusion

At the University of the Faroe Islands, there is a special department for development projects concerning peripheral islands with poor connections. The aim is to achieve better connections and development via networking, with a special focus on tourism. In 2013, the tourism sector received DKK 17 million (about US$3 million) from the Government, which will be used as an investment in MICE (Meetings, Incentives, Conferences and Events) marketing. This requires target groups, like business or non-governmental organisations.

For the Faroe Islands, there are two neighbouring clusters that are ripe for cooperation, especially within tourism development. One cluster includes the archipelagos of Shetland, Orkney and the Hebrides, with whom they share long-term historic connections: all populations on these islands are a result of Viking settlements from Scandinavia, especially Norway. History and 'islandness' connect them, even if architecture and language separates them. They have all been owned by the Norwegian king: the Hebrides until the 13th century; Shetland and Orkney until the 15th century (Grohse, 2013). For tour operators, there is a willingness to cooperate, but there is a lack of financial investment. The tunnel and road system (sometimes criticised by the local

Faroese people due to heavy costs and 'insular' lobbying) offers visitors easy access to the different islands, a situation rather unknown in other archipelagos. This condition has been used by incoming operators to market the Faroe Islands.

Even if the tourism organisation is not well synchronised, there is no evidence of a split view of what should be marketed. Each island may claim a different identity and need for special treatment, but there are no signs of a rivalry concerning the marketing of the Faroe Islands as a whole, a rivalry common between islands in warm water areas (Baldacchino and Ferreira, 2013). Perhaps it is the strong inter-connectivity of most of the islands that subdues such parochial sentiments. Moreover, cold water islands obviously have to stick together in order to get any visitors at all. There is no doubt that nature is the most estimated experience for the visitors of the Faroe Islands which include extrovert tourists like mountaineers, hikers, and anglers. So, are the visitors really visiting the Faroe Islands due to unspoiled nature? The authorities and tourism entrepreneurs believe so, but there are scant investigations to confirm this notion (Liu, Dietz, and Carpenter, 2007; Müller, 2013; Granquist, and Nilsson, 2013). Thereby, one important individual is not being involved; the presumptive visitor. What are his/her expectations of the Faroe Islands and the visit? Most evidence show that the presumptive visitor has no idea what can be expected of his or her visit other than remoteness. The impression mediated by all interviewed is, however, that a trip to the Faroe Islands is 'a lifetime experience'.

Sooner or later, as technology improves, investment financing becomes available, and engineering acumen mellows, it is possible that the complete Faroese archipelago will be connected. Such a seamless 'mainlanding' of the Faroes implies that there will be minimal challenges for living on any of its constituent island units. Otherwise, the remote island group would face the underlying trends of urbanisation that are impacting on many other island chains, leading to disproportional growth in its main city, along with a concurrent depopulation of remote rural settlements. Tunnel technology has strongly contributed to community sustainability in the Faroes, just as it has elsewhere (such as the Icelandic Westfjords region), and explains its broad public and political support, in spite of hefty price tags.

Meanwhile, the emergence of the Faroes as an attractive, cold water tourism destination has created an additional rationale and justification for this network of infrastructural connections. The distribution of, and local access to, sites, attractions and amenities represents an assortment of tourism experiences more akin to a continental state than an island archipelago. The disproportionate importance of Torshavn (as the main town, port, tourist accommodation and commercial centre) as well as Vágar (as the site of the only international airport) has not led to any tourist concentrations on their respective islands; as one may have expected in other archipelagic contexts. The tunnels are there, to share the traffic as much as the tourism revenues. Inter-island rivalry and jealousy have been strongly impacted and reduced, though not eliminated, with civil engineering. The tourism industry is not looked upon as something very important by the locals, just something with perhaps an added value. Fishing and sheep herding are sectors which the Faroese people respect. The unconnected islands have other priorities. For example, the people at Suduroy are mostly concerned to increase the number of inhabitants by attracting back-movers rather than visitors, after the serious population drop due to a considerable exodus to Denmark during the crisis in the 1990s. Concerning Sandoy, the tunnel is proof of the personal power of one particular Member of Parliament. However, in the future there may be more concerns about the tourism industry.

References

Ackrén, M. (2006). The Faroe Islands: options for independence. *Island Studies Journal*, 1(2), 223–38.

Baldacchino, G., and Ferreira, E.C.D. (2013). Competing notions of diversity in archipelago tourism: transport logistics, official rhetoric and inter-island rivalry in the Azores. *Island Studies Journal*, 8(1), 84–104.

Baldacchino, G. (2006). Studying islands: on whose terms? Some epistemological and methodological challenges to the pursuit of Island Studies. *Islands Studies Journal*, 3(1), 37–56.

Baum, T.G. (1998). Tourism marketing and the small island environment: cases from the periphery. In E. Laws, B. Faulkner, and G. Moscardo (eds), *Embracing and managing change in tourism: International case studies*, pp. 116–37. London: Routledge.

Baum, T.G. (1999). Decline of the traditional North Atlantic fisheries and tourism's response: the cases of Iceland and Newfoundland. *Current Issues in Tourism*, 2(1), 47–67.

Butler, R. (2006). Epilogue: contrasting cold water and warm water island tourist destinations. In G. Baldacchino (ed.) *Extreme tourism: Lessons from the world's cold water islands*, pp. 247–58. Amsterdam: Elsevier.

Faroese Main Road Authority webpage. (2013). Tunlar. Retrieved from http://www.landsverk.fo/Default.aspx?pageid=16215

Faroese infrastructure webpage. (2014). Infrastructure. Retrieved from http://www.faroeislands.fo/Default.aspx?ID=12314

Gaini, F. (2013). *Lessons of islands: Place of identity in the Faroe Islands.* Fróðskapur: Faroe University Press.

Granquist, S., and Nilsson, P.-Å. (2013). The wild North: network cooperation for sustainable tourism in fragile marine environments in the Arctic region. In D. Muller, L. Lundmark and R.H. Lemelin (eds), *New issues in Polar tourism: Communities, environments, politics*, pp. 123–32. London: Springer.

Grohse, I.P. (2013). From asset in war in to asset in diplomacy: Orkney in the medieval realm of Norway. *Island Studies Journal*, 8(2), 225–68.

Hall, C.M. and Boyd, S. (2005). *Nature-based tourism in peripheral areas: Development or disaster*, pp. 3–17. London: Channel View.

Holm, D., Helgadóttir, G., Arnason, S., and Nilsson, P-Å. (2012). *Back movers and in movers: A study of migration flows into small societies over time.* Hammerdal: Hammerdal Förlag.

Hovgaard, G. (1998). Coping with exclusion: a North Atlantic Perspective. In N. Aarsæther and J.O. Bærenholdt (eds), *Coping strategies in the North: Local practices in the context of global restructuring*, pp. 45–70. Copenhagen: Nordic Council MOST Project.

Jennissen, R. (2007). Causality chains in international migration systems approach. *Population Research and Policy Review*, 26(4), 411–36.

Liu, J., Dietz, T., and Carpenter, S. (2007). Complexity of coupled human and natural systems. *Science*, 317(5844), 1513–16.

Martin, T. (2001). *The reflexive community. Quest for autonomy as a coping strategy in an Inuit community.* In N. Aarsæther and J.O. Bærenholdt (eds), *The reflexive North*, pp. 41–70. Copenhagen: Nordic Council MOST project.

Müller, D. (2013). National parks for tourism development in sub-Arctic areas: curse or blessing? In D. Müller, L. Lundmark and R.H. Lemelin (eds), *New issues in polar tourism*, pp. 189–203. London: Springer.

National Geographic Travel webpage. (2013). Island destinations rated: introduction. Retrieved from http://traveler.nationalgeographic.com/2007/11/destinations-rated/intro-text

Nilsson, P.Å. (2007). Stakeholder theory: the need for a convenor. *Scandinavian Journal of Hospitality and Tourism*, 7(2), 171–84.

Nilsson, P.Å. (2008). Tourism in cold water islands: a matter of contract? Experience from destination development in the Polar North. *Island Studies Journal*, 3(1), 97–112.

NORA webpage. (2014). Welcome to the Northern Periphery Programme 2007–2013. Retrieved from http://www.northernperiphery.eu/en/home/

Nordin, U. (2005). Skärgården: en plats blir till. In G. Forsberg (ed.), *Planeringens utmaningar och tillämpningar*, pp. 215–34. Uppsala: Uppsala Publishing House.

Proctor, J. (2013). *Faroe Islands*. 3rd edn. Buckinghamshire: Bradt Travel Guides.

Rassing, C.R., and Sørensen, A. (2001). *Spørgeskemaundersøgelse af personer, der afrejser Færøerne, 15 maj 1999 – 14. Maj 2000.* Nexø, Denmark: Centre for Regional and Tourism Research.

Sandell, K. (2001). Några aspekter på svenska reservatsdilemmans förutsättningar. *Landskapet som arena*, No. 4. Umeå, Sweden: Umeå University Press.

Smyril Line webpage. (2014). Färöarna. Retrieved from http://www.smyril-line.se/foroyar.htm

Statistics Faroe Islands. (2014). *Arrivals to the Faroe Islands by air and ferry.* Retrieved from http://www.hagstova.fo

Visit Faroe Islands. (2014). The Faroe Islands: unspoiled, unexplored, unbelievable. Retrieved from http://www.visitfaroeislands.com/

Visit Tórshavn webpage. (2013). Visit Tórshavn. Retrieved from http://www.visittorshavn.fo/page.php?Id=139&l=en

Interviews (Held During 2013)

Biskopstø Olga, 1 September. Project leader for outer areas, University of Faroe Islands.
Hayfield Erika, 28 August. Minister of interior, Government of the Faroe Islands.
Hovgaard Gestur, 30 August. Researcher, University of the Faroe Islands.
Holm, Dennis, 28 August. Mayor, Vagur, Suðeroy.
Højgaard Guðrið, 28 August. Director, Visit Faroe Islands.
Højgaard Oddbjørg, 30 August. Hotel director, Hotel Hafnia, Torshavn.
Jacobsen, Friður, 2 September. Director, Green Gate Incomin Ltd.
Kreuzmann Theresa, 30 August. Director, Tourism information office, Kunnigarstovan.
Langgard Leivur, 29 August. Advisor, Parliament of the Faroe Islands.
Liknargøtu Henna á, 2 September. Marketing director, Smyril Line.
Meitelberg Jørgen, 3 September. Administrative director, University of the Faroe Islands.
Petersen Jogvar, 2 September. Hotel director, Klaksvik Hotel.
Skuvdal Gunnar, 30 August. Entrepreneur, Vestmanna Bird Watching.

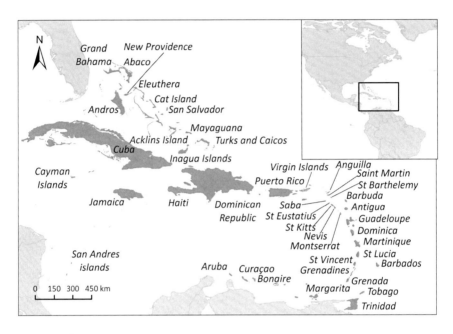

Figure 8.1   The Caribbean archipelago

Chapter 8

Navigating the Caribbean Archipelago: An Examination of Regional Transportation Issues

Sherma Roberts, John N. Telesford and Jennifer V. Barrow

Introduction

In the fifteenth and sixteenth centuries, the Caribbean Sea was a uniting medium for the Caribs, Arawaks and Amerindian people as they travelled via canoe to and fro a polyglot of islands in search of food, trade and community. The region also served as a pleasure periphery and a space of convalescence for many of the region's colonisers. Goulbourne (2009, p. xiv) recalls that the Caribbean was "a significant destination for the world's population: for settlement, colonisation, nativising, and of course, for visits and for gazing." The pre and immediate post independence era also witnessed increasing migration among Caribbean nationals travelling within the archipelago in search of family and most notably employment and improved quality of life (Thomas-Hope, 2001; 2009). This mobility was mainly by sea, using commercial shipping.

The growing democratisation of travel, the social and economic development of many Caribbean islands, and the importance that tourism has achieved within the region, have created an appetite for Caribbean residents to travel inter-regionally for the purpose of leisure and more recently, business. In 2012, regional travel and tourism accounted for US$48.4 bn and 2 million jobs (WTTC, 2013). Of equal importance is that, domestic travel contributed just over 30% of the direct travel and tourism GDP, making intra-regional travel a significant contributor to overall tourism earnings. While the growth in travel and commerce has been, to a large extent, facilitated by a modest increase in national, regional and short-lived itinerant air carriers, its potential has been stymied by the challenges associated with transport arrangements among Caribbean island and archipelago states.

This chapter evaluates the critical success factors needed to ensure the sustainability of one, or a combination, of, regional transportation modalities. The focus is therefore on intra-regional travel rather than international travel. The chapter argues that, key to the region's future competitiveness and the proposed integration movement propounded by Article 45 of the Revised Treaty of Chaguaramas (CARICOM, 2002), is the ability of its residents and its visitors to travel affordably *across* the region's island states, and not just *to* and *from* them. While the focus of the chapter will be on the Anglophone Caribbean, where necessary, examples and possibilities will be drawn from the wider Dutch, Spanish and French Caribbean.

The chapter begins by examining the contested notion of a Caribbean archipelago. The discussion then moves to the relationship between transport and tourism and its critical importance for destination development and competitiveness. The context of this chapter, which is the Caribbean region, is then discussed with specific reference to the current transport system and its challenges. Drawing upon elite interviews with government officials and transportation experts, as well as a survey of 760 Caribbean residents, the critical success factors for a sustainable regional transport system are discussed and recommendations proposed.

Benson and Whitehead (1985) suggest that a useful approach to analysing the significance of transport is to adopt a systems approach rather than viewing the modes as discreet entities. In this regard, they highlight four basic elements: modes (air, road, sea and rail); the way (airway, roadway, seaway, railway); terminals (points of interchange); and technology. The advantage of a systems perspective is that change in one specific transport mode is regarded in light of its impact upon the whole system, allowing for a more comprehensive treatment of the problem. The chapter therefore borrows a definition of transport based on this systems approach and articulated by Prideaux (1999, p. 56), which regards transport as a system of:

> ... operations and interactions between transport modes, ways and terminals that support tourism resorts in terms of passenger and freight flows into and out of destinations and the provision of transport services within the destination, and the provision of connecting transport modes in the tourism generating regions.

The Caribbean Archipelago

If one utilises the traditionally held definition of islands as pieces of land smaller than continents completely surrounded by water, then the Caribbean could be seen as a largely homogenous unit. However, the question of what constitutes the Caribbean remains inconclusive and highly contested, with its meanings "... not only invented but continuously reinterpreted in response both to external influences and internal currents" (Girvan, 2000: 34). Some have simply stated that the Caribbean is defined as all islands that are washed by the Caribbean sea, in a grand arc that starts from the Florida keys in the north-west down to Trinidad in the south-east (Blake, 2000). This definition is insufficient as it provides a geographical delimiter to the Caribbean experience and identity where the shoreline serves as boundary of containment (Hay, 2006). This position is necessarily insular and has been challenged by alternate notions of greater mobility, fluidity, permeability and possibility (Baldacchino 2005; Girvan, 2000). Moreover, within this geography, there are variations based upon size, language, distance and internal and external governance arrangements. Other perspectives on the Caribbean include that it is a largely political entity with islands being grouped according to their differing governance structure; for example, the French Overseas Territories of Guadeloupe, Martinique, St. Barthélemy and St. Martin; and the United Kingdom Overseas territories and English-speaking Turks and Caicos, Montserrat, Cayman Islands, and Virgin Islands. Adding to the political complexity are the islands of the Anglophone Caribbean that are largely made up of sovereign island states, each with their own constitution, legislature and emblems of sovereignty.

The cultural Caribbean has also been put forward as a way of defining the Caribbean (Blake, 2000). This definition suggests that the cultural historiography shared by many islands have shaped our political, economic and social realities over and above any political or geographical characteristics. These cultural identifiers (food, dress, language, religion, institutional structures) are seen as powerful enough to be able to define what it means to be Caribbean. Thus, unlike the geographical and the political definitions, the cultural Caribbean transcends space and time and joins the diaspora with those living within the boundaries of the islands. The cultural Caribbean is however highly and distinctly nuanced by the linguistic and indigenous groupings that occupy it. Thus, there is an Anglophone, Dutch, French and Spanish Caribbean and the Carib, Arawak, Ciboney and Mayan peoples that converse in a different *lingua franca* but yet share some cultural bonds based upon a common history.

The similarities and contrasts articulated above highlight the challenges and opportunities inherent to a Caribbean regional transport project. Given the greater commonalities among the Anglophone Caribbean countries and the authors' familiarity with these islands, this paper will focus attention largely on the Anglophone Caribbean countries that are members of the Caribbean Community (CARICOM).

Transport and Tourism

One of the key drivers of international tourism has been the transformation and development of transport technology since the late 1950s with the introduction of the jet engine (Culpan, 1987; Page, 1994; Honey, 1999; Sorupia, 2005). With the advent of faster, cheaper, more convenient and more comfortable transport modalities, there has been a concomitant change in the numbers and classes of persons engaging in both domestic and international travel. The World Travel and Tourism Council (2013) notes that, in 1950, there were 24 million international tourists and by 2000, arrivals had increased to 684 million, reaching the 1 billion mark in 2012. All transport modalities – air, sea, rail and road – have been posited as major factors in connecting generating regions to destination regions as advanced by Leiper's (1979) tourism system. This system has been critiqued for not examining in-destination transport, factors that may inhibit travel to and from the two regions, such as the interplay between demand and supply (Prideaux, 1999) and changes in motivations that may stimulate the demand for new routes (Hall, 2005); nevertheless, the critical importance of transport in international tourism flows must be recognised.

Transport infrastructure is also critical to destination development. Hall (1999) provides some insight into the different requirements of tourism transport, identifying four different roles that transport plays in destination development: linking the origin market with the tourist destination; providing access and mobility within a wide destination area (region or country); offering access and mobility within a tourist destination itself and finally providing travel along a recreational route. In one of the earliest works on the significance of transport to destination development, Kaul (1985) advances nine postulates governing the relationship between transport and tourism. These are:

- The evolution of tourism is influenced by developments in transport.
- The mass and individual nature of tourism requires transport infrastructure.
- Transport is integral for tourism to operate and its quality will influence the type of tourist flow.
- Planning and maintenance are key to a successful transportation system.
- Price competition influences the elasticity of demand which ultimately benefits tourism.
- The integration of domestic and international transport systems across countries has contributed to the growth in tourist flows.
- Technology impacts transportation systems and the consumer benefits from faster, more efficient and safer transport services.

- The accommodation sector needs to grow in step with the expansion in tourism numbers due to increasing transport modalities.
- Continuous innovation in transport fuels the continued growth of international tourism.

 These nine postulates have largely stood the test of time; evidenced by the growth in low cost carriers in the United States, Europe, India, New Zealand, Canada and Australia (Duval, 2007). However, there are many nuances with respect to governance structures, critical mass and transport financing modalities that impact upon the relationship between transport and tourism that the authors have not considered and may be of particular relevance to the Caribbean region.

Transport as a Requirement for Destination Competitiveness

Ritchie and Crouch (2007) argue that access to a destination via affordable and reliable transportation is integral to a destination's competitiveness. This view is supported to some measure by the Travel and Tourism Competitiveness Index (World Economic Forum, 2013) which identifies a number of indicators, including transport infrastructure, as aiding in a destination's competitive advantage and overall positive visitor experience (Page and Lumsdon, 2004). However, a number of factors impacting this transport indicator are worth examining. Khadaroo and Seetanah (2007) indicate that perspectives on transport capital are more heterogeneous than have been acknowledged. For example, they note that arrivals among European and American tourists to Mauritius were influenced by the availability of modern high quality transport infrastructure. In contrast, Asians and Africans to the same destination were not as bothered by the sophistication of the transport medium.
    The relative cost of transport to the destination can also impact on a destination's competitiveness and overall development. This cost is often relative to distance, and affects destination selection. Prideaux (1999) reminds us that, as distance increases, so does the cost of travel. In addition, the hidden costs associated with travel may alter one's transport choice as one mode is substituted for another. Complicating the distance-cost argument is the comfort factor, where Khadaroo and Seetanah (2007, p. 1027) argue that 'tourists [to Mauritius] preferred shorter to longer journeys so as to minimise discomfort.' These are quite reasonable assumptions in some island and mainland jurisdictions where the potential tourist has a choice in the medium of travel. In the Balearic Islands, for instance, while there are direct international flights to the three main islands (Mallorca, Minorca, Ibiza), the very proximate islands (Formentera and Cabrera) are isolated, with no inter-island flows because of an absence of transport infrastructure. Moreover, the air connectivity between the islands is short but expensive (Bardolet and Sheldon, 2008).
    Island archipelagos have their own slate of transport experiences. Travel between the islands is critical to trade and development; and the need for efficient regional and international transportation has become of vital importance to the survival of the tourism industry. Yet, linking islands through air and sea transport is a real challenge. This remains very much the case in the Caribbean, where there are few or no options available for intra-regional travel. The islands of Dominica, St. Lucia and Martinique are connected by a scheduled ferry service (Browne, 2013); but, by and large, travel within the region is by air. Many of the islands are between a thirty minute to a two hour flight away from each other, with airfare costs being largely influenced by government taxes (Browne, 2013), challenging

the distance-cost argument put forward by Prideaux. Moreover, the region's domiciled air transport sector is made up of a number of small commuter and jet airlines that are all very weak financially and continue to lose millions of dollars annually (Browne, 2013). The following section discusses transport within the context of the Caribbean region.

The Current State of Caribbean Regional Transport

Air transportation has been the mainstay of movement across and within the Caribbean region as it offers more options for international travel from North to South, as well as South-South movement within the region. As indicated above, there is presently no widespread use of ferries across the region. Notably there are some small operations within the British Virgin Islands (BVI) as well as from Tortola, BVI to the U.S Virgin Islands (USVI), particularly St. Johns and St. Thomas; between Martinique, Dominica, and St. Lucia; between Montserrat and St. Kitts and Nevis; and between Trinidad and Tobago. This dominance of the airplane versus the ferry goes against the prominence of seacraft in other archipelagos as projected by Hernandez (2002). However, the idea of a superferry as proposed at CARICOM Heads of Government level meetings, with the government of Trinidad and Tobago agreeing to fund a study on such a service for the Eastern Caribbean, has not gotten off the ground (Rambally, 2011; BN Americas 2008). As recently as 28 May 2013, the CARICOM Council on Trade and Economic Development (COTED) held a special transportation meeting in St. Vincent and the Grenadines where it indicated that the pilot programme of the fast ferry for the Southern region was put on hold, due to the high cost of the pilot project, estimated at over US$5 m (Government of the Republic of Trinidad and Tobago, 2013). This initiative is envisioned as a joint public/private investment project if it is to progress to reality. Without this fast ferry project moving forward, Caribbean nationals will continue to face the vagaries of one single and expensive mode of transport for intra-regional travel.

Meanwhile cruising, whilst not specific to intra-regional travel for residents, is a growing, popular mode for visitors to the region. Cruise visitors now surpass the number of stay-over visitors in various Caribbean island states (Caribbean Tourism Organisation, 2013). Caribbean cruise arrivals in 2012 totalled 21.2 million passengers, compared to stay-over visitors of 25 million, although growth in both areas shows fluctuations by individual destination (ibid.). The region accounts for some 37% of total global cruises, maintaining its position as the number one cruising region (CLIA, 2013). Countries such as Aruba, Barbados and Puerto Rico have long been established as home ports for various cruise lines; however, cruising has not overtaken air transportation for intra-regional travel by residents as it is not a high demand regional intra-Caribbean leisure/business transport option. Therefore, with no causeways and bridges and no full-fledged ferry service across the entire region, air transport becomes the mode of choice (or sheer necessity by default) for Caribbean residents and visitors to move from island to island.

LIAT – Leeward Island Air Transport

The people of the region have been able to island hop primarily on air services offered by LIAT (Leeward Islands Air Transport) which is owned by majority government shareholders of Barbados, Antigua and Barbuda and St. Vincent and the Grenadines and more recently, Dominica, in order of share holdings. This is the longest serving regional air carrier in the Caribbean, having been in continuous operation since 1956. The airline however continues to incur heavy losses, which are covered by the stakeholder governments (World Bank, 2006; Holder, 2011). The primary reason for these losses is the social welfare model of the airline rather than one operating on the strict basis of supply and demand (Holder, 2011; Browne, 2013). The airline flies daily to over twenty destinations within the region, but most of these routes are unprofitable; the necessary break-even load factors or critical mass at the destinations to warrant the service on commercial lines are severely lacking. The average time within LIAT's network is less than one hour based on the distance of the islands from each other. Also noteworthy is that many of the island populations served by LIAT comprise less than one hundred thousand residents each (Browne, 2013), making actual demand on a daily or even weekly basis substantially low.

The ongoing challenges of the post-2008 global economic crisis have led to a more deliberate attempt to increase intra-regional travel with Staycation packages being advertised to help drive hotel occupancies and keep tourism service suppliers viable. As a result, there have been increasing calls for LIAT (that has more than 75% of its traffic consisting of regional citizens and residents), to offer lower ticket prices and more reliable schedules. In response, LIAT's major shareholders have asked for a restructuring of the airline, advising of a need for new aircrafts due to the aging fleet of Dash-8s and have called for those member countries benefitting from the unprofitable routes/social services to contribute financially to the ongoing survival of the airline. It remains to be seen whether there will be additional national government contributions to the airline's operational costs or minimum revenue guarantees, or if a bold approach will be taken by existing shareholder governments to let non-contributors lose their access. In the meantime, LIAT has been able to secure financing through the Caribbean Development Bank and has moved ahead with replacing its old, high maintenance fleet of Dash 8s with a new fleet of ATR aircraft (Grant, 2013).

LIAT's constant bone of contention has been that Caribbean regional governments, generally through their tourist boards, have taken financial risks, in the form of revenue guarantees, with international carriers such as American Airlines but are yet to do the same for regional carriers such as LIAT (Holder, 2010). However, as noted by Bardolet and Sheldon (2008), with the multiple tiers and types of governance arrangements in an archipelago, each having different interests within the tourism sector, reaching consensus on certain critical matters is not easy.

Caribbean Airlines (CAL)

The other main intra-regional airline is the larger Caribbean Airlines (CAL) which was incorporated in 2006 after the winding up of its predecessor, British West Indian Airways (BWIA), set up in 1939, and fully owned by the government of Trinidad and Tobago. In contrast to its weekly and daily schedule to the UK, USA and Canada, CAL's intra-regional service provision is very limited when compared to that of LIAT (See Table 8.1).

It has been argued that the difference in regional reach by the two airlines has to do with national mandates. As stated by one Caribbean Tourism Minister,

> Caribbean Airlines' mandate is different to our mandate; their mandate is to make an efficient airline and just make money. They don't have a responsibility to make sure that there is interconnection. If a route isn't making money, they are going to stop it (The Barbados Advocate, 2010).

Table 8.1   Comparative analysis of Caribbean destinations served by regional airlines

Regional Destinations Served	Caribbean Airlines (domiciled in Trinidad and Tobago)	LIAT (domiciled in Antigua and Barbuda)
Antigua and Barbuda (Antigua)	Y	Y
The Bahamas (Nassau)	Y	N
Barbados	Y	Y
Belize	N	Y
Cuba	N	N
Dominica	N	Y
Dominican Republic	N	Y
Grenada	Y	Y
Guyana	Y	Y
Haiti	N	N
Jamaica	Y	Y
Montserrat	N	Y
Puerto Rico	N	Y
St. Kitts and Nevis (St. Kitts)	N	Y
St. Lucia	Y	Y
St. Vincent and the Grenadines (St. Vincent)	N	Y
Surinam	Y	N
Trinidad and Tobago (Trinidad)	Y	Y

Source: www.liat.com; http://caribbean-airlines.com.

Whilst there are other scheduled airlifts within the region – such as Bahamas Air, Surinam Airways, Cayman Airways and Cubana Airways – these offer very limited intra-regional service, covering only certain routes in the region. Of these scheduled airlines, only Caribbean Airlines and Surinam Airways are presently members of IATA (International Air Transport Association). There are also several small charter airlines in the region, but their size and schedules again do not permit mass movement of travelers at high enough frequency compared to scheduled regional airlines. These regional airlines are also confined by the frameworks of the different islands' air service agreements (Centre for Aviation, 2011). Specifically, the absence of liberal 'open skies' agreements means that countries are limited to bilateral air service agreements which impose restrictions based upon capacity, price, routes and the number of airlines which can use the agreement (Warnock-Smith, and Morrell, 2008).

Despite almost all islands having their own international airport, the regional airlines have established Antigua, Barbados, Jamaica and Trinidad as natural hubs due to their location (Bertrand, 2001). Meanwhile, other islands, such as Barbuda, Tortola (BVI), Montserrat, Dominica, Nevis and St. Vincent and the Grenadines do not have facilities for jet services, although St. Vincent has an international airport under construction. Moreover, language and history have to be taken into consideration when looking at airline hubs in the Caribbean archipelago. For example, the French islands use Fort-de-France, Martinique, as a hub; the Dutch use Aruba; and the English/Spanish use San Juan international airport in Puerto Rico. These types of organic transportation relationships based around language, and to some extent shared business and cultural practices, underpin the fractured nature of transport systems within the archipelago and militate against having a single or multiple transport modalities that are interconnected beyond cultural similarities. The exception being cases such as LIAT's and CAL's relationship with Puerto Rico and Dominican Republic where there is critical mass, and by extension greater viability.

Challenges to Intra-regional Travel

Absence of Facilitating Mechanisms

It is axiomatic that, with the limited number of scheduled airline options offering intra-regional access, there would be challenges such as a lack of code share agreements and reduced connectivity. The results are that regional travelers are not able to connect smoothly from one airline to another. Having to check-in again to access the connection for the onward journey entails additional security checks, which ultimately impacts the overall tourist experience. According to the Business Monitor International in its Caribbean Tourism Report (2012), the absence of a common aviation policy also has a negative impact on regional travel as there is a lack of cooperative action to support tourism development. The Caribbean Tourism Organisation's Aviation Task Force (CTO's ATF) established in September 2012 has further clarified that, in spite of there being a transport policy (Protocol VI in the 2001 Revised Treaty of Chaguaramas), there is no rationalised regional air transport policy from which airline operators and tourism officials can draw upon to inform practice. As such, the CARICOM Multi-lateral Air Services Agreement (MASA) remains the one, single framework for informing air transport negotiations, but with international rather than regional carriers (Bertrand, 2001).

Convenience and Affordability

Caribbean tourism needs transportation options that are reliable and affordable to both its residents and its visitors to optimise the potential for intra-regional travel. At present, there is growing concern by governments and increasing frustration by the travelling public over the lack of convenient access across the region. This challenge is exacerbated by inconvenient schedules in terms of the few code-sharing agreements in existence, ongoing government subsidies to airlines, and the high cost of travel within the region, with some fares being higher than travel from the region to the USA. In an attempt to better understand the challenges facing LIAT, the CARICOM Secretariat in 2009, commissioned a study which highlighted that a large portion of the airline ticket is made up of various government taxes to be used for airport enhancement and security that comply with the international requirements of such bodies as FAA, ICAO and IATA (Miller, 2009). The ability to tackle the high cost of travel needs political will and the financial support of CARICOM and wider regional countries to address the tax bundle in a more holistic way. More affordable travel would result in greater overall travel volume and tourism revenue to island destinations (Prideaux, 1999; Hanlon, 1986).

Methodology

The data informing the ensuing discussion was derived from eight face to face semi-structured interviews and 760 self-administered questionnaires, conducted and collected between September and October 2013. The interviews involved government officials with responsibility for transport and tourism and regional transport experts. The interviews sought to identify in some detail the major issues in Caribbean transport modalities, the main drivers of inter-regional travel, the factors impacting airline viability as commercial entities, the critical factors affecting airline ownership, the state of regional travel, factors impacting the quality of regional transport modes, and recommendations to help resolve regional transport challenges. The interviews were analysed using a thematic framework where consistently emerging themes/categories were coded (Collis and Hussey, 2003). The primary interview question dealing with the main concerns with the current state of regional travel indicated consensus around price, reliability of service and convenience as the greatest challenges to intra-regional travel. Moreover, based on the importance of tourism to the region and the push to grow intra-regional travel there was concern around customer satisfaction, with all respondents seeing the travel experience as pertinent to quality.

A self-administered survey was carried out at Grantley Adams International Airport (GAIA) in Barbados. This hub was chosen as it serves all international airlines and is a link between the Northern and Southern Caribbean islands. A total of 760 surveys were completed with the participants almost equally split between males (47%) and females (53%). Respondents indicated that the primary reason for intra-regional travel was vacation (59%), followed by business (51%), medical (11%) and events, sports, visa related trips and education (7%). For most respondents (80%), the preferred mode of travel is by air, while 4% chose sea, the rest expressing no particular preference. The survey data was triangulated with the interview data to provide a more comprehensive analysis of Caribbean transport issues.

Critical Success Factors

Need for a Different Ownership and Financing Model

There was consensus among all participants that the sole government funding model was not sustainable. The state regulatory framework was also identified unanimously as a major hindrance to alternative ownership of transport, particularly airlines. The concepts of 'protectionism', 'outdated ownership and control rules' and 'problems with regulatory perspective' were offered to the theme of regional transport problem resolution.

Rationalisation of Operational Costs

High operational costs coupled with short and frequent flights contributed to heavy wear and tear on the current aircraft fleet. This is compounded by government taxation in terms of landing fees, parking fees and air navigational system fees, among others. It was noted that, owing to these critical factors, the costs are then passed on to the customer, thereby impacting the cost of travel. This type of concern has been documented in research looking at other regions, but in some instances is welcomed, as state ownership might be the only plausible way for some residents to be able to travel out of, and back to, their island home.

In rationalising air transport costs, interview respondents suggested the introduction of an inter-island ferry service. However, a closer look at some factors – such as market size, attractiveness to Caribbean nationals, cost-benefit analysis, adoption of a mixed-use vessel, length of time – would be key determinants in making such a decision. This multi-modal option reinforces the argument that different modes can complement each other and should not be seen as mutually substitutable (Rigas, 1991).

Less Cumbersome Regulatory Environment

All interviewees agreed that the legal and regulatory framework hindered new entrants into the airline sector as well as inhibited the emergence of alternative modes of travel in the region. Respondents called for more public-private partnerships. Specific reference was made to the International Oversight System which calls for civil aviation systems to be self-financing: one respondent deemed these to be suitable for the region as these internationally imposed requirements have contributed to higher costs being passed on to the airlines and consumers.

'Open Skies' regulation was raised as an important factor by all participants. It was suggested that greater flexibility was needed in terms of an inter-modal approach allowing for collaboration which would encourage more players, and even some smaller players, to take on a role. According to one regional transportation expert:

> We are not sufficiently enthusiastic about the regional market to do decent market segmentation …We are still too linked with historic ties which have not changed … We do not have a region from a transport point of view, we have a series of sub-regions (personal communication).

The sub-regions being referred to – small archipelagos unto themselves – are defined by history and language.

Climate Change

The issue of climate change affecting regional travel was raised; one respondent dealt more specifically with airline emissions, another was clear that climate change is a factor affecting the tourism sector. This was with specific reference to rising sea levels and more intense weather systems. An interview respondent noted that the regional runways were relatively low lying and so would be impacted by rising sea levels. The matter of the Environmental Trading Scheme, which deals with airlines capping their emissions and/ or selling allowances to each other to increase emissions (Good, 2010), was broached but there was no resolution. Due to the mix of independent countries and overseas departments of European countries making up the Caribbean archipelago, it was stated that the impact of climate change on the region as a whole remained unclear due to the large differentials among the regional players.

Factors Affecting Residents' Decision to Travel

Affordability and Safety

The cost of travel was the primary factor influencing residents' decision to travel. Fifty four percent of survey respondents indicated that affordability was critical to their decision to travel and 46% reported that cost was the major influencer when thinking about transport mode. Respondents (50%) also rated safety as a crucial factor in their decision making. This is surprising, particularly given LIAT's and CAL's stellar safety record to date.

Reliability of Transport

Although this factor ranked fifth amongst those influencing travel decisions, the number of persons indicating that it is important (34%) is significant. Reliability (timeliness and frequency) is critical to the sustainability of any mode of travel within the Caribbean, as travelers will feel confident in deciding to leave their homes to travel to another Caribbean island. In this regard, the reliability of LIAT as the sole airline serving the greater part of the Caribbean region comes into question. The perception that the regional airline is unreliable has the potential to eat into its passenger numbers and obstruct commerce within the region; it does not augur well for taking that crucial decision to travel.

Destination Attributes

While respondents highlighted that affordability, safety and reliability were critical to their travel decision and choice of mode of travel, the survey results also revealed that destination attributes such as accommodation price (47%), destination attractiveness (41%) and availability of travel packages (25%) can enhance the demand for travel to specific Caribbean destinations. Respondents (33%) also pointed out that visiting friends and relatives (VFR) is important in choosing when and where to travel. However, all these factors seem to be secondary to the 'affordability to travel' option. Family visitation or event tourism in a particular island destination is seemingly prohibitive by the cost of getting there.

Choice of Mode of Travel

The majority of respondents indicated that their preferred mode of travel was by air. This response may be influenced by the fact that travel within the Caribbean is dominated by air, with few options for travel by sea. However, when asked what factors will most influence the choice of mode, the majority suggested that cost was the most critical factor. This is also congruent with cost of travel being the most important factor in making a decision to travel despite the mode. Safety and reliability of the mode were also offered as critical influential factors to be considered, and ranked second and third respectively. Aside from the cost of staying at a destination, 'safety and reliability' remained consistently important factors informing the decision to travel.

It was shown previously that the main reason for intra-regional travel is for vacation or tourism. In this regard the Caribbean region can be viewed as a regional tourism sub-system, consisting of the interplay amongst the generating regions, destination regions, a transit region (sea and air) and the environment in which these operate (Leiper, 1979). Taken as such, the Caribbean tourism system seems to be restricted by the cost to travel from a generating island to a destination island, and this despite the mode of travel used. But the Caribbean region is generally small and the proximity of the islands to each other is not prohibitive to travel either by air or by sea. But safety with the mode was the second important factor to be considered when making a choice of mode of travel. This factor brings into focus travel by sea, as there may be a general feeling, that travel by air is safer than travel by sea.

Conclusion

Intra-regional travel can be viewed as occurring within a Caribbean tourism sub-system, with Caribbean residents travelling for leisure, vacation and business. In this regard, islands interchange as tourism generating regions and destination regions. However, the decision to travel to a particular destination is dominated by 'mode of travel factors' with affordability to travel to a particular destination influencing both the reason to travel and the choice of mode of travel. Affordability is affected by the current state of the monopolistic nature of the mode of travel within the transit region. In the Caribbean, the one airline mode of travel, with its high operating costs and taxes, greatly affects intra-regional travel. However, and despite the fact that the majority of travelers suggest that flying is the preferred mode of travel, travel by sea must be considered as a viable option in the context of travel for leisure and vacation. Cost, safety, reliability and comfort and time to destination in that order are critical considerations to making the decision to choose between air and sea, should such a choice exist.

The Caribbean archipelago continues to face challenges with transport leading to partial accessibility and lack of options in mode choice. Moreover, where there is choice, there exists an unsatisfactory collaboration between modes of transport, or an implicit monopoly. This issue of lack of a seamless travel experience in some segments of the region is negatively impacting the competitiveness of Caribbean regional tourism. These issues are viewed as longstanding. High airfares, irregular schedules, impeding regulatory frameworks, inefficiencies encountered – in some cases due to dependency on state aid by state owned airlines – are prevalent issues. The continued high operational costs due to the proximity and/or distance between several small islands, the fragmentation of jurisdictional powers, the varying degrees of economic growth and development in the highly diverse member states with varied language and history, lead to some island destinations not offering viable air routes because of lack of critical mass and thwarting the economies of scale required to sustain routes profitably. This makes the majority of the routes non-viable under the present system and reduces regional transportation provision to a social good. This is the daunting reality which needs to be factored into the planning of transport modalities.

Involvement of the private sector via public/private sector partnerships to invest in a fast ferry service needs to be given serious consideration and resolved one way or another. Prominent among the recommendations proposed was the need for an Open Skies agreement and establishment of a regional single air space from a regional community of interest perspective, as practised by the Organisation of Eastern Caribbean States (OECS, 2006). Instead, various individual governments (such as Jamaica and Trinidad and Tobago) have made their own bilateral open skies agreements with the USA (Jamaica Observer, 2011; USDS, 2010). A collaborative approach could have opened the possibility of some of those social air-routes becoming more viable, with smaller aircraft more suited to the demand in specific areas to offer greater connectivity and access across the region.

Improved collaboration across the language/history sub-regions to increase hubs and multi-modal nodes would promote a wider dissemination of information and personnel exchange from one language sub-sector to another. For example, rather than travelling to Paris via London, a resident of the English speaking Caribbean could do so directly and daily via Martinique. Such and similar options would add greater credence to the free movement of people and enhanced regional integration.

It is also recommended that the regulatory framework be improved as it is presently seen as a stranglehold on the efficiency and effectiveness on travel options. There is also the need for a more enabling environment for prospective investors. This would of course call for less national protectionism within regional transport policy making. There is still no functional CARICOM regional air transportation policy, in spite of Protocol VI in the Revised Treaty of Chaguaramas that established the Caribbean Community (CARICOM Secretariat, 2002). There has been progress with the CARICOM Multilateral Air Services Agreement (MASA), recently redesigned allowing for a 'community of interest' and more liberal functioning along the lines of the ICAO international template for multi-national air services agreements CARICOM Secretariat, 2011a; 2011b). A number of transport policies drafted and agreed upon at regional level are yet to be ratified by member countries, or have been ratified but not yet implemented.

The implementation of MASA and the more recent revisions show some progress. The OECS sub-region appears to have set itself up for a speedier path of progress in enhancing the travel experience than the rest of the CARICOM member states due to more evenly dispersed development structure and a greater inter-island proximity in this grouping, lending to more commonality and therefore improved cooperation (OECS, 2013).

A sustained and sustainable regional transportation system is the fulcrum for Caribbean integration and intra-regional tourism travel. Yet, there appears to be a political inertia that has crippled deliberate action in forging a combination of transportation modalities to facilitate this movement. Addressing an audience of Caribbean scholars and regional Prime Ministers, Trinidad and Tobago's fourth Prime Minister, Basdeo Panday commented "it is now clear that some [Caribbean islands] must move at a pace different from others" (Panday, 2000, p. 2). As the Caribbean region stands at the crossroads of an uncertain future occasioned in large part by a deep global financial crisis and consequential diminishing tourism fortunes, it may be necessary for *some* islands to forge transport partnerships beyond the current institutional and policy architecture of CARICOM to ensure their destination's survival, competitiveness and sustainability. A critical function of these partnerships would be to seek out new and innovative financing arrangements for the envisioned transport project, which may even include a harmonised tax system. These partnerships may of necessity coalesce beyond the boundaries of geography, political arrangements and culture and would be at the vanguard of creating yet another definition of a Caribbean, one highlighted by heterogeneity, a creative imagination and political will.

References

Baldacchino, G. (2005). The contribution of 'social capital' to economic growth: lessons from island jurisdictions. *The Round Table: Commonwealth Journal of International Affairs*, 94(1), 31–46.

Bardolet, E. and Sheldon, P. (2008). Tourism in archipelagos: Hawai'i and the Balearics. *Annals of Tourism Research*, 35(4), 900–923.

Benson, D., and Whitehead, G. (1985). *Transport and distribution*. Harlow: Longman.

Bertrand, I. (2001). *Study of critical issues affecting the regional air transport sub-sector: Final report*. Madrid, Spain: World Tourism Organisation (WTO) and the United Nations Development Programme (UNDP).

Blake, B. (2000). The Caribbean: geography, culture, history and identity: assets for economic integration and development. In K. Hall and D. Benn (eds), *Contending with destiny: The Caribbean in the 21st century*, pp. 45–52. Mona, Jamaica: Ian Randle.

BN Americas. (2008). Cabinet approves US$1mn for ferry feasibility study. *Business Insight in Latin America*, 19 March. Retrieved from http://www.bnamericas.com/news/infrastructure/Cabinet_approves_US*1mn_for_ferry_feasibility_study

Browne, L. (2013). *The realities of intra-Caribbean tourism: Who gets it.* Presentation made in panel discussion in Martinique at the Caribbean Tourism Organisation's State of the Industry Conference (SOTIC) 17 October.

Business Monitor International. (2012). *Caribbean Tourism Report Q4 (2012)*. London: Business Monitor International Ltd. Retrieved from http://www.marketresearch.com/Business-Monitor-International-v304/Caribbean-Tourism-Q4-7147838/

Caribbean Tourism Organisation. (2013). Latest Tourism Statistics Tables. Retrieved from http://www.onecaribbean.org/statistics/latest-tourism-statistics-tables/

CARICOM (2002). *Revised Treaty of Chaguaramas establishing the Caribbean Community including the CARICOM Single Market and Economy*. Trinidad and Tobago: CARICOM Secretariat.

CARICOM (2011a). Significant development in regional cooperation in air transportation. Retrieved from http://www.caricom.org/jsp/community/regional_issues/regional_cooperation.jsp

CARICOM (2011b). Multilateral Agreement concerning the operation of air services within the Caribbean Community. Retrieved from http://www.caricom.org/jsp/secretariat/legal_instruments/agreement_multilateralairservices.jsp?menu=secretariat

Centre for Aviation. (2012). Lack of liberalisation in the Caribbean poses major roadblock to Redjet expansion. 20 January. Retrieved from http://centreforaviation.com/analysis/lack-of-liberalisation-in-the-caribbean-poses-major-roadblock-to-redjet-expansion-66501

Collis. J. and Hussey. R. (2003). *Business research: A practical guide for undergraduate and postgraduate students*. New York: Palgrave Macmillan.

Cruise Lines International Association. (2013). Cruise statistics for the Caribbean. Retrieved from http://www.cruising.org/sites/default/files/pressroom/CruiseIndustryUpdate2013FINAL.pdf

Culpan, R. (1987). International tourism model for developing countries. *Annals of Tourism Research*, 14(4), 541–52.

Duval, D.T. (2007). *Tourism and transport: Modes, networks and flows.* Clevedon: Channel View Publications.

Girvan, N. (2000). Creating and recreating the Caribbean. In K. Hall and D. Benn (eds), *Contending with destiny: The Caribbean in the 21st century*, pp. 31–6. Mona, Jamaica: Ian Randle.

Good, P. (2010). Tourism aviation and emissions trading. Paper presented at Caribbean Tourism Summit, Brussels, 14 March. Brussels: European Commission. Retrieved from http://www.onecaribbean.org/content/files/Philip-Good-European-commission.pdf

Goulbourne, H. (2009). Forced and free Caribbean migration: an understanding of modern diasporas. In: E. Thomas-Hope (ed.), *Freedom and constraint in Caribbean migration and diaspora*, pp. xi–xxiv. Mona, Jamaica: Ian Randle.

Government of the Republic of Trinidad and Tobago (2013). Council of Trade and Economic Development focuses on transportation, 28 May. Retrieved from http://www.news.gov.tt/content/council-trade-and-economic-development-focuses-transportation#.UuPr3rQ1jIU

Grant, J. (2013). Antigua Airline LIAT to replace Dash 8s with ATR 600s. *Daily Aviation News*, 22 July. Retrieved from http://aviationpaper.com/antigua-airline-liat-to-replace-dash-8s-with-atr-600s/

Hall, D.R. (1999). Conceptualising tourism transport: inequality and externality issues. *Journal of Transport Geography*, 7(3), 181–8.

Hall, C.M. (2005). *Tourism: Rethinking the social science of mobility*. Harlow: Pearson Education/Prentice Hall.

Hanlon, J.P. (1986). Indian air transport: factors affecting airline costs and revenues. *Tourism Management*, 7(4), 259–78.

Hay, P. (2006). A phenomenology of islands. *Island Studies Journal*, 1(1), 19–42.

Hernandez, L.J. (2002). Temporal accessibility in archipelagos: inter-island shipping in the Canary Islands. *Journal of Transport Geography*, 10(3), 231–9.

Holder, J. (2010). *Don't burn our bridges: The case for owning an airline*. Mona, Jamaica: UWI Press.

Honey, M. (1999). *Ecotourism and sustainable development: Who owns paradise?* Washington DC: Island Press.

Jamaica Observer (2011). Jamaica reaping benefits from Open Skies Agreement: Derby, 20 April. Retrieved from http://www.jamaicaobserver.com/news/Jamaica-reaping-benefits-from-Open-Skies-Agreement-Derby_8692383

Kaul, R. (1985). *Dynamics of tourism: A trilogy.* Transportation and marketing series, Vol. 3. New Delhi, India: Sterling Publishers.

Khadaroo, J. and Seetanah, B. (2008). The role of transport infrastructure in international tourism development: a gravity model approach. *Tourism Management*, 29(5), 831–40.

Leiper, N. (1979). The framework of tourism: towards a definition of tourism, tourist and the tourist industry. *Annals of Tourism Research*, 6(4), 390–407.

Miller, C. (2009). *Concept paper on a strategic plan on tourism services in the CARICOM Single Market and Economy*. Guyana: CARICOM Secretariat. Retrieved from http://www.caricom.org/jsp/single_market/services_regime/concept_paper_tourism.pdf

OECS (2006). Category One for OECS Civil Aviation. Organisation of Eastern Caribbean States. Press Release. Retrieved from http://www.oecs.org/index.php?option=com_content&view=article&id=390&Itemid=223&fontstyle=f-larger

OECS (2013). OECS Officials seek to put into practice an action plan to facilitate ease of travel. Organisation of Eastern Caribbean States. Press Release, 19 September. Retrieved from http://www.oecs.org/media-center/press-releases/trade,-economics-statistics/14-tourism/770-oecs-officials-seek-to-put-into-practice-an-action-plan-to-facilitate-ease-of-travel

Page, S. (1994). *Transport for tourism*. Sydney, Australia: Thomson Learning.

Page, S. and Lumsdon, L. (2004). *Tourism and transport: Issues and agenda for the new millennium.* Boston MA: Elsevier.

Panday, B. (2000). Reconfiguring the matrix of Caribbean development. In K. Hall and D. Benn (eds), *Contending with destiny: The Caribbean in the 21st Century*, pp. 1–6. Mona, Jamaica: Ian Randle.

Prideaux, B. (2000). The role of the transport system in destination development. *Tourism Management* 21(1), 53–63.

Rambally, R. K. (2011). Transport minister: low-cost inter-island ferry to benefit region. *The Guardian (TT)*, 24 September. Retrieved from https://guardian.co.tt/news/2011/09/23/transport-minister-low-cost-inter-island-ferry-benefit-region

Rigas, K. (2009). Boat or airplane? Passengers' perceptions of transport services to islands. The example of the Greek domestic leisure market, *Journal of Transport Geography*, 17(5), 396–401.

Ritchie, J.R. and Crouch, G. (2003). *The competitive destination: A sustainable tourism perspective.* Wallingford: CAB International.

Sorupia, E. (2005). Rethinking the role of transportation in tourism. *Proceedings of the Eastern Asia Society for Transportation Studies*, 5, 1767–77.

Thomas-Hope, E. (2001). *Skilled labour migration from developing countries: The Caribbean case.* Geneva: International Labour Office.

Thomas-Hope, E. (2009). Cultures of freedom and constraint in Caribbean migration and diaspora. In E. Thomas-Hope (ed.), *Freedom and constraint in Caribbean migration and diaspora*, pp. xxv–xlvi. Mona, Jamaica: Ian Randle.

USDS (2010). US reaches Open Skies Accord with Trinidad and Tobago, 3 May. United States Department of State. Retrieved from http://www.state.gov/r/pa/prs/ps/2010/05/141414.htm

Warnock-Smith, D. and Morrell, P. (2008). Air transport liberalisation and traffic growth in tourism-dependent economies: a case-history of some US-Caribbean markets. *Journal of Air Transport Management*, 14(2), 82–91.

World Bank (2006). *Caribbean air transport: Strategic options for improved services and sector performance.* Washington, DC: World Bank. Retrieved from http://documents.worldbank.org/curated/en/2006/09/7269187/caribbean-air-transport-strategic-options-improved-services-sector-performance

World Economic Forum (2013). *Travel and tourism competitiveness index: Reducing barriers to economic growth and job creation.* Geneva: WEF. Retrieved from http://www3.weforum.org/docs/WEF_TT_Competitiveness_Report_2013.pdf

World Travel and Tourism Council (2013). *Economic impact.* Retrieved from http://www.wttc.org/site_media/uploads/downloads/world2013_1.pdf

Chapter 9

The Bahamas: Individual Island Branding for Competitiveness in Archipelago Tourism

Sophia A. Rolle

Introduction: Tourism in the Bahamas

With population centres established on more than 30 major islands within a 700-island archipelago, The Bahamas, through its Ministry of Tourism, is committed to communicating the idea that this archipelago represents a series of independent and highly differentiated destinations where visitors can experience multiple island destinations offering unique island products and differential destinations on each island. While this concept represents archipelago tourism in its truest form, effectively promoting it has proven to be a monumental task for those charged with disseminating that information in the marketplace.

The Bahamas has long enjoyed the reputation for being the offshore destination of choice for the continental rich-and-famous, gamers and romantics and for being able to adeptly carve out an economy fueled by the tourist trade (Palmer, 1994). Nowadays, the local service industry (including offshore banking and construction-related tourism) is recognized as being the engine that drives the Bahamian economy, generating some 60% of total gross domestic product (GDP) (CIA World Factbook, 2013, para.1).

In the late 1940s, the Bahamian tourist industry was seasonal (operating for approximately six months of the year) and, as a consequence of this, those who worked in this sector had to resort to other activities like subsistence farming, fishing sponging and trading to survive the off-season. But seasonal tourism did not persist for long. The late Sir Stafford Sands, who served as Chairman of the Development Board (1949) and the country's first Minister of Tourism (1964), is credited with spearheading the policies that transformed The Bahamas "from a high-end quality destination to a mass tourist resort" (Thompson, 1979). Under his stewardship in 1950–1951, tourist arrivals to The Bahamas increased by 47% and in the ensuing years, the increasing numbers were referred to as startling (Fraser, 2001, p. 75). Lucrative resort developments ensued under his leadership from which Lyford Cay emerged in 1955 and Paradise Island in 1959.

By the mid-1960s, there were over 40 hotels and residential clubs established in the archipelago and visitor counts grew from 32,000 in 1949 to an estimated one million by 1968, thereby providing year-round employment for tourism/ hotel workers. Advertisements displaying the serene, idyllic, tropical, marine environs of The Bahama Islands appealed deeply to gregarious city dwellers in metropolitan USA, Europe and Canada and annual visitor patronage to the islands continued to surge until visitor arrival numbers outstripped available rental accommodations and hotel rooms (Bahamas Ministry of Tourism, 2011, para. 21). This encouraged the government to invest considerable resources in overseas marketing and advertising campaigns to ensure that tourism continued to retain its prominence as the centerpiece of the local economy. By 1982, annual visitor arrivals topped off at two million, registering the largest increase in stopover arrivals to The Bahamas

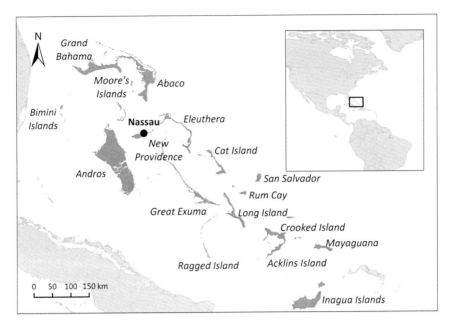

Figure 9.1   The archipelago of the Bahamas

in almost a decade. But it soon became apparent that the archipelago was not deriving maximum benefit from visitor patronage since the bulk of tourism related activities (such as casino gambling and sport fishing) were confined to just three of the 700 islands: New Providence, Grand Bahama and Bimini.

Traditionally, Nassau /Paradise Island and Grand Bahama, with the highest concentration of hotel rooms, have attracted most tourists to this archipelago destination; while islands such as Andros, the Abacos, those in the Exuma chain, Harbour Island and Eleuthera only welcomed a very small number of targeted visitors annually. Boutique resorts and eco-resorts are now found throughout the archipelago along with high-end specialized tourist facilities in the remote communities of The Berry Islands, Bimini, Walker's Cay, Long Island, San Salvador, Rum Cay and several of the Exuma Cays. The need to rethink the national approach to tourism was therefore inevitable and the obvious starting point was to develop a profile of the local tourist trade to identify the types of visitors attracted to this destination, their points of origin and an understanding of their spending patterns.

An Analysis of Visitor Patronage to the Bahamian Archipelago

The Bahamas finds it necessary to keep an accurate count of tourists to the archipelago in order to measure the impact that the industry has on the economy and to determine appropriate strategies for continuously growing this sector. Visitors to this destination are therefore grouped according to how long they spend in the destination either as "stopover visitors" or "cruise visitors". Stopover visitors spend more into the economy because those visitors sleep in a bed, eat at a restaurant, shop in the various outlets and require transportation and entertainment. Cruise passengers, on the other hand, generally arrive by

Table 9.1 Foreign air and sea arrivals to the islands of The Bahamas (first port of entry only) for 2012

	2012	2011	2011/12	2012	2011	2011/12
	Air and Sea		% Change Air and Sea		Air Only	% Change Air
Nassau/Paradise Island	3,285,035	3,006,077	9.3%	1,052,275	970,467	8.4%
Grand Bahama	839,490	818,289	2.6%	106,685	99,807	6.9%
Abaco	325,609	240,159	35.6%	76,994	75,596	1.8%
Andros	8,871	9,275	-4.4%	8,701	9,116	-4.6%
Berry Islands	642,309	614,063	4.6%	8,279	8,609	-3.8%
Bimini	54,036	53,216	1.5%	17,476	17,025	2.6%
Cat Cay	11,411	11,472	-0.5%	4,376	5,246	-16.6%
Cat Island	1,051	952	10.4%	1,048	921	
Eleuthera	248,348	296,940	-16.4%	31,892	33,817	-5.7%
Exuma	33,605	30,584	9.9%	32,917	30,017	9.7%
Half Moon Cay	472,892	488,925	-3.3%	-	-	
Inagua	734	779	-5.8%	175	251	-30.3%
Long Island	1,126	1,306	-13.8%	1,105	1,259	12.2%
San Salvador	- 15,653	15,551	0.7%	15,508	15,411	0.6%
Bahamas Total	5,940,170	5,587,588	6.3%	1,357,431	1,267,542	7.1%

Source: Immigration and Customs various ports of entry in The Bahamas.

a cruise ship to the destination and depart the same way, with many of their needs, including their accommodation, met on board.

One of the strategies of the "new push" initiatives is to entice cruise passengers to return to the destination as stopover guests in the future and thus utilise the growing cruise industry as an advertising tool for the destination. At the time this paper was written, the number of cruise visitors to the destination was at an all-time high and this was in part due to the phenomenal growth in the cruise industry and the eagerness of the cruise lines to capitalise on the archipelagic characteristics of The Bahamas. The biggest names in the cruise industry including Carnival, Celebrity Cruises, Disney Cruises, Royal Caribbean International, Norwegian Cruises and Holland American Cruises currently each offer their own private beach experiences for their cruise passengers on Bahamian "Out Islands" developed expressly for that purpose. Moreover, recent enhancements carried out to its port facilities now allow The Bahamas to accommodate the Genesis class cruise ships of the Royal Caribbean fleet, which boasts the world's largest cruise ships, such as the Oasis of the Seas: the largest ship afloat to date.

The data in Table 9.1 shows that the USA provides the largest market for visitors to the Bahamian archipelago, with Florida accounting for more than 21% of all visitors from the USA; this makes Florida a very important part of the conversation on tourism to various destinations in The Bahamas. Proximity, similarities in climate, cost of travel and other amenities seem to largely account for this demographic; while Canada and New York, where the weather is cold for a good part of the year and to whom the allure of the islands should appeal to most, only account for 9.2% and 9.45% respectively of all stopover visitors to The Bahamas (Bahamas Ministry of Tourism, 2012, p. 30).

Similarly, arrivals from countries in Europe with non-tropical profiles only accounted for 5.5% of annual stopover visitors to The Bahamas, but the number of European countries from which visitors come has increased to include the United Kingdom, Germany, Switzerland, Russia, Sweden, Austria, Denmark, Ireland, Finland, Turkey, Czech Republic, Luxemburg, Estonia, Lithuania, Serbia, Latvia, Andorra, Georgia, Belarus, Macedonia, Bosnia and Herzegovina, Moldova and Albania (Bahamas Ministry of Tourism, 2012, p. 30).

When the Florida market is subjected to further analysis, the figures show that the top Designated Market Areas (DMA) were Miami/Ft. Lauderdale, West Palm Beach/Ft. Pierce, Orlando/Daytona Beach/Melbourne, Tampa/St. Pete (Sarasota), Jacksonville and Ft. Myers/Naples. Some 48% or half of all the stopover visitors to The Bahamas from Florida in 2012 came from the Miami/Ft. Lauderdale DMA and approximately two in ten or 19% came from the West Palm Beach-Ft. Pierce DMA.

The "Out Islands" of The Bahamas

The hub of political, economic and social activities in the Bahamian archipelago is to be found in the capital city of Nassau on the island of New Providence. Initially New Providence was the most developed of all of the islands in the chain and prior to 1967, all the other islands were referred to as "Out Islands". Large-scale infrastructural enhancements did not spread to the other islands until slightly more than two decades ago.

In 1964, The Bahamas was granted self-governing status by Britain and attained majority rule in 1967. Shortly after, the political directorate agreed to seek political independence for The Bahamas and set out to galvanise national unity behind that movement. It was felt that the term Out Island was synonymous with isolation and exclusion and did not aid in creating the kind of united front that was necessary to advance the country to independence in 1973. The term "Family Islands" was preferred and subsequently adopted, hence providing a feeling of inclusion and togetherness for those residents who inhabited the remotest corners of the archipelago. For the most part, the Out Islands were remote, underdeveloped and sparsely populated – especially the South Easterly islands – and Inter-island travel was provided by subsidised weekly mail boat service. Movement between the islands otherwise was infrequent, prohibitively expensive and difficult to arrange. This was in itself an impediment to growth and development in the far flung communities of The Bahamas and prevented the active participation of the inhabitants of those communities in national initiatives – including participating in the vibrant tourist trade on their doorsteps.

Tourism finally spread to the Out Islands in response to the incentives offered under the Family Island Development Encouragement Act (2008). These incentives were primarily to support infrastructural development of the islands that eventually led to the building of small hotels and lodges for the purpose of hosting more visitors to those islands.

During the past two decades, all the principal population centres in the archipelago have received infrastructural upgrades inclusive of the installation of piped potable water, electricity, cable TV, and telephone and internet services to complement extensive upgrades to airports harbors and main roads, all of which are necessary precursors to touristic and industrial development. And now we have come full circle with respect to labeling the islands for in today's touristic environment the term "Out Islands" conjures up a feeling of peace and serenity and invites one to retreat to these places for solace and renewal. Therefore the use of the term "Out Island" is again en vogue when referring to the unspoiled Family Islands in promotional campaigns sponsored by The Bahamas Ministry of Tourism.

The task that lies ahead is how to preserve the rustic pristine state of those islands for they, like all island communities universally, are under attack. Scientists are discovering that natural and manmade activities are negatively impacting the oceans and reefs of the world and in the Bahamian archipelago, many of our vibrant native coral reefs that posed navigation hazards to shipping at one time are now declining as a result of being subjected to years of battering by intense cyclonic activity, tidal waves, man's own destructive actions, and more recently the impacts of climate change, global warming and rising sea levels. In spite of this, many a visitor to this archipelago agrees that the Bahamian Out Islands remain some of the most beautiful and remote natural wonders of the world: still sparsely populated, largely undeveloped, and rich in history (College of the Bahamas, 2011, pp. 39–43).

These attributes are what have led many in the Government and the Ministry of Tourism to conclude that future touristic and other developments in the archipelago should aim to promote the retention of this profile; islands rich in unspoiled ecosystems that offer world-class fishing, diving and any number of outdoor sporting activities, small or medium sized anchor developments that are on the one hand, economically viable and support the thrust of sustainability and eco-centric living and on the other hand, are compatible with the laid back way of life that local communities embrace.

Critiquing Traditional Archipelago Tourism in The Bahamas and the New Push

The Bahamas economy is tourism-based and is highly susceptible to the effects of external forces and shifting trends in the global market, such as recession, job losses and layoffs, premature closing of businesses, and in extreme cases, devaluation of currencies. External threats to the economy of The Islands of The Bahamas have prompted environmentalists and others to urge that future development in the Out Islands be of the kind that can mitigate the crippling impacts of natural and man-made disasters on local and regional tourist centric economies. The devastation caused to tourist-centric economies and the global reverberations of the 11 September 2001 attacks in the US is a case in point (Ishmael, 2001).

Tourism is supported to a great degree by impulse purchases, and anything that prevents this limits economic activity in the target area. Natural disasters also impact touristic activities. In 2012, Hurricane Sandy swept through the Caribbean region and traveled the length of the Bahamian archipelago, forcing cruise ships to either cancel their sailing to ports in the region or to be re-routed to unscheduled neighbouring destinations. This severely affected most island ports in The Bahamas and cruise visitor arrivals for that period fell by some 17% with a corresponding fall in revenue (Bahamas Ministry of Tourism, 2012, p. 30). The fall-out from the movement of hurricane Sandy had a rippling effect not only on the Islands of The Bahamas, but all along the Eastern shores of the United States.

External events can shatter fragile archipelago tourism efforts in other ways as well. The points highlighted below show how The Bahamas has been impacted by external forces:

- Expansions in the regional cruise inventory have forced cruise lines to pursue a deliberate intensification of efforts to attract land-based (stopover) visitors to take cruises. The cruise industry inducements include heavily discounted packages that offer a plethora of on-board activities for guests that previously would only be available at on-land hotel facilities.
- Cruise Industry purchases of private islands in The Bahamas for exclusive use by cruise passengers increase vacation options and offerings and encourage passengers to spend all of their funds with the cruise lines and avoid comingling with on-land entities. Hence this negates the need for cruise passengers to disembark while in port. This reduction in spending in the local economy negatively affects contributions to the overall GDP.
- Casino gaming, once considered a major competitive advantage for The Bahamas, has over the last decade proliferated throughout North America and is expanding throughout the Caribbean. The availability of onboard casino gambling is another activity that entraps cruise passengers to remain on the ship.
- The expansion of tourism development activities in the capital city of Nassau in particular has led to a high volume of leakage of foreign exchange that is used to import tourism products and services. This is accompanied by a high demand for talented personnel to work in the tourist industry in The Bahamas and leads to an abnormally high recruitment of a foreign workforce to supplement the shortfall of Bahamian workers.
- The Bahamas has lost market share to neighbouring destinations such as Cuba, the Dominican Republic and Puerto Rico. Hartnell (2012, p. 1) suggests that this is due in part to them being lower cost destinations and the extent to which Nassau resorts such as Sandals Royal Bahamian and Super Clubs Breezes took room inventory off-line post Hurricane Irene.

Aware of the impacts that external forces have had on the local tourism product, the Ministry of Tourism crafted a business plan in 2005 that outlined strategies for re-launching the tourism product to include marketing The Bahamas as a rebranded archipelago destination.

The plan articulated a concept styled the New Bahamas where unique tourism experiences would be offered on each island appropriately branded and featuring tourism products specific to that island. The rebranding took into account major tourism development on each of those islands where there were population centres; the creation of an effective "hub and spoke" transportation system that would provide adequate airlift between major out of country destinations to Nassau and the Out Islands, between Nassau and the Out Islands, and inter-island transport channels. The overarching objective of this exercise was to remain competitive in a region where the proliferation of lower cost destinations was threatening the very core of archipelago tourism in The Bahamas. An aggressive push to make the archipelago of The Bahamas more visible, attractive, accessible, affordable and convenient to potential visitors was launched in 2009.

In June 2012, Obediah Wilchcombe, Bahamas Minister of Tourisms, announced that the country intended to resurface as a regional leader in tourism and recover market share lost to countries like Jamaica, Barbados, Cayman Islands, Cuba and the Dominican Republic. At the centre of efforts would be focused attention on advancing the rebranding of the Out Islands of The Bahamas. One of the strategies to be employed would be to tap into new and emerging markets such as Latin America (specifically Brazil), Russia, India, and Asia (Knowles, 2012).

In March 2013, The Bahamas was reported as embarking on new initiatives aimed at attracting even more tourists (Caribbean Journal, 2013). The announced initiatives included the commissioning of a new digital platform that would allow visitors to conduct easier searches for airlift, car rentals and hotels throughout The Bahamas. Key industry stakeholders would also be more closely involved in key promotional opportunities in untapped markets across the hemisphere, especially in Latin America (ibid.). And participation in events such as the World Tourism Council Meeting 2013, which was held in Brazil, signaled the launch of the new aggressive promotional thrust for the Ministry of Tourism's hemispheric tourism campaign. It also signaled the rollout of the rebranding exercise and reintroduced The Bahamas as a variety of island destinations outside of the traditional Nassau and Paradise Island touristic offerings.

Comments by the President and CEO of the World Travel and Tourism Council's (WTTC), David Scowsill, confirming that Latin America will be one of the fastest growing regions in terms of travel and tourism, showed that The Bahamas' announced effort was indeed demonstrative of forward thinking (Turner, 2013).

The new initiatives addressed by government were really follow up activities in support of actions initiated much earlier on but never fully pursued. In 1992, the Government of The Bahamas had adopted a new market-friendly economic policy that was meant to encourage the expansion and diversification of the Bahamian economy (InterKnowledge Corporation, 2010). The policy targeted both Bahamian and international investors, particularly those interested in deepening the tourism product. Many incentives such as exemptions from paying real property taxes, customs duty on imported goods to granting crown land to locals to be used for tourism development projects were placed on the table in order to make investing in the tourism product an attractive proposition.

Under "The Islands of The Bahamas" initiative, unique experiences that could only be had in each island were identified by the Ministry of Tourism and enhanced so as to give each island a distinctly different destination flavour. The island of Bimini was dubbed the "Sports Fishing Capital of the World"; Andros Island the "Marine Naturalist Paradise" where one could explore the World's third largest barrier reef; the Island of San Salvador, one of the first to be discovered by Christopher Columbus, was billed the "Island of

Table 9.2 Estimated value added impacts of guided and non-guided angler expenditures (in US$)

Island	Guided Anglers Direct Value Expenditure Added		Total Impact	Non-Guided Anglers			Total Economic Impact
				Direct Value	Total Expenditure	Added Impact	
Abaco	2,669,922	2,723,320	5,393,242	7,675,267	7,828,772	15,504,038	20,897,280
Andros	4,778,994	4,874,573	9,653,567	18,854,535	19,231,626	38,086,160	47,739,727
Grand Bahama	1,090,177	1,111,980	2,202,157	4,324,248	4,410,733	8,734,981	10,937,138
Eleuthera	1,374,575	1,402,066	2,776,641	5,360,276	5,467,482	10,827,759	13,604,400
Exuma	631,839	644,476	1,276,315	2,904,607	2,962,700	5,867,307	7,143,622
Nassau/New Providence	2,331,957	2,378,596	4,710,552	8,935,499	9,114,209	18,049,709	22,760,261
Other Islands	1,869,609	1,907,001	3,776,610	7,027,389	7,167,937	14,195,327	17,971,936
Total	14,747,071	15,042,013	29,789,084	55,081,822	56,183,458	111,265,281	141,054,364

Source: Fedler (2010, p. 13).

Discovery". This island had already gained international acclaim for its natural unspoiled beauty and its use by American colleges and universities from the Finger Lakes area of North America to house an international research and field station. Since that institution was established, thousands of students have participated in research studies at the station and hundreds more jostle annually for the opportunity to travel to the island to conduct research on marine habitats and/or participate in geological digs. While many of the other islands possess similar eco-marine systems, proper field stations that would allow for institutional research activities have not yet been established there.

Evidence of the success of many of the islands rests on the degree to which they contribute to the overall national economy. A clear example of economic activity beyond the usual tourism fare on other islands of The Bahamas is bonefishing. The bonefishing flats of The Bahamas enjoy a positive reputation based on the quality of the bonefishing experience, a wide array of flats fishing opportunities on each of the islands, large populations of bonefish inhabiting the flats, access to the islands and, most importantly, unpolluted clear and clean waters. Data showing the overall economic contributions made by bone fishing activity by island is provided as Table 9.2.

While a fresh idea in the 1990s, "The Islands of The Bahamas initiative" had petered out by the dawn of the new millennium. The initiative failed mostly because a series of prerequisite supporting components were not in place when the concept was introduced. A major omission was the absence of adequate inter-island transport to move domestic and international visitors to and from the various advertised island destinations. Another oversight in this initiative was the fact that many of the advertised destinations lacked appropriate infrastructure to support the introduction of or to the growth of the tourist trade. Additionally, many native Bahamians who called these islands home, would in many cases, reject outright the notion of sustained tourist visits on their islands, and this situation further exacerbated the effort. Finally, the implementing agency did not take into account the staggering cost of infrastructural and super-structural development that was necessary to support tourism activity on any of these islands. Nevertheless, the Ministry of Tourism still forged ahead with the implementation of this initiative and the marketing and advertising campaigns continued unabated.

There is a widely held belief among key stakeholders and those responsible for marketing the destination of The Bahamas that the wholesale all-encompassing, cookie-cutter type advertising campaigns that have long been the standard used to sell this destination and many throughout the Caribbean have long lost their appeal and effectiveness in enticing tourists to visit these destinations. To this end, scholars, tourism officials and foreign consultants began to study the phenomena of 'paradise lost' and by early 2013, it was patently clear to them that a revised approach was desperately needed by the Bahamas Ministry of Tourism. To achieve this, the process that gave birth to the rebranding initiative that eventually gave way to the new push for archipelago tourism would need to be reviewed. The process is documented below.

In 2009, Vincent Vanderpool-Wallace, Minister of Tourism at the time, authorised the re-launch of the initiative to re-brand the Islands of The Bahamas. The re-launch unveiled a new advertising campaign that displayed sixteen new island-specific logos intended to brand the major island destinations in The Bahamas. Duffy & Partners (n.d.), a global design firm out of New York City, was contracted to create a branding solution for these islands. They were charged with creating a marketing message that moved away from the usual sun, sand and sea vacation generally depicted in many Caribbean destinations. What resulted was a multi-stepped process that provided answers to questions about brand differentiation, island appeal, and brand identity and architecture. A brand book featuring the new identity was made available to the people of The Bahamas. This book took one through the various phases in the logo design process (Duffy & Partners, 2004).

In July 2013, former Tourism Minister Vanderpool-Wallace indicated that the initial intention was to "create a mini Caribbean" portrait for the purpose of marketing The Bahamas as a destination, where visitors to each island would be feted to the uniqueness of that island with respect to food, indigenous culture, heritage and entertainment. It was anticipated that Island Directors would be appointed to give directed leadership to the implementation of the vision for each island and each island could expect its 'signature logo' to be prominently displayed on its very own dedicated web-based portal designed just for this level of branding exercise.

Several entities offered their opinions on the articulated vision and the results of its implementation. The Executive Director of the Nassau Paradise Island Promotion Board, Raymond Francis, offered a public interview in that regard which was rather critical of the success of the rebranding initiative launched under Minister Vanderpool-Wallace. Francis opined that the initiative was poorly communicated to key stakeholders on each of the islands. They were not sufficiently consulted on its development and implementation nor were they always aware of what was being intended for their island. In fact, in many cases, locals had formed their own views as to what should have been the brand logo for their island. Moreover, with many of the islands having more similarities than uniqueness, it became difficult to identify which island really ought to have laid claim to that which was being suggested by tourism officials.

Francis' position was similar to that articulated in the findings from the Destination Segmentation Report (Rozga and McKeeman, 2009) on The Bahamas commissioned by the Bahamas Hotel and Tourism Association (BHTA). The report provided an in-depth analysis of the challenge of "sameness" as opposed to uniqueness to be found on all of the islands in The Bahamas. The report also cited stakeholder-input on market trends and issues of diversification and segmentation of "unsung assets" on each of the islands. Unsung assets are those attractions or places on each island that were considered by the locals to be unique to that island. Another issue the report addressed was the wide range of prices charged for hotel/motel accommodations on the various islands and suggested that it seemed to be a glaring deterrent to increased visitor patronage to many of the Out Islands. Additionally, the report found that operators and stakeholders could not agree on what elements should be termed 'authentically Bahamian".

Subsequent to the release of the Destination Segmentation Report for The Bahamas (Rozga and McKeeman, 2009), it seemed that the Ministry of Tourism was making a deliberate effort to treat each of the islands as a separate destination with specific needs that could not be met with the mere swipe of a rebranding brush. This was particularly true of its efforts in Freeport (The Bahamas' second city) on Grand Bahama Island.

A new government was elected to office in The Bahamas in early 2012 and, through political and executive appointments that impact the Grand Bahama economy, this regime has demonstrated that it is patently aware of the important role that Grand Bahama plays in the national economy. One can infer that the decision to focus attention on Grand Bahama might have been spurred on by the fact that the present minister of tourism hails from that island.

Major touristic investments are now being launched throughout the archipelago. The opening of Resorts World Bimini Bay Casino has increased touristic offering for visitors to the island of Bimini with synergistic impacts in the economy of that community.

This includes the acquisition and commissioning of a Superfast Ferry capable of transporting 4,000 passengers between Bimini and the USA mainland. The operators of the new resort is the Genting/Resorts World Group, a leading international resort, gaming, cruise line, agriculture and energy conglomerate based in Malaysia. Such global connections will extend the marketing of this entity beyond the region's traditional marketing zone and hopefully will induce increased visitor patronage from newer untapped markets (The Bahamas Investor, 2013).

Mega resort developments catering to mass tourism in Nassau Paradise Island continue at unprecedented levels. A new venture dubbed The Baha Mar, a US$3.5 billion single phase resort development, will start receiving guests in December 2014. This edifice is located in Western New Providence and is billed as the largest resort development in the Western Hemisphere. When this comes on stream, it is expected that the national economy will receive a 12.8% injection to its annual GDP (Dean, 2013). The Baha Mar Resort Development is the second mega resort development to be constructed in the traditional centre of tourism for The Bahamas. The other, the Atlantis Resort, is located on Paradise Island which is connected to Nassau by a bridge.

"Owning a Piece of Paradise" is another marketing strategy that was introduced to the Bahamas within the last decade and a half. It was intended to attract visitors to the Islands of The Bahamas and keep them here. This was the result of Government repealing the Immovable Property Act, 1981 which required prior approval for the purchase, transfer, or inheritance of real property by non-Bahamians. The Immovable Property Act, 1981 has been replaced by the International Persons Landholding Act, 1994. The new act simplifies the process of foreign ownership of homes and real estate in the Commonwealth of The Bahamas; it is now easier for foreigners to purchase or build second homes in the country, particularly in the Out Islands (InterKnowledge Corporation, 2010).

Transportation: A Means to an End

A good transportation system is key to supporting and growing a vibrant tourist trade. Transportation impacts inter-island travel and the ease with which goods, commodities and passengers are moved between points. The movement of people between islands and the overall accessibility of the islands of The Bahamian archipelago continue to present somewhat of a challenge to local tourism.

Despite the challenges though, in recent years, there has been marked improvement in airlift and ferry services for domestic and international travelers within the archipelago. Some major carriers, such as American Airlines and Delta, are now servicing the Out Islands with direct flights from major hubs in North America, Canada and Europe. However, it is their interfacing with the local 'hub-and-spoke' transportation system that can be quite frustrating at times for their travelers.

Air Travel through the Archipelago

When compared with other ports, transportation costs for inter-island travel in the Bahamian archipelago can be unexpectedly high for spontaneous visitors who may take a fancy to hopping to another island while on vacation at a target island destination. Visitors soon find out that, in order to move from one island to another, they must first travel back to Nassau to access the inter-island hub. The Nassau hub serves as the major transit point for many of the international carriers calling on The Bahamas. The efficiencies gained involved in travelers getting to and from the Out Islands (such as access by air or ground transportation, US pre-clearance, and visa/passport controls) are seen as the critical factor for tourism's success in the rebranding programme.

While commenting on ease of travel between islands in The Bahamas, former minister of tourism challenge the next generation of tourism professionals to come up with better ways to maximise the proximity between The Bahamas and the United States. The reality is that in many cases it takes longer and is more expensive to get around many of our out islands (Rolle, 2009)

At present, Bahamas Air, the National Flag Carrier of The Bahamas, operates a hub-and-spoke system where passengers wanting to fly between islands, must first return to Nassau before flying onto their desired destinations. The challenges inherent in this become those of costs associated with having to (in some cases) purchase more than one airline ticket. There is also the question of wasted time when one has to return to Nassau (and in some cases overnight) before flying out again. Most international visitors are not aware of these costs until confronted with them.

In the last five years, efforts to improve the aviation industry in The Bahamas have produced an uptick in available flights to the Out Islands. Several local low-cost carriers have entered the market to provide both domestic and international airlift between islands. These include Sky Bahamas (which also services routes between several of the islands and South Florida), Western Air, Pineapple Air, and a myriad of small and medium-sized aircrafts offering charter flight services.

A number of marketing initiatives have been instituted to compliment the entry of low-cost carriers servicing the Out Islands that have helped to propel the Ministry of Tourism's re-branding exercise to new heights. One of the biggest success stories to date is the ambitious 'Air Credit' programme launched by the Ministry of Tourism in conjunction with the various tourism promotion boards in August of 2012 (Todd, 2012). This incentive programme offers to the potential visitor a US$200 credit for booking vacation stays to islands other than New Providence, of between three to five nights. Those who booked five or more nights received a US$350 credit. Initially the programme was intended to run for six months, but it was never discontinued and presently remains one of the most popular incentives for travelers to The Bahamas. It has also proven to be a strategic stimulant for attracting visitation to the Out Islands.

A second initiative, called the 'Fuel Credit Programme', has attracted a number of small and medium-size enterprises (SMEs). This was instituted by the Bahamas Out Islands Promotions Board (BOIPB, 2013). The Fuel Credit Programme targets licensed private pilots only. In order to qualify, pilots are required to stay at one of the participating BOIPB resorts or hotels for a minimum four-night, air-inclusive stay (with single or double occupancy). The US300 in fuel credit is given once the pilot satisfies the requirements and presents a copy of the stamped Bahamas immigration form in the name of the traveling party.

There are also incentive measures that target domestic tourism and the "Companion Fly Free Programme" is by far the most popular. It was instituted to encourage Bahamians to visit the Out Islands and to allay concerns about the high cost associated with travel to these islands (Bahamas Ministry of Tourism, 2011). Between the Ministry of Tourism and the participating Bahamian Hotels, US$31.7 million was spent in the first 18 months of the programme. This translated into 450,000 room-nights of business to hotels in Nassau, Paradise Island, Grand Bahama and the Out Islands. More than 26 resorts in various Out

Islands are participating in this programme. This level of economic stimulation especially in the Out Islands was hailed a success by many pundits (BahamasLocal.com, 2011).

Another new niche marketing area for The Bahamas involves efforts to court visitors who own private airplanes. At present, the government, through the efforts of the Ministry of Tourism, has taken steps to encourage owners to fly to The Bahamas and spend a few days enjoying the island of their choice. A number of FBO (fixed-based operators) are presently operating to and from The Bahamas.

Sea Travel through the Archipelago

The Fast Ferry Service

Along with air services, Bahamas Ferries operates the only inter-island, high-speed, waterborne transportation service in the country. They presently operate four high-speed, ocean-going craft: The Sealink, the Seawind, the Bo Hengy, and the Bo Hengy II. These crafts are modern vessels that are fully enclosed, and air conditioned. They are certified by the Bahamas Maritime Authority and the International Maritime Organisation's high speed codes, the highest international standard of safety. Passengers are provide with a unique 'by sea' experience at an affordable rate.

The "MailBoat Company" is another ferry option for inter-island travel. While limited in the number of ports it services, this craft takes longer to arrive at the destinations, but it also caters to both the domestic and international traveler. Perhaps this is not the most desirable mode of travel for a visitor to the islands because this boat is used primarily for the transshipment of freight and cargo. The MailBoat does however boast a seating capacity of 450 persons. Backpackers and allocentric tourist, those who enjoy adventure, enjoy meeting new people and often make their own travel arrangements, (Plog, 1967) may enjoy this mode of transportation to the Out Islands as it allows them more time to commune with nature and take in the scenic environments.

Mail Boats of The Bahamas

Mail-boats represent the original mode of inter-island transportation in the archipelago and are part of a fleet of state-subsidised motor tenders that ply the waters of the archipelago transporting passengers, mail, goods, vehicles, livestock, groceries, farm produce and anything that needs transporting between the islands. This system of inter-island travel has existed for as long there have been inhabitants on these islands and became of great importance during the days of prohibition and rum running. For many of the far flung or remote Islands and Cays in the country the mail-boat continues to be the only link there is with the centre of commerce in Nassau and some of their neighbouring islands.

Travel on the mail-boat is not high-speed and can be quite uncomfortable for some. They are not your fancy modern-day wonders of the water. And yet, more tourists are using them to island hop, especially the adventurous types.

Private Boats and Yachts

The continued development of the maritime industry in the country spawned the birth of many requests from foreign investors to develop private marinas on islands where there is also resurgence in second home development. These developments are often accompanied by the construction of private yacht docks. A cogent inclusion in travel data for The Bahamas is the impact that yachts and pleasure boats have on the local economy, particularly of the Out Islands. The presence of yachts, skippers, pleasure crafts, sailboats or fishing boats berthed in the harbours or marinas of the many populated and uninhabited islands is commonplace throughout the archipelago. Most of these craft are owned by or operated by visitors who spend extended stays in the archipelago living on their boats but spending into the local economies. This is welcomed especially in the Out Islands. Pleasure seekers and second home owners often fly to the destination to join their crafts. Few come by commercial airlines.

Best Practice Recommendations to Guide Out-island Development

It is likely that there will always be a demand for the traditional and high-end luxury offerings such as can be found in the mega resort towns in the United Arab Emirates, Las Vegas, and Nassau / Paradise Island and these may well persist as a mainstay of the mass tourism landscape.

The Bahamas Ministry of Tourism is being challenged to respond to declining visitor satisfaction with the overall Bahamian (tourist) experience and the need to offer a more diverse product to discerning visitors. The ministry's response has been to offer the "The Islands of The Bahamas" marketing concept, a new, vigorous and aggressive advertising campaign that seeks to highlight the variety of island offerings to be encountered on a Bahamian vacation experience.

Ecotourism measures are appealing to a larger number of visitors and islands that promote this component have already registered an increase in arrivals. The islands of Abaco, Bimini, Cat Island, Eleuthera, Harbour Island, Exuma, San Salvador and Long Island have been identified as experiencing unprecedented growth in tourist arrivals over the last decade, due in large part to the eco-resort and second home development activities on the islands. Apart from their pristine condition, unused beaches, rich tropical scenery and wildlife, these islands offer a rich heritage of eco-friendly hotel development and ecologically-friendly investments that ensure minimal trampling and low carbon foot prints in their fragile ecology. In fact, the government through its directed marketing efforts now offers favourable considerations and incentives to potential investors if they establish ventures that preserve the environment. The opening of the small boutique Tiamo Resort hotel in Andros; the upscale Delphi Club in South Abaco and the opening of the S&T Beach Club in San Salvador reflect the new trend in the Out Islands, with small exclusive, sustainable initiatives that are less prone to triggers in the world economy.

Local Bahamian investor groups and families with strong financial ties have also been courted to return to their birth-islands to develop small and medium-size enterprises with an island theme. Many of the new small resorts have incorporated environmentally friendly standards of operation. The Star Island Project located in Eleuthera is a prime example of these types of resorts (S.T.A.R. Innovation and Development, 2011).

All of the islands identified have modern and up-to-date infrastructure such as excellent roads, potable water, electricity, state of the art telecommunication facilities and most importantly, access to the islands by way of modern airports, marinas, and docking facilities. Thus, to underscore the seriousness of the government's intent in establishing these islands as the gateway to the new Bahamas, The Bahamas Investment Authority recently reported that the Inter-American Development Bank had announced the availability of funding for the establishment of environmentally-sensitive hotel and resort ventures in The Bahamas and that individuals or entities trying to access funding of this nature no longer required state guarantees to proceed (InterKnowledge Corporation, 2010).

Today's tourists are technology-savvy and spend a great deal of time surfing the internet. In order to reach potential clients, marketing must target them where they can be reached. The Out Island Promotions Board created the 'Out Islands of The Bahamas' website to do just that (BOIPB, 2013). Tranquility seekers looking for luxury eco-resort destinations are able to log onto this site and immediately access all participating eco-resorts on the Out Islands.

Conclusion

The extent to which archipelago tourism remains a successful venture in The Bahamas will be determined by the enlightened decisions of policy makers in the Ministry of Tourism who hopefully will be guided by leading-edge best practices that are linked to global industry trends.

Major shifts in what are motivating present-day and future travelers must be a prominent part of the tourism development conversation going forward. The World Travel Market Report, 2013 suggests that there are a few key indicators for tourist planners to watch out for. These include the new trend of inquires and bookings from a more exclusive and 'professional' clientele for luxury 'micro' stays at resorts where there are no children. Meanwhile, social media are playing a key role in linking travelers with destinations and an increasing number of travelers are opting to use low cost carriers to get to their destinations of choice. Tourist destinations would do well to note these trends and strategise appropriate responses (World Travel Market Report, 2013, pp. 12–14).

Growth in the cruise industry, particularly from the Chinese market, is expected to have a significant impact on those islands equipped to accommodate additional cruise ships and a large influx of cruise passengers from non-traditional markets such as Brazil, China, and other Asian/Eastern economies (Rokou, 2013). The implications for The Bahamas and other small island developing states are enormous; the greatest concern being that of sustainability – even the ability to continue to sustain low impact tourism.

Increase in visitor arrivals to all the islands of The Bahamas comes with the urgent mandate of finding ways of moving people economically to and from the various island destinations. This will require bringing focused attention to bear on the hub islands of Nassau and Grand Bahama; to review carrying capacity in these zones and to make appropriate adjustments to stay ahead of the game by improving infrastructure and supports services that favour development of all types.

Acknowledgements

Special thanks to my soul mate Kirk Lopez for his untiring assistance in editing this chapter, and to my colleagues, Margo Blackwell, Jessica Minnis and Antoinette Pinder-Darling, for their edits and fact checking.

References

Bahamaslocal.com. (2011). 'Fly free' promotion costs partners $32m, *Tribune*, 5 July. Retrieved from http://www.bahamaslocal.com/newsitem/25908/cable_bahamas/

Bahamas Ministry of Tourism. (2012). *The islands of the Bahamas: Arrivals report. "2012: The beginning of something great?"* Nassau, The Bahamas: Research and Statistics Department.

Bahamas Ministry of Tourism. (2011). History of the Ministry of Tourism. Nassau, Bahamas. Retrieved from http://www.tourismtoday.com/home/about-2/tourism-history/

Bahamas Ministry of Tourism. (2011). Launch of the domestic tourism programme. Nassau, Bahamas. Retrieved from http://www.tourismtoday.com/home/launch-of-the-domestic-tourism-programme/

Bahama Out Island Promotions Board. (2013). Private pilot offer: 300 fuel credit. Retrieved from http://www.myoutislands.com/USA-private-pilots.cfm

Bahama Out Island Promotions Board. (2013). Out Island eco-friendly resorts and hotels. Retrieved from http://www.myoutislands.com/natural-vacations/eco-travel.cfm

Caribbean Journal. (2013). Bahamas plans new tourism push. *Caribbean Journal*, 3 March. Retrieved from http://www.caribjournal.com/2013/03/03/bahamas-plans-new-tourism-push/

CIA World Factbook. (2013). *Bahamas: economic profile.* Washington DC: Central Intelligence Agency. Retrieved from http://www.indexmundi.com/the_bahamas/economy_profile.html

College of the Bahamas. (2011). *Alumni magazine.* Retrieved from http://www.cob.edu.bs/Publications/AlumniMag/AM_Fall11.pdf

Dean, R. (2013). BahaMar becomes a major driver of Bahamian economy. *The Bahamas Weekly.com*, 7 June. Retrieved from http://www.thebahamasweekly.com/publish/new-providence-bahamas/Baha_Mar_Becomes_A_Major_Driver_Of_Bahamian_Economy28818.shtml

Duffy and Partners. (2004). *Designer's workshop.* Retrieved from http://www.duffypov.com/assets/download/art130/BAH-DesignersWorkshop_june2004.pdf

Duffy and Partners. (n.d.). *Creating a branded experience.* Retrieved from http://www.duffypov.com/duffy-article/130/creating-a-branded-experience-the-bahamas

Family Island Development Encouragement Act 2008. (Commonwealth). Retrieved from http://laws.bahamas.gov.bs/cms/images/LEGISLATION/PRINCIPAL/2008/2008-0014/FamilyIslandsDevelopmentEncouragementAct_1.pdf

Fedler, T. (2010). *The economic impact of flats fishing in The Bahamas.* Report prepared for the Bahamian Flats Fishing Alliance. Retrieved from http://www.igfa.org/images/uploads/files/Bahamas_Flats_Economic_Impact_Report.pdf

Hartnell, N. (2013). Bahamas 'grew' stopover market share during 2012. *Tribune*, 4 January. Retrieved from http://www.tribune242.com/news/2013/jan/04/bahamas-grew-stopover-market-share-during-2012/

InterKnowledge Corporation. (2010). *A paradise for the Americas.* Retrieved from http://www.geographia.com/bahamas/investment/toursm01.htm

InterKnowledge Corporation. (2010). *Owning a piece of Paradise.* Retrieved from http://www.geographia.com/bahamas/investment/propty01.htm

Ishmael, O. (2001). The impact of the September 11 terrorist attacks against the United States on Caribbean political economy. Lecture held at Spelman College, Atlanta GA, USA, 28 November. Retrieved from http://www.guyana.org/Speeches/ishmael_112801.html

Knowles, K. (2012). Out Island promotions board gets millions for marketing. *Bahamas Journal*, 14 June. Retrieved from http://jonesbahamas.com/out-island-promotions-board-gets-millions-for-marketing/

Palmer, C.A. (1994). Tourism and colonialism: the experience of the Bahamas. *Annals of Tourism Research*, 21(4), 792–811.

Plog, S.C. (1974). Why destination areas rise and fall in popularity. *The Cornell Hotel & Restaurant Administration Quarterly*, 4(4), 55–8.

Rokou, T. (2013). Travel and tourism in a fast-changing world: new trends for 2014. *World Travel Market Report 2013*, 7 November. Retrieved from http://www.traveldailynews.com/news/article/57551/ravel-and-tourism-in-a

Rolle, C. (2009). Minister of Tourism updates: Minister challenges young Bahamians to advance tourism. *The Bahamas Weekly*, 6 July. Retrieved from http://www.tourismtoday.com/home/minister-challenges-young-bahamians-to-advance-tourism/

Rozga, Z., and McKeeman, J. (2009). *Destination segmentation report for the Bahamas*. Nassau, The Bahamas: WHL Consulting.

S.T.A.R. Innovation & Development. (2011). The world's coolest green address. Retrieved from http://www.starislandproject.com/

The Bahamas Investor. (2013). PM's remarks at Bimini casino opening, 1 July. Retrieved from http://www.thebahamasinvestor.com/2013/pms-remarks-at-bimini-casino-opening/ Thompson, A. (1979). *An economic history of the Bahamas*. Nassau, The Bahamas: Commonwealth Publishing.

Todd, J. (2012). MoT pumps 6M into air credits. *Nassau Guardian*, 2 November. Retrieved from http://www.tourismtoday.com/home/mot-pumps-6m-into-air-credits

Turner, R. (2013). *Travel and tourism economic impact 2013: Brazil*. World Travel and Tourism Council, Sovereign Court, London. Retrieved from http://www.wttc.org/research/economic-impact-research/country-reports/b/brazil/

World Travel Market. (2013). *World Travel Market Report 2013*, 7 November. Retrieved from http://www.hospitalitynet.org/file/152005208.pdf

PART III
Pacific Ocean

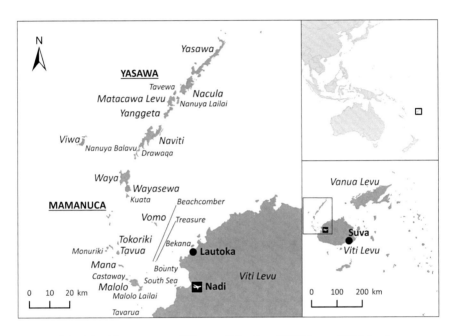

Figure 10.1   The Mamanuca and Yasawa Islands, off Viti Levu, Fiji Islands

Chapter 10
Competing Islands? The Mamanuca and Yasawa Islands, Fiji

John Connell

Introduction

In multi-island states, outlying islands are usually disadvantaged in terms of tourism, since they are beyond the standard tourist gaze (especially where the majority of tourists are from overseas), have limited infrastructure, and no effective means of marketing themselves. Additionally, they may have no particular attractions that differentiate them from larger, more central islands. Moreover the islands in many archipelagos within island states, such as Fiji, Tuvalu and Kiribati, are similar in culture and geography. How then do such islands enter the tourism economy – should they choose to do so – and what might they gain from it? Should they compete – indeed can and do they compete – to draw tourists to particular islands, or collaborate for the benefit of the archipelago as a whole? Will some islands benefit at the expense of others? This chapter seeks to examine these themes in the context of two archipelagos in Fiji where tourism has become of gradually increasing significance since the 1960s.

In the case of the two western Fijian archipelagos, the Mamanuca and Yasawa islands, how might tourists be drawn from the larger, more accessible island of Viti Levu (the location of most resorts, and the starting point of almost all tourists, given the location of the international airport), at what may sometimes be greater cost? Most small islands within small island states such as Fiji have limited opportunities for both development and livelihood diversity, hence tourism is usually regarded as a welcome means of some movement towards modernity. Indeed the smaller the island the more likely that tourism is seen as a panacea, however improbable that can be, for development. Achieving that condition normally poses considerable problems.

Tenuous Livelihoods

Both the Mamanucas and Yasawas are island chains of volcanic origin, some islands having peaks over 500 metres above sea level. Before tourism became established in Fiji the Yasawas, and to a lesser extent the Mamanucas, were some of the more remote and isolated outer islands in the country. In the colonial era, on the eve of the Second World War, the Yasawas had 'few contacts with the rest of Fiji. The population consists almost exclusively of Fijians, who practise subsistence agriculture and export some copra which is transported in small cutters to Lautoka' (Naval Intelligence Division, 1944, p. 255). Six of the islands were populated. The largest island, Yasawa, had a population of 610 in 1936. Naviti had 752, Waya had 544 and Nacula just 456 people. The smaller islands of Matacawa Levu and Yaqeta had 297 between them. These were therefore very small and fragmented island communities with only infrequent connections with the main Fijian island, or mainland, of Viti Levu. The smaller Mamanuca group is much closer to Viti Levu but had an even smaller population, with only three of the islands being populated and with Malolo having the largest population of 239.

Collectively, the two island archipelagos had less than 4000 residents, all of whom were then engaged in the same kind of mixed subsistence-cash agriculture as was described above for the Yasawas but with very narrow potential because of the limited availability of land and good soil (with such Fijian staples as taro and cassava, and also kava, being impossible to grow on most of the islands because of poor soils and inadequate rainfall), the price of copra (the lone cash crop), remoteness from the major port of Lautoka and small populations. While the islands developed sophisticated subsistence fishing economies, in comparison with most other parts of Fiji maintaining a viable and diverse livelihood was particularly difficult. After the war the two groups, like other outlying Fijian archipelagos to the east of the two main islands, gradually became sources of migration to the mainland, and populations began to steadily fall.

It was optimistically noted in 1951 that,

> Notwithstanding their isolation, the Yasawas are becoming known even outside Fiji. Scenes for the film *The Blue Lagoon* were taken on their beaches and the scenery and climate are both of a quality likely to attract the tourist if the necessary transport facilities and amenities can be provided' (Derrick, 1951, p. 214).

It took four more decades for that observation to become true. The two archipelagos boasted four key advantages for tourism. Small islands could be marketed as idyllic self-contained destinations, they were not too far from the international airport in Nadi, the climate was drier than other parts of Fiji, and the mountainous volcanic landscape was an attractive backdrop to blue seas. Disadvantages for other forms of development – low rainfall and poor soils – were no great disadvantage to tourism, and fishing skills proved valuable.

The Rise of Tourism in the Mamanucas and Yasawas

Tourism in Fiji effectively began in the 1920s. By the mid-1920s there were some 3,000 visitors and a Suva Tourist Bureau was established, but government indifference and distance limited the number of arrivals. In 1937 there were just 1,300 visitors and 6,400 cruise ship passengers. Accessibility improved substantially with the construction of a major airport at Nadi in 1940 and tourist numbers grew slowly through the 1950s. More aggressive national marketing (mainly by airlines) and the introduction of jet aircraft on Pacific routes in the 1960s (with Nadi as the central Pacific hub) laid the basis for a modern industry, that was primarily focused on the Coral Coast on the south coast of the main island of Viti Levu, and dependent on tourists from Australia and New Zealand, and, rather later, from North America (Britton, 1983, Lockhart and Chandra, 1997). Fiji became independent in 1970 at a time when tourism was growing rapidly and was recognised as a major plank in national development strategies. Tourist numbers grew for most of the subsequent forty years but at variable rates dependent on recessions in traditional markets, and political uncertainty – notably coups that reversed growth trends – with more diverse sources including Asia and Europe. Visitor numbers to Fiji increased from 110,000 in 1970 to 319,000 in 1994; thus passing the 300,000 that was once seen to be the maximum number that Fiji might reasonably accommodate, reaching 431,000 in 2003 and 675,000 in 2011. By then, tourism had overtaken sugar as the most important source of foreign exchange. Of the visitors in 2011, the majority (51%) were from Australia with the next largest group from New Zealand (15%). Smaller numbers came from Europe and America, with China (4%) for the first time passing the United Kingdom. Present growth is anticipated to involve a relative increase in the number of Chinese tourists. Almost all tourists still come from distant metropolitan nations with Australia being the largest source.

In the 1960s, most hotels were in the capital, Suva, where they had a business orientation, and near Nadi airport, where the biggest hotels were being developed. In the late 1960s roads were improved and the focus shifted to the Coral Coast, but by the early 1970s 'growing affluence among discretionary travellers led to demand for resorts that provided inclusive facilities in small high quality units. These were first developed on the Mamanuca islands' (Lockhart and Chandra, 1997, p. 308), where occasional yachts had previously visited. The first outer-island resort had been established by a local European entrepreneur on Plantation Island in 1966. Expansion into the Mamanucas was partly a function of boom conditions that lasted until the mid-1970s. As the boom slowed, national attention again focused on the Nadi area and the Coral Coast, and in the 1990s concentrated on the Denarau coastal area north of Nadi, where swampy areas could be reclaimed for large inclusive resorts operated by international companies such as Sheraton.

Although by the end of the 1970s a small number of tourist ventures had begun in the Mamanucas, it was two more decades later before tourism development effectively reached the Yasawas. By the late 1970s, it was estimated that the two archipelagos generated 4% of the tourist turnover in Fiji (with Viti Levu taking 94%) hence this was the only small island region where tourism was significant (Britton, 1983, p. 189) though then almost entirely confined to Malololailai, adjoining the nearest inhabited island to the mainland. Initially visiting the Yasawas was limited to rare cruise ships, with passengers not allowed to actually set foot on the islands until the 1950s, and land-based tourism ventures restricted until 1987. Development was then stimulated by local interest, with the government later providing an ecotourism startup fund and eventually the arrival of the Yasawa Flyer catamaran, early this century.

In the first edition of a series of Moon Publication Handbooks in 1985, three resorts were listed in the Mamanucas: Beachcomber Island, and Plantation Island and Dick's Place (later Musket Cove) on Malololailai. Each was oriented primarily at budget travellers and all offered dormitory accommodation. Beachcomber Island was seen as particularly attractive to young Australians – 'there's a sand floor bar, you can stroll round it in 10 minutes. There's no hot water but in this heat who needs it? Occasionally there is no cold either' (Stanley, 1985, p. 85). The larger Malolo island – accessible by foot from Malololailai at low tide – had no tourist accommodation. Allegedly 'Plans to build 3 hotels, 700 villas, a golf course, restaurants and shops on Malolo were vetoed by the villagers as it would have spoiled their fishing grounds, meant an end to their privacy, and besides, they didn't need the estimated million [dollars] a year anyway' (ibid.). If that was true then it was soon to change. By 1990 the Australian-owned Club Naitasi – which included private units developed under a time sharing scheme – had been established on the island.

In contrast, the 1985 Moon Handbook had little to say on the Yasawas:

> Small village guest houses have appeared on at least 2 islands, but even here a visit means taking along some yanggona [kava] which doesn't grow in the Yasawas and observing the conditions outlined in "staying in villages" above. You'll also have to take most of your

own food ... Unfortunately a lot of culturally insensitive people have been going over without taking anything with them lately, expecting to be fed by the locals for a week. This has created local food shortages and the reception has cooled (Stanley, 1985, p. 86).

At Waya, *bures* [traditional thatched houses] could be rented for A$5 (US$4) per head and on Tavewa two families accepted paying guests at A$6 (US$5) per head (extra with food) and were planning on building *bures* specifically for such visitors. Technically tourists were expected to get a permit from the Department of Agriculture in Lautoka, based on a letter of invitation from the village leader, except for Tavewa where land was held in freehold. The Handbook however suggested: 'There are always Yasawans around Lautoka market on Fridays. If you befriend someone or manage to persuade a boat captain, you might be able to go without bureaucratic sanction' (ibid.). Tourism in the Yasawas was in its absolute infancy. Five years later, little had changed but accommodation on Tavewa had expanded slightly. Permits were still required.

However, though Moon initially ignored it, the tiny island of Nanuya Levu, where the original *Blue Lagoon* had been filmed just after the War, was already known as the site of one of Fiji's most exclusive resorts: Turtle Island. In 1990, guests (mixed couples only) paid US$480 a night, with a minimum stay of six days, and arrived by seaplane at an extra US$480 per couple. The island was off limits to anyone other than hotel staff and guests.

Otherwise, most tourists simply saw the Yasawas from the decks of cruise ships that made day-long or three-day tours through the islands occasionally stopping at particular sites. Several of the villages had set up temporary markets on the beaches, selling shells, carvings, necklaces and mats. Commercial tourism was emerging. Thus, even by the end of the 1980s, not only had most of the islands in both archipelagos become at least tenuously accessible – though staying in the Yasawas was particularly difficult – but a degree of diversity had emerged between the backpacker dormitories of Malololailai, the *bures* of Tavewa and the luxury of Turtle Island.

During the late 1980s and 1990s, more of the islands, initially in the Mamanuca group, began to acquire tourist developments of some kind, many being established on hitherto unpopulated islands. Thus the Japanese-owned Mana Island Resort became the largest in the islands with 132 bungalows in 1990. Later the island was fiercely divided between this resort and locally owned backpacker accommodation (Stanley, 2007, p. 69). Nearby Matamanoa became the furthest resort from Nadi and Navini acquired a small resort. By the mid-2000s, almost every Mamanuca island of any size had acquired a resort of some kind though only Mana and Malolo were also inhabited by Fijian villagers. By 2005 Malololailai, with three resorts (one belonging to the Raffles Group), a marina, a nine-hole golf course and proposals for more time share condominiums, was seen as 'becoming overdeveloped' (Stanley, 2007, p. 63). Malolo was then developing similarly. Likuliku Lagoon Resort opened in 2007: the first luxury resort in the Mamanucas (with 'luxury' perhaps defined as being, like Turtle Cove, off limits to non-guests) with over-water '*bures*' at F$1,950 (US$1,100) per day. As the reference to *bures* indicates luxury resorts were designed to resemble, at least superficially, local village houses (despite villagers being anxious to move away from thatched roofing). The resort's website states:

> Once upon a time across the bluest of oceans, an island was born of lava and sand: an untouched paradise whose heart was a turquoise lagoon of unimaginable beauty and tranquility. The first visitors came and explored. To honour the magic of the place, they named it "Likuliku", meaning "calm waters". Likuliku Lagoon Resort Fiji is a haven of

subtle luxury and the first and only resort in Fiji with over-water bures. It is a unique and special place designed with integrity to Fijian cultural values, traditional designs and architecture, and is embraced by the renowned warmth of the Fijian people. From the water it looks like an ancient village, so traditional is the style. The beating heart of the Resort is a magnificent building in the design of a Fijian canoe house. Surrounded by sprawling ceilings, hand-woven thatch and an exotic mix of natural materials and modern elements, Likuliku embodies the richness of an ancient culture with vibrant present-day lifestyle touches. Welcome to Fiji's most unique luxury escape for couples. Welcome to your magical sanctuary (Likuliku Lagoon Resort, 2014).

Likuliku was a couples-only resort, the first in Fiji with over water accommodation, by then standard enough in the Maldives and French Polynesia. Chefs from New Zealand and Australia were producing a 'signature crabmeat omelet' matched by a 'fine wine list' balanced by a lagoon-facing spa (Kurosawa, 2013). A year afterwards Wadigi Island Resort was established nearby, at twice the price ('why book a hotel room when you can have an entire island'), and Tokoriki, Mama and Vomo islands all now host similar luxury resorts.

Tavarua, the southernmost tourist island became the 'South Pacific's' most famous surfing resort', with access to world-class breaks, catering to more affluent and more mature surfers. The Resort had even purchased exclusive rights to Fiji's most famous surfing spot, Cloudbreak, from the Fijian clan that held fishing rights (*qoliqoli*) there (Stanley, 2007, pp. 65–6), though a 2010 'surfing decree' annulled private leases over surfing areas. Even within the Mamanucas a considerable diversity was being established but with a growing focus on expense and exclusivity rather than the backpacker scene, beyond the Funky Fish Resort on Malolo, which increasingly catered to flashpackers (usually older backpackers, with bigger budgets and a preference for greater comfort), and Beachcomber and Bounty Islands (Stanley, 2007). Even so the backpacker scene grew again at the end of the decade as demand increased and small islands such as Bounty Island and South Sea Island, uninhabited because of the lack of water, became resorts.

In contrast, in the Yasawas:

> Only since 2000 have the Yasawans themselves recognized the money-making potential of tourism. Now a bumper crop of low budget 'resorts' has burst forth up and down the chain, as the villagers rush to cash in (Stanley, 2007, p. 172).

While that contradicts the agency of the Yasawa islanders described by the same author earlier, and reflects the considerable distance from tourist sources, the chronology is certainly correct. Finally the Yasawas were more formally involved in tourism, and a Nacula Tikina Tourism Association was coordinating development of locally owned backpacker lodges on the central islands (notably Tavewa and Nacula) surrounding the well-known blue lagoon. The backpacker resorts generally comprised a combination of two person *bures*, dormitories and spaces for camping, with generators or kerosene lamps providing the lighting. All are owned by local people, sometimes, as at Waialailai, by the entire nearby village, and sometimes by particular land holding groups (*mataqali*). Activities are similarly small-scale, dominated by walking, snorkelling and diving, with little significant impact on the environment.

Despite the proliferation of small backpacker oriented resorts, a number of more elite resorts have also been established, following the lead of Turtle Island. The Navutu Stars resort on Yaqeta is oriented to 'romantic couples' and usually excludes children under sixteen (Stanley, 2007, p. 182), while the Yasawa Island Resort was opened in 1991. As its website argues:

> **Yasawa Island Resort and Spa** is an exclusive retreat on one of the most remote and unspoiled islands of Fiji. Just 18 luxury bungalows are hidden among the palms, each just a few steps from a pristine white beach. Swim in crystal clear waters, dive on vividly coloured corals, connect with an ancient culture or indulge in Fiji's first beachfront spa. Whatever you choose to do at Yasawa, you'll do it in complete seclusion (Yasawa Island Resort, 2014).

Meanwhile, on Turtle Island:

> This entirely all-inclusive, exotic tropical paradise can be rented for a week at a time. Escape to Turtle Island with your company as an incentive or group meeting, have your dream wedding on the beach of the Blue Lagoon with all of your friends and family, invite the entire family for a reunion that you'll remember forever, or just get all of your best friends together for an island party of a lifetime! (Turtle Island, 2014a).

In a more limited way, the Yasawas have thus experienced some degree of diversification, and the 'upgrading' of initially basic backpacker resorts, as accommodation and food improved, has resulted in higher prices. Nonetheless, the primary market in the Yasawas is backpackers and the growing number of flashpackers, and air-conditioned dormitory rooms could still be booked online at the start of 2014 for A$8 (US$7) per day.

By the end of the 2000s, every populated island in the two archipelagos had at least one tourist resort however small. A few, like Mana and Malololailai, had more than one. Several resorts had been established on hitherto unpopulated islands and, within the constraints of small islands, resorts had been developed to suit most tastes. With few exceptions development was limited by the size of the islands and thus by access to land, water, labour and fresh produce (most of which in the Mamanucas came from Viti Levu but in the Yasawas included more locally grown produce). In the Mamanucas most destinations were developed by foreign entrepreneurs, occasionally very large corporate entities, but in the Yasawas only Turtle Island and the Yasawa Island Resort were not primarily local endeavours. Islanders simply sought to replicate what they had seen elsewhere, and draw the increasing number of tourists to their own particular island. There was both competition and collaboration.

Marketing the Periphery

Promoting Fiji as a tourist destination has generally involved three themes: tropical island South Seas imagery, cultural and scenic attractions unique to Fiji, and experiences distinct from urbanised metropolitan lifestyles (Britton, 1983, p. 36) and these have scarcely changed in half a century. The longest standing slogan has been 'Fiji: the way the world should be'. Promotion in major destinations like Australia is through television advertisements, feature stories in newspapers and brochures from travel agents. Only the latter two feature specific islands or island groups. At different time films have indirectly contributed to marketing Fiji, notably the first two *Blue Lagoon* films, partly filmed in the Yasawas, and *Castaway*, filmed on the small island of Monuriki, ironically one of the few

Mamanuca islands too small for tourism (except for day cruises). In 1995–96 the remake of *Swiss Family Robinson* as a TV series was shot on *Blue Lagoon*'s private island, Nanuya Lailai, and in 1996 the original movie *Contact* starring Jodie Foster was also located in the Yasawa island group.

Most tourism is undertaken through package tours, but alongside a significant independent, mainly 'backpacker' market. Most tourists thus book accommodation before reaching Fiji, with only limited familiarity with the country, and its diversity. Inevitably all Fijian island destinations are described in glowing terms, with the most obvious differentiation in brochures being in price and in range of activities (or the lack of them).

The national tourism agency's website has a map that ignores both archipelagos but markets tourism through of both places and themes: diving and snorkelling, action and adventure, backpacking, conference and incentives, cruising and sailing, family, sports and golf, and weddings and honeymoons. The majority of these categories are not linked to the archipelagos, but under 'action and adventure', within a range of possibilities, it is suggested: 'join a Jet Ski safari and be led on a fun, adventurous trip offshore by experienced guides around the Mamanucas'. Under 'cruising and sailing':

> … if you want to stay reasonably close to the mainland Viti Levu, the Mamanucas have a huge range of world-class resorts and activities to keep you going. Cruising these islands and 'resort hopping' is ideal for sociable types who love keeping busy and interacting with others. If a more laidback experience is what you're after, the nearby Yasawas are less developed but just as beautiful, giving you the opportunity to learn about Fijian culture and lifestyle with villages dotted throughout the group (Tourism Fiji, 2014a).

The national website is most effusive about the archipelagos under 'backpacking':

> The Yasawas boasts an impressive network of budget accommodations, all of which provide clean, comfortable amenities in stunning locations and are situated minutes from each other by boat. Each property is owned and operated by a local family, and offers authentic Fijian hospitality (Tourism Fiji, 2014b).

It provides a specific description of the Yasawas and also indicates that the Yasawas cater for flashpackers:

> The Yasawa Group of islands are more grand in stature than the nearby Mamanucas but are less commercialised, making them popular with backpackers. You won't find any shops, banks or medical services here, but with so much natural beauty you'll enjoy the break from civilisation. With gorgeous beaches, abundant sunshine and a range of backpacker resorts, this is the place to come for an affordable retreat in paradise (Tourism Fiji, 2014c).

By contrast the Mamanucas are rather less exotic and pristine

> The Mamanucas are a chain of 20 islands near Nadi and Denarau. One of the most established resort areas in Fiji, the Mamanukas (sic) provide a stunning array of activities for all types of travelers. In surroundings beautiful enough to star in 'Cast Away' and 'Survivor: Fiji' these islands offer parasailing, windsurfing, dolphin-watching, famous dives such as the Big W and Gotham City, some of the best surf breaks in the world, and

> just about any other activity you can do on or under water. Young or old, party animal or looking for a family holiday, there's an island for everyone (Tourism Fiji, 2014c)

The means of getting to both groups is described:

> There's really only one choice for traveling and fortunately they do it very well. Awesome Adventures will whisk you out of Nadi (Denarau Marina) on a huge and quite comfortable catamaran aptly named the Yasawa Flyer and you're off on a South Pacific adventure. The flyer's first stops are in the Mamanucas, and then three hours later, the first of the Yasawa Islands will appear on the horizon. You can choose 747 styled interior, air-conditioned seating or catch rays and ocean breezes on the expansive outside decks. Either way, you enjoy the trip and there's always another island coming along to keep your attention (ibid.).

Fiji is a rare example of a small island state where islands other than the main island are marketed in key source countries, and where backpacker resorts figure prominently in national advertising, and, to a lesser extent, are also included in the commercial brochures of large travel companies. That represents a deliberate attempt by Tourism Fiji to develop a more 'multifaceted and multilayered' approach to tourism, though this was in part a pragmatic response to limited interest from foreign investors in developing luxury resorts following uncertainty in the wake of the 2006 military coup.

Destination Branding

In both archipelagos, there are no differences in culture or ethnicity from place to place, and the islands are somewhat similar physically, differentiated by size, the existence (or not) of indigenous settlement and the presence of hills in the Yasawas. Certain characteristics of mainland tourism (such as urban shopping or rivers) are absent. While all destinations (except smaller backpacker places) have their own websites, the major travel companies are less concerned with encouraging a particular choice, but simply interested in a choice being made. There is then no necessary challenge in seeking to turn similarity into a distinctive island experience. Thus Viva Holidays' 2013/2014 brochure describes Treasure Island Resort thus:

> Set on a coral and sand-fringed atoll within a vibrant marine sanctuary, Treasure Island is one of Fiji's most iconic resorts, with extensive experience in providing hospitality and friendship to travellers from across the globe. This resort is specially designed for honeymooners, couples and families seeking a unique and unforgettable island holiday experience (Viva! Holidays, 2014).

On the next page of the brochure, Castaway Island is described as:

> … an iconic private island and is one of the most popular resorts in the Mamanucas. Surrounded by white sandy beaches with a pristine natural environment, vibrant coral reefs and a great resort atmosphere, Castaway Island is the perfect escape for families and couples alike (ibid.).

Typically, the extent of real differentiation between such resorts is slight. Generic descriptions and positive attitudes proliferate and degenerate into an amorphous mass of clichés, and the attributes of particular islands are minimised with reference to descriptions of the resort itself.

Some travel agents have made efforts towards differentiation. Rosie Holidays, the largest Fijian travel agency, differentiates the 63 destinations that it advertises in its overseas brochures according to six themes: weddings and honeymoons, family and friends, romantic escapes, pure indulgence, nature escapes and unique adventures. Of the seventeen destinations advertised for the Mamanucas (14) and Yasawas (3), and which exclude most basic backpacker places and some high end elite resorts, all but two are listed under 'romantic escapes', 10 are listed as 'family and friends' and 12 as 'weddings and honeymoons'. Most of these thus overlap. Only four are listed as 'pure indulgence', three as 'nature escapes' (all in the Yasawas) and only one as 'unique adventures'. Two destinations were listed under four categories. Ultimately room prices provide the most basic form of segmentation, while the costs of helicopter, seaplane and catamaran access are a further form of economic differentiation.

'Romance' and 'escape' are substantially more important than adventure. Many islands are marketed as honeymoon islands, and almost as many are marketed as possible places for weddings. Viva Holidays suggest that 'Your Fiji wedding can be a barefoot ceremony on the beach in a simple sunset setting or in a chapel with an escort of Fijian warriors' (Viva! Holidays, 2014). Others, including several in these two categories, are marketed as child-free (or at least for adults and mixed couples only) while others are marketed to families (and emphasise such things as clinics, nurses, creches and kids' clubs). Rosie Holidays, in their 2013/2014 brochure, note that a few resorts in the two archipelagos and elsewhere allow "exclusive access for schoolies for one or two weeks of the year" (Rosie Holidays, 2014, p. 8): a particularly Australian concept, where older high school students have what is often a wild week of partying at the end of the school year. Brochures necessarily seek to maximise the range of possibilities. Thus Beachcomber Island is listed by Rosie Holidays under three categories: 'weddings and honeymoons', 'family and friends' and 'unique adventure', but the actual description of the resort, on an island less than 200 metres across, notes that the 'resort is for the young and "young at heart" as it is known as the party island' with a barefoot bar, a nightly live band, and jet skiing. By contrast even the least discerning tourist may reasonably assume that tours and destinations labelled 'tropical awegasm' and 'the ultimate lei' (as in Awesome Adventures brochures) are designed for a more youthful segment of the market. Descriptions rarely change over time; Beachcomber has been for the 'young at heart' at least since the mid-1990s (King, 1997, p. 123).

Others are marketed according to the activities on offer – particularly surfing, diving and snorkelling and golf (although there are only two island courses) – or to the atmosphere – normally peaceful and relaxing (and privacy in elite resorts) but for backpacker islands centred on social activities, music, dance and bars. Food plays no obvious part in differential marketing – nor, beyond backpackers and schoolies, do demographic groups differentiated by age or sexuality. Otherwise, destinations in the two archipelagos market themselves to a broad population, and seek to imply that most resorts provide what most tourists want. Again therefore, with the exception of backpackers places in the Yasawas and high-end elite resorts, the extent of differentiation is minimal and choices are only lightly directed. Whilst branding may generally be 'a means to wrest social order and economic benefit from nature's unruly materiality and humanity's disorderly socioeconomic behaviour' (Bryant, 2013, p. 518), here it also imposes conformity while at the same time implying difference.

To a substantial extent, therefore, the establishment of resorts on small islands has imposed a considerable similarity on archipelagos that, despite minimal differences, were actually more different and distinct before the advent of what in the Mananucas at least is increasingly mass tourism. Islands may be different and each has particular attributes but all are subsumed under a pleasure periphery. Differences no longer matter greatly. Difference is shaped by the materiality of commerce rather than the nature of physical and social landscapes. Brochures rarely offer anything more than the most diagrammatic of maps. Space and time are obliterated. Distances are unimportant – even on the catamaran there is meant to be constant interest – hence choices need not be constrained by geography.

Island Hopping

A key element of tourism in the two archipelagos is island hopping, with tours oriented to those who wish to experience some or most of the islands and stay on more than one. Three different cruise companies (Captain Cook, Blue Lagoon and South Sea) operate in the region and Awesome Adventures sponsors the Yasawa Flyer. South Sea Cruises tour the ten Mamanuca islands. Captain Cook Cruises visit the 'remote and exclusive' Yasawa Islands, as do Blue Lagoon Cruises, in circuits of between three and seven days, visiting many and engaging in daily activities there (from snorkelling to eating and *meke* dance performances). Typically, as Blue Lagoon's website notes:

> We believe that, to experience the true essence of Fiji, you need to step ashore onto uninhabited islands, luxuriate in the warm tropical sea and discover the colourful world below. Meet local Yasawan villagers, savour traditional Fijian food, enjoy island walks, marvel at the most sacred of caves and of course, bask on the palm-fringed beaches! (Blue Lagoon Cruises, 2014)

In both of these cruises, accommodation is on board hence the direct economic impact on the islands is more limited.

In contrast, the Yasawa Flyer is oriented towards backpackers and promotes a *bula* ('hello') pass, ranging from five to 21 days:

> The Bula Pass is very simple ... you purchase the length of time that you need (for example, 10 days) and that entitles you to use the Yasawa Flyer to hop from island to island for the duration of the pass. Spend two nights at an island (or more, if you want), then hop on the Flyer next time it calls at that resort, and travel to the next. A fantastic way to see a lot in a short space of time, and at a reasonable price (Yasawa Flyer, 2014).

More formally, Awesome Adventures offers particular combinations, such as the Fiji Fling that covers 9 days and 8 nights staying at four different islands in the two archipelagos, and reducing the need for tourist choice. The Flyer voyages once per day and has a capacity of 267 travellers. Since the few other means of access to the Yasawas involve expensive small planes and helicopters, that number effectively represents the maximum number of tourists travelling to the Yasawas. Pressure on small islands and small destinations is thus limited.

Variable Impacts

Data are absent on the numbers of tourists who go to particular islands or to the two archipelagos as a whole. However the capacity of most islands is severely – and usually deliberately – constrained, hence tourist numbers are small. Tourism has consequently had a minimal environmental impact, partly because of small numbers and small-scale activities, even on islands such as Malolo and the tiny Bounty and South Sea islands. Environmental damage has primarily been the outcome of natural disasters. Along with most other areas of Fiji, the reefs of the Mamanuca Islands suffered from mass coral bleaching in 2000, and from cyclones in 1985, 2000 and 2012, creating physical damage at many different sites. Anthropogenic disturbances, such as sedimentation from land development, over-fishing and pollution (especially from liquid and solid waste disposal), have a limited presence and impact. Like other island groups in Fiji, coastal zone management is minimal; but some of the oldest private marine sanctuaries in Fiji were privately established around islands like Beachcomber.

Energy costs in the islands are high because of the expense of running generators. Access to fresh water is a severe problem and resorts, like Mana, have water shipped from the mainland on a daily basis, or have constructed desalination plants. The drier Yasawas pose even more problems for access to water, which is likely to be a constraint on size, and larger resorts have proclaimed their environmental credentials. The Mantaray Island Resort website states:

> Yasawa region is one of Fiji's driest. The porous volcanic rock means there is no fresh water accessible above ground and limited bore water. Rather than add stress to our environment we operate a desalination plant. A desalination plant converts salt water in to drinking quality fresh water. Our plant can produce up to 60,000 litres of fresh water every day! All of the toilets at Mantaray Island resort are odourless self composting toilets. Using bacteria and sawdust the waste naturally breaks down into compost which is in turn used on the resort gardens. This system does not require septic tanks and therefore eliminates the possibility of them leeching waste through the ground into our pristine marine environment. All of our waste water is treated by a revolutionary bio-gill waste water treatment system. All the waste water from our kitchen, laundry and showers is now treated using chemical-free, award-winning technology, developed in Australia, producing quality recycled water which is then reused on our gardens around the island. By treating our waste water to such a high standard, we are helping to keep our island, reefs, pristine waters and white sandy beaches: beautiful for all (Mantaray Island Resort, 2014).

Coastal management is absent in the Yasawas, and sewage disposal may become a problem, but village-based tourism has been held up as more successful there than in any other Fijian region – albeit limited elsewhere – on economic and environmental grounds (Campbell, 2010).

Substantial economic gains for Fijian islanders come from land ownership rentals, employment (mainly in resorts, including employment as tourist guides and kayaking and diving instructors), transport provision and small-scale marketing (of handicrafts, agricultural produce and fish). Incomes gained from tourism are vastly in excess of the very limited cash incomes available before the tourist era, and have resulted in many islanders retiring and returning from the mainland to participate in the tourist industry. Between 1976 and 1986, the village that owned Mana island almost doubled in size through return migration and the population had almost tripled by 1992 (Sofield, 2003, p. 299). On some islands, even where the presence of tourism is limited its impact may be considerable. On Nanuya Lailai island, the island's seven families have established six small backpacker resorts (with capacities of around 10–50 people) and also draw an income from cruise ship passengers visiting the Blue Lagoon Beach on the island, a dive shop and a small resort, with *bures* available from F$212 (US$120) to F$412 (US$230). Typically, the employees of resorts come from the villages and clans (*mataqali)* that own the land on which the resort was constructed – since priority must be given to them – hence wage incomes are highly localised. As in other parts of Fiji, local villagers also gain income from putting on dances for tourists, organising village (and other) tours and using left-over food in local pig husbandry (Connell and Rugendyke, 2008). Tourism has thus brought material rewards. Nacula Tikina villagers welcomed a modern boat, a generator, an improved village store, and the ability to maintain the church and pay school fees, while tourism was also the impetus for keeping a clean and orderly village (Kerstetter and Bricker, 2009). More intensive tourism on Mana, and lease fees alone, brought a range of benefits for traditional landowners; improved incomes brought modern houses and furniture, videos and TVs, boats with outboard engines, piped water and septic tanks, a larger church that doubles as a clinic, and an escape from poverty. The village subsequently developed its own backpacker resort on Mana island, and obtained extra income by hiring fishing boats to tourists, while fish and to a lesser extent agricultural produce have been regularly marketed to the resort (Sofield, 2003, pp. 302–3, 314, 318). This more sophisticated and complicated development thus represents the difference between the more established tourist scene in the Mamanucas and the still emerging scene in the Yasawas, where incomes still partly depend on non-tourist sources and the population turnaround has yet to happen.

Elite resorts in the Yasawas have played some role in supporting development beyond direct employment and marketing opportunities. As the Yasawa Resort points out

> After almost 20 years in Fiji on remote islands, assisting our local neighbours has become an integral part of all of our business dealings. It is the collaborative effort between the resort ownership, management, local staff and villages that has allowed Yasawa Island Resort and Spa to achieve the success that it has. Due to their remote location, Bukama Village and the other local villages on Yasawa Island struggle to obtain government assistance for necessities with respect to medical care, education, clean water and sanitation. Manasa's Foundation will primarily assist in educational and medical projects in Bukama Village. Foundation donations are used to purchase all necessary materials for each project (Yasawa Island Resort, 2014).

Likewise, on Turtle Island, the owner established the Yasawas Community Foundation in 1992 to generate funds for special projects considered to be important by the local people, which have included health, transportation and education. The Foundation sponsors medical and dental clinics to treat children and villagers from neighbouring islands, and enables the operation of a secondary school on the island for children from the seven villages, and scholarships for others to go to the mainland (Turtle Island, 2014b). Turtle Island has been held out as a model of community-based and conservation-oriented tourism (Figgis and Bushell, 2007). In the remote Yasawas, such support is particularly valuable.

Archipelago Tourism

Most smaller islands in countries that are tourist destinations, like neighbouring Vanuatu, have benefited little from tourism, since it is concentrated close to urban centres and airports. The Mamanuca and Yasawa Islands offer a partial exception though they have benefited from being relatively close to the international airport. More importantly, compared with Tuvalu and Kiribati, they have benefited from being within a country where tourism has long been of considerable significance, and has grown rapidly in the past two decades. What was regarded twenty years ago as overdependence on metropolitan countries for markets (King, 1997, pp. 93–103) has proved to be an advantage as tourism has continued to grow. The islands have benefited from unusually comprehensive and inclusive marketing by both government and the private sector.

Most small islands have few opportunities for development beyond tourism, therefore it is usually welcome. Elsewhere intervening opportunities, pre-booking in source countries and a lack of time are the bane of tourism development in small and outer islands (Connell, 2013), but these have been no disadvantage here. Indeed Fiji itself is littered with unsuccessful tourism development projects, mainly in the eastern islands (Campbell, 2010; Connell and Rugendyke, 2008), and the eastern archipelagos have not been nationally marketed. Cruise ship tourism has brought tourism development in some remote islands, such as Inyeug/Mystery Island in Vanuatu, but these are exceptions. Tourism in the Mamanuca and Yasawa Islands thus stands out as a distinctive example where intervening opportunities have not stood in the way of development (as they have for small eastern Fijian islands). Tourism in the archipelagos is both a recent overspill from the larger mainland and resorts, but also a contrast to that. Much like the Gili islands off Lombok, Indonesia, small islands have a particular allure to enough tourists from nearby much larger islands to ensure a distinctive market, especially when the overall tourism industry is growing.

Creating some degree of diversity from similarity has benefited the entirety of the archipelagos, with tourist brochures creating distinct 'alternative cultural geographies and alternative performances' that stretch the limits of what is possible in small islands, across continua from cheap to expensive and from relaxation and privacy to intense social activity. Potential tourists are spoilt for choice – as in Rosie's 63 destinations – creating a 'choice overload' (Park and Jang, 2013) that merely confuses and effectively devolves choice to the tourism industry. Ultimately only islandness is shared; but island nature has disappeared beneath the unnatural contrivances of island resorts.

Conclusion

In the 1970s, with limited tourism confined to the Mamanucas, islands and island resorts competed for tourists and success. Corporate involvement brought more overt capitalist development but no real sense of difference between islands. Increasing tourism numbers, new resorts, and extension to the Yasawas, meant greater collaboration, but effectively imposed from outside through mass marketing (on the government website and in corporate brochures) and through encouragement of island hopping. Brochures (and individual resort websites) offered a bland conformity ('something for everyone') rather than a sense of distinctiveness, where differentiation was marked primarily by price. As tourist numbers have grown, both competition and collaboration have largely been taken out of local hands.

Tourism has contributed to the economic recovery of both small island archipelagos. Population decline has ended, and return migration has brought new growth, especially in the Mamanucas, as island economies have been transformed from agriculture and fisheries to tourism and ancillary services. No other form of economic activity could have achieved this transformation, at minimal social and environmental cost, though the tourist life cycle is in an early stage especially in the Yasawas. Retaining land tenure and relatively small scale developments have contributed to local control, ownership and participation. This has enabled islanders to remain on their islands, in some contrast to eastern Fiji where island populations are falling, and to similar outer islands elsewhere in the Pacific, where tourism is also absent and infrastructure crumbling (Connell, 2013). Islands that had poor potential for any other forms of development have become newly productive (although environmental challenges – especially water supply – may limit future development). Over time every island in the two archipelagos has benefited from tourism. The nine populated islands are now linked to tourist development on more than thirty islands. Islanders have learned from the experiences of others, and have been in the fortunate position of not having to compete with each other as tourist numbers have steadily grown. Collaboration in marketing has replaced competition through geography and diversity and has brought unexpected development.

References

Blue Lagoon Cruises. (2014). Home page. Retrieved from http://www.bluelagooncruises. com/cruise-itineraries

Britton, S. (1983). *Tourism and underdevelopment in Fiji*, Monograph No. 31, Canberra: Development Studies Centre, Australian National University.

Bryant, R. (2013). Branding natural resources: science, violence and marketing in the making of teak, *Transactions of the Institute of British Geographers*, 38(4), 517–30.

Campbell, A. (2010). Strategic destination marketing, Nagigi style: Olivia's homestay in Fiji. In A. Lewis-Cameron and C. Roberts (eds), *Marketing island destinations: Concepts and cases*, pp. 97–108. Amsterdam: Elsevier.

Connell, J. (2013). *Islands at risk? Environments, economies and contemporary change*, Cheltenham: Edward Elgar.

Connell, J. and Rugendyke, B. (2008). Tourism and local people in the Asia-Pacific region. In J. Connell and B. Rugendyke (eds), *Tourism at the Grassroots: Villagers and Visitors in the Asia-Pacific*, pp. 1–40. London: Routledge.

Derrick, R.A. (1951). *The Fiji islands: A geographical handbook*. Suva, Fiji: Government Printing Department.

Figgis, P., and Bushell, R. (2007). Tourism as a tool for community-based conservation and development. In R. Bushell and P. Eagles (eds), *Tourism and protected areas: Benefits beyond boundaries*, pp. 101–14. Wallingford: CABI.

Kerstetter, D., and Bricker, K. (2009). Exploring Fijians' sense of place after exposure to tourism, *Journal of Sustainable Tourism*, 17(6), 691–708.

King, B. (1997). *Creating island resorts*. London: Routledge.

Kurosawa, S. (2013). Likuliku lagoon, *Wish (The Australian)*, June, pp. 80–81.

Likuliku Lagoon Resort. (2014). Home page. Retrieved from http://www.likulikulagoon. com/home.cfm

Lockhart, D., and Chandra, R. (1997). Fiji: crossroads of the South Pacific. In D.G. Lockhart and D. Drakakis-Smith (eds), *Island tourism: Trends and prospects*, pp. 302–22. London: Pinter.

Mantaray Island Resort. (2014). About Mantaray island Resort. Retrieved from http://www.mantarayisland.com/#!aboutus/c1jtn

Naval Intelligence Division. (1944). *Pacific Islands Vol. III: Western Pacific*, London: Geographical Handbook Series.

Park, J., and Jang, S. (2013). Confused by too many choices? Choice overload in tourism, *Tourism Management*, 35(1), 1–12.

Rosie Holidays. (2013). Fiji. Retrieved from http://www.oetravel.com.au/file/download/3251

Sofield, T. (2003). *Empowerment for sustainable tourism development.* Amsterdam: Pergamon.

Stanley, D. (1985). *Finding Fiji*. Chico: Moon Publications.

Stanley, D. (2007). *Fiji*. Emeryville: Avalon Travel.

Tourism Fiji. (2014a). Cruising and sailing. Retrieved from http://www.fiji.travel/information/guides/cruising-sailing

Tourism Fiji. (2014b). Backpacking. Retrieved from http://www.fiji.travel/information/guides/backpacking-0

Tourism Fiji. (2014c). Yasawa islands. Retrieved from http://www.fiji.travel/destinations/yasawa-islands

Turtle Island. (2014a). Once discovered, never forgotten. Retrieved from http://www.turtlefiji.com/Accommodation/Rent-the-Entire-Island/#.U68kYrGamdw

Turtle Island. (2014b). History of Turtle island. Retrieved from http://www.turtlefiji.com/About-Us/History-of-Turtle-Island/#.UsunS_vB_To

Viva! Holidays. (2014). Fiji 2014/15. Retrieved from http://www.vivaholidays.com.au/uploads/brochures/viva/fiji-2014-15.pdf

Yasawa Flyer. (2014). Awesome Adventures Fiji. Retrieved from http://www.fiji-budget-vacations.com/yasawa-flyer.html

Yasawa Island Resort. (2014). Welcome to Paradise. Retrieved from http://www.yasawa.com

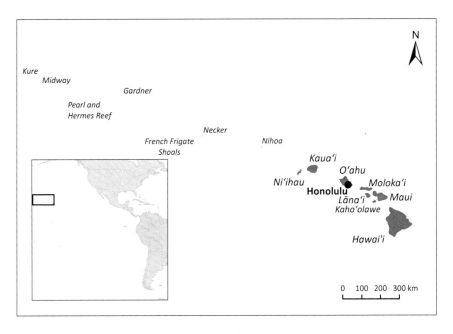

Figure 11.1   The Hawaiian archipelago, USA

Chapter 11
Travel Dynamics in the Hawaiian Archipelago, USA

Luciano Minerbi

Introduction

In the late 1980s, a surprising voice of opposition to tourism development was posted as a full-page advert in a US wide-circulation newspaper (See Figure 11.2). It was a bold stunt by some Hawaiian residents who wanted to protest against a proposed resort development on West Oʻahu. The advert featured a tin can, reminiscent of canned pineapple, a Hawaiian export staple, with the following writing:

> Don't Buy Aloha. Please don't visit Hawaii, until we are able to save what is left! Resort-travel-land interests are ruining us – and our islands – to get your money. Prices, taxes soar; wages diminish. You can't buy ALOHA! (Hawaii Residents Bureau, Honolulu, Hawaii; reproduced in Crocombe, 1989, p. 146).

The printed label on the can ironically described, in a brusque and tongue-in-cheek manner, the presumed fake content of tourism in Hawaiʻi:

> Instant Imitation – Aloha in Heavy Syrup – Distributed by – Friendly Skies Air Pollution Corporation. Ingredients: golden tail, sweet leilani, artificial leis and smiles – Electric ukulele, Nordic natives, plastic, high-rises, California fruit.

This advert revealed the sentiment of some island residents who felt left out from the planning and the profits of tourism and resort development, and were instead wary of its social, economic, and environmental costs. It demonstrates a keen awareness of the intersectoral linkages among finance, real estate, building construction, land development industries, and some islanders' own sense of economic marginalisation, physical displacement, and perceived environmental damage.

The important implication here is that tourism should not be planned and promoted in isolation, but must be balanced with other economic sectors so as to avoid an overdevelopment that harms residents and even impairs the long-term competitiveness of tourism itself. Moreover, studies focusing on tourism alone are inadequate for comprehensive and sustainable island planning when they ignore project externalities and distributional aspects (e.g. Office of the Auditor, 2011).

The promotion of, and opposition to tourism development in Hawaiʻi has continued apace, with increasing use of various media and settlement agreements both in and out of court. These settlements have grown from a few hundred to multi-million dollar packages for "community benefits" to mitigate adverse impacts, paid by developers to local

Figure 11.2   Don't Buy Aloha: please don't visit Hawaii

organisations in order to secure their support and to obtain government permits for their projects to proceed (Minerbi, 2012).

Hawaiʻi, the 50th state of the United States, provides an important case study where the usual tensions of archipelago tourism ride across a clash of cultures involving Western ideas of property, land and its commercialisation; indigenous and local notions of respect for the land and its relationship to family, community and heritage; and the mechanics of various levels of government that come into play to address such confrontations.

The Hawaiian Archipelago

The 'Hawaiian Islands' are thus introduced on the web pages sponsored by the State of Hawaiʻi's official tourist site:

> The fresh, floral air energizes you. The warm, tranquil waters refresh you. The breathtaking, natural beauty renews you. Look around. There's no place on earth like Hawaii. Whether you're a new visitor or returning, our six unique islands offer distinct experiences that will

entice any traveler. We warmly invite you to explore our islands and discover your ideal travel experience (Go Hawai'i, 2014).

In contrast, a native Hawaiian sovereignty group describes the same Hawaiian archipelago in a rather different and detailed way (Sovereign Nation State of Hawai'i, 1994):

> *Ka Pae 'Aina O Hawai'i Nei (the Hawaiian Archipelago)* comprises 132 islands, reefs and shoals, stretching 1,523 miles (2,451 km) southeast to northwest across the Tropic of Cancer between 154°40' to 178°25' W longitude and 18°54' to 28°15' N latitude, consisting approximately of a total land area of 16,642 km^2, including 1 percent of less than 10 km^2 of land area made up of islands off the shores of the main islands and the Northwestern Hawaiian Islands, from Kure Atoll in the North to Nihoa in the South, also Palmyra Island, Midway and Wake Islands, and all Lands that have resided with the Kanaka Maoli since time immemorial. The Hawaiian Islands form an Archipelago, which extends over a vast area of the Pacific Ocean, possessing a 20km Territorial Sea, and the 320km Exclusive Economic Zone, in accordance with generally recognised standards of international law.

This specificity is revealing because an archipelago is the realm of actual, potential, or virtual visitation by travellers (with the exception, in this case, of the Northern Hawaiian Islands, incorporated now in the Papahānaumokuākea Marine National Monument, a marine sanctuary, open only to scientists, and encompassing 360,000 km^2). Thus, the motivations of the two web pages are different, with the Hawaiian indigenous group presenting a political claim of first residence in the vast archipelago; while the tourist website limits its representation of the same cluster to just six visitable islands, all with a timeless lure that is ahistoric.

Tourism Economy in Hawai'i

The Hawai'i Tourism Authority (HTA) is the state tourism agency and is the main source of data for this chapter. It uses its research, industry and marketing expertise to implement the state's strategic tourism marketing plan, while supporting programmes that enhance and showcase Hawaii's people, place and culture to deliver a visitor experience that is second to none. Tourism is the largest single source of private capital on the islands. Total visitor spending in 2011 was US$ 12.5 billion, accounting for 145,000 jobs or 17% of total employment for the state and contributed US$ 1 billion of the tax revenue in 2010. This information does not however reveal how much tourism expenditure comes into the state, how much leaks out, how much circulates in the local economy (multiplier), how much is allocated to the public, private, and community sectors, and in which county jurisdiction and island. The average per capita income in the state of Hawai'i – inflation-adjusted for the years 2007–2011 – was about US$29,000. If all visitors' spending hypothetically went to the residents of Hawai'i, they would benefit from an additional US$9,000/person, or 31% of their per capita income.

In 2011, the state collected US$284.5 million in a transient accommodation tax, of which about 36% went to the counties, 30% to the Tourism Special Fund (to pay for the HTA), 21% to the state's General Fund, and 13% to the Convention Center Enterprise Special Fund. Thus, the larger share remains centralised at the state level. The HTA anticipated that 8.5 million visitors would be visiting Hawaii and spending some US$15.8

billion in 2013, or a 10.7% rise over 2012 (Schaefers, 2013). Aside from short term fluctuations and unforeseen events beyond local control, Hawai'i considers this tourism growth scenario and plans accordingly.

Tourist Plant and Accommodation by Island

Total visitor plant inventory in the state of Hawai'i is about 80,000 units, with 35,000 units on O'ahu alone, 21,000 on Maui, 11,000 on Hawai'i, 10,000 on Kaua'i, 500 on Moloka'i and 350 on Lāna'i. The order of receptivity of the islands by their importance is predictable: O'ahu, Maui, Hawai'i, Kaua'i, Lāna'i, and Moloka'i because visitors tend to go where the airlines take them and where accommodation is available. The single discrepancy is that Lāna'i has more tourists than Moloka'i but this is because Lāna'i has a luxury resort, while Moloka'i does not have a comparable one, not to mention some local opposition to tourism.

The 80,000 units state-wide consist mainly of hotels (55%), condominiums/hotels (16%), time-share (13%), individual vacation units (13%), with the rest including apartment hotels, bed and breakfast units, and hostels. This distribution shows a preponderance for tourist accommodations that provides high quality service to visitors resulting in the high state-wide hotel occupancy rate of about 73% in 2011.

Tourist Counts by Island

The number of tourists visiting Hawai'i in 2011 was a staggering 7.3 million, with the large majority coming by air and less than 2% by cruise ship (Hawai'i Tourism Authority, 2012). Almost two-thirds (65%) came from the continental US and Alaska, 16% from Japan, 7% from Canada, and 12% from other countries. First time visitors were close to 2.5 million, with the majority going to O'ahu, followed by Maui, Hawai'i (alias the Big Island), and Kaua'I (HTA, 2011). This is possible since there is more than one airport hub within the archipelago: the major international airport in the capital city of Honolulu, O'ahu, is now accompanied by three other hubs (two of them international airports) on the neighbouring islands that are served by direct transoceanic air routes.

Air visitors by island were distributed in such a way that almost half (5%) landed in O'ahu, 24% in Maui, 15% in Hawai'i, 11% in Kaua'i, and just 0.8% in Lāna'i, and 0.6% in Moloka'i. The average length of stay was close to 9 days, with an average daily spend per person of US$182, for total receipts of US$12,500 million. The Japanese and other Asian tourists are the biggest spenders. For the 124,000 visitors by cruise ship, the average length of stay was of 5 days, and the average daily spend per person was only US$51, for total receipts of just US$34 million (HTA, 2011; 2012). This explains the resistance to the growth of cruise ship tourism because their positive economic impact is less significant.

Visitor Carrying Capacity by Island

Comparing the number of visitors state-wide (in 2011) to the island counties' population (in 2010) gives a sense of the tourist pressure measured crudely as a ratio of visitors to residents: 6.6 visitors per resident is the state-wide average; 15:1 in Kaua'i; 14:1 in Maui; 7:1 in Hawai'i; and 4.6:1 in Honolulu city and its county of O'ahu. Thus, Kaua'i and

Maui are the counties with the greatest tourist pressure. However, Maui county actually comprises various islands: apart from Maui itself, it includes the islands of Moloka'i (site of a former leper colony, now a US federal park), Lāna'i, as well as the uninhabited island of Kaho'olawe, a pilgrimage site sacred to indigenous Hawaiians, and not easily accessible to tourists. (Indeed, the Hawaiian map on the Go Hawaii website deliberately excludes Kaho'olawe, as if it does not even exist).

Visitor Arrivals and Expenditures by Island

The state of Hawai'i is well served by airports. There are six, primarily commercial service airports in the four island counties, of which three are international, able to accommodate non-stop transoceanic flights because they have adequate runway lengths and ancillary facilities. Honolulu, Hilo, and Kona are international airports with runways of 12,000, 9,800 and 11,000 feet respectively. Kahului airport on Maui has a runway close to 7,000 feet. There are four other airports with scheduled passenger services: one relief airport on O'ahu, and three general aviation airports on the islands of Kaua'i, Hawai'i and O'ahu.

Table 11.1 shows that the bulk of visitors in 2011 landed in O'ahu, Maui, Hawai'i, Kaua'i, Lāna'i and Moloka'i, in that order. O'ahu received twice as many visitors as Maui, while Maui received twice as many as either Hawai'i or Kaua'i. Lāna'i and Moloka'i receive only a few thousand tourists per year. This pattern of arrivals is the result of the availability of direct transoceanic flights from the continental US and Canada to Hilo and Kona Airports on Hawai'i, Līhu'e Airport on Kaua'i, Kahului Airport on Maui, and Honolulu Airport on O'ahu.

Table 11.1   Visitor arrivals and expenditure by island (2011)

Year 2011	Hawai'i	Kaua'i	Maui	Lāna'i	Moloka'i	O'ahu	Totals
Visitor Arrivals (Millions)	1.3	1.0	2.1	0.075	0.055	4.4	8.93*
Name of Airport(s)	Kona & Hilo	Līhu'e	Kahului			Honolulu	
Expenditures (US$ million)	$1,500	$1,200	$3,200	$82,3	$28,7	$6,315	$ 12,326
Daily Spend per Person (US$)	$152	$155	$175	$312	$112	$194	
Tax Receipts (US$ million)	$19,1	$14,9	$23,5	–	–	$45,4	$102,9

*Inclusive of inter-island air trips

Each of the four islands that contain the airport hub is an important first destination in its own right and in turn can redistribute some of its visitors via local flights for islands hopping; a logistics model that is operational elsewhere (e.g. Costa, Lohmann and Oliveira, 2010).

An HTA survey in 2011 reveals which islands were the only ones visited. Out of about 3.4 million tourists who visited one island only, 1.8 million stayed only on

O'ahu; 822,000 only on Maui; 380,000 only on Hawai'i, 312,000 only on Kaua'i, 7,200 only on Lāna'i and 4,300 only on Moloka'i. Currently, over three-fourths of visitors to the state visit just one island (76.2%); and, in most cases, this island is O'ahu. Therefore, it is a natural challenge to explore ways to encourage tourists to visit (at least) an additional island by a careful consideration of its individual natural and cultural assets, while unfolding an accurate advertising campaign to inform tourists that such options exist, and that these align with their preferences and needs. Even if a shift from one to two or more islands does not materialise, the three different international airport hubs guarantee that different islands can be tourist destinations in their own right, thus retaining a diversification and decentralisation away from O'ahu.

Honolulu airport is currently the only one in the state that receives direct non-stop flights from outside North America. For an island airport to become an international destination requires complex and concerted design, building and planning (Minerbi, 2005). The required decision-making is well above the county level, involving international initiatives, federal approvals (US Department of Transportation and Federal Aviation Administration), active involvement of the state's tourism agency, and the foreign airlines that may have to provide the services and their marketing. Special charter flights can test the suitability to fly directly to the neighbourhood islands and prepare the way for regular air services in the future. Ancillary requirements include the facility and staffing of US customs and immigration services in these hub airports. Negotiations are underway with Japan Airlines to restart direct flights to Kona Airport that had been suspended in 2010. Other possible airlines include Korean Airlines, Qantas, Air Canada, (already serving directly Kahului and Kona airports from Vancouver, Canada) and WestJet (already serving Kahului and Lihu'e directly from Vancouver, Canada).

Inter-island Routes

Apart from those who have their own means of inter-island transport (using a private plane, pleasure sea craft or yacht), inter-island travel and island hopping is only feasible if the infrastructure that permits it is in place. This requires the operation of inter-island air carriers and/or sea ferry services.

Hawaiian Airlines, Go! Airlines, and Mokulele Airlines service the inter-island routes within the archipelago. Hawaiian Airlines alone offers about 200 daily inter-island flights; its route map boasts direct air connections among the major airports of Līhu'e, Honolulu, Kahului, Hilo and Kona, thus directly linking Kaua'i, O'ahu, Maui and Hawai'i islands. Go! Airlines offers similar connections as Hawaiian Airlines. A one-way non-refundable air trip from Honolulu Kaunakakai airport to Moloka'i is around US$91; between Līhu'e, Kaua'i and Kona, Hawai'i, costs may vary from US$160 to over US$300. Mokulele Airlines use smaller propeller planes; it also serves the big airports of Honolulu, Kahului, and Kona, but it also provides a capillary link to the smaller airports of Ho'holeua, Moloka'i, Kapalua, Maui, Lāna'i and Kamuela, Hawai'i. Fares range from US$39 to US$59 one-way.

But inter-island airlines can be eased out by strong competition, as in the case of Aloha Airlines, that ceased operations in 2008, with Go! Airlines stepping in to take its place (and slots). These inter-island air services provide residents with commuting travel for family, education, work and recreation, as well as serving tourists and the affluent and seasonal second homeowners who reside in rural and remote locations. However, stable travel by these airlines is by no means secure as they can go out of businesses and they may be bought and sold, resulting in periodic uncertainty and disruption to interisland schedules and accessibility for visitors, residents, and small businesses.

Visitor Experience and Activity Participation by Island

The distinct experiences an individual island offers, in order to better respond and appeal to the tourist type that it does, or could, attract, is revealed by its allegedly intrinsic and unique features, as well as by the data available on visitor profiles or preferences that document visitor behaviour (e.g. Baldacchino and Ferreira, 2013). Tourism planners typically sort visitor preferences by major market areas (MMA), lifestyle/life stages, segment and visitation status (first timers or repeat visitors), and the type of activity and facilities available by island. The MMAs for Hawai'i as a whole are: the US West, US East, Japan, Canada, Western Europe and Oceania.

For a more discriminatory analysis, the data suggests, for example, that the west coast of the island of Hawai'i is preferred over the east coast with the old capital of Hilo. US visitors, who are mostly independent travellers on self-guided tours (74%), tend to patronise urban facilities, supermarkets and artisanal shops. A sizable number are engaged in outdoor activities on neighbouring islands, particularly Kaua'i and Maui. The Japanese are substantially involved in all sorts of shopping and almost half travel in tour buses (44%). Canadians like sightseeing and active recreational activities (92% and 95%) concentrating on O'ahu and Maui; 81% of them rely on self-guided tours and car rentals. Europeans are heavily involved in recreational activities and shopping (95% and 96%). Visitors from Oceania behave similarly to Europeans and Canadians for entertainment, sightseeing, recreation and shopping and made use of bus tours, buses and taxi more than other visitor groups. Cultural activities, including parks, gardens, dance shows and historic sites, were well patronised by both Canadians and Europeans (83%). Hawaii's natural attractions also have their "potential perils", as accident statistics suggest (Vorsino, 2013).

The data on the differences in culture, budgets, characteristics, preferences, buying habits and actual percentages in activity participation by MMA are crucial for island planners and operators to fine-tune, customise, re-package and diversify their range of products for their diverse range of visitors. Moreover, Asian visitors from South Korea, Taiwan and the People's Republic of China are now increasing. Advertising in foreign languages on the web, at tourism offices and at the airports helps considerably in this task.

The Hawai'i Tourism Strategic Plan

The Hawai'i Tourism Authority completed its Hawai'i Tourism Strategic Plan 2005–2015 in 2004 and an update is in progress (HTA, 2004). It identifies policy level implications for the archipelago. Hawai'i tourism "strengths" include its people, natural attractions, allure, and quality accommodation. Its identified "weaknesses" include a lack of stakeholder consensus, limited visitor-resident interaction, inadequate infrastructure, and the volatility of the tourism and airline industry. Its "opportunities" include the expansion of the business, cruise ship, cultural and sport tourism segments, the marketing and customisation by geographic area, the improvement of resources and facilities. "Future threats" include anti-tourism sentiment, disrupting world events, the aging of infrastructure and the loss of identity and differentiation. The HTA seeks to address these matters for the archipelago by means of diversification, decentralisation, networking and specialisation. Thus the state of Hawai'i is suitably identifying the tourism issues that should be addressed and it is supporting individual islands developing as direct or specific tourist destinations in their own right. While strategic plans are in place for the various island counties (Hawai'i Tourism Authority, 2005a; 2005b), each island is considered on its own merits. There is an effort at discriminating one island destination from another; and this is done without necessarily imposing a contrived complementarity on the assemblage of island experiences.

Each island county has its own Visitor Bureau or Visitors Association and its own Hotel and Lodging Association seeking increased visitor expenditures and longer stay-overs while addressing any negative impacts caused by tourism. Hotels, airlines and travel companies shoulder the majority of the expenditure of tourism marketing. Their well designed, consistent, comparable and user-friendly web pages are linked and provide attractive information allowing tourists to learn, explore and consider what each county and each individual island offers. The HTA web page markets each county as well as each individual island as a possible destination by explaining the locale's basic characteristics, providing guidebooks, describing sub-regions and districts, illustrating possible experiences and events, and helping to plan a trip with details of amenities, facilities and activities.

The web site also probes the possible experiences that the visitor would seek and provides nested and specialised information while touting detailed options for family travel, health and wellness, recreation, sport, eco, agricultural and cultural tourism as well as weddings, honeymoons and romance. A willing tourist can end this web search by actually booking the desired product or service with a credit card.

Community Opposition to Tourism Development: The Inter-island Superferry

Some islanders have resisted central government and investor initiatives to develop their own island home as a tourism destination, and in some cases this has limited inter-island connectivity. Most Hawaiian residents seem to have accepted the presence of tourists and their contribution to the local economy; but tourists are expected to come visit and then go back; not to stay and buy property (see Figure 11.3).

Some islanders have blocked or protested against land sales, airport expansions, the construction of large resorts, and the operation of tour boats and ferry services. Molokai Ranch, that island's largest employer, said it was closing in 2008 because of years-long opposition to its residential development plan for La'au Point (Gomes, 2008). The interisland ferry is one other case illustrative of the impact of civic activism.

Hawaii Superferry was a transportation company that provided fast and regular passenger and vehicle transportation services between Honolulu Harbour on the island of O'ahu and Kahului Harbour on Maui (Hawaii Inter-Island Super ferry, 2014). This was Hawai'i's first regular inter-island passenger ferry service in more than 25 years; its US$5, one-way fares attracted more than 2,200 passengers when the service was inaugurated. But the project raised concerns among residents and environmentalists on various counts, including whale disturbances and collisions, invasive species and congestion (Leidemann, 2007). The inter-island ferry service commenced operations in December 2007 but was obliged to shut down in March 2009.

Super ferry operations between O'ahu and Maui were halted after the State Supreme Court ruled that the state had to conduct an environmental impact statement (EIS) before

Figure 11.3　Tourists are welcome, but tourists go home. © 2013 Luciano Minerbi, the author of the original is unknown

the ferry could be given permission to sail. Opposition was strong on Maui and other islands, but particularly on Kaua'i where 1,500 people protested against a top-down state government sponsorship of a private entrepreneur to establish a very fast, big and expensive commercial interisland ferry system, without completing the legally required EIS. Thus, while the 'ferry affair' was fought in the courts and the legislature, it garnered so many opponents that groups of boaters and surfers actually stopped the ferry from entering Nawiliwili Harbour in Kaua'i on 27 August 2007. The ferry had to return to the island of O'ahu without discharging passengers or cargo (Paik and Mander, 2009, p. 165). This turn of events unfolded in spite of the fact that a fast ferry service would also serve residents, and not just tourists. But the opposition had multiple unaddressed concerns: the State Government's disregard of existing EIS laws; the perceived adverse impact of additional visitors; of spreading invasive species; of encroaching on the whale and turtle breeding grounds within the archipelago; as well as opposition to the possible future use of the ferry by the US military. The situation escalated with the US Coast Guard cordoning the harbour and threatened fines of up to US$10,000 and jail time to the demonstrators.

A bill was introduced by the state government and passed in the state legislature to circumvent and nullify the Supreme Court ruling reiterating the need for the EIS. But the legal and the community fights, the protracted disagreement, and the national economic downturn, all thwarted the feasibility of this commercially driven, privately owned, interisland ferry. A public locally owned and operated small and slow inter-island ferry could have been a viable alternative (Paik and Mander, 2009, pp. 291–300). Meanwhile, proponents of the superferry, including a former Honolulu mayor, have not given up on the project (Grube, 2014).

The main lesson here is that legality of the process, genuine community participation, scientific knowledge of the archipelago ecosystem, design and use of small-scale appropriate technology and management should all be fully considered and vetted for interisland planning. To do otherwise ensures protracted conflict and robs Hawaiian residents of the benefits of long-term planning for a truly sustainable future.

Conclusion

Hawai'i is an archipelago where tourism remains a major component of the economy, even within the uncertain context of international political, economic and environmental events. Tourism is also the mainstay of private investment in the islands, but it must distribute its benefits and costs more equitably among the residents of Hawai'i (Minerbi, 1991, 1997). In fact, some opposition to tourism and development is enduring and it is evident on all islands.

Considerable investment in tourist resorts, facilities, infrastructure and services has already been committed on the major islands, making them premier tourist destinations for millions of tourists coming from major destinations in four continents every year. This significant tourist inflow is also possible thanks to the large airlines' seat capacity, the reach from different foreign countries, and the transoceanic airports that operate as hubs in the four island counties. Yet, Honolulu remains the primary hub. Inter-island air services link the four hubs to smaller airports supporting island hopping by tourists, resident and diasporic islanders, and seasonal residents.

This multi-hub airport system is crucial for promoting direct non-stop travel and landings to different islands, particularly for visitors who stay on one island only, while it also provides different options for island hopping and/or stay prolongation to visitors. But any increase and redistribution of visitors to neighbouring islands should be done in cognizance of physical, social and environmental carrying capacities, as the islands differ in size, ecology and fragility of ecosystems, as well as in their community needs and aspirations. Inter-island equity can be addressed via an intergovernmental transfer of tax revenues and not just a rerouting of tourists. Inter-island air routes require government support, otherwise they remain uncertain in viability, ownership, cost and frequency.

While O'ahu has the bigger share of direct visitors to Hawai'i – close to 50% – other islands also do fairly well. Intercontinental transoceanic flights use Honolulu airport on O'ahu as a main hub, but Kaua'i, Hawai'i and Maui islands have direct flights to and from mainland North America (US and Canada), so they already operate as independent hubs on their own merit. They too could expand and receive direct flights from Asia. And yet, this is an international endeavour that involves higher-level public-private approvals that an island county government cannot undertake alone, even if it has already secured the needed tourist infrastructure.

The tourists who converge on Hawai'i with their different characteristics and preferences offer challenges in meeting and satisfying their needs, as well as in the opportunities created to serve them across a wide range of interests, attractions and seasons. Periodic tourist surveys and fine-tuning of programmes and packages by specific islands can open or expand possibilities for more and better tourism experiences. The state tourism authority is already taking into consideration each individual island's peculiarities as opportunities. The industry also has a rich database by which it can profile tourism characteristics by visitor type and by island.

Differences in length of stay, expenditures, preferences and single and repeat visitations, plus the stability of a year-round tourism season, provide rich opportunities to government and industry for responding by encouraging diversification across the islands. Meanwhile, the HTA is updating its ten-year plan and monitoring spending, receipts, visitor and resident satisfaction; it can continue to refine its plan to each specific island county. Much more support for natural and cultural programmes that sustain local communities would result in improved visitor experiences and a higher acceptance by residents of the tourism industry in their midst. When communication among residents, government, and business improves, then concerns over the impact of tourism development, real estate, and construction are more likely to be addressed and translated into needed social contracts that benefit island people and protect the islands' fragile environments. Inappropriate and fast tracked tourism development creates mistrust and opposition, while participatory long range planning can chart a course that is supported by island communities and retains tourism as a viable economic activity.

References

Baldacchino, G., and Ferreira, E.C.D. (2013). Competing notions of diversity in archipelago tourism: transport logistics, official rhetoric and interisland rivalries in the Azores. *Island Studies Journal*, 8(1), 84–104.

Costa, T.F.G., Lohmann, G., and Oliveira, A.V.M. (2010). A model to identify airport hubs and their importance to tourism in Brazil. *Research in Transportation Economics*, 26(1), 3–11.

Crocombe, R. (1989). *The South Pacific: An introduction* (3rd edn.). Suva, Fiji: University of the South Pacific.

Go Hawai'i. (2014). Official tourist site, State of Hawai'i. Retrieved from http://www.gohawaii.com/

Gomes, A. (2008). Molokai Ranch closure leaves bleak prospect. *Honolulu Advertiser*. Honolulu HI, 26 March. Retrieved from http://the.honoluluadvertiser.com/article/2008/Mar/26/ln/hawaii803260433.html

Grube, N. (2014). Mufi makes it interesting, vows to bring back Hawaii superferry, 4 June. Retrieved from http://www.civilbeat.com/2014/06/mufi-makes-interesting-vows-bring-back-hawaii-superferry/

Hawai'i Inter-Island Super Ferry. (2014). Hawai'i Inter-Island Super Ferry. Retrieved from http://www.hawaiiinterislandsuperferry.com/

Hawai'i Tourism Authority. (2004). *Hawai'i tourism strategic plan 2005–2015*. Honolulu: HTA. Retrieved from http://www.hawaiitourismauthority.org/default/assets/file/about/tsp2005_2015_final.pdf

Hawai'i Tourism Authority. (2005a). *Hawai'i Island tourism strategic plan 2006–2015*. Honolulu HI: Hawai'i Tourism Authority. Retrieved from http://www.hawaiitourismauthority.org/default/assets/File/about/HawaiiIslandTSP.pdf

Hawai'i Tourism Authority. (2005b). *Kaua'i tourism strategic plan 2006–2015*. Honolulu HI: HTA. Retrieved from http://www.hawaiitourismauthority.org/default/assets/File/about/Kauai%20County%20TSP_FINAL.pdf

Hawai'i Tourism Authority. (2011). *Visitor satisfaction and activity report*. Honolulu HI: HTA.

Hawai'i Tourism Authority. (2012). Total visitor spending in July 2012 grew 17.8 percent while arrivals rose 7.8 percent. Honolulu: HTA, 29 August. Retrieved from http://www.hawaiitourismauthority.org/default/assets/File/research/monthly-visitors/July%202012%20Visitor%20Stats%20NR.pdf

Leidemann, M. (2007). High-speed ferry to connect Hawaiian islands. *USA Today*, 2 August. Retrieved from http://usatoday30.usatoday.com/news/nation/2007-02-08-hawaii-super-ferry_x.htm

Minerbi, L. (2012). Hawai'i, USA. In G. Baldacchino (ed.), *Extreme heritage management: The practices and policies of densely populated islands*, pp. 152–74. New York: Berghahn Books.

Minerbi, L. (2005). Organisation and planning of the tourist space. Paper presented at 2nd international congress on coastal areas and island tourism. Las Palmas, Spain: University of Las Palmas de Gran Canaria. 13–16 June.

Minerbi, L. (1992). *Impacts of tourism development in Pacific Islands*. San Francisco CA: Greenpeace Pacific Campaign.

Minerbi, L. (1991). *Alternative forms of tourism in the coastal zone: searching for responsible tourism in Hawai'i. Executive summary*. Eugene OR: National Coastal Research and Development Institute, March.

Minerbi, L. (1999). Tourism and native Hawaiians. *Cultural Survival Quarterly*, 23(2). Retrieved from http://www.culturalsurvival.org/ourpublications/csq/article/tourism-and-native-hawaiians-232

Minerbi, L. (1997). Isole Hawai'i: il turismo nelle isole: i rapporti con gli Hawaiiani. In G. Corna Pellegrini (ed.), *Annali Italiani del turismo internazionale: Il turismo tra le culture del mondo*, 2(2), 57–72. Milan, Italy: Department of Sociology, University of Milan.

Minerbi, L. (1996). Hawai'i. In C.M. Hall and S. Page (eds), *Tourism in the Pacific: Issues and cases*, pp. 190–204. London: International Thomson Business Press.

Office of the Auditor. (2013). State tourism marketing would benefit from improved plans, reporting, and oversight. Audit of major contracts and agreements of the Hawai'i Tourism Authority. Report No. 13-09, December. Honolulu HI: State of Hawai'i.

Paik, K., and Mander, J. (2009). *The superferry chronicles: Hawai'i's uprising against militarism, commercialism and the desecration of the earth*. Honolulu HI: Koa Books.

Schaefers, A. (2013). State tourism agency predicts huge influx. *Honolulu Star Advertiser*, Honolulu HI, 7 March. Retrieved from http://www.staradvertiser.com/s?action=login&f=y&id=195817391

Sovereign Nation State of Hawai'i. (1994). Proclamation of Restoration of Independence, 16 January. Retrieved from http://www.hawaii-nation.org/archip.html

Vorsino, M. (2013). Accidents kill visitors at unusually high rate. *Honolulu Star Advertiser*. Honolulu HI, 7 February. Retrieved from http://www.highbeam.com/doc/1P3-2886315731.html

PART IV
Indian Ocean

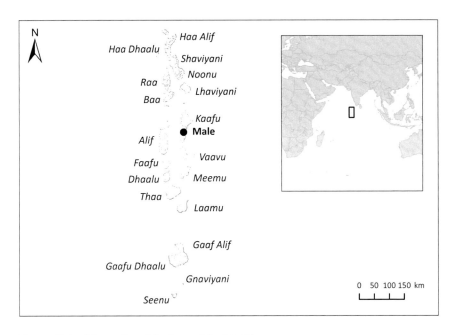

Figure 12.1   The atoll archipelago of the Maldives

Chapter 12

The Potential of Tourist Zones in the Maldives: Obscured behind the "sunny side of life"?

Fathimath Amira

Introduction

Islands possess distinctive and inimitable geographical features that immediately render images of paradise, and this is often perceived or presented as a brand in itself (Baldacchino, 2010). Warm water islands, in particular, are so deeply entrenched with their enchanting status that it is nearly impossible to disentangle their material actualities from their mythical illusions (Royle, 2001). This presence of a pre-conceived brand puts islands in a precarious position when it comes to marketing or branding a cluster of islands. Most islands possess unique and distinct geographical, cultural, historical and social characteristics that differentiate one from the other. Yet, the marketing strategy of an archipelagic state – especially if in nation-building mode and wary of secessionist tendencies – tends to gather all the islands within its sovereign territory, under the umbrella of a single, uncompromising and undiluted brand or image. When an archipelago is blanketed under a single marketing brand, however, the unique features of individual islands tend to be obscured and opportunities for their exposure could be lost.

This paper argues that diversification strategies that utilise the distinguishing features of islands are necessary to cater for various tourism market segments. In exploring the potential for differentiation between islands within an archipelago, this chapter assesses the extent to which existing policies and strategies for the marketing and promotion of Maldives are aligned to maximise the potential for a differentiation of the tourism experience within and between its newly established tourist zones. The islands of the Maldives may look similar at first glance: to the casual observer, they are – except for the capital Malé – sparsely populated, low lying atolls. However, a closer view reveals distinct geographical, historical, traditional and social differences. The islands differ from each other most significantly between the geographical atolls in their culture, dialect of the local language, cuisine, history and traditions. However, the official marketing policy of the Maldives, with the widely used slogan "Maldives – the sunny side of life", indiscriminately metes out the undifferentiating "sun, sand, sea" image to the country as a whole (Plate 12.1).

Marketing Archipelagos

An archipelago is a "large group of islands or a sea containing a large number of islands" (Bardolet and Sheldon, 2008, p. 902). For most tropical islands, their remoteness, finite island geography, small size of population and salubrious climate are key tourist attractions. While they often possess a wealth of unique cultural and historical attributes, more often than not these features come second in terms of their marketed touristic appeal. Islands, however small, possess their own special heritage, even those that belong to the same archipelago (Baldacchino and Ferreira, 2013).

The abundance of remote islands in archipelagos renders these as ideal settings for tourist enclaves, where tourist accommodation and activities are confined within a separate island or compound, protected from, but also protecting, indigenous cultural practices. Often, the key objective for enclave tourism development is to inhibit negative socio-cultural impacts to local societies; this strategy also restricts the opportunity for a multi-island experience. Tourists on an all-inclusive enclave resort may easily spend the entire duration of their holiday within the confines of a single compound or an island – a case of multiple insularity – where all their foreseeable requirements are catered for: accommodation, food, entertainment, live music, diving, swimming, gym, sports facilities, and any other activities. Most of these services are pre-paid in advance, limiting the motivation for tourists to venture out of the precinct or island and spend additionally on those services that are not included in their pre-paid package deal (Anderson, 2011).

To overcome the concentration of economic benefits within tourist enclaves and to provide a more equitable spread of tourist money among various communities, some tourism policies seek to encourage dispersal of development throughout archipelagos. One such strategy is the zoning of tourism development. Zoning determines areas for tourism development with exact delineation and boundaries with the aim of creating infrastructure and utilities, facilitate local job creation, and otherwise spreading tourism benefits within a region. While this strategy increases the benefits of tourism to wider communities, it creates challenges and issues as well. One contributing reason is that the establishment of different zones is not always accompanied by strategies to differentiate, or to acknowledge the existing idiosyncrasies of, the proposed zones. As a result, islands within an archipelago, irrespective of specific zones or atolls and their differing characteristics, end up being promoted under a single, official brand or logo. The unique features of the various atolls and the islands are buried behind the brand, resulting in fierce competition among resort operators for a larger share of the destination's tourist market. Long established islands gain the benefit from repeat visitors, and islands within the close proximity to the mainland or capital and to airports reap advantages over more remote resort islands that may require hours of sea and/or air travel. Where cooperation is more beneficial than competing in marketing and promotion for peripheral island destinations (Zhang, 2010), a possible solution and one that holds potential benefits for island resorts that fall within the various zones would be to leverage themselves on the unique heritage of the atolls and islands in which they are based. Yet, tourism promotion of the large majority of tropical islands is largely based on their natural and geographical features, while "local cultural traits and events are hidden or ring-fenced" behind "the island allure" (Baldacchino, 2012, p. 58). Official marketing materials of islands demonstrate a "stereotypical island imagery" that promotes what is perceived by the Western world as basic template for the distinctive warm water island setting (Berg and Edelheim, 2012, p. 84).

Not only is there a huge gap in the promotion of the heritage of these islands; the opportunity to experience those attributes is lost for any keen tourist due to the fact that inter-island travel is neither promoted nor easily accessible (Fonseca and Ramos, 2012). Marketing and promotion of tourism zones, or islands within an archipelago, based on differentiation of such tangible and intangible assets as historic buildings, monuments and archaeological sites, local traditions, histories, customs, folklore, arts and crafts and local ways of life, carries immense potential (Iliachenko, 2005). Differentiation centred on these features provides the opportunity to create and celebrate local identity and develop a uniquely identifiable image of the destination. Promotion of local heritage also opens up numerous pathways for wider communities to engage in and share the benefits of tourism.

Despite the fact that destination image is a crucial factor in the selection process for consumers (Kamenidou, Mamalis, and Priporas, 2009), standardisation of island brands traverses such varied destinations as Shetland, Malta and Channel Islands (Grydehøj, 2011). Particularly, in small island jurisdictions, sovereign or otherwise, it is relatively easy to bring on board various stakeholders to "sing the same tune" in consolidating a strong brand (Baldacchino, 2012, p. 59). Attention has flared on the concept of destination branding as a result of intensified competition among cities, regions and nations not only for a share of the tourist market, but for recognition, investment and prestige as well (Jansson, 2012); but destination branding itself is controversial due to the widespread public perception that nations cannot be branded in the same way as products or businesses (Vladimirova, 2011). The image of a nation is based upon its "geography, history, proclamations, art and music, famous citizens and other features" (Kotler and Gertner, 2001, p. 251). Hence, the branding of an island nation, even if effective, "is always going to be a partial and sanitised rendition of island life; it does not, it cannot, tell the whole story" (Baldacchino, 2012, p. 59). Conversely, the 'island brand' could be its own nemesis that threatens to drown the identity of islands in a homogenising and globalising world (Zhang, 2010, p. 408). A destination can develop a brand by combining its unique cultural heritage and its natural features to create a differentiated identity (Iliachenko 2005). Thus, it is important to veer away from homogenisation, to shed the bland 'island' image through differentiation.

"Branding is a powerful tool that can significantly improve the appeal of a tourist destination" (Iliachenko, 2005, p. 2). Since the brand of an island encompasses its identity, it should invoke a distinct image when used in tourism promotion (Zhang, 2010). Branding based on regional assets develops consumer expectations which, when confirmed on actual visitation, assists in encouraging repeat visits (Iliachenko, 2005). Increasing visitation was the key focus of conventional marketing studies that viewed tourism as a commercial good; hence, these studies were less likely to acknowledge the distinct, local, natural and cultural heritage of specific tourist destinations (Buhalis, 2000). Such strategies, as those employed by the concept of three-S tourism, may constrain island destinations' creative capabilities and eventually smother their appeal: "if an island destination is not considered different, it will lose its appeal" (Zhang, 2010, p. 428).

A place's identity is shaped by its residents, how they live and how they think (including what they think about themselves and about the residents of other places who visit as tourists). These and similar socio-cultural features could play a more crucial role than the natural or built environment in shaping place-based identity (Jansson, 2012). Thus, it makes more sense to create a brand around the local residents' way of life rather than make the residents conform to a concocted and contrived brand (ibid.). Escapism is not the only essential tourist motivation; novelty of experiences is a key motivation as well. Novel experiences can be developed by upholding islands' unique heritage (Freire 2005). According to (Hall, 1999, p. 230), any "symbol, slogan, name or design, or combination of these elements" should contain: 1) a unique image of the destination that clearly differentiates it from competitors; 2) a connection with quality that consumers can relate to; 3) a capability to sustain competitiveness; and 4) involves more than just environmental features. The execution of marketing strategies "does not mean the denaturing, or the reduction, of the historical or cultural value of the place; nor the destruction of a place's traditional cultural identity" (Metaxas, 2009, p. 1372). Hence, the only way to ensure the sustainability of a brand is to create one that achieves "self-recognition with the island's identity" (Zhang, 2010, p. 411). A balancing strategy that utilises available unique resources while leveraging the existing brand to shape a differentiated niche in the competitive island tourism market is probably the best way forward.

Maldives: An Overview

The Republic of Maldives is a chain of 26 natural atolls comprising 1196 coral islands situated in the Indian Ocean 500 km south-west of the southern tip of India (Bell, 2004). For administrative purposes the islands have been grouped into 20 atolls (Lutfy, 1995). A total of 196 islands are inhabited, while an additional 124 have been developed as tourist resorts (MOTAC, 2012). The rest are used for various agricultural and economic purposes.

The ethnic identity of the Maldivians is a blend of the early settlers (believed to have originated from Sri Lanka), southern India and Indo-Europeans (Lutfy, 1995). Over the centuries, sailors from East Africa, the Middle East and South East Asia anchored and left their mark which is evident in the development of Maldives (Amira, 2009). Islam is the official religion and the official and common language of the Maldivians is Dhivehi, whose foundations are based in Sanskrit and is closely linked to the Sinhalese language spoken in Sri Lanka (Maumoon, 2002). However, English is used widely in commerce and as the medium of instruction in schools. The Maldives has a population of 350,759 (in 2012) (Department of National Planning, 2012). With limited resources for economic development, the economy of the Maldives is dependent on tourism, fisheries and construction as its main sources of revenue (World Bank, 2006). The country relies on imports for products, staple foodstuffs, petroleum, construction materials and other goods required for the tourism industry. Tourism's contribution accounts for 34% (in direct benefits) and 75% (in indirect benefits) to the Gross Domestic Product (GDP), and some 52% of foreign exchange receipts (MOTAC, 2012). The wide disparity between tourism's direct and indirect contribution indicates the spillover of tourism revenue into other economic sectors. Economic growth (measured via the gross domestic product) has maintained an average of almost 8% per year for more than a decade, except in 2005 when the 2004 Asian Tsunami caused GDP to contract by 5.5% (World Bank, 2006).

The Maldives has a unique culture, developed over many years in harmony with the island environment and its official Muslim religion. The influences are evident in the boats used for travelling between islands, design and construction of houses, food, cooking, rituals, music, clothing, dance and social norms (Maumoon, 2002). A striking feature of the Maldives is that, while the islands may be practically identical in their physical features, distinctive differences in cultural aspects are evident between the atolls, as any local would know. The dialects of the local language, clothes, food, handicrafts and rituals are good examples. The country has been promoted under the slogan of "Maldives – the sunny side of life" for the last 12 years (Naseem, 2011), except for a short period of time during 2011 when, with a change of government and consequent changes made to the tourism promotional authority, the slogan was changed to "Maldives – always natural". However, concern from the industry about the consequences of ditching the long standing "Sunny side of life" slogan brought it quickly back to official use in 2012.

Tourism Development

Tourism was officially initiated in the Maldives by George Corbin, an Italian tour organiser who came across the Maldives while searching for new tropical destinations. With the collaboration of three Maldivian businessmen, Ahmed Naseem, Mohamed Umar Maniku and Hussain Afeef, two island resorts with a bed capacity of 280 were opened as late as 1972 (Zulfa and Carlsen, 2011). The initial years saw tourism being developed largely according to unplanned individual initiatives (Dowling, 2000), with modest and simple facilities and services due to limited infrastructure and a lack of trained human resources (Sathiendrakumar and Tisdell 1989). Tourism marketing was initially handled jointly with Sri Lanka, and with a strong focus on diving. However, during the early 1980s Maldives emerged as an independent destination which the 1TMP described as a "beach relaxation" image (MOTAC, 2012b, p. 26). From the start, tourism development has been led by the private sector which took the pragmatic approach of focusing development around existing infrastructure and the only international airport. This resulted in 47% of the total number of resorts in the Maldives being located in the mid-region of the Maldives (MTCA, 2008).

Tourism development in the Maldives has leapt forward in the last four decades in terms of facilities and services to meet the increasing volume of tourist arrivals. Where only 1,000 tourists arrived during 1972 (the year that tourism officially began), in the year 2012 Ministry of Tourism predicted tourist arrivals to exceed 1 million, although that target was closely missed by roughly 42,000 (Powell, 2013). According to law, tourists to the Maldives can only stay at a facility registered with the Ministry of Tourism, Arts and Culture (MOTAC). The most popular accommodation consists of resorts that are built to the concept of "one-island-one-resort" facilitated by the sheer abundance of small islands. By the end of October 2012, a total of 124 resorts with a bed capacity of 24,432 were in operation along with roughly 2,000 beds in guesthouses and live-aboard vessels (MOTAC, 2012); another 53 resorts were under construction (see Table 12.1). Guest houses provide accommodation for budget-conscious travellers; while 'Safari Vessels' provide live-aboard accommodation combined with on-board holiday: while cruising around different islands and travelling to secluded marine parks and dive or surfing spots, they offer adventure activities such as scuba diving, wave surfing and game fishing. By the end of 2011, there were 157 safari vessels with a capacity of 2,514 beds (ibid.).

Throughout the history of Maldives tourism, Europe has been the market leader, contributing 70–80% of tourist arrivals until 2011. However, a decline of almost 4% drove total arrivals from Europe down to 54% in 2012. Asia and the Pacific has now become the number one market, where the growth rate in arrivals has increased nearly 22% from 2008 to 2012. And an increase from nearly 23% to more than 40% of all arrivals in 2012 have placed China and Russia as the new emerging source countries (MOTAC, 2013). The economic downturn in Europe, the rise of an affluent Chinese middle class and a Russian elite, are seen as the main reasons for this change. Profound implications on

Table 12.1   Development of tourism facilities across the atolls (including leases under development)

Upper North Province		Central Province		South Province	
Haa Alif Atoll	6	Meem Atoll	3	Gnaviyani Atoll	1
Haa Dhaal Atoll	5	Faaf Atoll	1	Seenu Atoll	5
Shaviyani Atoll	4	Dhaal Atoll	5		
North Province		**South Central Province**			
Noon Atoll	10	Thaa Atoll	3		
Raa Atoll	12	Laam Atoll	7		
Baa Atoll	12				
Lhaviyani Atoll	6				
North Central Province		**Upper South Province**			
Malé (Capital)	17	Gaaf Alif Atoll	11		
Kaaf Atoll	50	Gaaf Dhaal Atoll	9		
Alif Alif Atoll	11				
Alif Dhaal Atoll	16				
Vaav Atoll	3				

Source: MOTAC (2012b).

visitor trends have been evident due to this increase in Asian markets. Honeymoon trips used to consist of a large portion of arrivals; this has experienced a decrease consistent with the drop in arrivals from the European market. The diving segment has registered a similar downward trend which, according to the MOTAC is attributed to growth of the Chinese market in which diving comprises only a small percentage. Another substantial variation is the decrease in occupancy rates (from 82.5% in 2007 to 77.5% in 2012) and the average length of stay at resorts and hotels (from 8.5 nights in 2007 to 6.8 nights in 2011). This is blamed on the faster rate of growth in supply than demand, combined with the growth of the Chinese market whose average length of stay is just 3–4 nights (MOTAC, 2012b).

Development of Tourism Zones

Since 1982, successive tourism master plans have provided guidance and strategy for the sector. The First Tourism Master Plan (1TMP) made the first call for the creation of 'tourism development zones' by allocating resorts in all the atolls of the archipelago as a vehicle for social and economic development and to spread tourism benefits more equally throughout the atolls. To create new 'hubs' or 'growth poles', the establishment of three separate zones were proposed: one in the north, one around the island of Malé (the capital city) and one in the south. It was advocated that local handicraft products should be used for regional differentiation between the three zones. By the end of the decade (1982–1992), the envisaged new 'hubs' did not occur; instead, the private sector-led growth continued to expand around Malé and the neighbouring Ari Atoll. The new remote zones did not thrive as expected because the complementary strategies intended by the government to provide the necessary infrastructure, especially in sea and air transportation, were lacking. As a result, risk wary private investors continued with the expansion of existing facilities, on islands with existing tourism infrastructure (MOTAC, 2012b).

The Second Tourism Master Plan (2TMP), covering the years 1996 to 2005, continued the guidelines for decentralisation and expansion of tourism, and endorsed that Maldives should position itself as a "premium marine-eco destination" (MOTAC, 2012b, p. 12). The Third Tourism Master Plan (3TMP), launched in 2008 and covering 2007 to 2011, placed strong emphasis on sustainable tourism, proclaiming that the steady growth pattern of Maldives tourism development should be an example of social and economic sustainability. 3TMP called for the industry to aim for excellence in global sustainable tourism and pledged to develop infrastructure to support tourism development in the new zones, emphasising that tourism should be viewed as a vehicle for social and economic development "that benefits all Maldivians in all parts of the country" (ibid, p. 15). Branding Maldives as an exclusive destination with innovative products was proposed to help maintain its position as a top tourism destination in South Asia. It was also acknowledged that the rich culture, heritage and history of the Maldives are not well integrated into tourism and called for cultural and heritage tourism to be better promoted, together with the key core attractions of sun, sand and sea: "Cultural and heritage tourism has not taken root in the Maldives despite the fact that the country is rich in culture, heritage sites, and history" (MTCA, 2007, p. 59).

New policies that came to effect under the Strategic Action Plan 2009–2013 released islands for resort and hotel development across the archipelago, including plots of land on inhabited islands for hotel and guest house development with the aim to bring direct benefit to those island communities. At the same time, a policy and regulatory review was called for to support these new products. To date, however, no operations have commenced on any of the plots released under the new policy. Some of those that started development chose for a land swap due to dissatisfaction with the land, lack of government's support to develop transportation, and the uncertainty around the issue of being able to serve alcohol in the new sites. Currently, the allocation of land on inhabited islands for tourism activities has been stopped awaiting a review of regulation. Uncertainties around demand, lack of attractions and restrictions on beach attire and alcohol consumption have constrained their progress (MOTAC, 2012b). To respect the hundred percent Muslim population, tourists are instructed to dress modestly and refrain from wearing bikinis and bathing suits while on an inhabited island (MMPRC, 2012).

Current Policies

In the absence of a current economic development plan, authorities count on the tourism sector for development, job creation and the justification for infrastructure development in the outer atolls (MOTAC, 2012b). The objectives outlined in the Draft 4TMP for the next five years indicate the ambition to further increase tourism development as well as visitor numbers while engaging more locals in tourism activities:

- Maintain an annualised 10% growth rate.
- Increase average duration of stay from 6.8 days to 7.2 days.
- Increase occupancy from 73% to 85%.
- Increase bed capacity from 25,000 to 35,000.
- Maintain average growth of annualised bed nights at 10% per annum (from the current 6.5 million to 12 million).
- Increase local, tourism-related employment from 11,000 to 19,000 workers.
- Increase the percentage of local employees per resort from 45% to 50% (MOTAC, 2012a, p. 18).

However, several problems stand in the way of achieving those ambitious objectives. Previous policies to keep tourism development separate from local communities have made it challenging to integrate tourism into the local society. Even with policies that decree that the employment of foreign workers must not exceed that of locals, most of the technical jobs continue to be filled by expatriates. Combined with the large percentage of foreign owned resort operators, a significant share of tourism benefits are still leaked out of the Maldivian economy, with relatively little ripple effects from tourism revenue reaching local communities (Amira, 2009). The Maldives tourism industry is faced with the dilemma of protecting the success story of the existing tourism product which is the engine of the state's economy, while at the same time needing to acknowledge the urgent need for fresh approaches to create growth in other areas of the society and economy. However, neither the existing marketing policies nor the locals' ideas for engaging differently with tourism hint at the provision of a solution to these problems. Locals do not seem to view opportunities for engaging in tourism beyond that of a resort island, city hotel or guest house: "even an island council with an attractive new airport, health centre and marina will tend to focus on developing a new resort rather than seeing other opportunities" (MOTAC, 2012b, p. 23). At the same time, marketing policies and activities have continued to leverage the destination's limited, natural attractions. From the time of 1TMP during the 1980s, visitor perceptions have revolved around the image of a tropical island Eden. Although consecutive Tourism Master Plans advocated slight changes with recommendations for local culture to be integrated into tourism, the crux of all promotion and marketing has remained essentially the same for four decades. Key competitors throughout the years have been destinations that exhibit similar product offerings as the Maldives such as the Caribbean, Indonesia, Philippines, South Pacific, Seychelles, Mauritius, Thailand and Fiji. Nonetheless, authorities proclaim that the appeal of this proposition would be "permanent and sustainable" among the long-standing markets (MTCA, 2007, p. 49). MOTAC firmly believes that the idyllic tropical island imagery extensively used in print and electronic media by official marketing bodies and tourism operators will sustain the position of Maldives as attractive to both the Western and Asian markets. This, despite the strong and increasing tourist demand and expectation for contact and interaction with the local culture and nature of the destinations that they visit (Yu and Lee, 2014). The strategic marketing plans proposed in the 4TMP claims that the "visual impact" of the "beach-fringed, reef-surrounded, atoll islands" will remain "strong and enduring", while at he same time acknowledging the fragility of the islands' distinctive "geography, topography and biodiversity": "Protection of the pristine natural environment is a priority of the highest order, determining the form and degree of development that can be permitted" (MOTAC, 2012b, p. 80).

The official destination marketing organisation, Maldives Marketing and Public Relations Corporation's (MMPRC), in its current strategy, envisions the Maldives to become:

a. The best tropical island destination in the world.
b. The most exclusive destination in South Asia.
c. The top tourism earner in South Asia.
d. An example of sustainable tourism development in small island nations (MOTAC, 2012b, p. 76).

The draft 4TMP advocates retaining and continuing to centralise destination marketing by riding on the brand of "the Sunny Side of Life", with variations off the main slogan to suit different market segments, as follows:

a. The romantic side of life: for honeymooners and couples to depict complete privacy associated with the Maldives product.
b. The colourful side of life: for underwater devotees to portray the attractiveness of the reefs and marine life.
c. The thrilling side of life: for watersports and adventure enthusiasts to communicate the variety of adrenaline pumping activities on offer.
d. The spiritual side of life: for tourists who seek revival of body and mind to portray the spa and wellness product.
e. The human side of life: for tourists interested in combining a beach holiday with interaction with local communities (MOTAC, 2012b).

Thus far, the Maldives has been doing well in terms of visitor numbers (MOTAC, 2013); but the impact on tourist flows from the economic decline that most European countries are experiencing, along with increasingly sophisticated destination competition in the region, cannot be ignored. The benchmark predicted by MOTAC to exceed one million visitors in 2011 was not realised. Throughout 2012, performance of growth rate was below average except in January, even during the usually peak periods from February to May. Justification by the Minister of Tourism that Maldives should not be compared to destinations such as Sri Lanka or Seychelles, because the Maldives' "tourism market is very different" and is of "high-value" (http://www.dailymirror.lk), is of little consolation in the face of imminent threats. As cautioned in the 4TMP, development of similar tourism products to that of the Maldives, in neighbouring countries, and at lower prices, should be of serious concern to the Maldives and leaves no room for complacency. The threat posed by simillar destinations who can offer a much wider range of tourism activities, such as Sri Lanka and Indonesia, and the development of resort products such as Koh Samui in Thailand which target high-end markets, cannot be dismissed or ignored.

During the past decades, Europeans who prefer relaxation with passive recreations more than active ones, used to be the leading markets. However, at present, Chinese tourists who desire multiple activities are the market leaders. A 2011 MOTAC visitor survey revealed that around 10% of beach-oriented tourists, regardless of source market, expect to experience some interaction with local culture. At the same time, the most enjoyable activity for 10% of tourists was found to be visiting other islands (MOTAC, 2011). However, less than two in five actually do visit inhabited islands. As acknowledged by MOTAC: 'This demonstrates that, even among Maldives' existing visitor base, there exists a demand for more involvement with local populations and their cultural heritage' (MOTAC 2012b, p. 58).

Opportunities for Maximising Potential of Tourist Zones

Being so central to the economy of Maldives, tourism zonal development seems a plausible way to facilitate regional growth, and to spread the benefits of tourism across many more of the atolls of the archipelago. As more resorts become established in remote atolls within the tourist zones, opportunities need to be explored to maximise the potential of the different zones. It is essential to seek ways to overcome existing challenges and explore further prospects if the future objectives of existing policies and strategies are to be realised. While the zonal strategy proved to be initially challenging to implement, the successful establishment of a number of resorts and supporting infrastructure illustrates the diligence and resilience of the industry. To sustain growth in the newly developing zones, robust development need to be maintained. Draft 4TMP recommends that the most advantageous option would be to embrace strategies "that complement the surrounding mainstream industry rather than attempt to present an alternative to it" (MOTAC 2012a, p. 45) Therefore, maximising potential opportunities that the zones present needs to be pursued.

Promoting the unique characteristics specific to each zone could prove to be viable and sustainable way to nurture and enhance the competitiveness, vibrancy and diversity of the Maldives tourism experience. The natives of the atolls are the experts and custodians of their culture, history and heritage; hence they are the ideal advocates and champions for the interpretation of thse local features. The promotion of differentiating cultural characteristics, could pave the way to better engage local communities, and also foster an awareness and appreciation of cultural resources as assests among the locals themselves as well as those from other atolls who may thus be encouraged to follow their example. The variety of activities would shift the thrust of potential local entreprenuers from solely focusing on operating a resort, hotel or guesthouse, and reveal a truer identity, complexity and authenticity of the Maldives.

Conclusion

As is already evident from the establishment of resorts and ongoing development of infrastructure in the newly established tourist zones, the zoning strategy seems an appropriate tool for both effectively creating a regional development policy as well as distributing tourism benefits to local communities more equitably. However, for the strategy to be successful and sustainable, some key challenges need to be addressed. The limitation of product range is a drawback for Maldives tourism. Untapped opportunities exist in the unique diversity of both physical and heritage characteristics of the atolls and islands. Such differences can be observed in the populations of the various islands in their appearance and customs which is attributed to the diverse places of their settlers' origin (Mohamed, 2012). With the wide dispersion of the islands, the diction and jargon of the native language vary from atoll to atoll (SAARC Tourism Maldives, 2014). In addition, local crafts, arts and customs exist that are specific to a particular atoll or island. One of the most distinctive of Maldivian handicrafts is wooden lacquer ware – ornamental objects of various shapes made from hollowing out pieces of wood which are lacquered in red, yellow and black resin with intricate patterns. The experts of this craft belong almost exclusively to Thulhaadhoo Island in Baa Atoll. Another special craft is the intricately woven reed mats, a craft exclusive to the southern atolls. The specific reeds that grow in the islands of these atolls are dried in the sun and dyed using natural dyes to create intricately patterned mats. Traditionally used for seating, praying or sleeping, these mats formed royal gifts from Sultans of the Maldives. Handloom or weaving and embroidery of traditional garb have been part of the Maldivian culture that dates as far back as 1340s. Eydhafushi in Baa Atoll is famous for *'feyli'* weaving – a wraparound with brocades of black, brown and white worn during the monarchy era by both men and women (Ministry of Economic Development and Trade, 2007). Local cuisine illustrates some of the most signifcant and interesting differences where dishes and preparation methods vary across the atolls and islands (Amira, 2009). Similarly, some islands are famous for their traditional folk dances. An example is *Kadhaa Maali*: a form of traditional music and dance that is performed only in Kulhudhuffushi in the Baa Atoll (Ministry of Economic Development and Trade, 2007).

These unique aspects are largely on the brink of extinction and most local crafts and customs are dying traditions. Even though potential opportunities exist in leveraging these differences in tourism, culture is a component that is, thus far, glaringly absent in tourism promotion and development. The variations in heritage across the atolls and the zones hold huge benefits and immense potential as a point of difference between the atolls and the tourist zones. In addition to contributing to fill the void of cultural aspects from tourism, the zones would provide differentiation not only for the Maldives tourism product, but between the zones as well, thus easing competition and introducing some badly needed complementarity and synergy among the zones.

With increasing numbers of resorts and their development spread across the archipelago, with no differentiation in products or activities on offer, the Maldives tourism industry runs the risk of creating and intensifying internal competition among the resorts for existing markets. Tourism industry is the engine of Maldives' economy and the largest source of job and income creation for which opportunities for further involvement and engagement from locals are needed. And yet, while enthusiastic for involvement in tourism industry, many Maldivians fail to recognise the benefits arising from activities aside from operating resorts, hotels or guest houses. To maximise the benefits from the tourist zones, the unique differentiating features of the zones need to be researched and profiled. The possibilities of using the zoning strategy for the best advantage from the perspectives of operators, marketers, policy makers and locals should be further explored. The inherent vibrancy of the Maldives, the exclusive differences between the different atolls and tourist zones, should no longer remain obscured and shunned behind "the sunny side of life".

References

Amira, F. (2009). The role of local food in Maldives tourism: a focus on promotion and economic development, AUT University.

Anderson, W. (2011). Enclave tourism and its socio-economic impact in emerging destinations. *Anatolia: An International Journal of Tourism and Hospitality Research*, 22(3), 361–77.

Baldacchino, G. (2010). Island brands and 'the island' as a brand: insights from immigrant entrepreneurs on Prince Edward Island. *International Journal of Entrepreneurship and Small Business*, 9(4), 378–93.

Baldacchino, G. (2012). The lure of the island: a spatial analysis of power relations. *Journal of Marine and Island Cultures*, 1(2), 55–62.

Baldacchino, G., and Ferreira, E.C.D. (2013). Competing notions of diversity in archipelago tourism: transport logistics, official rhetoric and inter-island rivalry in the Azores. *Island Studies Journal*, 8(1), 84–104.

Bardolet, E., and Sheldon, P.J. (2008). Tourism in archipelagos: Hawai'i and the Balearics. *Annals of Tourism Research*, 35(4), 900–923.

Bell, H.C.P. (2004). *Maldive Islands.* New Delhi, India: Asian Educational Services.

Berg, I., and Edelheim, J. (2012). The attraction of islands: travellers and tourists in the Cyclades (Greece) in the twentieth and twenty-first centuries. *Journal of Tourism and Cultural Change*, 10(1), 84–98.

Buhalis, D. (2000). Marketing the competitive destination of the future. *Tourism Management*, 21(1), 97–116.

Daily Mirror (Sri Lanka). (2013). Maldives falls 40,000 short of million tourist target for 2012, 15 January. Retrieved from http://www.dailymirror.lk/business/other/24997-maldives-falls-40000-short-of-million-tourist-target-for-2012.html

Department of National Planning. (2012). *Statistical Yearbook 2012*. Malé, Maldives: Department of National Planning.

Dowling, R. (2000). The Maldives. In C.M. Hall and S. Page (eds), *Tourism in South and Southeast Asia: Issues and cases*, pp. 248–55. Oxford: Butterworth-Heinemann.

Fonseca, F.P., and Ramos, R.A.R. (2012). Heritage tourism in peripheral areas: development strategies and constraints. *Tourism Geographies*, 14(3), 467–93.

Freire, J.R. (2005). Geo-branding, are we talking nonsense? A theoretical reflection on brands applied to places. *Place Branding and Public Diplomacy*, 1(4), 347–62.

Grydehøj, A. (2011). "Making the most of smallness: Economic policy in microstates and sub-national island jurisdictions. *Space and Polity*, 15(3), 183–96.

Hall, D. (1999). Destination branding, niche marketing and national image projection in Central and Eastern Europe. *Journal of Vacation Marketing*, 5(3), 227–37.

Iliachenko, E.Y. (2005). Exploring culture, history and nature as tourist destination branding constructs: The case of a peripheral region in Sweden. The VIII Nordic-Scottish conference on rural and regional development in association with the 14th Nordic symposium in tourism and hospitality research, Akureyri, Iceland, pp. 1–11.

Jansson, D. (2012). Branding Åland, branding Ålanders: reflections on place identity and globalisation in a Nordic archipelago. *Place Branding and Public Diplomacy*, 8(2), 119–32.

Kamenidou, I., Mamalis, S., and Priporas, C.-V. (2009). Measuring destination image and consumer choice criteria: the case of Mykonos Island. *Tourismos: An International Multidisciplinary Journal of Tourism*, 4(3), 67–79.

Kotler, P., and Gertner, D. (2001). Country as brand, product and beyond: a place marketing and brand management perspective. *Brand Management*, 9(4–5), 249–61.

Lutfy, M.I. (1995). *Dhivehiraajjege jografige vanavaru*. Malé, Maldives, G. Sosuni.

Maumoon, Y. (2002). *A general overview of the Dhivehi language*. Malé, Maldives: National Centre for Linguistic and Historical Research.

Metaxas, T. (2009). Place marketing, strategic planning and competitiveness: the case of Malta. *European Planning Studies*, 17(9), 1357–78.

Ministry of Economic Development and Trade. (2007). *Handicraft in the Maldives.* Male', Maldives: Ministry of Economic Development and Trade, Enterprise Development Unit.

MMPRC. (2012). *Maldives visitors guide*. Malé, Maldives: Zebra Cross Private Ltd.

Mohamed, N. (2012). The First Dhivehin. *Dhivehi Observer*. Retrieved from https://archive.today/o/yPMn/http://www.dhivehiobserver.com/history/papers/First_Dhivehin_1708200612.htm

MOTAC. (2011). *Maldives visitor survey 2011 report*. Malé, Maldives: Ministry of Tourism, Arts and Culture.

MOTAC. (2012). *Tourism Yearbook 2012*. Malé, Maldives: Ministry of Tourism, Arts and Culture.

MOTAC. (2012a). *Fourth Tourism Master Plan 2013–2017, Volume 1: Strategic action plan*. Male', Maldives: Ministry of Tourism, Arts and Culture.

MOTAC. (2012b). *Fourth Tourism Master Plan 2013–2017, Volume 2:* Background and analysis. Malé, Maldives: Ministry of Tourism, Arts and Culture.

MOTAC. (2013). *Tourism Yearbook 2013*. Malé, Maldives: Ministry of Tourism, Arts and Culture.

MTCA. (2007). *Maldives Third Tourism Master Plan 2007–2011*. Malé, Maldives: Ministry of Tourism and Civil Aviation.

MTCA (2008). *Fathuruverikamuge tharahgyge 35 aharu*. Malé, Maldives: Ministry of Tourism and Civil Aviation.

Naseem, A. (2011). An indepth analysis of the march towards Maldives-Always Natural slogan. *Maldives Today*. Retrieved from http://www.maldivestoday.com/2011/10/26/the-new-marketing-slogan-of-maldives-appears-to-be-a-copy-of-the-ocean-conservancy-organization/, http://www.maldivestoday.com.

Powell, L. (2013). Maldives falls 40,000 short of million tourist target for 2012. *Minivan News*. Retrieved from http://minivannews.com/travelandarts/maldives-falls-40000-short-of-million-tourist-target-for-2012-51075

Royle, S.A. (2001). *A geography of islands: Small island insularity*. London: Routledge.

SAARC Tourism Maldives. (2014). Maldives Culture. Retrieved from http://maldives.saarctourism.org/maldives-culture.html

Sathiendrakumar, R., and Tisdell, C. (1989). Tourism and the economic development of the Maldives. *Annals of Tourism Research*, 16(2), 254–69.

Vladimirova, M. (2011). The brand image of Malta as a tourism destination: a case study in public relations and corporate communication practice. *The University of West London Journal*, 1(2), 44–61.

World Bank. (2006). *The Maldives: Sustaining growth and improving the investment climate*. Washington DC. World Bank.

Yu, J., and Lee, T. J. (2014). Impact of tourists' intercultural interactions. *Journal of Travel Research*, 53(2), 225–38.

Zhang, J.J. (2010). Brand(ing) Kinmen: a tourism perspective. *International Journal of Entrepreneurship and Small Business*, 9(4), 407–33.

Zulfa, M., and Carlsen, J. (2011). Planning for sustainable island tourism development in the Maldives. In J. Carlsen and R.W. Butler (eds), *Island tourism: Sustainable perspectives*, pp. 215–27. London: CABI.

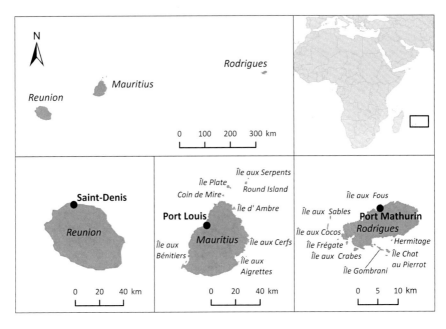

Figure 13.1   The Mascarenes: Reunion, Mauritius and Rodrigues, plus smaller islands

Chapter 13
Travelling the Mascarenes: Creoleness in Tourism Policies and Practices on La Réunion, Mauritius and Rodrigues

Carsten Wergin

Introduction

The Mascarenes, like many other archipelagos, moves on a bumpy road towards sustainable tourism development. There are numerous stakeholders involved that have to deal with complexities fuelled by resident sentiments about socio-cultural fragility, different political climates and geographical characteristics. Hierarchical government structures (island – archipelago – mainland) generate diverse community rivalries. For the French Overseas-Department (DOM) of La Réunion, these extend 11,000km north to continental France; while the relationship between the autonomous sub-island Rodrigues and its mainland Mauritius is traditionally spiced with racial tension.

My focus in this chapter is on Creoleness as a cultural marker that caters for particular tourist products to outline some of these differences. The text discusses the ways in which apparently common denominators of creolisation and colonialism have different impetus in tourism policies and practices on La Réunion, Mauritius and Rodrigues. Writing as a sociocultural anthropologist, it compliments other contributions to this volume that focus more on economic vectors and quantitative analysis. I draw on material collected during fieldwork in the Mascarenes between 2003 and 2009. This leads me to investigate how La Réunion, Mauritius and Rodrigues sell their Creoleness to potential tourists. How complimentary and/or different are their Creole 'products'?

Cultural conflicts are often camouflaged in official narratives about tourist spaces. On the islands of the Mascarenes, touristified enactments of Creoleness are grounded in individual island histories of colonialism, and the particular significance for their island identity within the archipelago. With Baldacchino and Ferreira (2013, p. 85), I ask,

> To what extent are such discourses, and the harmony they infer, constructed and hyped versions of an altogether different practice: one driven by intense inter-island rivalries, one characterized by too similar island destinations competing for the same tourists, one where there are other differences between and within islands which may be socially and historically more relevant than what is officially portrayed, but which are dismissed as not appropriate or 'incorrect' for branding and marketing purposes?

The Mascarene archipelago is made up of three islands. The largest in terms of land area, La Réunion, has 2,512km² of land and about 838,000 inhabitants (INSEE 2012a). This is followed by Mauritius with a size of 2,040km² but 1,233,000 inhabitants (Government of Mauritius, 2011). Finally, the Rodriguan population of about 40,400 lives on a total land mass of only 109km² (ibid.).

All three islands were unpopulated before colonisation. They form an archipelago like no other because of the long distances between them and the uneven distribution of wealth. This promotes particular tourism policies and practices. Inhabitants of the richer island, La Réunion, are targeted by poorer islands, Mauritius and Rodrigues, as potential visitors. As a result, large parts of the general archipelago tourist clientele stem from the islands within the archipelago itself: in 2012, annual passenger traffic by country of original embarkation on Mauritius showed 257,000 arrivals and 248,000 departures from La Réunion, and 67,000 arrivals from Rodrigues with an almost identical amount of departures (Government of Mauritius, 2013). People from La Réunion are heavily targeted by Mauritian tourism marketing and traditionally make up the majority of visitors to Mauritius: In 2004, La Réunion led the category of international arrivals to Mauritius with 96,510 visitors, followed by visitors from South Africa (52,609) and the Malagasy Republic (8,256). Of the Asian contingent, Indians made up the majority with 24,716, followed by the Chinese (6,127). (Schnepel, 2009, p. 296). Mauritians, on the other hand, make up the majority of visitors to Rodrigues. Domestic travel is comparably cheaper for them, and local Rodriguan products such as honey and *piment* paste are very popular among the Mauritian population. Finally, of the few places that Rodriguans (can) afford to visit, Mauritius figures first, while their inter-island travel is to a large extend stimulated by family visits, student exchanges and other obligations, also medical reasons such as operations.

Related economic differences can be attributed to the different histories of decolonisation of these islands. While in 1946, La Réunion received the same status and rights as other French DOMs, Mauritius became independent from British rule only in 1968. Rodrigues forms part of the country of Mauritius as a sub-island jurisdiction and was only granted the rights of an autonomous region in 2001. Some Rodriguans told me during fieldwork that they would even today prefer to have remained part of the British Empire, largely because they see their interests under-represented within Mauritian national politics. As a consequence, the socio-economic set up of La Réunion differs greatly from that of Mauritius and Rodrigues, also with regards to public funds that stream in each year from continental France, as well as the Franco/European healthcare and school system standards.

Another fundamental reason for these differences is that, in contrast to La Réunion whose inhabitants are French citizens, on Mauritius/Rodrigues the idea of a "rainbow nation" is actively promoted. This image of a diverse but unified whole provides the ideological setting for the formation of a national identity that is distinct from that of La Réunion in its understanding of Creoleness. To further illustrate this, I draw on a theoretical setting outlined by two academics from La Réunion, Carpanin Marimoutou and Françoise Vergès. In their manifesto *Amarres: Créolisations India-Océans* (2003), they define La Réunion in relation to its geographical location within the Indian Ocean. The latter for them is,

> ... a space without specific supranationality or territorialisation. It is a cultural space, made of several overlapping space-times in which temporalities and territories are constructed and deconstructed. An ocean that links continents and islands. An Afro-Asian, Muslim, Christian, animist, Buddhist, Hindu space; a space of Creolisations. An ocean of trade winds and monsoons, cyclones and winds. (Vergès, 2006, p. 44, translated from the original french).

Carpanin Marimoutou was a representative of this "space of Creolisations" at a 2002 conference in St. Lucia in the West Indies entitled "Créolité and Creolisation". He gave an account of the relationship between place (*le lieu*) and the connections between places (*les liens*) and argued that these two concepts remain inseparable when trying to define "the Creole". In order to outlines this, he compared definitions for being Creole first in a Mauritian, then in a Réunionese context.

In Mauritius, Creole denotes those who are defined as being neither French, English, Indian, nor Chinese, but descendants of African slaves with no identifiable national roots. The term Creole is to describe those whose history is lost and cannot be retrieved. On La Réunion, the development of the term took a different route. After the official abolition of slavery in 1848, and the beginning of the transfer of indentured labourers from India, the term "Creole" came to describe foremost those who had been born on La Réunion. To some extent, it even excluded the descendants of slaves by focusing on poor white peasants, the so-called *Kréol Blancs*.

In contrast to Mauritius, being Creole on La Réunion from the nineteenth century referred to possession of a concrete origin, thus creating a connection between the island and its inhabitants, and distinguishing those from whoever came afterwards, notably indentured labourers from India. As a consequence, while on Mauritius being Creole meant having lost a connection to a concrete place of origin, on La Réunion being Creole came to mean establishing a connection with the island. Creoleness on La Réunion therefore describes an affirmative construction of relations leading to new fictions of a common island identity. While for the Mauritian context, the definition of what a Creole is remains a highly controversial topic, as the term continues to separate a socio-economically disadvantaged part of the population from the Hindu-Mauritian ruling class (Vaughan, 2005).

As Vergès and Marimoutou argue, the Mascarene Archipelago is set in an ocean of diversity, and, as I will argue in this chapter, La Réunion has successfully grounded itself in it through the affirmative engagement with its Creoleness. In other words, affirmative cultural action – in the cases presented below 'affirmative musical action' – has helped to establish Creoleness on La Réunion as a cultural marker with which by now many people identify. Contrary to this, Mauritius/Rodrigues has not grounded itself in Creoleness but continues to use Creoleness to present its elites as different from former slaves. In La Réunion, therefore, Creole culture is organic and interwoven with local politics and aspirations. In Mauritius, Creoleness remains a locus for conflict, as it is used to imagine 'the other' against which the Hindu-Mauritian ruling class positions itself.

In recent years, parts of the younger generation of Mauritians have, similar to the Réunionese, become more open to other impulses and ideas for self-expression, 'adopting a more cosmopolitan approach in their self-definition' (Boswell, 2006, p. 208). The question remains, whether tourism policies and practices are used effectively to promote those more cosmopolitan approaches that reach the island and become implemented within cultural production and self-expression. Tourism might generate images that bring the islands of the Mascarenes closer together, as it fosters Creoleness as a distinctive attribute in the realms of cultural performance, music and food. However, as will be seen below, more often than not, such apparent similarities brought forth in tourist advertising foreclose more complex layers of difference.

This is the focus of the anthropological reading I present in this chapter. It puts an emphasis on the distinct cultural marker of Creoleness to show how policies and practices in tourism are to a large extent 'policies and practices of visibility'. Those cater for a particular image of a destination, partly influenced by a local population, partly a product of history, and partly a product of a touristification of a place through which history becomes actively rewritten.

Touristifying Creoleness on La Réunion

A holiday on La Réunion leads visitors to explore volcanic landscapes, including visits to a still active volcano. They can watch whales and swim with dolphins, do adventure walks in tropical jungles in the three *Cirques*; enclosures by high mountains that account for 50plus micro-climates, or of course, there are possibilities to surf or relax at the beach. Since La Réunion is an integral part of France and the European Union, its population of roughly 840,000 people use the euro as their currency, has European licence plates on its cars, and (apart from its Creoleness) is still taught in school to be Gallic in origin.

Apart from the different takes on Creoleness in Mauritius/Rodrigues and La Reunion that I discuss in this chapter, the above is linked to another powerful contrast at work that strongly impacts on their tourism industries: La Reunion is part of France and maintained by French transfer payments. As a result, its tourism is almost exclusively domestic, since only continental French can bear the 5-star prices charged for what compared to the neighboring island Mauritius often amounts to only a 3-star service. Mauritius, on the contrary, is much better served by international flights since tourism is a substantial contributor to its general economy. This necessitates tapping as many markets as possible. As a result, the gap between La Reunion and Mauritius, in terms of tourist arrivals and general growth of the industry, has increased since the 1980s (Gay, 2012, p. 1638).

In 2011, 471,000 people visited La Réunion, which is the highest number ever recorded for this Creole island. However, it is still only about half of the number of visitors that travelled to Mauritius in the same year. The great majority of visitors to La Réunion again came from continental France (81%). This lessened the benefit to the local hotel and accommodation industry since 44% of visitors stayed with family or friends. However, there was also an increase of 14% of tourists from other European countries (INSEE, 2012b). In 2012, visitor numbers to La Réunion dropped by 5.3% to 446,500. That same year, Mauritius was visited by 965,000 people. Visitor numbers were still 6.2% higher than 2010, while 2011 was 12.1% above the numbers from the previous year (INSEE, 2013). The French bureau of statistics (INSEE) estimates that tourism is still on the rise in La Réunion, but this remains to be confirmed in the coming years.

Ancestors of the general population of La Réunion came from Africa, India, Southeast Asia and Europe, especially continental France as its main colonising power. Since its discovery by Portuguese sailors in 1507, La Réunion has consistently seen the arrival of new migrants, the latest wave coming from the Comoro Islands, as well as from Europe, notably retirees. This has produced a cultural richness that caters for numerous possibilities to visit cultural events and local village feasts.

The aforementioned postcolonial theorist Françoise Vergès, herself born on La Réunion, describes the way in which the island was perceived during colonial times as 'the "bastard" child of the colonial empire' (Vergès, 2003, p. 167) in contrast to contemporary tourist postcards and glossy brochures. In previous works, my attempt has been to understand processes of Creolisation through an analysis of musical practices, focussing on the ways in which local musicians represent their Creole life-worlds (Wergin, 2010). I will draw on this to illustrate this image of the "bastard child" and how it is used affirmatively today for the enactment of local culture.

In 1981, the Réunionese musicians Danyèl Waro published his remarkable album *Batarsité*. In the title track he defined his island identity as "not white, not black", but with its roots in *batarsité* ("bastardhood") (ibid.). Waro was born, lives and works on Réunion. Son of a poor white peasant, who would be categorized as *Kréol Blanc* (see above), he

Figure 13.2   Celebrations at Danyèl Waro's house, La Réunion, 20 December 2003
Photo: The author.

began his career in the late 1970s, after he had returned from imprisonment in continental France. He was jailed for refusing to fulfil his army service. During that time, he began to write poems and songs in Réunionese Creole.

Figure 13.2 shows friends and family of Danyèl Waro (front right) who celebrate the Réunionese 'Abolition of Slavery Day' in his home. They surround him, dance and sing along to his music, the Maloya. All participants sing and dance for the special occasion of a public holiday that was introduced to commemorate what the people of La Réunion have successfully overcome: 20 December is to demonstrate that Réunionese social reality has gone beyond its violent colonial past.

For tourism policies and practices, this is fortunate for various reasons. The holiday falls into the high tourist season when Europeans aim to escape the cold winter months on this subtropical island. Consequently, many visitors are encouraged to celebrate 20 December and with it Maloya. Both cultural markers have become local attractions for global audiences. Both are celebrated throughout the island and foster the understanding of a successful Réunionese struggle for recognition of cultural difference grounded in Creoleness at home and abroad. The music, Maloya, has become a recognizable medium for a Réunionese society after the experience of 'violence, brutality and exile' during the island's creolisation process (Vergès, 2006, p. 36).

A similar argument can be made for the musical equivalent to Maloya on Mauritius and Rodrigues, which is called Séga. Here also, musical celebrations of a unique social reality are standard repertoire in tourism policies and practices for audiences who seek imaginaries of places that are exotic and different, but at the same time peaceful and harmonious

**Figure 13.3   Séga dance performance with groups from La Réunion and
Rodrigues, Pointe Venus Hotel and Spa, Rodrigues, 2009**
Photo: The author.

"rainbow nations". Their "staged authenticity" (McCannell, 1973) extends beyond the realm of the local, since global economic interest supports cultural resources such as a particular musical product of Creoleness. Waro and fellow musicians are successful on World Music stages, at international festivals and local cultural events due to the value of showcasing 'real Creoleness'.

For events in hotels such as the one shown above (Figure 13.3), local music is used to emphasize the qualities of a picturesque holiday destination with happy people in colourful dresses, dancing and singing on white, sandy beaches. Such techniques of what, with reference to Said's (1979) concept of 'orientalism', can be termed 'tropical-islandism' are ever-present not only in the Mascarenes but also in other regions in the Indian Ocean, and beyond (Amira, this volume). Meanwhile, an image of Creoleness is created for the demands of an industry that nurtures imaginaries of western travellers who seek authentic environments and the whitewashed tranquility of "a peaceful, safe and equitable society" (New Adventures, 2014, n.p.).

When Hobsbawm (1995) argues that 'the economic-technological base provides to some extent the framework, the limitations, within which culturally a variety of different forms of organisation can develop', this is also true for how Creoleness is fostered within the tourism sectors on La Réunion, Mauritius and Rodrigues. Resources and networks have led to closer interconnections between hosts, guests, representations and perceptions of the islands and their Creole foundations. In some instances, tourism policies and practices have incorporated Creoleness into their repertoire as cultural marker. On La Réunion, this is nurtured by the affirmative engagement of a local population with its violent colonial past. On Mauritius and Rodrigues, this development has been quite different, as the values of Creoleness for tourism policies and practices are only on the verge of being discovered.

Mauritius and Rodrigues: Creoleness from Below

Mauritius is an island state that has a very particular history of colonial and postcolonial integration. After the British had conquered French *Isle de France* in 1810, they renamed it Mauritius. Subsequently, the island became part of their Empire in the Treaty of Vienna of 1814. Britain granted the Franco-Mauritian ruling class rights to pursue their cultural practices and keep vestiges of the former legal-political structure (Neveling, 2012, p. 6). As on La Réunion, in the early to mid-19th century, slavery was gradually replaced by indentured labour from India when the plantation economy moved from coffee crops to sugar cane production.

Since 1968, Mauritius is an independent democratic state. This encompasses Rodrigues, which in 1528 was discovered by the Portuguese sailor Diego Rodriguez. The volcanic land of the significantly smaller island dependency is partly surrounded by a 90km² coral reef. On 20 November 2001, Rodrigues received the status of autonomy which gives its Chief Commissioner the right to spend money from a yearly budget allocated to him by the Mauritian authorities.

Since in 1970, Mauritius was opened up to foreign investors, the number of tourist arrivals has constantly increased, from around 72,000 in 1974, to 150,000 in 1985, to 536,000 in 1997, 906,000 in 2007, and 965,000 in 2012 (Schnepel, 2009, p. 292; Government of Mauritius, 2013). La Réunion continues to provide the highest share in arrivals to Mauritius with 139,000 people in 2012, followed by South Africa (89,000), the UK (87,000), India and Germany (both 55,000) (Government of Mauritius, 2013).

In contrast to the prosperous development of the Mauritian tourism sector, fundamental problems for people living on Rodrigues remain a lack of development and, related to this, a high unemployment rate. As in other archipelago contexts, the dependence of Rodrigues on Mauritius is linked to a 'tightly coordinated, top-down, centre-periphery logistic relationship' (Baldacchino and Ferreira, 2013, p. 86). Thanks to the autonomy status of Rodrigues, its branding is today accomplished by a local tourism agency, all be it in close collaboration with state departments who allocate the necessary financial support. This is what slightly differentiates the Mauritius-Rodrigues relationship from the general centre-periphery dependency on many other archipelagos in the Indian Ocean such as the Seychelles or Maldives (Baldacchino and Ferreira, 2013, p. 87).

Rodrigues caters for popular tourism imaginaries of a place 'frozen in time' and 'unspoiled by development'. One reason for this is its geographical isolation. Inter-island links with La Réunion that do not involve Mauritius have been tried but not kept up, because Air Mauritius holds a monopoly on the route Mauritius-Rodrigues and does not offer flights that do not include a stop on the mother(is)land. In addition, the closest container harbour is Port Louis, on Mauritius, roughly 36 hours away. However, satellite TV, Internet and mobile phones constantly bring information to the island. This not only influences interests, identity and culture of the people living on Rodrigues, but also their particular ways in which they represent themselves and their cultural differences within the archipelago and the nation-state of Mauritius.

The second reason for a characterisation of Rodrigues as 'unspoilt by development' is the cultural and economic neglect that its Creole population is said to experience from the

Hindu-dominated mother(is)land. One way of classifying the general composition of the Mauritian population is to state that, of the nation's total of 1.2 million citizens, 68% are of Indian origin, 27% are Creoles, 3% Chinese, and 2% French. However, certain other criteria are used in the government census from 1982 that are relevant to further outline the meaning of Creoleness in the Mauritian context. Here, the population is given as consisting of 52% Hindus, 16% Muslims and 3% Sino-Mauritians, with 29% belonging to the category of the "General Population". While the first two categories were created along religious lines, the third reflects country of origin (China), and the fourth includes Creoles, French and "Coloureds" (i.e., "mixed" descendants of French and Creoles) (Schnepel, 2009, p. 297).

The resulting Creole minority is traditionally considered under-represented within the Republic of Mauritius (Eriksen, 1998). Politically, the Hindu majority dominates Mauritius, while the Franco-Mauritian minority still owns most of the land (Eisenlohr, 2006; Mukonoweshuro, 1991). In the 1982 census, the term Creole was used to describe all those Mauritians who are descendants of African slaves, and as such described a minority. However, this caters for a significant distinction between Mauritius and Rodrigues. While in the Republic of Mauritius Creoles are a minority and make up about 27% of the total population, they account for 97% of the population on Rodrigues. To discuss resulting cultural differences and ethnic rivalries, I return once again to the topic of musical enactment of Creoleness for tourist audiences.

In 2009, I conducted fieldwork on tourism development on Rodrigues and had brought my saxophone with me in order to get in closer contact with local people. Some of the musicians I met and with whom I started to collaborate on a regular basis were directly involved in the tourism sector. As described for the Réunionese context, they also were important contributors to the tourism industry since musical entertainment is a vital part not only of all-inclusive hotel packages but the tourist experience in general; the performance of traditional song and dance during or after dinner (Figure 13.4).

I visited Rodrigues for the first time in 2003. Back then, I was doing fieldwork on La Réunion and wanted to take a few days of vacation in a place, I was told, "like La Réunion 30 years earlier." This image is repeatedly invoked, even in academic publications. A few years earlier, David Picard had conducted his research on La Réunion for a book that was to be published in 2011 and in which he develops his notion of 'cultivating the human garden' (Picard, 2011). Like a gardener would cultivate flowers, local development policy, nature conservation, and museum initiatives dramatize social life so as to evoke modernist paradigms of time, beauty and nature. Islanders who live in this human garden are thus placed in the ambivalent role of 'human flowers', embodying ideas of authenticity and biblical innocence, but also of history and social life in Creoleness (ibid.). La Réunion is, for the various reasons outlined above, not the tropical island destination one expects from related tourist advertisements. It does not even advertise itself as such, but as an 'île intense' with volcanoes, drastic climate changes and high mountains. Picard and his publishers must have felt the need to counteract this 'shortcoming' and to apply their own 'magic' to his 2011 book when they chose a painting of fishers at the beach near Point Cotton on Rodrigues (!) for its cover.

In light of the above, destinations acquire a culture of self-aestheticisation by the light of which they apply makeup, speak of their beauty, parade specificities, and display hospitality. In 2003 Rodrigues, tourism had already been identified as the main field from which to generate alternative income for its inhabitants, who largely remain dependent on agriculture, fishing and social benefits from the mother(is)land. But when I returned to

Figure 13.4   Dinner evening with traditional dancers, Hotel Mourouk Ebony, Rodrigues, 2009

Photo: The author.

Rodrigues in 2009, self-aestheticisation and cultivation of its 'human garden' seemed to only take shape very slowly. What caught my attention, however, was the large and diverse support of international organisations. Those had started a wide range of development initiatives linked to the preservation of the island's spectacular lagoon, or the re-introduction of former endemic plants and animals such as turtles from Madagascar.

In conjunction with the tourism industry, strong emphasis was put on sustainable development and nature conservation. It was this "ideology of sustainability" that became one of my central concerns. I began to wonder how local people reacted to international expert policy that came to teach them about sustainable fishing techniques and alternative livelihoods as wildlife guards or tour guides. As mentioned above, the common fear for many Rodriguans remains that important decisions are taken somewhere 'outside' Rodrigues, i.e. on Mauritius, without consulting with Rodriguans. Rodriguans are to behave according to the expectations of others. Similar to the music of Danyèl Waro and other Réunionese artists of the 1970s, many songs that are sung today on Rodrigues articulate this complaint in a partly localized manner, sung in Rodriguan Creole, but using a very international style: reggae.

There seemed to be an interesting tension between such local music and the policies and practices of international organisations: the music and musicians internationalized but emphasized 'collaboration', while international development aid was based on 'education'. In terms of Creoleness, there was another tension visible in the reggae performances. In order to articulate their distinctive Creole message, they had to withdraw

Figure 13.5 **"Rodrigues, ki to lavenir (…what will be your future)? Maurice, as tu du cœur (…do you have a heart)?" Nou touris, mort; nou pep enteré (… without tourism we are dead, our people might as well be buried). 2009 demonstrations on Rodrigues for better support of the local tourism industry by the Mauritian government**

Photo: The author.

to a different musical style, adopted from Jamaica in the Antilles, another archipelago. They could not use Séga, as their local music had already been claimed by the tourism industry as a symbol of peaceful diversity within the 'rainbow nation'. Instead, they sought musical collaboration with another Creole setting, the Antilles. Meanwhile, international development aid was educating them about possible changes that would make representations of their local culture and environment more profitable, tailored to the demands of the international market.

On Rodrigues, tourism entrepreneurs remain among the most educated and most sensible to such lucrative international intervention. In their work, they strongly influence the perception of the environment, of traditions and landscape, and also of Creoleness. In accordance with the demands of the market, tourists are invited to spend their holiday in an 'authentic' Rodriguan home, with a family that shares its dinner with them. In this way, the entrepreneurs become actors in an internationally informed process that restructures the whole island. When, for example, the unique biodiversity of the island's lagoon (a promising tourist attraction) is under threat of extinction through destructive fishing practices, protective measures are implemented so that fishers and not fish are eliminated (Wergin, forthcoming).

Here again, market segmentation is of particular importance for Rodrigues. In many places, the lack of adventure tourism can be partly compensated by an increased effort to promote local heritage (Bardolet and Sheldon, 2008). On Rodrigues, it is a particular landscape – the lagoon, endemic forests, and dry plains – that became heritage sights/ sites. Likewise, a diverse range of Rodriguan traditions, artisan products, cooking recipes, music and dance performances of various kinds – all of which advertise an element of Creoleness – are 'rediscovered' for tourism marketing. However, as has been shown elsewhere, such markers of difference, that are constructed by marketing professionals, do not always meet local approval (Baldacchino and Ferreira, 2013). Once more, MacCannell's notion of "staged authenticity" resonates here. As musician, I became a member of such staged authenticities. I was also backstage when they were designed. From this particular perspective, tourism development on Rodrigues proves to be something contested and constantly 'in the making'.

Development policies and practices work at a different speed to the general public, which does not always agree to give up fishing in order to take tourists sight/site-seeing in their fishing boats. Furthermore, while the island and its Creole population need to demonstrate a lot of flexibility towards new policies and practices, its infrastructure, environmental and cultural fragility only support a limited numbers of tourists. The local political authority, the Rodrigues Regional Assembly (RRA), outlined various measures to tackle these obstacles. Notably, it aims for a maximum of 100,000 tourists per year (RRA Magazine, 2010). A key factor to attain this goal is accessibility. As elsewhere, travel between the islands in an archipelago is critical to their tourism development (Bardolet and Sheldon, 2008, p. 902). This is where Creoleness and ethnic rivalry once again return into the picture.

During my fieldwork in 2009, the Rodriguan population protested against the Mauritian government over a conflict for cheaper airfares to the island. The then Chief Commissioner argued that the problem was more fundamental than the price of airfares, since the Mauritian government would generally not respect the autonomy of Rodrigues. In early 2009, the price for a ticket to India was at 15,000 MUR return, while a ticket to Rodrigues was at 8,000 MUR for a domestic journey that was significantly shorter. This for him proved the point.

As illustrated in Figure 13.5, when negotiations with government representatives about cheaper airfares to Rodrigues ran the risk of failure, the Rodriguan population did what I have elsewhere called 'trump the ethnic card' (Wergin, 2012). In a threat to go public with their accusations against the Mauritian government that this was in fact not an economic but a racial conflict derived from a general disregard for the interests of Mauritian Creoles, they created significant pressure on their opponents, since one cannot advertise Mauritius as a peaceful 'rainbow nation' if its government is said to undermine the rights of parts of its population that consequently take to the streets. Such negative publicity would cause tremendous damage to the tourism imaginary so carefully crafted in over 40 years of promotion activity.

The two groups found a compromise that included a special package for Mauritians to stay for a minimum of three nights in a Rodriguan hotel, and at a reduced price. The offer was not made available on the international market but emphasized the already existing dependency of Rodrigues tourism on domestic travellers from the mother(is) land. Despite creative international tourism marketing and development aid, state support kept the industry on the Creole island limited to inter-island travel, while international arrivals to date are to stay on the main island and not to travel further.

Conclusion: The Creole Archipelago

This chapter has discussed some of the uneven geographies created by colonialism and tourism development in the two-state, triple-island, Mascarene archipelago. It has done so by probing into some of the cultural nuances related to Creoleness as it is expressed in inter-island conflicts, on World Music stages and as used in tourism marketing strategies. On La Réunion, Creoleness is an accepted part of local culture. The violent struggle associated with it is put into song, celebrated and turned into a cultural marker that distinguishes the island from continental France. On Mauritius and Rodrigues, Creoleness is also represented in tourism contexts. It is used to 'exoticize' the place, present beautiful dancers, different food and a general imaginary of happiness within the 'rainbow nation'.

While on La Réunion there is a certain truth to the image transported in Maloya about a Creole culture that has reached a common understanding, the cases of Mauritius and Rodrigues suggest that, under the touristifications of Creoleness, ethnic conflict and racial rivalry remain. These close readings of different appropriations of Creoleness present local culture and communities within the archipelago as a complex 'geo/biographically mixed space' (Mignolo, 2002). It follows that tourism policies and practices can trigger more diverse localised processes than many theorists tend to acknowledge. Hence, only by paying attention to historical specificities (such as Creoleness) as the foundations for archipelago tourism policies and practices, can the 'in the making' of tourist destinations be represented appropriately.

In many archipelagos, including the Mascarenes, the interest of visitors in nature and culture can enhance the pride of people in their traditions, but it also widens the sphere of influences on the local even more. As seen in the case of Rodrigues, the valorisation of a tradition can greatly change under the impact of international tourism and development programmes. Meanwhile, the musical examples and manifestations for cheaper airfares also show that depth and sophistication of Mascarene cultures and their engagement with Creoleness are more than the official tourist narratives suggest, and also more than standardized tourism policies and practices can cater for.

The diverse actors presented here create complexity, surely also some confusion, in regard to the meanings of Creoleness in the archipelago. In addition, the three islands are at different stages of tourism development and require distinct product and market policies. As in other archipelagos, the islands aim to distinguish themselves (cf. Bardolet and Sheldon, 2008, p. 902). Even if part of the same republic, as is the case of Mauritius and Rodrigues, competition between them can result in political tension. But, as the example of La Réunion shows, the difference that is grounded in Creoleness can also be used productively. It can become a cultural marker that could make both island destinations, Mauritius and Rodrigues, more attractive for their visitors.

Here, I follow Baldacchino and Ferreira (2013) in their suggestion that, if archipelagos wish to promote diversity, tourism policies and practices need to 'become more anthropologically sensitive to actual and historically valid forms of difference' (ibid., p. 101; also Grydehøj, 2008). There is much potential in recognizing Creole diversity in the Mascarenes, beyond official discourse or glossy tourist brochures; especially if this resonates more closely with political history, colonialism and contemporary socio-cultural practice. Tourism policies and practices continue to impact on how these processes develop in the future, and do so in significant ways that intertwine and create further distinctions between the three islands of La Réunion, Mauritius and Rodrigues. As such, their diverse ways of appropriating Creoleness as cultural marker and means for tourism promotion, whether in music, art or tourist brochure, remains open for further, critical investigation.

References

Baldacchino, G., and Ferreira, E.C.D. (2013). Competing notions of diversity in archipelago tourism: transport logistics, official rhetoric and inter-island rivalry in the Azores. *Island Studies Journal*, 8(1), 84–104.

Bardolet, E., Sheldon, P.J. (2008). Tourism in archipelagos: Hawai'i and the Balearics. *Annals of Tourism Research*, 35(4), 900–923.

Boswell, R. (2006). *Le malaise créole: Ethnic identity in Mauritius*. New York: Berghahn Books.

Eisenlohr, P. (2006). *Little India: Diaspora, time, and ethnolinguistic belonging in Hindu Mauritius*. Berkeley CA: University of California Press.

Eriksen, T.H. (1998). *Common denominators: Ethnicity, nation-building and compromise in Mauritius*. Oxford: Berg.

Gay, J.-C. (2012). Why is tourism doing poorly in Overseas France? *Annals of Tourism Research*, 39(3), 1634–52.

Government of Mauritius. (2013). *Annual digest of statistics 2012*. Ministry of Finance and Economic Development. Retrieved from http://statsmauritius.gov.mu/English/Publications/Documents/Regular%20Reports/annual%20digest/annualdig12.pdf

Government of Mauritius. (2011). *Population census: Main results*. Ministry of Finance and Economic Development. Retrieved from http://www.gov.mu/portal/goc/cso/ei977/pop2011.pdf

Grydehøj, A. (2008). Branding from above: generic cultural branding in Shetland and other islands. *Island Studies Journal*, 3(2), 175–98.

Hobsbawm, E. (1995). *A talk with Eric Hobsbawm*. Retrieved from http://www.ciaonet.org/wps/hoe01

INSEE (2013). Après le boom de 2011, le tourisme marque le pas. Retrieved from http://www.insee.fr/fr/themes/document.asp?reg_id=24&ref_id=19768

INSEE (2012a). *Estimation de population au 1er janvier, par région, sexe et grande classe d'âge*. Retrieved from http://www.insee.fr/fr/themes/detail.asp?reg_id=99&ref_id=estim-pop

INSEE (2012b). Une année record pour le tourisme réunionnais. Retrieved from http://www.insee.fr/fr/themes/document.asp?reg_id=24&ref_id=18597

MacCannell, D. (1973). Staged authenticity: arrangements of social space in tourist settings. *American Journal of Sociology*, 79(3), 589–603.

Marimoutou, C., and Vergès, F. (2003). *Amarres: Créolisations India-Océanes*. La Réunion: Éditions K'A.

Mignolo, W. (2002). The geopolitics of knowledge and the colonial difference. *The South Atlantic Quarterly*, 101(1), 57–96.

Mukonoweshuro, E. (1991). Containing political instability in a poly-ethnic society: the case of Mauritius. *Ethnic and Racial Studies*, 14(2), 199–224.

Neveling, P. (2012). A periodisation of globalisation according to the Mauritian integration into the international sugar commodity chain, 1825–2005. Retrieved from http://www.open.ac.uk/Arts/ferguson-centre/commodities-of-empire/working-papers/WP18.pdf

New Adventures. (2014). New Adventures about Reunion Island. Retrieved from http://www.newadventures.com/vacation/reunion-island/about-reunion-island

Picard, D. (2011). *Tourism, magic and modernity: Cultivating the human garden*. Oxford: Berghahn Books.

RRA-Magazine. (2010). *Magazine of the Rodrigues Regional Assembly*. Retrieved from http://www.gov.mu/portal/sites/rra_portal/download/rramagazine/tourist.pdf

Said, E.W. (1979). *Orientalism*. New York: Vintage.

Schnepel, B. (2009). Two beaches: the globalisation of Mauritian waterfronts. In V.Y. Hookoomsing, R. Ludwig, and B. Schnepel (eds), *Multiple identities in action: Mauritius and some Antillean parallelisms*, pp. 287–317. Berlin: Peter Lang.

Vaughan, M. (2005). *Creating the creole island: Slavery in eighteenth-century Mauritius*. Durham NC: Duke University Press.

Vergès, F. (2006). Creolisation and the Maison de Civilisations et de l'Unité La Réunionnaise. *Journal of Visual Culture*, 5(1), 29–51.

Vergès, F. (2003). The island of wandering souls: processes of creolisation, politics of emancipation and the problematic of absence on Reunion Island. In R. Edmond. and V. Smith (eds), *Islands in history and representation*, pp. 162–76. London: Routledge.

Wergin, C. (forthcoming). Reconstructing nature for tourism development: ethnographic accounts from a World Heritage Site in the making. In M. Gravari-Barbas, L. Bourdeau, and M. Robinson (eds), *World Heritage sites and tourism: Global and local relations*. Farnham: Ashgate.

Wergin, C. (2012). Trumping the ethnic card: how tourism entrepreneurs on Rodrigues tackled the 2008 financial crisis. *Island Studies Journal*, 7(1), 119–34.

Wergin, C. (2010). *Kréol blouz: Musikalische inszenierungen von identität und kultur*. Cologne: Boehlau.

Conclusion
Archipelagic Tourism: Synthesis and Reflections

Dimitri Ioannides and Evangelia Petridou

Introduction: Desiring Islands

During the recent economic crisis, the European Union has obliged cash-strapped Greece to find unorthodox ways of raising capital, including the sale of both state and privately owned property and real estate (Moya, 2010). Thus, in the past few years there have been several cases where wealthy persons have acquired Greek islands for their private use. The Qatari emir, for instance, has purchased several uninhabited islands, forming their own tiny archipelagic cluster known as the Echinades, which lies between Ithaca and the Greek mainland, in the Ionian Sea (Squires, 2012).

The desire of the rich and famous to acquire private islands hardly constitutes a novelty. Richard Branson owns Necker Island in the British Virgin Islands – which explains the origins of his brand name – described on its website as "my home and favourite hideaway" (Necker Island website, 2014). An internet search reveals sites dedicated to offering private islands for rent and purchase (e.g., Private Islands Online, 2014). This reminds the reader of Dubai's ambition to create a cluster of artificial islands known as 'The World', shaped in the continents of the world (Henderson, 2006). Although this project has been bedeviled by financial and technical difficulties, when it was first announced it drew much attention and several celebrities made bids to buy their own personal island. Meanwhile, for the many others who cannot afford buying them, island hopping becomes the closest best thing (Royle, this volume).

It is not only individuals who acquire and develop small islands. The Maldives is famous for encouraging the development of more than 100 of its own islands as enclave luxury resorts (Amira, this volume). This allows the devout Muslim country to generate the much needed income from tourism while avoiding as much as possible the interaction of locals and visitors in highly populated areas to reduce the possibility of cultural contamination (Domroes, 2001; Henderson, 2008; Scheyvens and Momsen, 2008). It is also well worth mentioning that cruise companies are in the business of leasing uninhabited islands. Louis Cruise Lines has leased an island in the Maldives (Vora, 2009) while the Disney Cruise company leases and has developed a Bahamian cay it has named Castaway Cay for the use of its own ships (Castaway Cay, 2014). Meanwhile, officials in the Bahamas defend leasing out cays and islands to the cruise industry as sound business practice. Their argument is that, when a cruise company invests in developing the leased island, it is likelier to demonstrate loyalty to that particular island nation; according to the Bahamian Director of Tourism, the cruise companies that make use of private islands in the Bahamas always require their ships to call in either New Providence or Grand Bahama, that country's two main ports-of-call (Bonimy, 2010; also Rolle, this volume).

The above examples attest to situations where top-down decisions, taken at either a national or a regional level, have had repercussions on several small islands throughout the world. The issue, of course, is that most (if not all) such islands are constructed from scratch or uninhabited to begin with and, thus, there are no local inhabitants that must be convinced about the merits of such decisions. It would be far harder, though not impossible, to convince inhabitants on a populated island of the potential benefits of being sold or leased out to a private corporation or individual as there are always local factions which would not condone such a move.

The fascination that wealthy individuals and companies have with leasing or buying islands for their own use, especially when these are located in the midst of archipelagic clusters, is somewhat ironic considering these places are often not too far away from populated islands whose inhabitants have long battled the handicaps of small size (in terms of land area and population), isolation, and peripherality. In other words, while isolation for short periods of time can be a major reason why the wealthy are attracted to small out-of-the-way uninhabited islands, by contrast, the same characteristic is often a major handicap for the long-term inhabitants of populated islands. This is especially the case for remote islands within large archipelagic clusters where evident development inequities are manifest. Thus, one could excuse the residents of an island, which has long battled economic decay and severe depopulation, for being envious when their own homeland is bypassed and a nearby island is suddenly purchased for private use, especially when this investment does not create a tangible long-term benefit for the islanders.

Regional Disparities

Such a discussion highlights a common thread emerging in this volume, namely regional imbalances, some of which are severe, affecting islands and island clusters. Since this volume is focused specifically on tourism, clearly each island, especially when dealing with archipelagos, witnesses varying levels of development and success as a destination. Explanations for this have been offered in this volume and elsewhere, essentially boiling down to variations in geographical features and historical trajectories, affecting each of the islands differently (Ioannides, 1994). More importantly, it is the degree of accessibility an island has to the outside world and, in the case of archipelagos, to other islands that determines whether it flourishes as a tourism destination or not. While all islands by their very nature of being surrounded by water suffer limited accessibility opportunities in the first place, clearly some islands are more accessible than others. In turn, this affects the degree of visitation an island receives. One expects tourists will flow in steady streams to Santorini and Rhodos, both of which are well served daily with flights from many parts of Europe as well as several domestic flights from Athens. In contrast, the opportunities for accessing an island like Simi, off the coast of Rhodos in the Dodecanese, are substantially reduced since this destination lacks an airport and has only infrequent ferry connections to Rhodos or the mainland (Karampela et al., this volume).

In this collection, the Faroe Islands feature as an interesting exception in that they are an archipelago where the authorities have a long-term policy to link many of the islands through a costly project of bridges and tunnels (Ankre and Nilsson, this volume). In this respect, the Faroes are unusual in that much of this archipelago has effectively been transformed into a single mainland destination, allowing tourists to rent cars and drive around from island to island. The positive effect is that this high level of connectivity between many of the Faroese islands allows tourists to spread out to some of the more peripheral areas and not concentrate heavily in one community. Nevertheless, most archipelagos lack this high level of connectivity either because of the absence of funds or because their geography means their islands are simply too far away from each other to have fixed links between them.

Double Insularity, Nested Peripherality

Clearly, in these cases, many archipelagic islands are subjected to a condition of double insularity or nested peripherality (Weaver, 1998; Spilanis, Kizos, Vaitis, and Koukourouvli, 2012; Cannas and Giudici, this volume). To illustrate this situation, let us examine the flows of tourists from key markets like those in Western Europe to islands in the Mediterranean or elsewhere. Especially in cases where the tourists are cost-conscious, largely concerned in having a good time anywhere, as long as it is a beach destination in the sun away from the dreary weather of their own home country (Butler, this volume), flows are often largely controlled by major tour operators. The latter include key players such as the British-German company Thomson-TUI or the Scandinavian outfit Apollo, who promote products guaranteeing a high volume of sales and profits and demonstrate no particular loyalty to any one destination as long as it is well connected to the market and offers adequate lodgings and infrastructure. This means their focus, especially in the case of sun-seeking mass tourism, is not so much on specific destinations, whether these are islands or not, but holiday type, meaning that they can often substitute one destination for another when they perceive the terms to no longer be in their favour (Ioannides, 1998). Thus, where one goes on holiday, especially when one is not so bothered about the identity of the destination as much as what the destination offers in terms of facilities and entertainment, often rests in the hands of gatekeepers such as tour operators and airlines based in key markets. This situation, in turn, renders many coastal destinations and particularly islands in an especially vulnerable position: these places end up assuming most of the risk of failure when tour operators or airlines decide to pull out.

While all island destinations are, to some degree, vulnerable to events unfolding and decisions made in the major markets well beyond their shores, in contexts where an island destination is one of many within a larger archipelago, we tend to end up with a second layer of peripherality. This means that only one or a handful of islands draw the majority of tourists, simply because these key destinations have the airport(s) or seaport(s) with direct access to their markets, as well as the ferry or airline companies that service them (e.g., Baldacchino and Ferreira, Johnson, Roberts et al., this volume). Weaver (1998, p. 306) dubs such key islands the archipelago's "internal core", since it is in these places where most of the local decisions ultimately affecting the fortunes of other more peripheral islands are made. For instance, if a foreign consortium wants to develop a major resort on one of the peripheral islands of an archipelago state, negotiations and decisions as to which island will ultimately be selected usually take place in the core island. This point has been aptly fleshed out in this collection, where we observe, for example, the existing uneven relationship between Gozo and Malta (Chaperon and Theuma, this volume). Similarly, through its marketing activities, the destination management company, normally based in the major island and administrative capital of the archipelago, can have a major impact as to which of the secondary islands are promoted as tourist destinations … and which are not (Connell, this volume).

Some Islands are More Equal than Others

Apart from the issue of nested peripherality, we must also consider the concept of intervening opportunities (Connell, this volume). When international tourists visit an archipelago, in addition to arriving in the main island where the major point of entry exists, if they are looking for an island hopping experience, they will undoubtedly visit the islands with the best connections. This means that, if two or more outer islands that are almost identical in a topographic and a cultural sense offer the opportunity for what effectively are conceived as similar experiences, most tourists are likely to only visit the one that is most convenient to get to. To be sure, over time, either because of the actions of individual entrepreneurs – whether these are located on the main island or one of the outer islands – or because of a new focus in terms of transportation policies, some islands might rise in popularity as others reach maturity or begin to wane. This, of course, is an issue affecting all places as existing or potential destinations and not just islands. In an evolutionary sense some islands will see their popularity grow, others will retain or manage to rebrand/recover their attraction, and yet others will see a decline that they can do little about.

Several questions lead from this. To begin with, does it ultimately matter if inequities exist in terms of islands' attractiveness as tourist destinations? Even though this may be an odd question to ask in a book concerned with archipelago tourism, does every island have to strive to become a tourist destination, just because this seems to be the Holy Grail for places with few alternative development options in the 21st century? From the locals' perspective, is tourism a development option that is always welcome? And, if the inhabitants do see tourism as a potential means of diversifying their economy, the question is what type of tourism should be encouraged so as not to end up with each island destination being a copy of the next? What sort of tourism will ensure that the destination maintains its environmental quality, avoids the commodification of local cultures, and distributes any benefits equitably, rather than seeing them end up in the hands of a few major players, including exogenously based entrepreneurs? These kinds of questions have often been asked when referring to the role tourism that can play in the development of peripheral regions, including islands. They break surface intermittently in this collection (e.g. Marcelino and Oca González, Rolle, Minerbi, Wergin, this volume); but it is not our intention to solve them here.

Ultimately, one must consider what is best from the perspective of those individuals who happen to live on archipelagic islands. When considering that many of these environments are some of the most peripheral territories in the world, it is clear that life is not always easy there. Opportunities for economic activity may be few and, in some locales, the original sources of livelihood may have dwindled, as has often happened in the cases of fishing or agricultural communities. Added to this is the looming threat of global environmental change, including the threat of rising sea levels that impact low-lying (coral atoll) islands especially hard. For instance, there are serious fears that Caribbean coral reefs are in danger of vanishing over the next two decades and this, of course, has dire consequences both for many islands' maritime food sources as well as their tourism industries (Morelle, 2014). Unsurprisingly, the easy (though hardly ideal) solution in many islands facing handicaps such as these is for people, usually the young, to leave their place of birth and seek better opportunities elsewhere, either in a neighbouring larger island or in another country: island diasporas are already significant. Nevertheless, others choose to stay, because after all this is home; while some émigrés choose to return after years away. All these people surely deserve better than to be penalized simply because of where they are from, and for something they hardly had a part in causing.

For Spatial Justice?

The statement above is normative, in the sense that it prescribes the 'right' thing to do and – much like sustainable development or world peace – it is a state towards which we should strive knowing that it is unlikely to be ever attained in practice. The challenges we have referred to are a function of uneven development and the spatial inequalities deriving from it; any location in space comes with a relative advantage or disadvantage (Soja, 2010). It is true that social processes do not happen uniformly over space and, therefore, "there will always be some unevenness in the geographies we produce just as there are always variations between individuals in their socio-historical development" (Soja, 2010, p. 71). The question then becomes not how to eliminate uneven development (the ubiquity of which is uncontested) but how to combat the injustices stemming from it.

To better illustrate this point, we turn briefly to the European context where, as part of the Lisbon Strategy, the concept of territorial cohesion has been adopted and has equal salience as economic and social cohesion (e.g., Faludi, 2006). The themes running through territorial cohesion are equality, fairness, and (territorial, spatial) justice. Petridou and Ioannides (2012) have demonstrated how the concept of spatial justice, especially as treated by Soja (2010), relates to the European concept of territorial cohesion. More specifically, Soja foregrounds injustices stemming from asymmetric socio-spatial human geographies inflicted on disadvantaged urban populations. Territorial cohesion as used in the European policy-making arenas encompasses all geographies, including declining or marginalized urban areas as well as rural and peripheral regions (mountains, islands, sparsely populated areas in the extreme north, border areas) challenged because of intrinsic characteristics stemming from their geographies.

This is not to say that levelling the playing field is necessarily going to stem from top-down decisions and payment transfers. Rather, spatial justice is more efficiently achieved when regions reflect on existing traits that could give them a competitive advantage and develop them in the specificity of their regional culture. Petridou and Ioannides (2012) discuss, for example, how collective artistic arrangements in the periphery of Sweden can contribute, in a bottom-up fashion, towards territorial cohesion by promoting the unique character of the region for residents and tourists alike. Meanwhile, using resilience theory, Hamzah and Hampton (2012) reflect that actors on small islands are not exactly passive when it comes to the imposition of exogenous decisions that may alter the tourism product. For instance, on the Malaysian island of Perhentian Kecil, rather than disappearing, many long-term family businesses catering to backpackers and independent travelers have managed to adapt and stay in business, despite the aggressive one-way stance on the part of federal and state authorities to develop a luxury-end resort as a means to alter the tourism product. This situation indicates that decisions affecting individuals on peripheral island communities must not be imposed in top-down fashion without recognizing the rights and desires of the inhabitants and protecting elements that are truly unique to the destination.

In spite of the European roots of territorial cohesion, the idea of fairness and equality among places – a sort of territorial justice – easily extends to the context of archipelagos and connects to the questions we raised earlier. The pronounced diversity of islands within and across archipelagos in terms of geographies and geopolitics renders one-stop-shop policy recommendations ineffective. In addition to a more pronounced diversity, islands and archipelagos face idiosyncratic challenges caused by the single feature, which powerfully defines their identities: the water surrounding them. Apocalyptic narratives have become more frequent as the ubiquity of crisis is taken for granted and islanders are starting to see the consequences of climate change (e.g., Guilford, 2014; Morelle, 2014). Thus, the normative concept of territorial justice as a way of thinking about spatialities should be mainstreamed in policy making efforts: how can policies benefit an archipelago as a whole as well as its constituent elements? Archipelagos are more than the sum of their parts as they encompass the linkages among their nodes (the islands) and the linkages to the main is(land)s. It is through these linkages and place-specific social relationships that the potential of a region can be realized because the strength of regional identity and the uniqueness of regional culture are vehicles for regional economic development and foster feelings of trust, creativity and entrepreneurship among citizens (Süssner, 2002; also Robert, 2007, p. 25).

One example of turning an element of distinct regional culture into a clear tourism-generating opportunity is the knitting culture existing on the various islands of Shetland, Scotland, UK. To be sure, knitting has traditionally been a component of reproductive labour and thus highly feminised and often unpaid or underpaid (Abrams, 2006; Arnold, 2010); whereas now, it appears that it has been transformed into one of the key products that has firmly established the Shetland Islands as a tourism destination (e.g., Baldacchino and Vella Bonnici, 2006). The different traditions of knitting each island has (fine lace, colourful patterns of sweaters, and so on) are showcased in the Shetland Textile Museum, while knitters visit the Shetlands from Japan, New Zealand and the U.S. (Shapiro, 2014; Shetland Museum and Archives, 2008). The act of knitting as a cultural artefact not only highlights the uniqueness of the islands, but is also embedded in the community know-how transmitted from the older generation of residents to younger cohorts of residents and tourists alike. This is the kind of creativity among citizens that can offer a competitive advantage to a destination, crucial in the absence of the '3S's.

Conclusion

As a parting note, we wish to suggest the mainstreaming of territorial justice in policy making processes. Archipelagic regions, especially ones plagued by extreme peripherality, stand to benefit from increased representation in the decision-making process that directly affects their future. Consequently, special attention must be paid to their specific regional culture – manifested in architecture, art, food, and traditions – in guiding, for example, policy making decisions regarding transportation networks, tourism infrastructure, as well as branding and marketing strategies. What is more, if an archipelago is viewed not as just a group of islands but rather as a network of islands (Baldacchino, this volume), then there is room to take into account the relationship among the nodes and the fact that these relationships might change. The centrality or relative importance of some islands will undoubtedly alter over time, thus changing the nature of the linkages among the islands and repivoting the archipelago's geopolitical relations. This fluidity we deem an important characteristic to keep in mind especially when the safety and security of a small island, not to mention its image of a safe haven, remains beyond most islands' control.

References

Abrams, L. (2006). Knitting, autonomy and identity: the role of hand-knitting in the construction of women's sense of self in an island community, Shetland, c. 1850–2000. *Textile History*, 37(2), 149–65.

Arnold, C. (2010). An assessment of the gender dynamic in Fair Isle (Shetland) knitwear. *Textile History*, 41(1), 86–98.

Baldacchino, G., and Vella Bonnici, J. (2006). *Successful small business from small islands*. Valletta, Malta: The NISSOS Project.

Bonimy, J. (2010). Director General of tourism defends leasing cays to cruise lines. *Caribbean News*, 15 April. Retrieved from http://www.caribbeannewsdigital.com/en/noticia/bahamas%E2%80%99-director-general-tourism-defends-leasing-cays-cruise-lines

Castaway Cay. (2014). Castaway Cay: Location Bahamas. Retrieved from http://disneycruise.disney.go.com/cruises-destinations/bahamas/ports/castaway-cay/

Domroes, M. (2001). Conceptualising state-controlled resort islands for an environment-friendly development of tourism: the Maldivian experience. *Singapore Journal of Tropical Geography*, 22(2), 122–37.

Faludi, A. (2006). From European spatial development to territorial cohesion policy. *Regional Studies*, 40(6), 667–8.

Guilford, G. (2014). An entire island nation is preparing to evacuate to Fiji before they sink into the Pacific. *Quartz*, 1 July. Retrieved from http://qz.com/228948/an-entire-island-nation-is-preparing-to-evacuate-to-fiji-before-they-sink-into-the-pacific/#228948/an-entire-island-nation-is-preparing-to-evacuate-to-fiji-before-they-sink-into-the-pacific/

Hamzah, A., and Hampton, M.P. (2013). Resilience and non-linear change in island tourism. *Tourism Geographies*, 15(1), 43–67.

Henderson, J. (2010). The politics of tourism: a perspective from the Maldives. *Tourismos: An International Multidisciplinary Journal of Tourism*, 3(1), 99–115.

Henderson, J. (2006). Tourism in Dubai: overcoming barriers to destination development. *International Journal of Tourism Research*, 8(1), 87–99.

Ioannides, D. (1998). Tour operators: the gatekeepers of tourism. In D. Ioannides and K. Debbage (eds.), *The economic geography of the tourist industry: a supply-side analysis*, pp. 139–58. London: Routledge.

Ioannides, D. (1994). *The state, transnationals, and the dynamics of tourism evolution in small island nations*. PhD Dissertation. New Brunswick, NJ: Rutgers University.

Morelle, R. (2014). Caribbean coral reefs 'could vanish in 20 years'. *BBC News online*, July. Retrieved from http://www.bbc.com/news/science-environment-28113331

Moya, E. (2010). Greece starts putting island land up for sale to save economy. *The Guardian*, 24 June. Retrieved from http://www.theguardian.com/world/2010/jun/24/greece-islands-sale-save-economy

Necker Island (2014). Necker Island: Sir Richard Branson's Private Island. Retrieved from http://www.neckerisland.virgin.com/

Petridou, E., and Ioannides, D. (2012). Conducting creativity in the periphery of Sweden: a bottom-up path towards territorial cohesion. *Creative Industries Journal*, 5(1–2), 120–38.

Private Islands Online. (2014). The Private Island Marketplace. Retrieved from http://www.privateislandsonline.com/islands/the-world-islands-dubai

Robert, J. (2007). The origins of territorial cohesion and the vagaries of its trajectory. In A. Faludi (ed.), *Territorial cohesion and the European model of society*, pp. 23–35. Cambridge, MA: Lincoln Institute of Public Policy.

Scheyvens, R., and Momsen, J.H. (2008). Tourism and poverty reduction: issues for small islands. *Tourism Geographies*, 10(1), 22–41.

Shapiro, A. (2004). NPR, All things considered. Radio broadcast, 2 July 2014. Retrieved from http://www.npr.org/blogs/parallels/2014/07/02/327709376/a-scottish-yarn-a-knit-in-time-saves-the-fabric-of-shetland-life

Shetland Museum and Archives. (2008). Home page. Retrieved from http://www.shetlandmuseumandarchives.org.uk/index.html

Soja, E. (2010). *Seeking spatial justice*, Minneapolis MN: University of Minnesota Press.

Spilanis, I., Kizos, T., Vaitis, M., and Koukourouvli, N. (2012). Measuring the economic, social and environmental performance of European island regions: emerging issues for European and regional policy. *European Planning Studies*, 21(12), 1998–2019.

Squires, N. (2012). Qatar royal family buys Greek island of Oxia for knockdown 5 million euros. *The Telegraph*, 25 April. Retrieved from http://www.telegraph.co.uk/finance/newsbysector/constructionandproperty/9226844/Qatar-royal-family-buys-Greek-island-of-Oxia-for-knockdown-5m.html

Süssner, J. (2002). Culture, identity and regional development in the European Union. In *Informationen zur Raumentwiklung*. Vol. 4/5. Bonn: BBR.

Vora, K. (2009). Louis Cruise India becomes first cruise company to lease island in Maldives. TravelBIZ monitor. Retrieved from http://www.travelbizmonitor.com/louis-cruises-india-becomes-first-cruise-company-to-lease-island-in-maldives-8847

Weaver, D.B. (1998). Peripheries of the periphery: tourism in Tobago and Barbuda. *Annals of Tourism Research*, 25(2), 292–313.

Index

For Product Safety Concerns and Information please contact our EU representative GPSR@taylorandfrancis.com Taylor & Francis Verlag GmbH, Kaufingerstraße 24, 80331 München, Germany

Printed and bound by CPI Group (UK) Ltd, Croydon, CR0 4YY

08/05/2025

01864549-0001